THE
PARTICIPATING
READER

THE
PARTICIPATING
READER

Susan Wittig
University of Texas at Austin

Franklin Holcomb
University of Texas at Austin

Anne Dunn
University of Nebraska–Lincoln

Prentice-Hall, Inc., *Englewood Cliffs, New Jersey* 07632

Library of Congress Cataloging in Publication Data

WITTIG, SUSAN
  The participating reader.

  Bibliography: p.
  1. English language—Rhetoric. 2. College readers.
3. Reading comprehension. I. Holcomb, Franklin (date)
joint author. II. Dunn, Anne (date)
joint author. III. Title.
PE1408.W6238   808'.0427   77-2998
ISBN 0-13-650200-8

PRENTICE-HALL SERIES IN ENGLISH COMPOSITION
James C. Raymond, *Series Editor*

Printed in the United States of America

10 9 8 7 6 5 4 3 2 1

Prentice-Hall International, Inc., *London*
Prentice-Hall of Australia, Pty. Limited, *Sydney*
Prentice-Hall of Canada, Ltd., *Toronto*
Prentice-Hall of India Private Limited, *New Delhi*
Prentice-Hall of Japan, Inc., *Tokyo*
Prentice-Hall of Southeast Asia Pte. Ltd., *Singapore*
Whitehall Books Limited, *Wellington, New Zealand*

Acknowledgments

Unit 1

page 3   From Susanne Langer, "The Lord of Creation," *Fortune Magazine*, January 1944. Reprinted by permission of Time Inc.

5   From *Tristes Tropiques* by Claude Levi-Strauss. Translated by John and Doreen Weightman. New York: Atheneum, 1974, p. 298.

7   From "How To Mark A Book" by Mortimer Adler. In *Saturday Review*, July 6, 1940.

12   "Different readers. . . ." From *Read with Speed and Precision* by Paul D. Leedy. New York: McGraw-Hill Books Co., Inc., 1963.

18   "The definitions given. . . ." From *Language in Thought and Action,* Third Edition, by S. I. Hayakawa, copyright © 1972 by Harcourt Brace Jovanovich, Inc. and reprinted with their permission.

18   "Words display. . . ." From "Verbal Communication" by Roman Jakobson. In *Scientific American*, September, 1972, p. 78. Reprinted by permission of the publisher.

18   Samuel Johnson's description of the difficulty of making definitions appears in his Preface to *A Dictionary of the English Language*, published in April, 1755.

19   "One of the most important. . . ." From "Animal Communication" by Edward O. Wilson. In *Scientific American*, September, 1972, p. 60. Reprinted by permission of the Publisher.

20   The poem was written by John Donne. Its title is "A Valediction: Forbidding Mourning."

20   "We may agree. . . ." From *Symbol, Status, and Personality* by S. I. Hayakawa. New York: Harcourt, Brace and World, 1963.

21   Excerpts from Tom Wolfe's article "The Birth of the New Journalism." Copyright © 1972 by the NYM Corp. Reprinted with the permission of *New York* magazine.

page 22   The cloze test paragraphs are taken from *Writing: Man's Greatest Invention* by J. Hambleton Ober. Copyright 1965 by The Peabody Institute of the City of Baltimore.

25   Practice 2 is from Mario Pei, *What's in a Word?* New York: Hawthorn Books, 1968, p. 142.

Unit 2

29   From *Gift of Tongues* by Margaret Schlauch. Copyright 1942 by Margaret Schlauch. Reprinted by permission of The Viking Press.

30   Alfred Korzybski's concept of map and territory appears in *Science and Sanity: An Introduction to Non-Aristotelian Systems and General Semantics.* Lancaster, Pennsylvania: The International non-Aristotelian Library Publishing Co., 1933.

33   Excerpted from William Golding's essay entitled "Party of One—Thinking as a Hobby." First published in Holiday Magazine, August, 1961. Reprinted by permission of Curtis Brown, Ltd. Copyright © 1961 by The Curtis Publishing Company.

35   Practice 1(B) From Walter Schramm's book, *Men, Messages, and Media.* New York: Harper and Row Publishers, 1973, p. 137.

37   "In 1900. . . ." and "Man in the automotive age. . . ." were both written by John Keats, in *The Insolent Chariots.* Philadelphia: J. B. Lippincott Co., 1958.

40   "The San Bernadino Valley. . . ." is taken from Joan Didion's essay, "Some Dreamers of the Golden Dream." Reprinted with permission of Farrar, Straus & Giroux, Inc. from *Slouching Towards Bethlehem* by Joan Didion, Copyright © 1966, 1968 by Joan Didion.

41   "Dolor," copyright 1943 Modern Poetry Association, Inc. from the book *The Collected Poems of Theodore Roethke.* Reprinted by permission of Doubleday & Company, Inc.

41   Practice 3(1). This passage is taken from Aldous Huxley, *Brave New World Revisited,* chapter 6. New York: Harper and Row, 1958.

42   Practice 3(2). From *Middletown* by Robert S. and Helen M. Lynd, copyright, 1929, by Harcourt Brace Jovanovich, Inc.; copyright, 1957, by Robert S. and Helen M. Lynd. Reprinted by permission of the publisher.

44   This metaphor is from *The Eco-Spasm Report,* by Alvin Toffler. New York: Bantam Books, Inc., 1975, p. 4.

45   Practice 4(2). Reprinted with permission from the August 1974 issue of *Texas Monthly* Magazine. Copyright 1974 by Mediatex Communications Corporation, Post Office Box 1569, Austin, Texas 78767. Subscriptions $12.00 per year.

46   Practice 4 (3A). From Edward O. Wilson's "Animal Communication." In *Scientific American,* September, 1972, p. 54. Reprinted by permission of the publisher.

46   Practice 4 (3B). From *The Lives of a Cell* by Lewis Thomas. Copyright © 1971, 1972, 1973 by the Massachusetts Medical Society. Reprinted by permission of The Viking Press.

Unit 3

page 47 The headnote is taken from Irving J. Lee, *Language Habits in Human Affairs.* New York: Harper and Row Publishers, Inc., 1941.

50 "The Age of Wordfact" by John Kenneth Galbraith. Reprinted by permission of the author. Copyright © 1960, by The Atlantic Monthly Company, Boston, Mass. Reprinted with permission.

52 Otto Friedrich's account of wordfact from "There are 00 Trees in Russia." Harper's, October, 1964. Reprinted by permission of author. Copyright © 1960 by *Harper's* Magazine.

53 Practice 2(1). From *Who's Who in America,* 38th Edition, 1974–1975. © Marquis Who's Who, Inc.

54 "The Short Happy Life of Aris Rutherford." In *Newsweek,* March 17, 1975. Copyright 1975 by Newsweek, Inc. All rights reserved. Reprinted by permission.

57 The excerpt is from a UPI story printed Feb. 13, 1975.

60 "The 'new' student liberalism. . . ." From "Beyond the New Leftism" by Steven Kelman. Reprinted from Commentary, by permission; copyright © 1969 by the American Jewish Committee.

62 Practice 5 (1A). "Ecology—The Safe Issue," was written by the editors of *Ramparts,* in *Ramparts,* May 1970, p. 3. Copyright 1970 by Ramparts Magazine Inc. Reprinted by permission.

62 Practice 5 (1B). "Brutalized Language" appeared as an editorial in the Baton Rouge State-Times. Reprinted by permission of The Baton Rouge State-Times.

64 Excerpts from *Culture and Commitment* by Margaret Mead. Copyright © 1970 by Margaret Mead. Reprinted by permission of Doubleday & Company, Inc.

64 The two short quotations about Mick Jagger are from the article "On and On Mick's Orgy Rolls," by Albert Goldman, in *The New York Times Magazine,* Nov. 23, 1969.

65 These excerpts are from Douglas MacArthur's last West Point speech.

66 These three short quotations about ecology and science are from Lynn White's essay, "The Historical Roots of Our Ecologic Crisis," in *Science,* March 10, 1967.

67 Practice 6. "A 28-year old Queens Woman . . . had no clues" is from *The New York Times,* March 14, 1964, p. 26. © 1964 by The New York Times Company. Reprinted by permission.

67 "The neighbors had . . ." is by Robert Parella, from *The New York Herald Tribune,* March 14, 1964, p. 10.

68 Article entitled *Queens Barmaid Stabbed, Dies,* by Thomas Pugh and Richard Henry. Appeared in *The New York Daily News,* March 14, 1964, p. 5. Reprinted by permission of the New York Daily News. (The previous three news stories also are reprinted in *Language and the Newsstand,* edited by Thomas F. van Laan and Robert B. Lyons. New York: Charles Scribner's Sons, 1968, pp. 97–100.)

Unit 4

page 70 The unit headnote is Richard Wilbur's poem "Mind." From *Things of This World*, © 1956, by Richard Wilbur. Reprinted by permission of Harcourt Brace Jovanovich, Inc., from *Poems 1943–1956*.

72 The three quotations are taken from the editorial page of the Dec. 31, 1975 San Francisco *Chronicle*. The first and third are from an article entitled "The Politics of Failure," by James Kilpatrick; the second is from the editorial, "Moscone's Call for Resignations."

74 Robert Penn Warren's simile-laden description is from "The Patented Gate and the Mean Hamburger," in *The Circus in the Attic and Other Stories*. New York: Harcourt Brace Publishers, 1947. .

75 "I'm going back to New York . . ." by Mary McLaughlin, appears in her essay, "Goodby Suburbs," in *Today's Living*, from the *New York Herald Tribune*, 1958.

76 "There were the houses. . . ." is from *Inishfallen, Fare Thee Well*, by Sean O'Casey. New York: The Macmillan Co., 1949.

77 Practice 1 (2A). This paragraph is taken from Julian Huxley's "Man's Challenge: The Use of the Earth," in *Horizon*, September, 1958.

77 Practice 1 (2B). From Susanne Langer, "The Lord of Creation," *Fortune* Magazine, January 1944. Reprinted by permission of Time Inc.

77 Practice 1 (2C). From John G. Mitchell, *Ecotactics: A Sierra Club Handbook for Environmental Activists*. New York: Sierra Club Pocket Books, division of Simon and Schuster, 1970. Copyright 1970 by The Sierra Club. Reprinted by permission of Simon & Schuster, Inc. Pocket Books division.

77 Practice 1 (3A, 3B, and 4). From *The Lives of a Cell* by Lewis Thomas. Copyright © 1971, 1972, 1973 by the Massachusetts Medical Society. Reprinted by permission of The Viking Press.

78 Practice 1 (5). The metaphoric comparison of wit and humor is from Charles Brooks' *Chimney Pot Papers*. New Haven: Yale University Press, 1919, pp. 129–30.

79 "The event-making man. . . ." from Sidney Hook's *The Hero in History*. New York: Humanities Press, Inc., 1943.

79 "Churchill too loves. . . ." is taken from "Mr. Churchill," by Isaiah Berlin. It first appeared in *The Cornhill Magazine*, September, 1949.

79 "I would set out . . ." is written by John Updike. It appears in "The Blessed Man of Boston, My Grandmother's Thimble, and Fanning Island." From *Pigeon Feathers and Other Stories*, by John Updike. New York: Alfred A. Knopf, Inc., 1962.

79 "The decade being tragic. . . ." is by E. M. Forster from *Two Cheers for Democracy*. New York: Harcourt Brace, 1951.

81 Practice 3 (A). The sentence is from Jacob Brackman's "Onward and Upward with the Arts: the Put-on." In *The New Yorker*, June 24, 1967.

81 Practice 3 (B). The sentence is from Wallace Stegner's *Beyond the Hundredth Meridian*. Boston: Houghton Mifflin, 1962.

81 Practice 3 (C). The sentence is from Edmund Wilson's *The American Earthquake*. Copyright 1958 by Edmund Wilson. Garden City, New York: Doubleday, 1958.

page 81 Practice 3 (D). The sentence is from *The Encantadas or Enchanted Isles* by Herman Melville.

81 Practice 3 (E). The sentence appears in Malcolm Bradbury's "Can We Bring Back the Old-Fashioned Bank Robber?"

81 Practice 3 (F). Lewis Mumford wrote this sentence in *Technics and Civilization*. New York: Harcourt Brace, 1934, 1962.

82 The comparison of Newton's and Einstein's ideas on the space-time continuum is from Lincoln Barnett, *The Universe and Dr. Einstein*. New York: Harper and Brothers, 1948.

82 Practice 5 (1). This description of the expanding universe was written by Fred Hoyle, "When Time Began," *The Saturday Evening Post*, February 21, 1959.

83 Practice 5 (2). This passage by Richard Hughes appears in his book *In Hazard*. Published by Peter Smith. It is reprinted by permission of David Higham Associates Limited.

84 From *Fables for Our Time*, published by Harper and Row. Copr. © 1940 by James Thurber. Copr. © 1968 Helen Thurber. Originally printed in *The New Yorker*.

86 From *Preface to Critical Reading*, Fourth Edition, by Richard D. Altick. Copyright © 1946, 1951, © 1956, 1960 by Holt, Rinehart and Winston, Inc. Reprinted by permission of Holt, Rinehart and Winston.

88 This collection of clichés comes from Sidney J. Harris' "A Pretty Kettle of Clichés," from *Leaving the Surface*. Boston, Mass.: Houghton Mifflin Company, 1968.

89 Twain's mixed metaphor comes from *Life on the Mississippi*, Chapter III.

89 Practice 6 (A). This metaphor is from Frank Deford, "Everybody Gets into the Act," in *Sports Illustrated*, Feb. 16, 1976, p. 65.

89 Practice 6 (B). Tom Shales wrote this metaphor; it appeared in the *Austin, Texas American Statesman*, Feb. 14, 1976. Reprinted by permission of the *Austin American Statesman*.

89 Practice 6 (C). This metaphor appears in Jacques Barzun, *God's Country and Mine*. Boston: Little Brown and Company, 1954, p. 1.

89 Practice 6 (D). Harrison E. Salisbury wrote this short passage in "Travels through America,' *Esquire*, February 1976, p. 29.

89 Practice 6 (E). The passage is from Lou Maysel's column in the *Austin, Texas, American Statesman*, January 4, 1976. Reprinted by permission of the *Austin American Statesman*.

90 Practice 6 (F). These sentences were written by Richard Selzer, "The Drinking Man's Liver," *Esquire*, April, 1974, p. 126.

90 Practice 6 (G). The passage is from an article called "Peach Buds Are Confused," written by Nat Henderson, in the *Austin, Texas, American Statesman*, Feb. 21, 1976. Reprinted by permission of the *Austin American Statesman*.

90 Practice 6 (H). This short piece is from an article called "New York: Rising Red Ink," in *Newsweek*, Feb. 23, 1976, p. 65. Copyright 1976, by Newsweek, Inc. All rights reserved. Reprinted by permission.

90 Practice 6 (I). The sentences are from a sports column in the *Austin, Texas, American Statesman*, March 18, 1976, p. E1. Reprinted by permission of the *Austin American Statesman*.

page 91   Practice 7 (1B). The paragraph is taken from Norman Mailer's *Miami and the Seige of Chicago*, p. 11. Reprinted by permission of the author and the author's agents, Scott Meredith Literary Agency, Inc., 845 Third Avenue, New York, New York 10022.

   92   The allegory about the man in the cage is reprinted from *Man's Search for Himself* by Rollo May, Ph.D. By permission of W. W. Norton & Company, Inc. Copyright 1953 by W. W. Norton & Company, Inc.

   94   Oscar Wilde wrote this short parable, "The Doer of Good." It appears in *The Portable Oscar Wilde*. Edited by Richard Aldington. New York: The Viking Press, 1953. © 1946.

Unit 5

   127   The unit headnote is taken from Benjamin Lee Whorf's book, *Language, Thought, and Reality*. Cambridge: MIT Press, 1956.

   130   "The problem that most. . . ." is taken from Thomas Landon Thorson's *The Logic of Democracy*, New York: Holt, Rinehart and Winston, 1962, p. 151.

   133   This sentence is the opening sentence in William Faulkner's *Absalom, Absalom!* New York: Random House, 1936.

   133   "Danny is an educated man. . . ." was written by Peter Carlson, *Newsweek*, June 3, 1974. Copyright 1974, by Newsweek, Inc. All rights reserved. Reprinted by permission.

   134   George Wald's statement is excerpted from his article, "A Generation in Search of a Future." From *The New Yorker*, March 22, 1969. From "Notes and Comment" in *The New Yorker*. Reprinted by permission; © 1969 The New Yorker Magazine, Inc.

   135   Practice 1. Table "Average Sentence Length in Words" is from page 38 in *The Art of Plain Talk* by Rudolf Flesch. Copyright 1946 by Rudolf Flesch. By permission of Harper & Row, Publishers.

   136   Practice 1 (2). Excerpt from pp. 56–7 "The Ring of Time–Fiddler Bayou, March 22, 1956" in *The Points of My Compass* by E. B. White. Copyright © 1956 by E. B. White. Originally appeared in *The New Yorker*, and reprinted by permission of Harper & Row, Publishers.

   137   Excerpts from *Culture and Commitment* by Margaret Mead. Copyright © 1970 by Margaret Mead. Reprinted by permission of Doubleday & Company, Inc.

   137   "If too many. . . ." is from a book by Ramsey Clark, *Crime in America*, p. 151. Copyright © 1970 by Ramsey Clark. Reprinted by permission of Simon & Schuster, Inc.

   139   The sentence, "Another means. . . ." is by John Bardach, "Rivers and History," *Downstream*. New York: Harper and Row, 1964.

   139   George Plimpton/Everybody Can't Be First String/*Sports Illustrated* December 18, 1972. © 1972 George Plimpton.

   139   Francis Christensen, in *Notes Toward a New Rhetoric*, wrote the passage about the cumulative sentence. New York: Harper and Row, 1967, p. 6.

   140   Practice 2 (A). This sentence is from *Crime in America*, by Ramsey Clark, p. 38. Copyright © 1970 by Ramsey Clark. Reprinted by permission of Simon & Schuster, Inc.

page 140   Practice 2 (B). This sentence was written by Martin Meyerson, in an article called "The Ethos of the American College Student," in *Higher Education and Modern Democracy,* ed. Robert A. Goldwin. Chicago: Rand McNally, 1967.

140   Practice 2 (C). This is another example from Ramsey Clark's *Crime in America.*

141   Practice 2 (D). David O. Hill wrote this sentence, in "Goodbye to the Great Whales," in *Audobon,* January, 1975.

141   Practice 2 (E). The sentence is taken from an article, "Drugs and Student Values," written by Kenneth Kenniston and presented to the National Association of Student Personnel Administrators, Nov. 7–8, 1966.

141   Practice 2 (F). This sentence appears in Arthur Koestler, *The Trail of the Dinosaur.* New York: Macmillan, 1956. © 1955.

141   "Travel is no cure. . . ." is also from Koestler, *The Trail of the Dinosaur.*

141   The paragraph of antithetical sentences is from Bernard Shaw's *Man and Superman.* New York: Brentano's 1903. Reprinted by permission of The Society of Authors on behalf of the Bernard Shaw Estate.

142   The sentence, "The more you live. . . ." was written by Marya Mannes in *But Will It Sell?* Philadelphia: Lippincott, 1964.

142   This example of repetition in sentence structure is also from Marya Mannes, *But Will It Sell?* Philadelphia: Lippincott, 1964.

143   Martin Luther King, Jr.'s sentence came from his "Letter from Birmingham Jail, April 16, 1963" published in *Why We Can't Wait.* New York: Harper and Row, 1963.

144   "Of all the ills. . . ." appears in Barbara W. Tuchman's "The Missing Element: Moral Courage," from *In Search of Leaders: Current Issues in Higher Education,* ed. G. Kerry Smith. American Association for Higher Education, 1967.

144   James Baldwin's description of ghetto dwellers comes from *Notes of a Native Son.* Boston: Beacon Press, 1955.

145   Practice 3 (A). This example was taken from *The Declaration of Independence.*

145   Practice 3 (B). Walter Lippman wrote this passage in "The Indispensable Opposition." Copyright © 1939, by The Atlantic Monthly Company, Boston, Mass. Reprinted with permission.

145   Practice 3 (C). This passage appears in Robert Moses' article "Are Cities Dead." Copyright © 1962, by The Atlantic Monthly Company, Boston, Mass. Reprinted with permission.

145   Practice 3 (D). This passage comes from William G. Carleton's "The Passing of Bughouse Square." Copyright © by the Antioch Press. First published in the *Antioch Review,* Vol. XX, no. 3. Reprinted by the permission of the editors.

145   Practice 3 (E). G. K. Chesterton wrote this passage about virtue, mercy, and chastity in *Tremendous Trifles.* New York: Dodd, Mead and Co., 1909.

146   Practice 3 (F). This sentence by John G. Mitchell comes from one of the Sierra Club Pocket Books, *Ecotactics: A Sierra Club Handbook for Environmental Activists.* New York: Sierra Club Pocket Books, division of Simon and Schuster, 1970. Copyright 1970 by The Sierra Club. Reprinted by permission of Simon & Schuster, Inc. Pocket Book division.

Unit 6

page 148   The unit headnotes are taken from Simeon Potter's *Our Language*. Baltimore: Penguin Books Ltd., 1961, and Pascal's *Penseé*. New York: Modern Library, 1941, p. 11.

150   These two series of short sentences—"Our scientists. . . ." and "We can't do it. . . ."—were adapted from Ira Mothner's article, "Cities," in *Look* magazine, June 11, 1968.

156   William Butler Yeats wrote this coordinated passage in his *Autobiography*. New York: Macmillan Co., 1936.

157   Marya Mannes uses semicolons to coordinate these sentences in *But Will It Sell?* Philadelphia: Lippincott, 1964.

157   This passage by Diana Trilling is taken from her article "The Death of Marilyn Monroe" in *Claremont Essays*. New York: Harcourt Brace, 1965.

158   "The ancient Egyptian. . . ." comes from John L. Foster's "On Translating Hieroglyphic Love Songs." *Chicago Review* 23, no. 2 Autumn, 1971.

158   This example of coordination—"We must cease to talk in abstractions. . . ."—appears in E. Merrill Root's "What Is the Battle." In *Collectivism on the Campus*. Old Greenwich, Conn.: Devin-Adair Co., 1955.

159   Practice 3 (A). Ernest Hemingway wrote this passage in "The Short Happy Life of Francis Macomber." From *The Fifth Column and the First Forty-Nine Stories*. New York: Charles Scribner's Sons © 1936, 1938.

159   Practice 3 (B). Excerpts from *Culture and Commitment* by Margaret Mead. Copyright © 1970 by Margaret Mead. Reprinted by permission of Doubleday & Company, Inc.

159   Practice 3 (C). E. Merrill Root strikes again with another example from his popular article, "What Is the Battle," in *Collectivism on the Campus*.

159   Practice 3 (D). "A Student's Aims in Education" by Philip Werdell. From *Dialogue on Education*, edited by Robert Theobald copyright © 1967 by The Bobbs-Merrill Company, Inc.

159   Practice 3 (E). "A Student's Aims in Education" by Philip Werdell. From *Dialogue on Education*, edited by Robert Theobald copyright © 1967 by The Bobbs-Merrill Company, Inc.

160   Practice 3 (G). Germaine Greer's discussion of female economic influence appears in *The Female Eunuch*, © 1971, McGraw-Hill. Reprinted by permission of the publisher and Granada Publishing Ltd.

160   Harvey Cox considers the economics of erotic fantasy in this excerpt from "Playboy's Doctrine of Male," *Christianity and Crisis*, 1971.

161   (a) This example of the restatement pattern appears in *Newsweek*, August 25, 1975, p. 44.

161   (b) "The pitcher's windup. . . ." comes from Murray Ross's "Football Red and Baseball Green," *Chicago Review* 22, nos. 2–3, January-February, 1971.

161   (c) Kenneth Keniston wrote this sentence in "Drugs and Student Values," a paper presented to the National Association of Student Personnel Administrators, Nov. 7–8, 1966.

161   (d) Excerpted from *Culture and Commitment* by Margaret Mead. Copyright © 1970 by Margaret Mead. Reprinted by permission of Doubleday & Company, Inc.

page 161   (e) Serge Chermayeff and Christopher Alexander collaborated to write this sentence in *Community and Privacy*. Garden City, New York: Doubleday, 1963.

162   (f) "The small tribe of Iks. . . ." From *The Lives of a Cell* by Lewis Thomas. Copyright © 1971, 1972, 1973 by the Massachusetts Medical Society. Reprinted by permission of The Viking Press.

162   Lewis Thomas also wrote this longer example of the restatement pattern in *The Lives of a Cell*, pp. 16–17. New York: Bantam Books, 1973.

163   "A Student's Aims in Education" by Philip Werdell, from *Dialogue on Education*, edited by Robert Theobald, copyright © 1967 by The Bobbs-Merrill Company, Inc.

164   Practice 5. Example A comes from *U.S. News and World Report*. February 2, 1976, p. 45.

164   Practice 5 (B). This sentence was written by Rachel Carson in *The Eye of the Sea*. Boston: Houghton, Mifflin, 1955.

164   Practice 5 (C). Robert Claiborne's sentence appears in his article, "Future Schlock," in *The Nation*, Jan. 25, 1971.

164   Practice 5 (D). This example comes from Andrew M. Greeley's "A Christmas Biography," in *The New York Times*, December 23, 1973.

164   Practice 5 (E). In July 1974, *Harper's* printed this sentence by Lucian K. Truscott in his article, "Notes on a Broken Promise."

164   Practice 5 (F). Henry Winthrop wrote this magnificient sentence in "Portents of a Coming Counter Culture." *Colorado Quarterly*, XIX, No. 2 Autumn 1970. Reprinted by permission.

165   This example was written by T. E. Lawrence in *The Seven Pillars of Wisdom*. London: Jonathan Cape, 1926.

165   "The tall stalk had fallen. . . ." appears in Hal Borland's "Perfection" from *Sundial of the Seasons*. Philadelphia: J. B. Lippincott Co., 1953.

165   Rachel Carson wrote "The new earth, freshly torn. . . ." in *The Edge of the Sea*. Boston: Houghton Mifflin, 1955.

166   "The hawk. . . ." comes from Walter Van Tilburg Clark's short story, "Hook." *The Watchful Gods and Other Stories*. New York: Random House, 1940.

166   George Plimpton/Everybody Can't Be First String/*Sports Illustrated*, December 18, 1972 © 1972 George Plimpton.

166   "Life on an air-conditioned mountain top. . . ." appears in Serge Chermeyeff and Christopher Alexander's *Community and Privacy*.

167   This example is from Marya Mannes' *But Will It Sell?*

167   This paragraph by Martin Luther King, Jr., also appears in Unit 5.

168   Practice 7 (A). George E. Hollister wrote this passage for his article "With Legs Like These . . . Who Needs Wings?" in *National Wildlife Magazine*, August/September, 1973.

168   Practice 7 (B). Virginia Woolf wrote this passage about moths in *The Death of the Moth and Other Essays*. New York: Harcourt, Brace, Jovanovich, 1942, 1970.

168   Practice 7 (C). This passage appears in Larry McMurtry's "Take My Saddle from the Wall: A Valediction." From *In a Narrow Grave*. Austin, Tx: Encino Press, 1968.

168   Practice 7 (D). This discussion of witchcraft is from Gilbert Highet's *A*

Clerk of Oxenford: Essays in Literature and Life. New York: Oxford University Press, Inc., 1954.

page 169   Carl Sagan wrote this example of the qualifying pattern in *The Cosmic Connection: An Extraterrestrial Perspective.* Garden City, New York: Doubleday & Company, Inc., 1973.

169   This example, "During the more or less . . ." is also from Sagan's *The Cosmic Connection: An Extraterrestrial Perspective.* Garden City, New York: Doubleday & Company, Inc., 1973.

169   Two examples—"Under the pressure . . ." and "In some cities it's already hard . . ."—were written by Edmund Flatermager in "Who Will Do the Dirty Work Tomorrow?" *Fortune,* January, 1974.

170   a. "When there is considerable evidence . . ." is also from Sagan's *The Cosmic Connection.*

170   b. James Wellard wrote "The main camps and forts . . . in "The Lost Cities." *The Great Sahara.* London: Curtis Brown Ltd., 1964.

170   c. Lewis Mumford wrote this sentence in *The Conduct of Life.* New York: Harcourt Brace Jovanovich, 1951.

170   d. This example comes from H.V.J. Edgen's "The Uses of History." *Michigan Quarterly Review,* 8 Winter, 1969.

171   Practice 8 (A). This passage appears in Jules Henry's *Culture Against Man.* New York: Random House, Inc., 1963.

171   Practice 8 (B). This passage was adapted from "TV as Babysitter," by Jerzy Kosinski. Jerzy Kosinski on NBC's "Comment." © Jerzy Kosinski. Reprinted by permission of the author and NBC.

171   Practice 8 (C). From *The Lives of a Cell* by Lewis Thomas. Copyright © 1971, 1972, 1973 by the Massachusetts Medical Society. Reprinted by permission of The Viking Press.

172   Practice 8 (D). This passage by John Voelker appears in "Testament of a Fisherman," from *Anatomy of a Fisherman.* New York: McGraw-Hill, 1964.

Unit 7

173   The headnote for this unit is taken from I. A. Richards' essay, "Structure and Communication," in *Structure in Art and in Science,* ed. Gyorgy Kepes. New York: G. Braziller, 1965.

176   Carl Jung's paragraph appears in his book *Man and his Symbols.* London: Aldus Books Ltd., 1964.

176   This paragraph comes from Ralph Ross' *Symbols and Civilization.* New York: Harcourt Brace Jovanovich, 1962.

177   Rhoda B. Nathan and Judith S. Neaman wrote this more difficult paragraph in *The American Vision.* Glenview: Scotts Foresman, 1973.

178   Practice 1 (A). This example is from Rachel Carson's *The Sea Around Us.* New York: Oxford University Press, 1951.

178   Practice 1 (B). Sheldon Cheney wrote this paragraph in *A New World History of Art.* New York: Holt, Rinehart and Winston, 1956.

178   Practice 1 (C). From Margaret Mead, "Women: A House Divided," *Redbook,* May 1970. Reprinted by permission of the publisher.

page 179   Practice 1 (D). This example comes from Joseph Fletcher's "The Patient's Right to Die." Harper's Magazine, October, 1960. Reprinted by permission of author. Copyright © 1960 by Harper's Magazine.

179   Lewis Thomas wrote this extended restatement pattern. From *The Lives of a Cell* by Lewis Thomas. Copyright © 1971, 1972, 1973 by the Massachusetts Medical Society. Reprinted by permission of The Viking Press.

180   "I have almost reached. . . ." Excerpt from *Culture and Commitment* by Margaret Mead. Copyright © 1970 by Margaret Mead. Reprinted by permission of Doubleday & Company, Inc.

180   The restatement paragraph, "Almost anything that an animal. . . ." is also from Lewis Thomas' *The Lives of a Cell.* p. 24.

181   This example also appears in *Culture and Commitment* by Margaret Mead.

183   Practice 2 (A). Martin Meyerson wrote this paragraph in "The Ethos of the American College Student" from *Higher Education and Modern Democracy,* ed. by Robert A. Goldwin. Originally published by Rand McNally, Chicago, 1967. Reprinted by permission of the Kenyon Public Affairs Forum, Washington, D. C.

183   Practice 2 (B). This paragraph by Bergan Evans was quoted in Francis Christensen's *The Christensen Rhetoric Program.* New York: Harper & Row, 1968.

183   Practice 2 (C). This example by Polly Redford appears in "Our Most American Animal," *Raccoons and Eagles.* New York: E. P. Dutton, 1965.

185   Neil H. Jacoby wrote this paragraph about technological change in "The Environmental Crisis," *The Center Magazine,* December, 1970.

187   This more complicated paragraph comes from Irving and Harriet Deer's *The Popular Arts: A Critical Reader,* p. 3. New York: Charles Scribner's Sons, 1967.

188   Practice 5 (A). This paragraph appears in *The Essential Lippman.* Edited by Clinton Rossiter and James Lane. New York: Random House, Inc., 1963.

189   Practice 5 (B). Kenneth Keniston wrote this paragraph in "Heads and Seekers: Drugs on Campus, Counter-cultures, and American Society," in *The American Scholar,* vol. 38, no. 1 Winter, 1968–69. Reprinted by permission of the author.

189   Practice 6 (A). Ramsey Clark wrote this paragraph about riots in *Crime in America.* Copyright © 1970 by Ramsey Clark. Reprinted by permission of Simon & Schuster, Inc.

190   Practice 6 (B). This example appears in Albert E. Elsen's *Purposes of Art.* New York: Holt, Rinehart, and Winston, 1962, pp. 32–33.

190   Practice 6 (C). This paragraph comes from Alexis de Tocqueville's *Democracy in America,* vol. II. Translated by Reeve, Bowan, and Bradley. New York: Alfred A. Knopf, Inc., 1945.

190   Practice 6 (D). Henry Steele Commager wrote this paragraph in "The Crisis of the Universities," *Newsday,* June 7, 1969. Reprinted by permission of the author.

190   Practice 6 (E). From Susanne Langer, "The Lord of Creation," *Fortune* Magazine, January 1944. Reprinted by permission of Time Inc.

191   From "The Secret Life of Walter Mitty" in *My World and Welcome to It,* published by Harcourt Brace Jovanovich. Copr. © 1942 James Thurber. Corp. © 1970 Helen Thurber. Originally printed in *The New Yorker.*

page 191 This descriptive paragraph appears in Joan Didion's "Some Dreamers of the Golden Dream." Reprinted with the permission of Farrar, Straus & Giroux, Inc. from *Slouching Towards Bethlehem* by Joan Didion. Copyright © 1966, 1968 by Joan Didion.

192 "I think I'll write. . . ." is cited in Peter Elbow's essay "Freewriting" from *Writing Without Teachers*. New York: Oxford University Press, 1973.

193 Practice 7 (A). James Baldwin wrote this paragraph in "Fifth Avenue Uptown: A Letter from Harlem," from *Nobody Knows My Name*. New York: The Dial Press, 1961. Reprinted by permission of The Dial Press.

194 Practice 7 (B). This paragraph appears in Tom Wolfe's "The Birth of the New Journalism" *New York* 5, no. 7 February 14, 1972. Copyright © 1972 by the NYM Corp. Reprinted with the permission of *New York* Magazine.

194 Practice 7 (C). This passage is from William Faulkner's "Impressions of Japan," in *Essays, Speeches, and Public Lectures,* edited by James B. Meriwether. New York: Random House, Inc., 1965.

194 Practice 7 (C). This paragraph was taken from James Wellard's "The Lost Cities" in *The Great Sahara*. London: Curtis Brown Ltd., 1964.

194 Practice 7 (E). Jaime De Angulo wrote this account of the Pit River Indians in "Indians in Overalls." Reprinted by permission from *The Hudson Review,* Vol. III, No. 3 (Autumn, 1950). Copyright © 1950 by The Hudson Review, Inc.

195 Practice 7 (F). This paragraph appears in George Orwell's "A Hanging" from *Shooting an Elephant and Other Essays*. New York: Harcourt Brace Jovanovich, 1945.

195 From Dr. Graham Blaine, "Why Intelligent Young People Take Drugs," *Journal of Iowa Medical Society,* January, 1969. Reprinted by permission of the publisher.

197 This two-paragraph sequence about contemporary music comes from J. L. Simmons and Barry Winogard's *It's Happening: A Portrait of the Youth Scene Today*. Santa Barbara, California: McNally and Loftin, Publishers, 1967.

Unit 8

219 The first headnote for Unit 8, from *Language in Thought and Action,* Third Edition, p. 155, by S. I. Hayakawa, copyright © 1972 by Harcourt Brace, Jovanovich, Inc. and reprinted with their permission.

219 The second headnote, from Ludwig Wittgenstein's *The Blue and Brown Books,* originally published by Harper & Row, New York, 1958, p. 27. Reprinted by permission of Basil Blackwell Publishers, London.

224 These paragraphs describing the anthropologist's difficulty with a "point-to" definition are cited in Lionel Ruby and Robert E. Yarber's *The Art of Making Sense,* Third Edition. Philadelphia: J. B. Lippincott Company, 1974, p. 39.

225 Louis B. Salomon's explanation of a circular definition appears in *Semantics and Common Sense*. New York: Holt Rinehart Winston, Inc., 1966, p. 54.

225 Monroe Beardsley's remarks about circular definition are taken from his book, *Thinking Straight*. Third Edition. Englewood Cliffs, N.J.: Prentice-Hall, Inc., 1966, p. 254.

page 225   Ambrose Bierce's "The Devil's Dictionary" is included in *The Collected Writings of Ambrose Bierce.* New York: The Citadel Press, 1946, p. 301.

226   This qualification of the average city dweller's need for definitions appears in *Webster's New World Dictionary.* New York: The World Publishing Company, 1972, p. xxvii.

226   The statement of editorial policy for "This present dictionary. . . ." is also taken from *Webster's New World Dictionary.* New York: The World Publishing Company, 1972, p. xxvii.

227   Bernard de Voto produced this descriptive definition of a buffalo in *Across the Wide Missouri.* Boston: Houghton Mifflin Company, 1947.

227   This definition of a "technetronic" society appears in Zbigniew Brzezinshi's "America in the Technetronic Age." London: *Encounter,* January, 1968.

228   "Marital complaints today. . . ." reprinted by permission of *Psychology Today* Magazine. Copyright © 1976 Ziff-Davis Publishing Company.

229   This extended definition is reprinted from *Life Against Death,* by Norman O. Brown. Copyright © 1959 by Wesleyan University. Reprinted by permission of Wesleyan University Press.

230   "What Is a Recession?" *Time,* March 4, 1974. Reprinted by permission from *Time,* The Weekly Newsmagazine; Copyright Time Inc., 1974.

232   "The pipe under. . . ." Reprinted by permission of *Psychology Today* Magazine. Copyright © 1976 Ziff-Davis Publishing Company.

233   Practice 2 (A). Excerpt from "When Is Death?" by Leonard A. Stevens, *The Reader's Digest,* May 1969. Copyright 1969 by The Reader's Digest Assn., Inc.

233   Practice 2 (B). This startling announcement first appeared in *Newsweek,* March 22, 1976, p. 85. Copyright 1976, by Newsweek, Inc. All rights reserved. Reprinted by permission.

233   Practice 2 (C). E. H. Gombrich developed this definition in "The Visual Image." *Scientific American,* September 1972, p. 92. Reprinted by permission of the publisher.

234   Practice 2 (D). This definition is taken from Ernest R. Kretzmer's "Communication Terminals." *Scientific American,* September 1972, p. 131. Reprinted by permission of the publisher.

234   Practice 2 (E). "Plovers" are defined in *Birds of North America: A Guide to Field Identification* by Chandler Robbins, B. Bruun, and H. Zim. New York: Western Publishing Company, 1966.

234   Practice 2 (F). William G. Carleton included this definition in "The Passing of Bughouse Square." Copyright © by The Antioch Press. First published in the *Antioch Review.* Vol. XX, no. 3. Reprinted by the permission of the editors.

236   The first definition of "The American Dream" appears in Herman Spivey's "Can—Should—the American Dream Survive?" *Phi Kappa Phi Journal,* Winter, 1976, p. 3. Reprinted by permission of the author and the publisher.

237   Spencer Brown wrote this example in "The Younger Generation." *The New York Times,* Nov. 27, 1966. Copyright 1966 by The New York Times Co.

238   "The little verb. . . ." Reprinted by permission of *Psychology Today* Magazine. Copyright © 1976 Ziff-Davis Publishing Company.

239   The four advertisements from *Time* all appeared in the May 19, 1975 issue, pp. 18, 19, 22, 76–77, and 64.

page 240   Will Rogers' playful definition of "a conference" is quoted in "Quotable Quotes," *Reader's Digest*, November 1975, p. 145.

240   Merle Miller quotes Harry Truman's explanation of valuable learning in the Truman biography, *Plain Speaking*. New York: G. P. Putnam's Sons, 1975.

240   Mary H. Waldrip created this definition of "rumor" in the Dawson County, Georgia, *Advertiser and News*.

240   Anecdote from "All in a Day's Work" (RD 8/75) by L. H. Crum in the August 1975 *Reader's Digest*. Used with permission.

240   Practice 4. Ambrose Bierce returns with more definitions from "The Devil's Dictionary." *The Collected Writings of Ambrose Bierce*. New York: The Citadel Press, 1946.

241   This comparison of the impact of two different populations on their land is from Wayne H. Davis' article, "Overpopulated America," *The New Republic*, January 10, 1970, p. 13. Reprinted by permission of *The New Republic* © 1970, The New Republic, Inc.

Unit 9

244   The first headnote is from Loren Eiseley's "The Cosmic Prison" in *The Invisible Pyramid*. New York: Charles Scribner's Sons, 1970. Reprinted by permission of the publisher.

244   The second headnote is from Ludwig Wittgenstein's *Philosophical Investigations*. Originally published by Macmillan & Co., New York, 1958. Reprinted by permission of Basil Blackwell Publishers, London.

249   Kenneth Boulding explains the role of individual value systems in perception in his book *The Image*. Ann Arbor, Michigan: University of Michigan Press, 1956.

252   The example of the Chinese teacher-on-a-holiday and the explanation of the spread of the rumor are from Gordon Allport and Leo Postmen's *The Psychology of Rumor*, pp. 134, 136–137. New York: Henry Holt and Company, 1947.

253   Practice 3. Newspaper accounts about the fall of Antwerp during World War I are cited in Arthur Ponsonby's *Falsehood in Wartime*. London: E. P. Dutton and Company, Inc., 1928.

254   "How Real Is Our Reality?" by Albert Rosenfeld appears in *Saturday Review/World*, October 5, 1974, p. 51. Reprinted by permission of the publisher.

258   This prediction of the rate of economic recovery is taken from *Time*, May 26, 1975, p. 70.

262   Practice 5 (A). Mark Twain created this dialogue about language differences in Chapter 14 of *The Adventures of Huckleberry Finn*.

262   Practice 5 (B). This example appears in *The American Rifleman*, December, 1969.

262   Practice 5 (C). Thomas Reid developed this argument in "Essay I" from *Essays on the Intellectual Powers of Man*. Originally published 1785.

262   Practice 5 (D). Excerpts from "The Most Exhaustive Survey on Smoking & Disease" from *Time*, December 8, 1963. Reprinted by permission from *Time*, The Weekly Newsmagazine; Copyright Time Inc., 1963.

page 263   Practice 5 (E). Ramsey Clark characterizes "youthful crime" in this excerpt from *Crime in America*. © 1970 by Ramsey Clark. Reprinted by permission of Simon & Schuster, Inc.

263   Practice 5 (G). This passage appears in *Business Week,* February 16, 1976, p. 20. Reprinted by permission of the publisher, McGraw Hill and Co., New York.

263   Practice 5 (H). John G. Mitchell wrote this passage about the decline of available land in *Ecotactics: A Sierra Club Handbook for Environmental Activists*. New York: Sierra Club Pocket Books, division of Simon and Schuster, 1970. Copyright 1970 by The Sierra Club. Reprinted by permission of Simon & Schuster, Inc. Pocket Books division.

264   Ludwig Wittgenstein's description of problem-solving is taken from *Philosophical Investigations,* edited by George Pitcher. Garden City, New York: Doubleday and Company, 1966.

264   This passage by Loren Eisley appears in "The Cosmic Prison" in *The Invisible Pyramid*. New York: Charles Scribner's Sons, 1970. Reprinted by permission of the publisher.

264   Eisley's further comment about the power of unstated assumptions is also from "The Cosmic Prison."

Contents

III STYLE AND STRUCTURE

IV LANGUAGE AND CONCEPTUAL STRUCTURES

Foreword

A foreword is exactly what it says it is. It is a word about the book, offered to readers before they begin to read. The foreword serves as a kind of guide, to help them organize the book, to help them form expectations about it. If readers know what to predict, the reading becomes easier.

So here is our foreword. We are writing a book about reading, designed to help you improve your reading skills. But first we should tell you what the book is *not* designed to do. It is not designed to help you read faster, for we are more concerned with the skills of interpretation than with speed. It is not specifically designed to help you improve your reading vocabulary, although we believe that your ability to comprehend and respond to words will be improved. It is not designed to help you learn to skim-read, nor to paraphrase what you have read. In short, this book is not like most books you will find in reading labs and in developmental reading courses.

This book about reading is different from most others because it asks you to do two things at once: it asks you to learn to read a text carefully and responsively; and it asks you to learn to *watch* yourself reading carefully and responsively and to understand *why* you respond as you do. Doing these two things at once is difficult, of course. It is rather like watching yourself watch yourself in a mirror. Nevertheless, most sophisticated thinkers have learned this self-reflexive habit of mind and practice it every day—and find that practice makes this difficult pattern of thinking much easier.

Before we go on, it might be helpful to say *why* the three of us decided to write this book. We've been teaching for about fifteen years, if you add it all up together. During these years, we have learned in our classrooms and in our conversations outside of class that most of our students can handle the mechanical tasks of reading fairly competently and with some efficiency. They can read a page in a reasonable period of time, can understand most of the information it conveys, and can paraphrase it with some accuracy. But what happens when the information that is being paraphrased is of less importance than the emotion or belief that is being conveyed? And what happens when the writer uses metaphoric language, or when he or she implies something without actually stating it—or states it indirectly?

Our college students have a great deal of difficulty at these points in their reading—primarily, we believe, because they are *passive* readers. They let the pages slip by under their eyes, gleaning the information printed there, but not questioning that information in any significant way. They don't ask whether indeed it *is* information, or something else altogether; they don't inquire about how it is presented, in what kind of organization and style, with what effect on their perceptions; they don't wonder about the kinds of assumptions and beliefs and values it is based on. Our college students, for the most part, are not *participating* readers, reading with a full understanding of what reading is all about.

This book is designed to help you become a participating reader. It is designed to help you understand the process of reading—the part of reading that is related to perception and the part of reading that is related to the making of meaning, or interpretation. It is designed to help you understand how reading is similar to all of the other meaning-making activities in your life. When you have finished this book and have achieved the goals that are outlined at the beginnings of each of the chapters, or *units*, you will find yourself reading more critically, with greater attention to language, to pattern and organization, to logic and idea.

If you'll take a quick look at the Contents, you'll be able to see something of the book's organization and structure. The first section defines some important terms—the term *reading*, for instance, and the phrase *the participating reader*. It focusses on the ways we read the world around us and how that kind of "reading" is similar to the reading of printed marks on the page. It also raises the question of the importance of writing in our media-oriented culture. Section II, you'll notice, is divided into three units. In each of these units, we take up one important aspect of language use: language used to inform, language used to express belief and to persuade, language used metaphorically. In Section III (which is also divided into three units), we are concerned with the way structure—the style of sentences, the organization of paragraphs, the relationship of paragraphs to one another—creates meaning in the reader's mind. Finally, Section IV (composed of two units) takes up the question of conceptual structures—structures of belief and assumption—that organize all writing and reading. It also discusses inductive argument, examining the strategies with which writers present argument and the tests readers can apply to make sure those arguments are sound.

The organization of the book is probably fairly clear to you by now: we begin with the whole act of reading, then turn to the way words have meaning, the way sentence and paragraph structures organize the reader's perception of meaning, and the way beliefs and attitudes influence both writing and reading. Throughout, our focus is on *you*: on your meaning-making activity and on your interaction with the text you're reading.

But the overall content organization isn't the only thing that you need to know about, because the book is built on another important structure: a *learning* structure. To get an overview of that learning structure, turn to Unit 2, p. 30, where you'll find a list of learning goals outlined—activities you should be able to perform when you've finished studying the unit. Notice that in this unit (the first unit in Section II), you'll be carrying out relatively simple tasks—learning definitions, finding examples, practicing the recognition of important concepts. Turn now to p. 48 and look at the learning goals for the next unit. Here, you'll deal with more difficult tasks, discussion and describing, as well as defining. In the last unit of this section (Unit 4, p. 71), you are asked to perform the most difficult task of all—evaluating language on the basis of its appropriateness. In this text, the organization of learning is built on a sequence of simple-to-difficult tasks.

Within the units themselves, practice problems in both close reading and in writing about what you've read help you to develop your skills and to evaluate your learning. At the end of each section, a group of readings gives you an opportunity to synthesize what you've learned and to apply it to the complex operation of reading whole essays and articles. These readings are meant to be discussed in class, so that you can match your ideas about each reading against those of the other students. As you engage in these discussions and as you work through the study questions, we hope you'll find yourself doing what we described in the beginning of this foreword: watching yourself reading, and at the same time under-standing how and why you read.

Forewords serve one other purpose: to allow authors to thank the people who help their books pass from idea to print. We want first of all to thank the two hundred or so students who have shared with us their enthusiasm and skepticism over the two years this book has been in the making, and who have so cheerfully submitted to the torture of blue dittoed pages. We also want to thank the reviewers, James Raymond and Susan Miller, whose painstaking readings and most helpful advice shaped and reshaped and re-reshaped our thinking—right up to the final hour. We are also grateful to Bill Oliver and Martin Tenney, of Prentice-Hall, for their patient encouragement. And we owe a special thanks to two other people: to Barbara Babcock-Abrahams, whose ideas on self-reflexivity and participation in the interpreting act are reflected so frequently in these pages; and to Jim Blake, for allowing us to take over his home, his drafting tables, and his dinner hour with our books and papers. We are in your debt.

SUSAN WITTIG
FRANKLIN HOLCOMB
ANNE DUNN

THE
PARTICIPATING
READER

I

INTRODUCTION

UNIT 1
The Participating Reader

UNIT I

The
Participating
Reader

Of all born creatures, man is the only one that cannot live by bread alone.
He lives as much by symbols as by sense report, in a realm compounded of
tangible things and virtual images, of actual events and ominous portents, always
between fact and fiction. . . . By the agency of symbols—marks, words, mental
images, and icons of all sorts—he can hold his ideas for contemplation long
after their original causes have passed away. Therefore, he can think of things
that are not presented or even suggested by his actual environment. By associating
symbols in his mind he combines things and events that were never together in
the real world. This gives him the power we call imagination. Further, he can
symbolize only part of an idea and let the rest go out of consciousness;
this gives him the faculty that has been his pride throughout the ages—the power
of abstraction. The combined effect of these two powers is inestimable. They are
the roots of his supreme talent, the gift of reason. (Susanne K. Langer)

What Is Reading?

Have you ever stopped to think how many different activities we could classify under the general term "reading"? For example, I may *read* the clouds to discover whether it's going to rain; or I may *read* my neighbor's face to decipher his intentions after I have backed over his favorite magnolia bush; or I may *read* tea leaves, the tracks of an animal, tarot cards. In all of these reading activities, I have seen and interpreted a *sign* * or a group of signs that have meaning for me, and I may even decide upon a course of action based on my reading. (I may put on a raincoat before I go out, or I may flee hastily to the other side of the fence away from my neighbor.) *Reading,* * then, can be broadly defined as the active process of making meaning out of signs and symbols—not just alphabetic symbols, but anything that can be interpreted: any natural event or any cultural artifact.

There are many excellent reasons why it would be useful for us to look at the many things we interpret and at the many ways in which we read the world around us. But reading language is a vitally important means of gaining experience beyond our own immediate abilities to see and make sense out of the physical world. For instance, only if we can read the printed symbols that represent language do we know how important discoveries were made when we weren't there to witness them. We know so many things out of the past—how Edison developed the phonograph, how radium was discovered, what Newton thought about the workings of the universe, what Abraham Lincoln said at Gettysburg—only because somebody took the time to write about them and we've taken the time to read what has been written. If we can't read printed symbols, it has often been pointed out, we are in a very real sense prisoners of our own time and our own place. Claude Lévi-Strauss, a French anthropologist, describes writing as a way of gaining power:

* Throughout this book, words marked by a single asterisk are defined in the glossary beginning on p. 312. Double asterisks are noted at the bottom of the page.

4

Gesturing to communicate—scratching your head, biting your nails, wiggling your foot—is one of the most important nonverbal languages that humans "speak." However, as this cartoon indicates, it is also a language that is open to all kinds of "readings." Putting communication into words narrows down the possible interpretations a reader might give. (Drawing by C. E. M.; © 1961 The New Yorker Magazine, Inc.)

Writing is a strange invention.... The possession of writing vastly increases man's ability to preserve knowledge. It can be thought of as an artificial memory, the development of which ought to lead to a clearer awareness of the past, and hence to a greater ability to organize both the present and the future. After eliminating all other criteria which have been put forward to distinguish between barbarism and civilization, it is tempting to retain this one at least: there are peoples with, or without, writing; the former are able to store up their past achievements and to move with ever-increasing rapidity towards the goal they have set themselves, whereas the latter, being incapable of remembering the past beyond the narrow margin of individual memory, seem bound to remain imprisoned in a fluctuating history which will always lack both a beginning and any lasting awareness of an aim.

In fact, as Lévi-Strauss goes on to point out, writing is a way of setting a people free; at the same time, it also enables a nation that possesses writing to exert power over another nation that does not. Whichever way we choose to look at the issue, one thing is clear: reading and writing—the basic tools of literacy—give us control over the world and over our lives.

Because of the importance of printed materials as a source of knowledge about the world, this book will focus primarily on the process of reading writing. Other kinds of reading experiences are necessary before the printed words begin to make sense to us, however. (How would it be possible to understand a writer's observation that "the low clouds on the horizon signaled rain" unless we have already learned to read clouds for ourselves?) When we talk in this book about the process of reading printed words in the pages of books, magazines, newspapers, you should keep in mind that we are dealing with only one small aspect of the act of reading.

Why Do We Read?

We pick up reading materials for all kinds of reasons. We read fiction and poetry for entertainment, for escape, for pleasure. We read articles, essays, and nonfiction pieces for information necessary to our physical comfort, our professional or personal advancement, our psychological well-being. We read both fiction and nonfiction because we're interested in other people's beliefs, or because we want to understand how other cultures in other times thought and believed and acted, or because we would like to learn about the structure of the physical and social universe. There are as many different motives and opportunities for reading as there are readers.

People who read widely develop a number of different reading strategies to deal with the different materials they read. These strategies have to do with how deeply involved the reader is in the act of reading

GASOLINE ALLEY—By Moores

In our culture, other communications media appear to be replacing the book in importance. Is this statement true, in your experience? How much time do you spend reading, compared to the length of time you spend watching TV or listening to the radio? If the statement is true, what might be the consequences for our culture? Do you think those consequences might be good or bad? (Reprinted by permission of The Chicago Tribune. Copyright 1975. All rights reserved.)

and how fast he or she can read the material. When you're reading for fun, you may gobble up a whole novel, from beginning to end, in one evening. When you're browsing through the current issue of *Time* or through the morning paper, you may read a little bit here, another little bit there—you may scan the page quickly, looking for something that interests you, but you may never finish a single article and read without real concentration. In both these cases, you're probably a fairly *passive reader,*° watching the words "go by" on the page, not deeply engaged with your reading.

On the other hand, when you're reading something you're really interested in or something you know you must remember in detail, you become a *participating reader;*° you may even read with pencil in hand, marking major points in the text or taking notes on a sheet of paper. Your degree of active participation in your reading—your level of concentration, your interaction with the material (marking the page, taking notes), even the speed of your reading—varies from one kind of reading task to another. It depends, primarily, upon your motivation and your purpose for reading. In general, readers who participate *fully* in the reading act— who engage all their mental resources in the business of interpretation —are much more likely to retain what they've read. Mortimer Adler, commenting on the act of participating in reading, observes that making notes on the pages of a book is much more likely to increase the reader's understanding:

> But, you may ask, why is writing necessary? Well, the physical act of writing, with your own hand, brings words and sentences more sharply before your mind and preserves them better in your memory. To set down your reaction to important words and sentences you have read, and the questions they have raised in your mind, is to preserve those reactions and sharpen those questions.
>
> Even if you wrote on a scratch pad, and threw the paper away when you had finished writing, your grasp of the book would be surer. But you don't have to throw the paper away. The margins (top and bottom, as well as side), the end-papers, the very space between the lines, are all available. They aren't sacred. And, best of all, your marks and notes become an integral part of the book and stay there forever. You can pick up the book the following week or year, and there are all your points of agreement, disagreement, doubt, and inquiry. It's like resuming an interrupted conversation with the advantage of being able to pick up where you left off.

This book contains a wide selection of *kinds* of reading materials, although some kinds have been intentionally either omitted or slighted. (We haven't included many stories or poems, for instance, because our focus here is not primarily on reading for entertainment.) Our concern in this book is the informative and persuasive reading you will be doing in your college work, and it is specifically designed to help you develop some strategies that will be useful to you every day, as you read through the various assignments your college instructors will make. The purpose for reading that we have assumed here is a *critical* purpose; we think that you will find it necessary during most of your college work to be a person who examines carefully and analytically what you read.

Take a moment now to think about the reading practices and habits you've already begun to develop. Here are a few of the questions you might ask yourself as you work through the tasks suggested below: What kinds of reading do I do? Is my reading primarily in assigned texts, or do I read for recreation? How is my reading related to the many other things I do in my life? How could I plan to do more (or more different kinds of) reading?

practice 1

SOME WRITING AND REVIEWING TASKS FOR READERS

1. Find the definition of reading in the paragraphs you've just finished. Use it as a basis for a short paragraph in which you describe the different kinds of reading you do—other than reading written materials. (Reading people's faces and actions, reading nonverbal signs, and so on.)

2. On the next page, you'll find a guide for a reading journal. Keep the journal for five days, noting the titles of the pieces you read, the number of pages you read, the time you spend reading, and your reasons for reading. Include any comments you might have on the material itself.

3. After you've finished your journal, make a list of the kinds of things you've been reading: newspapers, magazines, books, and so on. Did you read any short stories? plays? poetry? science fiction? With your teacher or with a group of your classmates, use the format on p. 10 to make another list—this time a list of things you'd like to read during the course of the semester—and a reading schedule that will help you to organize your planned reading. A copy of a book review magazine (*The New York Review of Books* is available at most college bookstores) may help you and your classmates decide which books you'd like to put on your list.

What Happens When You Read?

Reading the printed page is a complicated process that involves us in a half-dozen activities at once. Some of us may believe that reading is a *watching* process, that all we have to do is look at the page and let it "soak" into our consciousness. That belief, however, may lead us into

Reading Journal

Day	Date	Title	Pages/Time Spent	Reasons for Reading	Comments
1					
2					
3					
4					
5					

NAME _____

READING SCHEDULE

FROM _____

To _____

Title	Begin/Finish	Buy? Borrow?

Nonfiction

Fiction

Poetry

Drama

Other

trouble, for nothing could be further from the actual fact of the matter: reading is in fact an active process—or rather, an *interactive* process—that involves the reader in many ways. Reading isn't accomplished on the page, but in the *interaction* between the words on the page and the reader's mind.

Some of the processes of reading are physiological and neurological; they happen automatically, whether we are thinking about them or not. Others are mental exercises that require our active participation in what's going on: to pay close attention to the page, to remember what we've been reading, and to think ahead to what's coming next. Still others are higher-level conceptual activities that involve thinking about the process of thinking. This activity may require us to examine closely the systems of beliefs out of which we as readers make judgments. All of these operations take place almost simultaneously when we encounter the written page. People who understand what's happening as they read have important advantages over those who don't. For one thing, when they experience reading difficulties, they know that the trouble may lie with themselves (maybe they are too tired or too distracted or too disinterested to participate fully in their reading). But they also know that the trouble may lie with the material—with its level of difficulty or with its appeal or with its presentation on the page—and that they can regulate their reading activity to cope with the material and with their attitudes toward it. Reading isn't easy—it is one of the most demanding mental ventures that we engage in, requiring all our resources. Readers who know what they're doing are way ahead of the game.

The Physical Act of Reading

The physical process of reading a page involves your eyes and your brain—your neurological system—in a complex set of cooperative activities. Right now your eyes are following a pattern that your brain taught them a long time ago, when you first began to read: they are moving quickly from left to right, from the top to the bottom of the page, scanning the printed symbols. (So long ago that you probably can't remember it, you learned that in our language we read only in one direction, across the page, and that letters are grouped into words and words into sentences from left to right, from top to bottom. Your eyes have remembered that knowledge ever since, and operate automatically when they meet the printed page.)

According to reading experts, "good" readers have trained their eyes to move as rapidly as their understanding of the material will allow. However, their eyes don't move across the page linearly, encountering every word: they have learned to let their eyes pause on a ten-word line perhaps only twice in the length of it, so that instead of seeing and recognizing ten single words, they see two five-word clumps. In fact, the actual path of an efficient reader looks something like this:

> Different readers   take in varying amounts   of print   at a glance.   Some grasp   only one word   at a time;   their eyes feed the mind   information in tidbits.   Each word is   a separate mental   and physical effort,   and cumulatively,   the result of such activity   is fatigue and   loss of interest.   The physical effort   is simply too great   to be justified   by the result.   The rapid reader,   on the other hand,   scoops up *groups* of words   at a single glance.   His eyes travel   across a line of print   in three or four jerks   and then return   along the white alley   between the rows   of printed characters   to the beginning   of the next line.   To each three or four stops (fixations) per line   for the rapid reader,   the less efficient reader   makes eight, ten, or twelve   separate pauses.

Skilled readers, then, don't actually, physically *see* every word on the page. And, equally important, their eyes don't actually *see* or discriminate every letter of every word. Instead, they see word-shapes, configurations of letters, first and last letters instead of whole words. These "graphic cues" are added to other kinds of important information that the reader is processing, so that the whole word is recognized, even though the reader may have glimpsed only the slightest of visual cues.

To prove to yourself that you don't make use of all the graphic or printed information that the page gives you, try this experiment with the lines below, in which letters have been deleted from some words. If you can fill in the blanks with the missing words and letters, you know that the information you processed to understand those missing graphic cues came from somewhere else in the reading process.

> Recognizing whole wo -shapes is   important factor in reading eff ncy. Beginning re   rs wh are un amiliar wi   the way words look on p er treat each series   letters as a n w pr lem; ski   ed readers respond   word-wholes, even whole phrases. They do   t need to loo at wor -parts.

You see, you really don't need to look at everything on the page in front of you in order to reconstruct the message the writer wanted to send. In fact, readers who attempt to make use of *all* the information at their disposal are usually inefficient, and their inefficiencies slow up their reading progress considerably.

The rate at which your eyes move, the number of times you allow them to pause in mid-line, and the length of these split-second pauses are all factors that influence your reading speed. If your eye movements

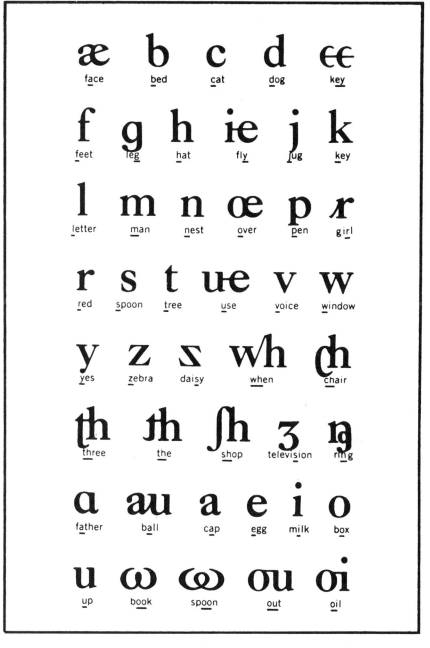

æ   b   c   d   ee

face   bed   cat   dog   key

f   g   h   ie   j   k

feet   leg   hat   fly   jug   key

l   m   n   œ   p   ʀ

letter   man   nest   over   pen   girl

r   s   t   ue   v   w

red   spoon   tree   use   voice   window

y   z   ʒ   wh   ch

yes   zebra   daisy   when   chair

th   th   ſh   ʒ   ŋ

three   the   shop   television   ring

a   au   a   e   i   o

father   ball   cap   egg   milk   box

u   ω   ω   ou   oi

up   book   spoon   out   oil

Not even all *English* alphabets look alike! Many children have learned to read books printed in a new alphabet, called the Initial Teaching Alphabet (ITA). Some critics have suggested, however, that although the new alphabet does encourage better reading, it creates unusual spelling habits in later life. *(Copyright by Initial Teaching Alphabet Publications, Inc.)*

are efficient (if you scan the line quickly enough to catch all the meaningful word shapes, perhaps actually resting on the words only once or twice in the line) your reading speed is likely to be fairly high. On the other hand, if your eye movements are inefficient (if you scan the line word by word, or linger momentarily over one word or another) your reading speed is apt to be fairly low.

The ability to recognize words in a split second can be measured with an instrument called a *tachistoscope,* * a machine that looks like a slide viewer. The tachistoscope displays words or phrases for a preset length of time; it is used as a teaching tool to encourage readers to look at whole clumps of words, rather than at single words in the line. However, researchers are finding out that the use of machines as reading aids is not as helpful for most college-age readers as the conscious, deliberate effort to improve skills related to *critical* reading. This appears to be true because most readers can read the words on the page; their difficulties arise from an incomplete knowledge of the significance of these words and the way the words and sentences have meaning.

practice 2

EXERCISES FOR READERS

To test our comments here about line-scanning, take a page from a magazine (the page should have full-width columns) and poke a hole in it with a pencil. Ask a friend to begin reading ten lines immediately above the hole and go on past it for ten lines while you watch the scanning action of his or her eyes through the hole in the paper. How many pauses per line can you count? Now, have your friend measure your scansion rate and compare notes.

Your college probably has a reading lab, and most reading labs own at least one tachistoscope. Ask the person in charge if you can test the speed of your reading reflexes by using the tachistoscope. See if you can discover the shortest length of time you require to read a three- or five-word phrase. How do your reading reflexes compare with those of other students in your class?

Conceptualization and the Reading Process

The connection between what your eyes see and what your brain registers is in many ways a scientific mystery, and we aren't really interested here in the technical explanation of its physical characteristics. Let's simplify the problem by saying that the optic nerve transmits the image—the size, shape, and general configurations of the printed letter-clumps that have been registered on the retina of the eye—to the brain, where a rapid-fire sorting operation goes on that *decodes* the visual image of the letters and makes meaning out of it. It's the decoding process that we're interested in here, the process of translating the shapes of printed letters into ideas. We can call it the process of *conceptualization*.

What Are Concepts?

Concepts * are mental images or categories that are built out of our experiences with concrete things, with events in everyday life, with people: they are ideas through which we understand the physical and social worlds we live in. For example, concepts such as *democracy, socialism,* and *communism* allow us to categorize and classify some forms of socializing activity that enable large groups of people to live together, sharing particular beliefs and ideologies about the social and economic nature of their coexistence. Other concepts, such as *honesty, truth, loyalty,* help us to describe particular character traits that make coexistence in the social world comfortable and pleasant. Still others (*symphony, march, aria*) make it possible for artists to talk about certain products of their musical imagination while others (*Phasianidae, Colinus virginianus*) allow scientists to classify certain kinds of wildlife.

Human beings aren't born with a fully developed ability to conceptualize, or to build mental categories. This is an ability that matures as we grow older, and it is related to our expanding vocabulary and our ability to use language. Learning specialists tell us that we learn gradually, over a period of years, to construct mental categories—patterns of ideas about the way the world works—and to test them against our experience. Younger children build relatively simple concepts that allow them to adequately understand their relatively limited experiences, while adults must build very complex concepts in order to cope with the complicated world they live in. A child's concept of the *abstraction* * *"punishment,"* for example, may include only spanking or being told to stand in a corner; an adult's concept of punishment may range from simple to complex forms of physical punishment to political or social exile to imprisonment—even to capital punishment. The adult's concept is built on a long-time experience with many events in the world—and events that he or she has read about; the child's concept is built on a much briefer experience with the world, and does not often include reading.

But the problem doesn't end there, for in fact most adults whose activities require them to perform several different kinds of jobs or to work with abstract ideas rather than with concrete things must develop concepts *about* their concepts—intricate mental filing systems which enable them to understand and think critically about decisions they have made and plans they want to put into action. These filing systems, built out of concepts-about-concepts, perform the necessary function of helping them to organize what they know, so that they can examine the

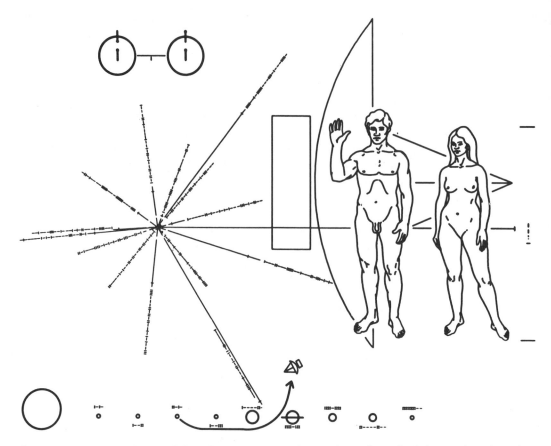

This message appears on the outer hull of the *Pioneer* spacecraft. It is designed to tell inhabitants of another solar system where the craft comes from and who sent it. Do you think that these symbols can communicate the message that is intended? What concepts would a "reader" have to possess in order to decipher it? What would make it difficult to "read"? *(Pioneer spacecraft graphic message. Reprinted by permission of the publisher.)*

outcomes of their decisions. For example, an employer hiring a worker must know not only the activities the worker is to perform, but the educational background and motivation level the worker must have— he must know "what kind" of a worker he wants to hire.

But there is an unfortunate difficulty with our concepts-about-concepts, for our filing system may keep us from making certain kinds of intelligent choices. For instance, our employer may have a concept-about-concepts that tells him that no woman could perform the tasks the job requires or possess the necessary educational background or motivational level; the concept "woman" can't be filed under his concept of "what kind" of worker he wants to hire. In this case, the employer's concept-about-concepts keeps him from carrying out certain actions that might be very beneficial to him. Further, we are often unaware of our concepts-about-concepts; they operate at a subconscious level, frequently passed along from generation to generation without ever being closely examined. These concepts are what we often call our *cultural myths.**

How Is Reading Related to Concept-Building?

Our ability to read is very clearly related to our abilities to build organized concepts, to construct mental categories that include pieces of information we have picked up here and there, and to group them systematically according to principles of understanding that make sense to us. Reading *is* concept-building, in fact: it begins with our physical encounter with the words on the page and our recognition and decoding of them, and ends in the larger understanding of the relationship between the author's ideas and our own. Our ability to read is also related to our "record-keeping" abilities: our capacity to keep track of what we think is important, to check our understanding of these significant pieces of information we already have against the incoming information from our reading.

If our mental records are efficient and adequate and if we arrange them so that we can get at them easily, we can continually add to our conceptual categories—and our reading ability will be continually improved. If we examine our concepts-about-concepts carefully, and test them against our experiences and the recorded experiences of others, we can keep them from operating invisibly. Because all our concepts reside in language, the close study of words, their meanings, and their social functions is necessary to make our concepts visible to us. In this book, we will spend some time with this task, in order to see how concepts are passed along to us through the language of the books we read.

The Guessing Game: Predictions and Inferences

Have you ever noticed that you can *predict* * the end of a friend's sentence, once he or she has begun it? Or have you ever watched a performer whose performance consists of mimicking another speaker—a split second *before* the word is spoken? These are only two examples of the ability of human beings to predict speech patterns and to guess what's going to come next. It is possible to predict a speaker's next words both because we are familiar with the speaker and know his or her speaking habits (you know your friend very well) and because we know the language *code* * (the words and the way words are combined in English sentences) .

Readers also predict language patterns a split second before they actually recognize the word-shapes on the page. Their ability to make informed guesses about what's coming next on the page contributes to their ability to read quickly and efficiently. However, the ability to anticipate what the writer will say is related to the level of difficulty of the reading material. We can easily read the following passage from a college textbook, for instance, partly because we recognize all the words and partly because the words are combined with one another in sentence patterns we have learned to expect:

> The definitions given by little children in school show clearly how they associate words with situations; they almost always define in terms of physical and social contexts: "Punishment is when you have been bad and they put you in a closet and don't let you have any supper." "Newspapers are what the paper boy brings and you wrap up the garbage with it." These are good definitions.

Our abilities to predict the words and sentence patterns in this passage enable us to read it quite easily. As you probably noticed, some of the patterns sound very much like speech. (As a rule, the closer writing is to talking, the easier it is to read. That doesn't always make it the best writing, however!) But take a look at the following passage, excerpted from an article in *Scientific American*. It is much more difficult: the words are new and we may need to look up a half-dozen terms before we can begin to decode it:

> Words display two patently distinct kinds of semantic value. Their compulsory grammatical meaning, a categorical relational concept or group of concepts that words constantly carry, is supplemented in all autonomous words by a lexical meaning. Like grammatical meanings, any general lexical meaning is in turn an invariant that under diverse contextual and situational transformations generates what Leonard Bloomfield (1887–1949) precisely defined as "marginal, transferred" meanings. They are sensed as derivative of the unmarked general meaning, and these tropes either stand in agreement with the verbal code or are an *ad hoc* digression from it.

Unfamiliar words are not the only things that keep us from anticipating what's coming next in the sentences we read. Unfamiliar sentence structures, complicated combinations of words in the sentence, also make it hard for us as readers to anticipate what's about to happen on the page. Look at this passage, in which the great dictionary-maker Samuel Johnson complains about the difficulties of making definitions:

> When the nature of things is unknown, or the notion unsettled and indefinite, and various in various minds, the words by which such notions are conveyed, or such things denoted, will be ambiguous and perplexed. And such is the fate of hapless lexicography, that

not only darkness, but light, impedes and distresses it; things may not be only too little, but too much known, to be happily illustrated. To explain, requires the use of terms less abstruse than that which is to be explained, and such terms cannot always be found; for as nothing can be proved but by supposing something intuitively known, and evident without proof, so nothing can be defined but by the use of words too plain to admit a definition.

Tough? You bet! College-level readers know most of the words in this passage (with the exception perhaps of *lexicography* (dictionary-making) and *abstruse* (difficult), but Johnson's *syntax* *—the way he combines the words in the sentence—makes predicting very difficult and makes the passage exceptionally hard for modern readers.

One other factor often makes prediction difficult. That factor is abstractness, the level of generality at which a particular author works. For an example, compare the following two passages and decide which is easiest to read:

One of the most important and most difficult questions raised by behavioral biology can be phrased in the evolutionary terms just introduced as follows: Can we hope to trace the origin of human language back through intermediate steps in our fellow higher primates. . . . ?

Maxwell, a monkey who lives in a University of California laboratory, may help us answer an important question about the evolution of human language. By watching Maxwell learn to use symbols— colored blocks of different shapes—biologists hope to trace human language, step by step, back to our nearest animal neighbors, apes and monkeys.

If you're like most readers, you'll find the second passage much easier to understand, even though the two vocabularies are very much the same. The first passage, as you've probably already noticed, is highly abstract, while the second uses a specific example that helps the reader to visualize clearly what is being said. Instead of having to think about "fellow higher primates," the reader is invited to consider Maxwell the monkey and his adventures with symbols.

Related to the use of abstraction is the use of *metaphor,* language that provides a comparison between two different things. Clichéd metaphors like *dead as a doornail* and *beet red* don't usually give readers difficulty because they are easily predicted. However, highly original metaphors, like John Donne's famous comparison of two lovers to a drawing compass, are likely to cause problems for inexperienced readers:

If they [the lovers] be two, they are two so
    As stiff twin compasses are two,
Thy soul the fixed foot, makes no show
    To move, but doth, if the other do.

And though it in the center sit,
    Yet when the other far doth roam,
It leans, and harkens after it,
    And grows erect, as that comes home.

The reading problem here originates in the difficulty of the metaphor,*
which challenges the reader to full participation in the reading act. No
once-over-lightly will work here, for the passive reader can't cope with
the intricacy of the metaphor. The reader who spends the effort required
to understand what the poet is saying will be amply rewarded. In Unit
Four, we'll discuss at length some of the problems presented by metaphor
in reading.

From Prediction to Inference

Predicting (guessing what's going to appear next on the page) is
immediately related to *inferring* * (guessing what's going on in the
writer's mind). Inference-making is probably the single most difficult
kind of participation that readers must undertake, and it demands conceptual skills that we may not even realize we possess.

Let's describe it this way. Writers can't tell readers *precisely* what
they mean, because language is not a perfect communication tool, as you
know from your own experience. Our communications are full of ambiguities, misstatements, and unstated assumptions; further, because we
speak out of our past experiences, we may be talking about something
different even when we appear to agree. S. I. Hayakawa describes this
problem:

> We may agree as to what the term "Mississippi River" stands for,
> but you and I recall different parts of the river; you and I have had
> different experiences with it; one of us has read more about it than
> the other; one of us may have happy memories of it, while the other
> may recall chiefly tragic events connected with it. Hence your
> "Mississippi River" can never be identical with my "Mississippi
> River." The fact that we can communicate with each other about the
> "Mississippi River" often conceals the fact that we are talking about
> two different sets of memories and experiences.

To make matters more complicated, some writers (usually the most
sophisticated writers) don't *want* to tell readers precisely what they
mean, because readers who get the point themselves, by carefully figuring it out, and by understanding clearly how it is related to their *own*

experiences, are more likely to fully understand the message. Tom Wolfe, a famous contemporary journalist, has remarked:

> I liked the idea of starting off a story by letting the reader, via the narrator, talk to the characters, hector them, insult them, prod them with irony or condescension, or whatever. Why should the reader be expected to just lie flat and let these people come tromping through as if his mind were a subway turnstile?

Participating readers, who take charge of their reading, are much more likely to understand what's going on. Even if they are momentarily confused, readers who stop to figure things out are better off than readers who are "spoon-fed" with the writer's ideas. Furthermore, readers who have to work to understand the writer's message are more likely to agree with the writer's point of view.

The reader's task is to try to decipher *through inference* what the writer means. At the beginning of the reading, we can say, writer and reader don't share the same concepts, the same understanding. In the

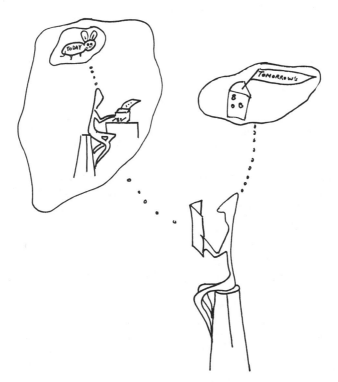

The Reading Process: A Matter of Inferences.
"Worry is Today's Mouse Eating Tomorrow's Cheese"

process of reading, readers bring their conceptual models—filing systems of concepts—into line with the writer's conceptual model: the writer teases the readers into guessing what these concepts are (inferring them, from the bits and pieces of evidence on the page). The readers, if they are actively participating in the reading activity, respond by trying to infer what the writer is thinking. If they're right, these inferences will probably be supported in some way in the next few lines, and they'll feel satisfied. If they're wrong, and their inferences or guesses are not matched by the writer's next few statements, they go back and try again.

Do you remember that "lost" feeling you've experienced (we *all* have) when you're reading along and suddenly you don't have the foggiest idea of what the writer is saying? At that moment your conceptual model, built on your inferences, has slipped out of alignment with the writer's model. You *are* lost, and in order to decipher or decode the passage, you must go back and try again, testing out a new set of inferences. You repeat this task until the passage "makes sense." Generally, getting lost like this happens because you momentarily stop participating. Maybe something has distracted you, or maybe the predictions become too difficult (because of vocabulary, sentence structure, or level of abstraction). We hope in this book to help you discover some specific strategies for dealing with these problems in your everyday reading.

practice 3

A TEST FOR READERS WHO WANT TO
MEASURE THEIR PARTICIPATION

Cloze testing * is a technique that measures a reader's ability to predict the next word he is about to read and his ability to make inferences about the writer's meaning in a particular line or passage. Here are two "cloze" passages from which some words have been deleted. Your task is to "close up" the empty spaces by supplying the word you think the writer used. As you supply these missing words, ask yourself what clues you are relying on most heavily to help you predict the word that has been left out. Which of the two passages is the more difficult?

Passage 1

In this twentieth _____ we take the _____ of our alphabet as much for _____ as the air we _____. We _____ to write at such an early _____ that we seldom stop to _____ about the importance of _____ to mankind. How many of us realize _____ writing alone has _____ possible the greatest civilizations and cultures, the _____ empires of the _____ race? _____ Lincoln once _____ that writing has enabled us _____ "converse _____ the dead, the absent, the unborn at all distances _____ time and space."

Passage 2

There _____ two distinct and _____ ways of writing, _____ using pictures, the other _____ syllables or _____ to express sounds. But do _____ be misled _____ thinking that ancient picture-_____ was dropped when sound-writing _____, for we make use of pictures _____ with our alphabet today. We also find good use _____ the devices employed by _____ for communication after he _____ to write. Transition _____ the stages in the development of _____ was gradual. One stage was _____ abandoned when the _____ began. They were intermingled. This means _____ we find _____-writing and _____-writing coexisting _____ the same system.

Passage 1: Original Version

In this twentieth century we take the letters of our alphabet as much for granted as the air we breathe. We learn to write at such an early age that we seldom stop to think about the importance of writing to mankind. How many of us realize that writing alone has made possible the greatest civilizations and cultures, the great empires of the human race? Abraham Lincoln once said that writing has enabled us to "converse with the dead, the absent, the unborn, at all distances of time and space."

Passage 2: Original Version

There were two distinct and different ways of writing, one using pictures, the other using syllables or letters to express sounds. But do not be misled into thinking that ancient picture-writing was dropped when sound-writing began, for we make use of pictures along with our alphabet today. We also find good use for the devices employed by man for communication before he learned to write. Transition between the stages in the development of writing was gradual. One stage was not abandoned when the next began. They were intermingled. This means that we find picture-writing and sound-writing coexisting in the same system.

How successful were you in predicting the writer's word choices? Some words, of course, have several possible synonyms. In the first passage, for instance, you might have substituted *vast* or *greatest* (or some other adjective suggesting size) for *great;* you might also have substituted *in* or *through* for *of* in the last blank. In Passage 2, you might have used *are* rather than *were* in the first blank; *varying* instead of *different; started* or *appeared* for *began;* and so on. Check with your classmates to see what words they used, and how your predicting abilities compare to theirs. Generally speaking, more experienced readers who are more familiar with the writing code (vocabulary, sentence structure, sentence-to-sentence organization) are more successful in predicting word choices and may be more completely involved in their reading. A low score on this predicting practice (in comparison with the scores of your classmates) may indicate that you need more practice in reading, and a higher level of participation in the reading process.

How is it that we are able to make predictions like these? As a reader, you are responding to two kinds of signals: *structural signals* * that help you decide what part of speech—what sentence component— should fill the empty slot; and *meaning signals* * that help you choose among the several alternative words that might fill the slot. Sometimes we only have to respond to one of these signals. In the following sentence, for instance, only the structural signal tells us that we need the word *that* to close up the empty space:

> This means _____ we find picture-writing and sound-writing co-existing in the same system.

In the following sentence, however, we need to pay attention to the meaning signals as well, so that we can choose among the several possible verbs that might fill the slot (the structural signal tells us that a verb would appropriately follow a noun):

> We ~~wanted~~ *learned* ~~hoped~~ ~~decided~~ to write at such an early age that we seldom stop

to think about the importance of writing to humankind.

The structural signal tells us that we need a verb; the meaning signal tells us *which* verb would make sense out of the phrase *to write at such an early age*. In our search for meaning signals, we respond to the whole sentence context—even to the context of several sentences, if necessary. All our predictions are the result of the structural and meaning signals that we process as we read.

Of course, this whole complicated process goes on automatically, and we're hardly ever conscious of it. But we do become aware of it— sometimes uncomfortably aware—when our predicting machinery isn't working very well. As we said earlier, unfamiliar vocabulary, complicated sentence patterns, and the use of abstract or metaphoric language make prediction difficult, slow our reading, and frustrate us. But while we can't change the writer's habits (we can't make the writer give us a simpler, more concrete vocabulary or easier sentence patterns), we can adjust our own habits to the writing. Each of the units of the text that follows is designed to introduce you to ways in which you can learn to make these adjustments in your reading so that you will find it easier and more pleasant to read.

practice 2

TWO WRITING TASKS FOR READERS

1. In *What's in a Word?* Mario Pei writes about the importance of the written word in the cultural evolution of the human race:

   > Books represent the accumulated wisdom of the human race. They are the repositories of mankind's experience, in the six thousand and more years that have elapsed since it first occurred to man to record that experience in permanent form. . . . It is books that give us access to all the varied forms of thought of the past and present—religious, philosophical, artistic, poetic, fictional, scientific.

   In a short essay, describe several of the ways in which writing has made possible some of our major cultural developments. You may also want to comment on what the human race would have been like if humans had not learned to read and write.

2. In the same essay, Pei comments that the gift of writing has seemed so precious that every ancient culture that possessed it created the legendary explanation that it had been bestowed by the gods. For instance, the Hindus said that Brahma invented letters by tracing out the seams of the human skull with his finger. The Egyptians claimed that the bird-god Thoth invented writing, and always pictured him with a reed brush and an ink palette in his hands, drawing the hieroglyphics that served as the Egyptian alphabet. Invent your own legend for the origin of the alphabet, and write down your narrative. (You may invent an alphabet, too, if you like.)

II

LANGUAGE AND MEANING

UNIT 2

From the World to the Word: Real Territories and Verbal Maps

It is impossible for any two persons ever to have learned the same word under precisely the same circumstances; occupying as it were, the same space in time, and apprehending the new term with precisely the same background. Therefore each will take it into his consciousness ringed about with a special context of associations, differing from the associations of everyone else hearing it. This is what Hermann Paul means when he says that each linguistic creation—and re-creation—is, and remains the work of an individual. Yet procedures repeat themselves and approximations of understanding do occur. Our speech is a compromise between the ultimate incommunicability of one person with another and the conventional communication values attached to certain symbols. *(Margaret Schlauch)*

Evaluating Your Learning

When you've finished this unit, you should be able to demonstrate your knowledge of what you've read by

- defining the terms "territory" and "verbal map"
- defining the terms "language of fact," "language of belief," "language of metaphor"
- pointing out examples of these three uses of language in selected readings and in your own reading

A Look Back and a Look Ahead

In Unit One we discussed the reading act as a whole, setting up a context for the analytic study of important skill areas. In the next three units we'll be concerned with one of those areas—the study of words and meaning. In this unit, we'll begin by describing the relationship between words and the things they refer to and then begin to review three ways in which this relationship influences the meanings of words. We'll see that words can be used *informatively*, to refer more or less directly to the world of things; that they may be used *emotionally*, not only to refer to things but to reflect beliefs and attitudes; and that they can be used *metaphorically* as well, to refer to more than one thing or idea. In order to explain these kinds of language use, we'll borrow the concepts of *map* and *territory* from Alfred Korzybski.

The Map and the Territory

John and Margaret are talking together about the car John has just bought. "It's a 1965 Porsche with 60,000 miles on the speedometer," John says, patting its red hood. "It's in top-notch running condition and it has three new tires." Margaret shakes her head. "Those tires look to me like retreads," she says doubtfully. "I'm always afraid of used cars—they're more trouble than they're worth." John isn't listening. "Gets up and goes like a jack rabbit," he says fondly, gazing through Margaret and into a distance filled with jack-rabbit starts and Porsches.

The simple story of John and Margaret and John's red Porsche illustrates the three different uses of language that we will be studying in this chapter: *the language of fact,* * *the language of belief,* * and *the language of metaphor.* * John is using (or appears to be using) the language of fact when he gives several details about his car: "It's a 1965 Porsche with 60,000 miles on the speedometer." Margaret is using the language of belief when she says, "I'm always afraid of used cars—they're more trouble than they're worth." And John is using the language of metaphor when he compares the way his car starts with a jack rabbit's running habits.

You can probably think of a number of examples of each of these uses of language that you have found in your own reading—a textbook you are currently studying that uses language in a primarily factual way; an editorial in a news magazine that uses language to influence the reader's beliefs; a poem that uses language metaphorically, to give the reader a new perception of the events and objects the poet is describing. And you can probably think, too, of the ways in which these categories overlap in any piece of writing. Editorials give facts, poems make us change our beliefs and opinions, textbooks and scientific documents use metaphors. Language is the most complex of all human activities, and these three categories cannot completely describe all its uses—especially because writers often seem to deliberately stretch them. For instance, one writer may use what appears to be factual language, and yet his "facts" have no basis in reality. Another writer's opinion statement may be closer to the actual truth of the matter (if indeed the truth can be known!). A third writer's metaphor may give us more actual knowledge than either factual language or a statement of opinion. However, if we use them wisely, these categories of language—the language of fact, of belief, and of metaphor—do help us to understand some very important things about the way words function in relationship to the world they appear to describe.

In order to better understand the relationship between words and the world of things they refer to, let's borrow Alfred Korzybski's description of language as a map. Korzybski considered all of human experience and knowledge and all of the things in the real world as a potential *territory* * for which a speaker or a writer may make a verbal *map* *—not a line-map or a picture-map, but a map in words. Although this word-map can never be precisely identical with the territory of things, events, and ideas it represents, it can nevertheless represent a territory in any of the three ways we described in the paragraph above.

a. To describe the territory precisely, the writer ** uses factual language that corresponds as closely as possible to the territory that it refers to. In our earlier example, John's statement that his car is a 1965 Porsche *maps* the territory (the car itself) factually. It does not, however, tell *everything* about the car; no map can represent everything about the territory it describes.

b. To reveal his or her feelings about a particular territory, or to persuade the reader to have certain feelings about a territory, the writer uses a language of belief—forceful or more subtle emotional language. Margaret's statement that used cars are more trouble than they're worth is a map that tells more about her feelings than about the actual territory—used cars.

c. To help the reader become familiar with territory that he or she may not immediately recognize, or perhaps to evoke or express emotion as well, the writer may employ metaphoric language, comparing a less familiar map to a more familiar one. John creates a metaphoric map when he says that his car "goes like a jack rabbit." His metaphoric map is an attempt to describe his car's speed (an unknown) by comparing it to the well-known speed of a certain swift animal; at the same time, it is an expression of his pride in his new car, and an attempt to impress his listener.

Meaning and Response

Before we go on, let's take up once more a topic that was introduced in the first unit, the reader's meaning-making activity. *Meaning,** we sometimes think, resides *in* language, and it is the hearer's or reader's task to dig it out, almost like a squirrel digging for a buried nut. We talk about a writer's meaning being "hidden" or "lost" or (on a good day) "discovered"—as though the meaning of a particular statement were something constant, solid, almost tangible. We think that meaning is "locked" inside a word or a phrase and we believe that we must read to find the key that "unlocks" it.

The fact of the matter, however, is that the word or the phrase does not *contain* meaning, requiring us to find the key to gain access to it. Instead, the word or phrase is a key that unlocks meaning inside *us*, as hearers or readers, and gives us access to the meaning that lay within the author. Each of us is a unique collection of experiences, beliefs, memories, plans, hopes—the word-keys that we read open our experiences and cause us to respond, just as they opened the author's experiences and caused him or her to respond. The task of the reader is not to "discover"

** Since our concern is primarily with the written word, we'll use the term *writer* here, although what we have to say goes for speakers too.

a "hidden" meaning in the words, but to *uncover* the meaning the words have for him or for her, and to match that with the meaning the words seem to have had for the writer.

Let's look at an example of this kind of meaning-making. In an essay entitled "Thinking as a Hobby," William Golding writes

> It was the headmaster of my grammar school who first brought the subject of thinking before me—though neither in the way, nor with the result he intended. He had some statuettes in his study. They stood on a high cupboard behind his desk. One was a lady wearing nothing but a bath towel. She seemed frozen in an eternal panic lest the bath towel slip down any farther; and since she had no arms, she was in an unfortunate position to pull the towel up again. Next to her, crouched the statuette of a leopard, ready to spring down at the top drawer of a filing cabinet labeled A-AH. My innocence interpreted this as the victim's last, despairing cry. Beyond the leopard was a naked, muscular gentleman, who sat, looking down, with his chin on his fist and his elbow on his knee. He seemed miserable.

How would you read these three *symbols* *? What meaning do they unlock in you? Do you share with Golding his small-boy perception that the lady is about to lose her towel, that the filing cabinet is being attacked by the leopard, that the gentleman is miserable? Or do you have, within you, another meaning, built out of your cultural experiences? Golding's headmaster (the principal of his school) had such a different meaning within himself:

> ... they symbolized to him the whole of life. The naked lady was the Venus of Milo. She was Love. She was not worried about the towel. She was just busy being beautiful. The leopard was Nature, and he was being natural. The naked, muscular gentleman was not miserable. He was Rodin's Thinker, an image of pure thought.

For the small boy, the statuettes unlocked memories of his own experience or experiences available to him. The headmaster, however, didn't realize that his grammar school charges might not be able to "read" the symbols as he intended them to be read—as Love, Nature, Rational Thought. His reading grew out of his education and his reading, a background that the boys had not yet come to share. You can see, then, that the "meaning" of these three symbols, just like the "meaning" of a printed word, lies not in the symbols themselves, but in the perceiver's experience of them, an experience that is unlocked by the symbols.

In this sense, you don't "discover" meaning on the page as you read. Instead, you are creating meaning out of your own past experiences. And you are coming to understand how various authors have created meaning within themselves, as well, and have left traces of that meaning in the words they chose. If there is a "discovery" of meaning through reading, it occurs when the reader comes to recognize what meanings the words must have had for the writer, what experiences he or she must have had.

This brings us to a question that many readers ask when they begin to think about the process of meaning-making. "Well, then, if the meaning is in me, not in the words themselves, what keeps me from making *any* meaning I choose to make?" By the very nature of the written language, meaning is a product of the reader's interaction with the printed symbols on the page. Because language is abstract, because the words are not *directly* related to the things they stand for, and because meaning is a product of our past experiences, it is not possible to pin down the *meaning* of a given word, sentence, or paragraph. But that meaning is to a great degree "fenced in" by the *denotations* * of the words, the agreed-upon meanings that have been given to the symbols by speakers and writers of the language. As you read, you are giving meaning to the symbols out of your understanding of their denotations; you are responding to the shared, agreed-upon meaning that other language-users would create. You *are free* to make any meanings you choose, but if your meanings don't line up with the shared community meanings and with the meanings the author experienced, you are not likely to receive the message the author wanted you to receive, nor the message other readers might receive from the same page.

Now let's turn from our discussion of the reader's share in the meaning-making process to a discussion of the writer's share, and see how writers use language factually, emotionally, and metaphorically. We'll begin with the language of fact.

Language Used Factually

The language of fact is used to describe or report a territory as clearly and specifically—and accurately—as possible. This kind of language informs the reader of the unambiguous, "reportable" characteristics of a thing, a person, an event, a concept. It tries to avoid judgments, opinions, and guesswork as much as possible—or at least appears to avoid them by maintaining a neutral, objective attitude toward the subject. It also attempts to confine the possible meanings that the reader might assign to the statement by using terms that are as precise as possible. Here are some brief examples of the language of fact:

In a right triangle, the sum of the squares of the two sides equals the square of the hypotenuse.

Richard Nixon resigned the office of the presidency in August 1974.

Christopher L. Schales invented the modern typewriter in 1867. In 1932, August Dvorak rearranged the keyboard for greater efficiency. Dvorak's keyboard system, called the American Simplified Keyboard, is now available in some typewriters.

You'll notice that the writers of these passages have used neutral words, words that neither evoke any special kind of feelings in a reader nor express any of the writer's feelings or beliefs. They are *fact* words, chosen to report information accurately and objectively. They are verbal maps that correspond as nearly as possible to the territory they describe.

Because factual language adheres so closely to the thing or concept that it refers to, the properties or facts of that territory limit the terms that may be used. If, for example, a nuclear scientist claims to write a report about a nuclear reactor, he must describe that reactor as it is— not as he wants it to be or as he thinks it should be. If he describes a cracked pipe as a whole pipe, then his map stops resembling the territory it purports to represent, and a radioactive cloud might testify to the mistake. We can define factual language, then, as *language that is used to represent verifiable facts and that can be tested for accuracy against other factual statements or against physical evidence.*

The factual use of language occurs most frequently in scientific reports, directions or instructions, records of known events, and definitions. You might look for it in textbooks, in newspaper accounts of events, in dictionaries, in cookbooks. However, because factual language is an attempt to establish a close relationship between the world and the word, it excludes a great portion of the writing that you encounter—unless you read nothing except cookbooks and *Scientific American.* This is true because most writers want to do more than simply report the world to their readers; they usually want to persuade them to feel a certain way about it.

We will have much more to say about the factual use of language and its relationship to the language of belief and of metaphor in Unit Three. For the moment, let's summarize this introduction to factual language by reviewing its distinctive characteristics. It has a *neutral tone,* neither expressing the writer's attitudes nor deliberately evoking the reader's feelings. It creates *clear, careful description,* an effect that often results from the use of documented evidence or statistics. It attempts to be accurate, an attempt that you can verify or disprove only if you know other, related facts. Factual language attempts to provide an accurate map of the territory it refers to.

practice 1

Read the following two passages and decide whether or not they fit the definition of factual language. What problems do you encounter when you begin to look closely at language that appears to be factual? How would you go about testing the validity of these maps—that is, how well they match the territory they purport to describe?

A. In 1920, women made up 20 percent of the labor force; by 1966 the figure had risen to 40 percent. The majority of women workers are either women without

"Pardon me, sir, could you
tell me where I am?"

• •

"Seventy-three degrees fifty-eight minutes west,
forty degrees forty-five minutes north."

• •

What kind of information did the questioner in this cartoon want? What kind did he get? How is this response related to the map/territory concept we've been discussing? Why is it funny? Do you know of other jokes or cartoons that function in this way? (*Drawing by Stan Hunt;* © 1971 *The New Yorker Magazine, Inc.*)

children or mothers whose children are in school, but the number of working mothers with children still at home has risen sharply.

B. What do the mass media themselves cost? Books and periodicals each have been grossing in the neighborhood of $2.5 billion per year. Television's total time sales for 1970 were reported by the FCC at $3.2 billion and radio's at $1.3 billion. Daily newspapers are estimated by the American Newspaper Publishers Association to have grossed $8.498 billion in 1970. In other words, the mass media are something like a $20 billion industry, even excluding related expenses for items such as receiving sets and maintenance.

Language Used to Express an Opinion or Create a Belief

Factual language, as we have said, serves a limited purpose, and you will probably not encounter such language by itself very often in your daily reading. Usually, you will find instead words and phrases used factually in combination with words and phrases used to express or create opinions and beliefs—a combination that allows the writer both to describe some territory and to express his attitudes or attempt to influence the reader's attitudes concerning that territory. For an example, look at these two descriptions:

In 1900, there was hardly enough paved surface in North America to fill a tooth; today there exists enough to cover New England. In other words, 40,000 square miles of our New World is now under pavement. Our new roads, with their ancillaries, the motels, filling stations and restaurants advertising Eats, have made it possible for you to drive from Brooklyn to Los Angeles without a change of diet, scenery or culture, and this, too, is a gift of Detroit.

Man in the automotive age? He is everywhere. Here comes another, Richard Masters by name, encapsulated in chromium, ruler of three hundred and fifty horses which are now drawing him at sixteen miles an hour through downtown Washington, D.C.—for sixteen miles an hour is Washington's top average downtown speed, our traffic scientists say. Masters has entered the world of no U turn, no left turn, no right turn, right turn only, stop, go, one way, slow, no parking from 8:30 A.M. to 6 P.M. and no standing. He is looking for a place to park, along with 350,000 other people.

Both of these descriptions seem to present verifiable facts, using words and phrases that directly describe real territories (*40,000 square miles, three hundred and fifty horses, sixteen miles an hour*). However, the language of these passages does considerably more than that. The writer mixes together fact and fiction, verifiable statements and personal opinions, in a way that is probably so familiar to you that you ordinarily don't even distinguish these uses of language. Yet, as you read the paragraphs, you may have recognized in the words a map of your own worries and apprehensions about man's effect on his environment. If so, you can see that the writer is doing at least two different things at once: first, he is describing a current state of affairs—a territory—by appearing to build a factual map of it; second, he shows his own feelings about that territory and persuades you to agree with them by using emotional language. For example, he shows his disapproval (and attempts to cultivate yours) by commenting wryly upon the sameness and blandness of the American highway scene: "Our new roads ... have made it possible for you to drive from Brooklyn to Los Angeles without a change of diet, scenery, or culture. ..." He shows his concern about the way the automobile rules our movements (and hopes to waken your concern) by adding up all the regulations that a driver meets in a short ride: "no U turn, no left turn, no right turn, right turn only, stop, go, one way, slow, no parking from 8:30 A.M. to 6 P.M. and no standing." Of course, what we respond to here is not individual words, but words and phrases that combine to build a context that is loaded with feeling. The words, by themselves, may even appear factual, but when the reader examines them in combination, they are seen to make a highly emotional statement. You can see, then, that language may be used emotionally at the word and phrase level, and that it may also be used to build an emotional context—through the combination of elements not by themselves powerfully emotional.

The language of belief, which affects the reader's opinion or reveals the way in which something has affected the writer's opinion, may be apparent in such obviously emotionally charged words as *love, hate, evil, innocent, dirty, clean.* These and other opinion words carry such a powerful appeal that we all recognize their message immediately. The writer may also affect the reader's opinion more subtly, however, by the process of verbal association or *connotation.**

As we said, all words have a dictionary meaning—their *denotation.* At the same time, each word, through centuries of use, has acquired a whole set of *connotations*, or suggestions (the contemporary slang term "vibration" or "vibes" is a good synonym). These connotations, together with the word's denotation, make up its whole meaning. For example, compare the two words "grizzly" and "panda" (one a species of bear, the other a large, bearlike mammal). Because of certain associations these words have acquired in our culture, the word "grizzly" evokes an image of awesome, ferocious power, while the word *panda* may remind us of something warm and cuddly—even when we are confronted by the snarling, four-footed variety of Giant Panda that prowls the Tibetan slopes.

Writers use connotations skillfully, as painters use certain colors, to

The words "dog food" have different connotations for Charlie Brown and for Snoopy. How does this comic distinction illustrate the difference between public and private connotation? (© 1957 United Feature Syndicate, Inc.)

evoke feelings, and readers have to be alive to the many suggestions that (together with the words' denotative meanings) make up the message. For example, imagine for a moment that you've been given the task of defining the term "communism." If you are using language factually, to build an objective map, you might define communism as "a political theory that depends on the equal distribution of all wealth in a society in which all people belong to the same social class." On the other hand, if you want to affect your reader's emotions indirectly, you might exploit some of the inevitable connotations of the term by associating it with other terms that might arouse your reader's negative responses. You might define communism as "an economic system in which free enterprise is stifled." Or, if you wanted to engage your reader's emotions more directly, you might say, "Communism is an evil dictatorship." Thus, any writer using the term "communism" may manipulate the unwary reader by exploiting built-in emotional associations of which the reader is only partially aware, creating a powerful emotional context with only a few strategically placed words.

This example of connotation stresses the public associations of words that many people in a language community may share. A great number of words—such as "America," "democracy," "motherhood"— possess connotative powers that arise from long years of shared community habits, or from intense community feelings about certain issues. Our culture and the many language communities within it share certain ready-made concepts and public attitudes. Writers, then, frequently employ these *public connotations* * to influence our opinions and/or to express their own. A good example of public connotation used in description appears in this paragraph from an essay by Joan Didion:

> The San Bernadino Valley lies only an hour east of Los Angeles by the San Bernadino Freeway but is in certain ways an alien place: not the coastal California of the subtropical twilights and the soft westerlies off the Pacific but a harsher California, haunted by the Mojave just beyond the mountains, devastated by the hot dry Santa Ana wind that comes down through the passes at 100 miles an hour and whines through the eucalyptus windbreaks and works on the nerves. October is the bad month for the wind, the month when breathing is difficult and the hills blaze up spontaneously. There has been no rain since April. Every voice seems a scream. It is the season of suicide and divorce and prickly dread, wherever the wind blows.

In this paragraph the author contrives to enlarge in a specifically emotional way on the meaning of one term, the San Bernadino Valley, a real point in a real territory. She builds more subtly on the connotative powers of language by creating a map of this territory that associates the San Bernardino Valley with the forbidding, frightening Mojave desert, with the Santa Ana wind (a wind that is said to drive people mad), with suicide and divorce. She further reinforces the negative tone by weaving into the description phrases that refer to uncomfortable physical states: "works on the nerves'" "prickly dread." These connotations combine to create a feeling of foreboding in the reader, a feeling that is reinforced as the essay goes on.

In addition to public connotations shared by members of a speech community, words often take on *private connotations* * which belong only to individuals. Both public and private connotations function in the same way, deriving their strength and usefulness from the wide range of associations between different words and emotional responses to those words. Private connotations, however, are not the common property of a whole community; rather, they are built up and developed through the private experiences of each person. You have developed a large number of private connotations out of your own experience. For example, you may feel uncomfortable when you hear the word "dentist"; perhaps this uneasiness can be directly traced to an early unfortunate experience with one. For you, the word has strongly negative connotations, although you probably don't use these connotations deliberately in your writing, because you can't depend on anyone else's sharing your feelings or even knowing what you're talking about. However, private connotations are frequently the basis for literary expression because they allow the writer to explore his own feelings about certain objects in his world. Here is an example of the private connotations that may surround objects, in a poem written by Theodore Roethke.

DOLOR

> I have known the inexorable sadness of pencils,
> Neat in their boxes, dolor of pad and paperweight,
> All the misery of manila folders and mucilage,
> Desolation in immaculate public places,
> Lonely reception room, lavatory, switchboard,
> The unalterable pathos of basin and pitcher,
> Ritual of multigraphy, paper-clip, comma,
> Endless duplication of lives and objects.
>
> And I have seen dust from the walls of institutions,
> Finer than flour, alive, more dangerous than silica,
> Sift, almost invisible, through long afternoons of tedium
> Dripping a fine film on nails and delicate eyebrows,
> Glazing the pale hair, the duplicate gray standard faces.

Do you share Roethke's private associations of sadness with pencils and dolor with pad and paperweight, or misery with manila folders and glue? Probably not—or at least not at the beginning of your reading of this poem. But what happens when you encounter the more public connotations of the phrase *lonely reception room?* (Probably everyone has had to wait alone in a public place, wondering apprehensively what was going to happen next.) Does the use of the public connotation help you to understand what the writer is doing and increase your willingness to agree with his other perceptions? Much of the power of the poem depends upon the poet's ability to bring you to share in his private connotations, and to agree that under some conditions, pencils and pads and paperweights and manila folders are indeed "desolate" and do represent the "endless duplication" of lives governed by bureaucracies and institutions.

practice 3

A WRITING TASK FOR READERS

1. Read the following passage carefully, noticing the language that Aldous Huxley uses to affirm the public connotations of two words, "democracy" and "dictatorship." Write a short paragraph pointing out his use of connotations and discussing his use of the language of belief.

   The survival of democracy depends on the ability of large numbers of people to make realistic choices in the light of adequate information. A dictatorship, on the other hand, maintains itself by censoring or distorting the facts, and by appealing, not to reason, not to enlightened self-interest, but to passion and prejudice, to the powerful "hidden forces," as Hitler called them, present in the unconscious depths of every human mind.

2. The following paragraphs were written by a husband-and-wife team of sociologists well known for their study of American middle-class life in the 1920s. Study the paragraphs closely, and write a short commentary on the way the writers create the comparison through connotation. Does some of the language seem "dated" to you? Have the connotations of some of the words changed since the essay was written? How could these changes in connotation have come about?

> The poorer working man, coming home after his nine and a half hours on the job, walks up the frequently unpaved street, turns in at a bare yard littered with a rusty velocipede or worn-out automobile tires, opens a sagging door and enters the living room of his home. From this room the whole house is visible— the kitchen with table and floor swarming with flies and often strewn with bread crusts, orange skins, torn papers, and lumps of coal and wood; the bedrooms with soiled, heavy quilts falling off the beds. The worn green shades hanging down at a tipsy angle admit only a flecked half-light upon the ornate calendars or enlarged colored portraits of the children in heavy gilt frames tilted out at a precarious angle just below the ceiling. The whole interior is musty with stale odors of food, clothing, and tobacco. On the brown varnished shelf of the side- board the wooden-backed family hair brush, with the baby bottle, a worn purse, and yesterday's newspaper, may be half stuffed out of sight behind a bright blue glass cake dish. Rust spots the base-burner. A baby in wet, dirty clothes crawls about the bare floor among the odd pieces of furniture.
>
> The working man with more money leeway may go home through a tidy front yard; whether his home is of the two-floor variety, a bungalow, or a cottage, there are often geraniums in the front windows, neat with their tan, tasseled shades and coarse lace curtains. A name-plate of silvered glass adorns the door. The living room is light, with a rather hard brightness, from the blue- and pink-flowered rug, bought on installment, to the artificial flowers, elaborately embroidered pillows and many-colored "center pieces." The furniture is probably straight-lined "mission" of dark or golden oak or, if the family is more prosperous, "over stuffed." The sewing machine stands in the living room or dining room, and the ironing board with its neat piles of clothes stretches across one corner of the kitchen. . . . There may even be a standing lamp with a bright silk shade, another recent installment purchase and a mark of prestige. Some magazines may be lying about, but rarely any books.

Language Used Metaphorically

The use of both public and private connotations invites, or even requires, the reader to associate one verbal map with others and to link these maps with his feelings about them in a complicated pattern of word-associations. Similarly, *metaphoric* language extends the meaning of a term by directly comparing it to another term. The central logical operation underlying metaphoric language, then, is *comparison* *— bringing two or more different things together as a single idea. Samuel Johnson, whose concern for language spurred him to write the first

English dictionary, summarized the process of metaphor by saying, "It gives you two ideas for one." You can also think of a metaphor as a "double exposure," giving you two different maps, superimposed. For instance, in the example that began this unit, John gave us a metaphoric double exposure when he brought car and jack rabbit together in one imaginary creation. You can easily see how this process works if you take a look at the diagram and then turn back quickly to the poem in Unit 1, p. 19. In that poem (part of which is quoted here) the poet compares the lovers to a pair of compasses, in order to show their inseparability and dependence on one another. In the mind of the reader, these two images, or maps, are fused together, so that the concept is a "double exposure."

Writers resort to metaphor when they want to clarify an abstract idea by giving it life, in order to make you imagine it more concretely, more vividly. They use metaphor when they want to expand the significance of an idea by linking it to another idea—or when they want to make you feel a certain way about a certain territory by comparing it to some other territory that you already know and have feelings about. The only restriction that metaphor-map-makers face in making their comparisons is that the territories being compared must be similar enough so that the comparison makes sense to the reader—yet different and unex-

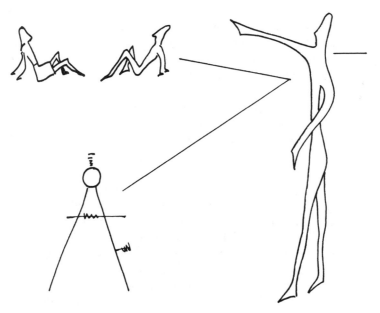

Compass Lovers
If they be two, they are two so
As stiff twin compasses are two,
Thy soul the fixed foot, makes no show
To move, but doth, if the other do.

pected enough to expand the significance of the term. For example, this discussion of three kinds of language use that you've been reading employs a metaphor. By comparing events, objects, and ideas with a real-world territory, and by comparing words to maps of territories, we are relying on your ability to associate simple, concrete things (territories and maps) with more complex, abstract things (the world and words). We're relying on a metaphor, one that (we hope) will make it easier for you to *see* what we mean.

The metaphoric process can be a simple, almost automatic one, as when you describe someone with a commonly used metaphoric expression like *wise as an owl, dirty as a pig, blind as a bat, drunk as a skunk.* These expressions represent comparison at its simplest, least effective level, because the maps that are superimposed—the map describing a person's wisdom and the map describing an owl's wisdom—have been put together so many times that we hardly recognize them as being metaphors. These "ready-made" metaphors are clichéd, tired, worn out.

However, the process of metaphoric language can also be a complex, highly imaginative one in which the comparison of different maps explains a complex process or idea in a way we had not thought about before. In this description by Alvin Toffler (from his book *The Eco-Spasm Report*), the author depends on such a process. Toffler wants to show that modern economics is a muddled, confused science, operating with out-of-date theories and without any sure sense of direction or real knowledge of how to control the economy. To strengthen this criticism, Toffler compares economists to generals—generals who are using antique equipment to fight a modern war:

> Like generals, economists are busy fighting the last war. Their stabilizers and tools seem increasingly like some cobwebbed, economic version of the Maginot Line—a mighty fortress with guns pointing in irrelevant directions.

Toffler's metaphor, to which he returns several times in the book, underscores his point in an interesting and memorable way. In fact, it may be true (as some writers believe) that readers tend to recall metaphoric language more vividly than factual language or opinion statements—perhaps because of the effort *they* must make to get the point.

And that is precisely the difficulty with metaphoric language, of course: because the relationship between the two terms of the metaphoric map are not specified, because the writer doesn't spell everything out, readers have to work to make the connection. Toffler, for instance, doesn't tell us *how* economists are like generals, or *how* their economic theories are like the Maginot Line (a good dictionary will help you to decipher *that* historical allusion, if you don't already know it); he leaves it to your imagination to complete the comparison, and it is as rich and multifaceted as you are able to make it. Readers who fail to recognize the metaphoric map, or who explore it only in a very quick and superficial and *passive* way, deprive themselves of much of the significance of their reading. Only in the simplest of elementary and high school textbooks does the writer make everything immediately available to all of his or her readers. Mature writers, writing for intelligent, *participating* audiences, use all their resources to challenge the imagination and the intellect. The most challenging of these resources is the language of metaphor.

practice 4

THREE WRITING TASKS FOR READERS

1. One of the ways that metaphoric language differs from factual and emotional language is that it is much less direct but at the same time more concrete. These two qualities make it useful for certain purposes—advertising, for instance. Consider these hypothetical advertisements for a laundry detergent:

   factual: Whiz is a detergent that removes dirt from your clothes.
   emotional: People who care about being clean use Whiz for their laundry.
   metaphoric: Whiz makes your clothes flower-fresh, as clean as a meadow washed by a spring rain.

   Leaf through a few magazines and find three advertisements that seem to you to use language in the three ways we've described in this unit: factually, emotionally, metaphorically. Write a short analysis of the relative effectiveness of any one of the ads you found. Why do you think the writer chose to use language in that particular way? Does the choice of language depend on the kind of audience the writer is trying to reach?

2. Writers often use language in several ways in a single short passage. In this paragraph from the essay "Redneck!" by Larry L. King, which words or phrases or sentences strike you as being factual? which designed to play on your emotions or your beliefs? which metaphoric? Can you detect any public connotations in the words he uses? Do any of these terms have private connotations for you? How do the metaphors contribute to the overall meaning? Write an essay describing and commenting on the use of language in King's paragraph.

   There are "good" people, yes, who might properly answer to the appellation "redneck": people who operate Mom-and-Pop stores or their lathes, dutifully pay their taxes, lend a helping hand to neighbors, love their country and their God and their dogs. But even among a high percentage of these salts-of-the-earth lives a terrible reluctance toward even moderate passes at social justice, a suspicious regard of the mind as an instrument of worth, a view of the world extending little further than the ends of their noses, and only a vague notion that they are small quills writing a large history. They are often friendly in their associations and may sincerely believe themselves to accept "ever" feller for what he is; generally, however, they own more prejudices than a U-Haul could carry.

3. Here are two short passages describing the same event: the reaction of a male moth to the chemical agent bombykol, a glandular secretion that is (for moths) a powerful sexual stimulant. Both are written by scientists, both are intended to inform their audiences about the use of this chemical—but the two are very different. Study the two passages carefully. What kinds of uses of language do you find? Which piece do you think is the more interesting? What is the source of its power? Write a paragraph describing your responses to each passage.

A. Bombykol is a remarkably powerful biological agent. According to estimates made by Dietrich Schneider and his co-workers at the Max Planck Institute for Comparative Physiology at Seewiesen in Germany, the male silkworm moths start searching for the females when they are immersed in as few as 14,000 molecules of bombykol per cubic centimeter of air. The male catches the molecules on some 10,000 distinctive sensory hairs on each of its two feathery antennae. Each hair is innervated by one or two receptor cells that lead inward to the main antennal nerve and ultimately through connecting cells to centers in the brain. The extraordinary fact that emerged from the study by the Seewiesen group is that only a single molecule of bombykol is required to activate a receptor cell. Furthermore, the cell will respond to virtually no stimulus other than molecules of bombykol. When about 200 cells in each antenna are activated, the male moth starts its motor response. Tightly bound by this extreme signal specificity, the male performs as little more than a sexual guided missile, programmed to home on an increasing gradient of bombykol centered on the tip of the female's abdomen—the principal goal of the male's adult life.

B. The messages are urgent, but they may arrive, for all we know, in a fragrance of ambiguity. "At home, 4 P.M. today," says the female moth, and releases a brief explosion of bombykol, a single molecule of which will tremble the hairs of any male within miles and send him driving upwind in a confusion of ardor. But it is doubtful if he has an awareness of being caught in an aerosol of chemical attractant. On the contrary, he probably finds suddenly that it has become an excellent day, the weather remarkably bracing, the time appropriate for a bit of exercise of the old wings, a brisk turn upwind. En route, traveling the gradient of bombykol, he notes the presence of other males, heading in the same direction, all in a good mood, inclined to race for the sheer sport of it. Then, when he reaches his destination, it may seem to him the most extraordinary of coincidences, the greatest piece of luck: "Bless my soul, what have we here!"

UNIT 3

Context and Meaning

. . . the phenomenon of language is different from the non-verbal phenomena which we represent by it. We live in two worlds which must not be confused, a world of words, and a world of not-words. If a word is not what it represents, then whatever you might say about anything will not be *it*. If in doubt, you might try eating the word *steak* when hungry, or wearing the word *coat* when cold. In short, the universe of discourse *is not* the universe of our direct experience.   *(Irving J. Lee)*

Evaluating Your Learning

When you've finished this unit, you should be able to demonstrate your knowledge of what you've read by

- identifying in any reading selection examples of the ways in which context controls the meaning the reader creates
- discussing the distinction between word and thing, map and territory
- discussing the distinction between factual and emotional language and finding examples of passages in which the two are used together
- defining the terms "wordfact" and "self-fulfilling prophecy" and discussing examples of them
- describing, in any piece of writing, the different ways the writer has controlled the reader's meaning-making process: through the selection of detail, word choice, and emphasis

A Look Back and a Look Ahead

Remember John and Margaret and John's red Porsche, an example we used in the last unit? There we defined three uses of language: language used factually, language used to create belief or opinion, and language used metaphorically. These kinds of language can be viewed as three different kinds of map-making activities, we suggested. Writers use words factually, to create a map that corresponds as closely as possible to the real territory they describe. This short statement is a factual map:

> The earth dam now under construction will contain a reservoir of 652.4 square acres, at a constant depth of 627 feet above sea level. It is estimated that private and commercial use of the land in the area will increase by 65%.

On the other hand, writers use the language of belief and opinion, emotional language, to "color" the maps they present to the reader, in order to create a particular meaning-response in the reader. Compare this statement to the more factual one:

> The earth dam now under construction will create an immense lake, threatening the wildlife in the river basin and inviting commercial pollution of an untouched wilderness.

Finally, writers use metaphoric language to compare different maps, in an attempt to make one more familiar to the reader or in an effort to make the reader consider an idea in a different way. Metaphors are frequently used to evoke a particular kind of response in the reader, as well:

> The earth dam now under construction may be as devastating to the life of this valley as a nuclear weapon.

Readers who confuse the factual and emotional uses of language, or who fail to explore fully the metaphors they encounter, run the risk of missing a big part of the message—or even worse, of being deceived by what they read. The ability to distinguish these three uses of language, then, is a necessary reading skill.

Man's Verbal Environment

Human beings alone, unlike all other creatures, are capable of significantly altering their environment. In fact, man has modified his environment to such a degree that now it is mostly of his own making. This man-made environment includes not only the technological developments that we depend on for physical comfort but also the signs and symbols that we depend on for communication and social interaction. When you stop to think of it, you may be surprised by the extent to which our environment is dominated—even controlled—by words. You might be able to go a day without talking, but could you go on longer than that? What would happen to our educational system, to our government, and to our economy if people could suddenly no longer speak to one another? We are surrounded by words—we *swim* in words, one writer has said, the way fish swim in the sea; and, as water must be to a fish, our verbal environment is largely invisible to us.

That very invisibility is the source of a great part of our difficulty with words, for we frequently forget that we live in the context of language, just as we live in the world. We confuse language and the world, the map and the territory, and forget that the words we use are merely stand-ins for something else. If the words we read *look* factual, if they *appear* to refer to a real territory, and particularly if they are supported by statistics, we tend to accept the words as if they were the real thing, ignoring the fact that language, as Irving Lee has said, "can be manipulated independently, without corresponding to any non-verbal facts."

The Map Is NOT The Territory

As readers, we shall not have difficulty keeping our verbal environment separate from our physical environment if we remember Alfred Korzybski's famous warning: *the map is not the territory*. Language is a system of arbitrary signs that are not, and cannot be, identical with the things, events, or concepts they stand for. No matter how hard you try, you won't be able to find any consistent relationship between the word and the thing it refers to. Small words can represent large things—"sky," for instance—and large words can represent small things: "microscopic." Nothing about the word "waffle" would help a visitor from Mars to associate the word with the butter-and-honey-coated thing it refers to. There is no quality of the word "red" that would give a clue to the color it depicts. Words are arbitrary signs that, through use, have come to stand for certain things.

What can happen if we forget that a map is a representation of a territory and not the territory itself? We may come to believe, for instance, that pouring out words about diminishing famine will feed the hungry. We may think that our description of a political assassination as an "action of extreme prejudice" clears up the matter. John Kenneth Galbraith has defined this map-territory confusion by coining the term *wordfact**, pointing out that we have a tendency to want to change whatever we can't live with simply by calling it something else:

> The wordfact makes words a precise substitute for reality. This is an enormous convenience. It means that to say that something exists is a substitute for its existence. And to say that something will happen is as good as having it happen. The saving in energy is nearly total.

Galbraith goes on, in a rather ironic tone, to provide some familiar examples of wordfacts:

> It is no longer easy to think of unemployment as a misfortune. It reflects the *introduction of needed and desirable slack in the system*. No properly run economy can be without it. The drastic decline in farm income in recent years has become a *manifestation of the vitality of the market system*. Though farmers have been leaving their farms at an unprecedented rate, the forces making for this migration have been favorably described by the Secretary of Agriculture in a book with the agreeable title *Freedom to Farm*. Bad

Rich and poor: Too many words, not enough deeds? (Reprinted by permission of the Boston Globe.)

television programs were strongly defended early this year by the Federal Communications Commission as a *precious manifestation of the freedom of speech*. The networks found this a more than satisfactory substitute for any improvement in their programs.

According to Galbraith, the wordfact is a way of using a map to change one territory into another territory—a sleight-of-hand trick that careful readers are always on the lookout for.

Another related result of the confusion between map and territory is the *self-fulfilling prophecy* *—some maps are so powerful that they can actually change the territory. The media provide us with complex examples of this phenomenon every day. Reports of the failing economy, it is frequently charged, actually depress the economy even further—a powerful press can convince spenders that they ought to be more conservative in their plans, investors that they ought to hold on to their money, builders that they ought to hold up on construction. Their financial conservatism (caused by the report that the economy is depressed) results in a depressed economy. The prediction fulfills itself.

There are other examples. In the race riots of the late 1960s, media reporting of rioting led to even more rioting, and newscasters' vivid descriptions of what was going on, accompanied by on-the-scene camera shots and interviews with rioters and victims, incited others to participate. We might question, too, the role of the opinion poll in the voter's decision to cast a ballot for a particular candidate. Could a report that a majority of voters favor Candidate X cause some voters to vote for that candidate on election day? Otto Friedrich gives a very funny (but rather frightening) example of the same thing. It seems that a *Newsweek* researcher, writing an article on Sudan, needed to know the size of the Sudanese army. She called the Sudanese Embassy in Washington, but no one there knew the answer either. After some other unproductive attempts to get the information, the frustrated researcher was stymied. In Freidrich's words:

> As the weekly deadline approached, an editor finally instructed the checker to make "an educated guess," and the story appeared with a reference to something like "the 17,000 man Sudanese army." There were no complaints. The *Newsweek* story duly reached Khartoum [the capital of Sudan] where the press complaisantly reprinted it and commented on it. Digests of the Khartoum press returned to Washington, and one day a Sudanese Embassy official happily telephoned the *Newsweek* researcher to report that he finally was able to tell her the exact number of men in the Sudanese army: seventeen thousand.

Both the wordfact and the self-fulfilling prophecy are common, particularly in the media, and they frequently confuse us to such an extent that we can no longer distinguish between our verbal environment and our physical environment, between the word and the thing or event the word refers to. Careful, critical readers who have learned to distinguish language from reality are less apt to be confused than those who unthinkingly accept the writer's wordfact and who may even enable the self-fulfilling prophecy to come true.

practice 1

Some manufacturers have made fortunes by recognizing our tendency to confuse words and things. The word *Jell-O*, for instance, is a trade name for a particular brand of fruit-flavored gelatin dessert. Through effective advertising, however, many people have become accustomed to identify *all* fruit-flavored gelatin desserts as "Jell-O," even though they carry different brand names. Do you think that 7-Up's campaign to identify itself as the *Un*-Cola has anything to do with this concept? Further, some brand names seem to be designed to make us believe that a product has a certain characteristic: *Ideal* Dairy Products, for instance, or *More* and *Kool* cigarettes. Collect several other examples of this

BERRY'S WORLD

© 1974 by NEA, Inc.

"... As you can see, the profit picture for oil companies isn't all THAT bright ..."

Reprinted by permission of Newspaper Enterprise Association (or NEA).

kind of deliberate map-territory confusions and bring them to class for discussion.

practice 2

TWO WRITING TASKS FOR READERS

1. "Wordfacts," which confuse the distinction between language and reality, can appear in even the most carefully guarded public statements and records. A recent example of such confusion concerns a biographical entry in *Who's Who in America,* an annual listing of prominent Americans. This description from the 1974–75 edition seems to report the background and accomplishments of a 45-year-old chemist, writer, and sports enthusiast:

RUTHERFORD, ARIS MACPHERSON, educator; b. Strath Spey, Scotland, April 10, 1930; s. Archibald MacPherson and Ephygeneia (Aristeides) R.; diploma Strath Spey and Glenlivet Inst. Distillation Engring., 1948; B. Tech., Billingham Coll. Engring. and Tech., 1952, D.Eng., 1955. Came to U.S., 1956, naturalized, 1961. Chief design engr., tester Strath Spey Distillation Co., Ltd., 1955–56; chem. engring. cons., Chgo., 1956–60. . . . Author: Sampling Techniques, 1957; American Football—A Guide for Interested Scots, 1960; Distillation Procedures, 1963. Office: U Minn Sch Chemistry Minneapolis MN 55455.

Yet the following account from *Newsweek* reveals that "Aris Rutherford" is a wordfact rather than a prominent citizen:

The Short, Happy Life of Aris Rutherford

It pops up on page 2,672 of the current edition of *Who's Who in America,* a thirteen-line biography set between those of James Merle Ruth ("food co. exec.") and David Ross Rutherford Jr. ("educator"). The luminary is Aris Mac-Pherson Rutherford, a Scottish-born professor who graduated from the "Strath Spey and Glenlivet Institute of Distillation Engineering," is a trustee of the "Scottish-Greek Friendship Foundation" and has written a book called *American Football: A Guide for Interested Scots.*

Aris MacPherson Rutherford is also a phony. For the first time in its 78-year history, *Who's Who,* that fusty arbiter of American celebrity, has been victimized by a hoaxer. The confessed perpetrator is Rutherford Aris, 45, a normally no-nonsense professor of chemical engineering at the University of Minnesota. A while back, Aris, who was already listed in *Who's Who,* received a biographical form from the reference book's publisher addressed to "Aris Rutherford." Aris assumed correctly that the name transposition was a computer error and let it pass, but a rather pompously insistent follow-up letter convinced him that *Who's Who* was "begging to have its leg pulled." Since Aris Rutherford sounded Scottish, the professor meshed the fictional specialty of "distillation engineering" with the name of Glenlivet, a label familiar to lovers of unblended malt whiskey. . . . After the Minneapolis *Star* exposed the hoax, Aris sent an apologetic letter . . . , although he had already submitted an update on Rutherford's record to include the title of his latest book: *American Baseball: A Guide for Interested Englishmen.*

The same tactic employed by government officials and the heads of corporations produces frequent public scandals. Consulting your memory and some news sources, compile a collection of wordfacts that have been revealed as more word than fact, and write an essay summarizing your findings and commenting on them.

2. In your everyday reading, collect one or two examples of what you consider to be self-fulfilling prophecies. Using these as evidence, write an essay describing how such a process might work and what its results might be.

Contexts and Meanings

If the map is not the territory, if we must nevertheless use the symbol to stand for the thing, and if we want to be able to communicate with others through symbols—what can we do? The obvious answer, of course, is to agree upon the *meaning* of symbols. To establish that necessary agreement is the purpose of dictionaries, but even dictionaries present us with problems, as we suggested earlier. Can a dictionary tell us how we understand the meaning of the following pair of descriptions?

> 1a. He draped the coat around her slender form.
> 1b. He hung the coat on her thin frame.

We recognize that these sentences are similar and yet somehow different. What is the source of that difference? Would you agree that the first sentence might be found in the context of a love story and that the second would be more likely to appear in the context of a melodrama about an orphaned child? Would you also agree that those contexts (even though they are absent from our example) exert some influence over the meaning the reader sees in each sentence? The *contexts* * in which words are regularly used shape our understanding of their meaning. Writers, understanding this fact, make use of it to control their readers' responses. Now look at these two sentences:

> 2a. The old man looked pale but hearty.
> 2b. The old man looked hearty but pale.

This time, the order in which the words occur *within* the sentence controls our perception of their meaning. The first sentence presents an encouraging picture, within the emphasis falling on the word "hearty"; the second sentence implies that something ominous is about to happen— the emphasis falls on the word "pale." In this case, our awareness of the sentence context in which the word is placed shapes our understanding of it. Even dictionaries, useful as they are, can't always tell us in any absolute way the meaning of a word, because that meaning is controlled by the context in which the word is found. To read well, you must understand not only the dictionary definition of a word but also its "contextual" definition.

For example, in the last chapter we offered this sentence as a short instance of factual language: "Richard Nixon resigned the office of the presidency in August, 1974." By itself, the sentence is an uncomplicated map of an unambiguous territory, a simple use of factual language. However, consider the same sentence in a larger context:

> As the months passed following the discovery of the burglary of the Democratic headquarters, public sentiment turned gradually against Nixon. Those who accused him of complicity in the break-in and perpetration of the ensuing cover-up demanded with increasingly strident voices that he resign; such a resignation, they said, would simultaneously improve the nation's political health and stand for all time as Nixon's clear confession of guilt in the two crimes. Finally, bowing to such pressure, Richard Nixon resigned the office of the presidency in August, 1974.

In this context, the surrounding circumstances change the sentence from simple statement to damning indictment. The president's resignation is seen to be a "clear confession of guilt." Moreover, consider how we can further manipulate the meaning the reader might take from the sentence by changing just one phrase: Richard Nixon *finally relinquished* the presidency in August, 1974. Even factual language, or language which by itself could be considered to be a statement of fact, can become opinion-laden in certain contexts. As we mentioned earlier, this is the kind of language that we must be wary of; it often appears factual when it is really aimed to control the reader's meaning-making, to control his or her emotions and beliefs.

Contexts and Control

You might easily spend the rest of your life investigating all of the social, cultural, historical, and personal definitions that words acquire in their contexts and in discovering, personally, their meaning for you. Your task as a reader, however, can be simpler, for seldom does a writer give you the freedom to find all of those meanings in the words he or she uses. You'll recall that earlier we discussed the question, "What keeps me, as a reader, from making *any* meaning I choose to make?" Writers use many devices to reveal their own meanings and to control the meanings their readers create—to make sure that the reader builds a meaning close to the one the author intended. This control over the meaning-making process, often called *slant*,* is an inevitable part of any act of writing, and readers need to be aware of the ways in which writers guide and direct their perceptions.

The Devices Writers Use to Establish Control

Everything that we read, from the list of ingredients on a cereal box to a chemistry textbook to a philosophical treatise or a newspaper editorial, is a product of the writer's selection. The writer has chosen the symbols he or she wants and has organized them for three purposes: to convey information, to express the writer's beliefs, to impress the reader and evoke feeling. This control is achieved through three different kinds of slanting techniques:

1. The selection of facts and details
2. Word choice
3. Emphasis

The Selection of Facts and Details

If you're looking for "unbiased" facts, for straight factual language, you can always depend on the newspaper. Right? Wrong. The news is written by people who must *choose* the kind and amount of information they include in any story. That act of selection, of leaving out some facts and including others, automatically moves any piece of writing away from the primarily factual use of language and along the continuum toward the language of opinion. Consider as an example this UPI story printed February 13, 1975:

> PHNOM PENH (UPI)—Communist forces besieging Phnom Penh fired at least ten rockets into the Cambodian capital and its airport Wednesday. One rocket exploded near the central market, killing five persons and wounding ten others, military sources said.

The story would have an entirely different effect on readers if the writer had included some other information that might have been available. Let's add one more "fact":

> One victim, an elderly woman buying a portion of rice for her family, died hours after the metal fragments from the bomb tore into her body. She was found with her tiny granddaughter still clutching her neck.

The second paragraph adds a detailed account of one of the victims. Do you as a reader respond differently to the story when this detail is added? How do the different presentations of this event—one rather general and abstract, the other intensely personal—influence your feelings?

Experienced writers are fully aware that they constantly choose the details they present and that they are controlling the reader's perceptions through that choice. They may choose to slant a piece of writing either for or against some point of view, or they may try to include enough different kinds of details, presented from a variety of perspectives, to give an impression of *balance.** Even balanced writing necessarily omits something, for to include every possible detail would clearly be impossible.

Experienced readers are constantly aware that the writer is slanting the report by selecting only those facts that seem important, depending on his or her attitude toward the subject. A careful reader, aware of this, decides whether to seek additional details from another source or to rely on what the writer has presented. Here are some important things to consider when you are reading language that appears to be used factually:

1. Even when all the reported facts are verifiable, the choice of details to be presented establishes a controlled, or slanted, context.
2. Depending on the writer's purpose, the slanting can produce either a positive or a negative effect, or it can produce the effect of balanced impartiality.
3. Different writers produce different verbal maps for the same territory.
4. The reader must constantly analyze what appear to be the "facts" in any writing and must evaluate their selection.

practice 3

A WRITING TASK FOR READERS

Below are two statements which, without any context, appear to be neutral *— without any slant. Choose one statement and create additional facts about the event. Then write three paragraphs in which you use those facts to create three different contextual meanings—one positive*, one negative*, one balanced*. Remember that you are attempting to control the reader's perception through the device of selection of details and facts, making three different maps of the same territory.

a. Charles Solo, 18, of 5173 Hilldale Avenue, was issued a magistrate's warning Wednesday for reckless driving.

b. City Council members met in a closed session for two hours last week, debating whether to submit the sewer bond issue to voters in the next election.

practice 4

Choose a partner and go out on a street where you can observe people in action. For the space of several minutes, watching the same scene, you and your partner should jot down what you see. Compare your maps. What things or events did you report differently? What things or events appeared in both your reports? What is the source of the similarities and the differences in the two maps of the same territory?

Word Choice

Like the details writers select, the words they use are also inevitably the product of a particular perception and a particular intention: writers choose words because those words have a meaning for them and because they intend to create a similar meaning in the minds of their readers— that is, to control the meaning the reader makes. A reader *is* under the writer's control. He or she can see only the words the writer has chosen, words that have a powerful cumulative effect on the perceptions. However, experienced readers know that writers use words in this way and they try to "see through" the writer's language to the intentions beyond. How can you evaluate the linguistic choices made by a writer?

It would be impossible to divide all the words in a dictionary into lists according to their positive, negative, or neutral effect, although such a list would simplify the reader's task considerably. The list, however, could reflect only personal judgment, and that judgment would become meaningless once the words began to operate in any context. We've already seen, for example, how a sentence that appears to be factual can become emotionally laden within a different context (remember the sentence about the presidency?). That factual language may even assume different emotional characteristics from context to context.

If readers can't consult lists of words to watch out for, what can they do? The best answer is that a reader can learn to be sensitive to the connotations of words and to understand the emotional effect that language can carry. Look again at the short news article quoted above in the discussion of slanting by selection of detail:

> PHNOM PENH (UPI)—Communist forces besieging Phnom Penh fired at least 10 rockets into the Cambodian capital and its airport Wednesday. One rocket exploded near the central market, killing five persons and wounding ten others, military sources said.

Since the article appears in the context of a newspaper, and since news supposedly avoids slanting, we can assume that the article is relatively free from a strong positive or negative viewpoint. Or can we? The writer's choice of details, as we have seen, influences the meaning and the effect of the statement in the reader's mind. And its appearance in the context of an American newspaper supported by local business influences its meaning even further. Accordingly, we can expect that these contexts will produce certain kinds of slant that can be seen if we look closely enough, from a more impartial perspective. Are these words and phrases really neutral?

Communist, besieging, at least ten rockets, exploded, killing, wounding, military sources

"Besieging," for example, is a charged word within this context, though it might be neutral in a different context, not involving people's lives ("The storm besieged the deserted island for over two hours").

Nevertheless, we can demonstrate that along a continuum even this slanted language is closer to factual than to emotional language. Here's the same story, rewritten in two ways:

> PHNOM PENH—Communist soldiers battering this ancient city attacked both the capital and its airport Wednesday, rocking heavily populated areas with a barrage of missiles. When one rocket exploded near the crowded central market, it killed five people and crippled ten more, survivors said.

> PHNOM PENH—Loyal troops of the Khmer Rouge, attacking the foreign-held capital of Cambodia, advanced their cause Wednesday by firing about a dozen rockets into the capital city and its airport. One rocket struck a market next door to the American Embassy, killing five employees and injuring several others, pro-Western government officials admitted to newsmen.

The information in all three versions of the story is almost identical, but the word choices slant the meanings significantly. What is the difference, for example, between "Communist forces," "Communist soldiers," and "loyal troops"? What perspectives are revealed in the phrases "this ancient city" and "the foreign-held capital"? From what points of view do you think each of these versions might have been written?

Let's look at another, more complicated example, in which the writer has taken up a negative view of his subject, the student liberal movement, sometimes called the New Left. Through his choice of words, he shows his disapproval of the attitudes of this group toward the trade unions and middle-class trade-union members. See if you can tell just how the writer is attempting to control the meaning you make out of this passage:

> The "new" student liberalism has accepted and propagated the opinion that rank-and-file members are largely reactionaries and even "honkies." It has blamed rioting and crime in the Negro community on a generalized "white racism" or, more specifically, on the police, rather than on real-estate interests, low-wage employers, and political conservatives whose policies have been responsible for ghetto conditions in the first place. It permits those who went to high school in the suburbs or to prep school in New England to sneer "racist" at low-income whites who are rightly concerned with

crime, living conditions, or keeping their jobs—and to cop out on the more difficult task of providing alternative answers to these problems from those presented by the Nixons and Wallaces.

The writer's negative attitude is clear from his selection of descriptive detail: for example, the young liberals, he suggests, who "sneer" at white middle-class workers, are the product of upper-class suburban high schools and prep schools in New England. (Does the word "sneer" have any special effect on you? What does the writer suggest when he says that these students went to "prep school"? Does that suggestion have any effect on your understanding?) But his negative attitude is even more apparent in the way he characterizes the liberals by their word choice. He borrows words directly from the student liberals, saying (in effect) "Here's how these people *sound*. Here are their beliefs, expressed in their *own* word choices. They believe the white lower class is 'honky,' that it is 'racist,' and that the trade unions are reactionary." It is clear that the writer believes these words to be poorly chosen and misapplied—and

"Generally comprehensive and incisive, but with an excessively negative tone over-all, wouldn't you say?"

(Drawing by D. Reilly; © 1971 The New Yorker Magazine, Inc.)

that he wants you to form a negative opinion about the people (the New Left) who use language to overgeneralize and to stereotype. His slanting device—borrowing words from those he is describing—is very effective, and unwary readers may easily be taken in by it. Your ability to "see through" the writer's language and to evaluate the kinds of words presented to you is important to your ability to read carefully and critically. If you accept everything on the page without understanding precisely how the writer has controlled your acceptance, you will be taken in by many writers with whom you might otherwise disagree.

practice 5

1. In the following passages, note the words or word groups that seem to you to have been chosen by the writers to control your perception as a reader. Do you think the choices are effective? Why or why not? How do you respond to these passages?

A. Look at the values which galvanize energies and allocate resources in the business system: pursuit of money, enrichment of self, the exploitation of man— and of nature—to generate still more money. Is it surprising that a system seeking to turn everything into gold ends up turning everything into garbage? The market is master. Business makes money meeting consumer demands; it makes even more money creating new demands. More money is spent on advertising and sales promotion in America, on planned obsolescence and consumer manipulation, than on all education—public and private, elementary school through the university. This is pollution of the mind, and it has its own costs. Some students estimate that socially useless, ecologically disastrous waste products make up nearly half of the Gross National Product.

B. The great instrument of the English language has been encrusted with words and word forms derived from penitentiary inmates, slum dwellers, vagabonds called "street people" and the "pop" music and drug worlds.

Increasingly, men and women exposed to a college education resort to crudities in order to express their states of mind.

Too many people delude themselves by insisting that they simply are adopting more natural modes of expression. They disdain the genteel as archaic and unsophisticated. In this process, literature as a distinctive, higher expression of thought and feeling is overwhelmed by gutter words and gutter attitudes.

In a few years, movie goers have come to accept all the Anglo-Saxon expletives. In fact, about all that is Anglo-Saxon that seems acceptable today are the expletives; their use is commonplace in movies, is becoming more so in television and, increasingly, in general conversation.

Millions of people with advanced educational backgrounds, and assuredly of respectable backgrounds, have come to accept and to laugh at the use of terms once commonplace only in barracks, prisons and locker rooms.

A university professor, a scholar of semantics, terms all this a degradation of language. He says a vast number of students have only rudimentary vocabularies. They communicate, he says, in abbreviated "hip" jargon, grunts and Anglo-Saxon expletives.

One significance in all this is that people think in terms of language. The English language is the result of hundreds of years of expansion and growth in communication. Intelligently used, it allows communication of subtle and noble relationships and ideas. The brutalization of the language means a whole people are getting away from the moral sensitivity associated with the precise definition of relationships and principles.

Under Stalin, the higher forms of the Russian language were debased so that those barriers to totalitarianism, complex forms of speech and verbal decencies, could be razed. Adolf Hitler, for the same reason, did the same thing to the language of the German people.

Decent speech is not a Victorian fetish. It is an effort by a society to prevent men and women in that society from viewing themselves strictly in animalistic terms. Filthy speech leads to filthy views of humanity. It is a short step from acceptance of brutal speech to participation in brutal acts. Those who don't believe this might consult with Charles Manson—if they can get permission from prison authorities to see him.

2. In your own reading, find a short passage that demonstrates how writers attempt to control the meaning the reader attributes to a given sentence or passage through the choice of words. Do you think the writer has made the best possible choice, given his or her intention? Why or why not?

Emphasis

As with slanting by the selection of detail and the choice of certain words, slanting (or controlling the reader's perceptions) by *emphasis* * results inevitably from the process of placing words in the context of other words. Word emphasis is perhaps more apparent in speech than in writing, though it is equally important in both. In speech we can vary the stress we place on some words by changing the volume and pitch of the voice and the speed at which we speak. Further, we have a wide range of body language, facial gestures, and hand motions—all of which help us to emphasize spoken language. In speech, you can easily slant statements in different ways, controlling your listener's understanding, by emphasizing different words. To see how this works, try saying each of the following sentences out loud, emphasizing the italicized word:

He said that the judge *was* an honest man. (That is, the judge once was honest, but may not be so now.)

He said that the judge was an *honest* man. (That is, the judge is absolutely honest.)

Can you hear the differences in meaning that result from the differences in emphasis? Try emphasizing the rest of the words, one at a time, and see what different meanings result. Which words can most radically change the meaning of the sentence when they are emphasized? Which emphases make the least difference? Why?

Just as spoken emphases change the meaning of a statement, so do written devices of emphasis. It's easy to see how graphic devices like underlining or italics can serve this function. For instance, the writer whose description of student liberalism we looked at earlier adds this comment to his charges:

> ... student liberals frequently ... make statements like, "The unions are *the* most reactionary force in this country," only to retreat embarrassedly when reminded of the role of corporate business.

The speaker's emphasis on *the* makes it appear that there is only one reactionary force—a belief, the writer claims, that is in error. Here is another example in which a threatening emphasis is placed on important words:

> There are still parents who answer a child's questions—why must I go to bed? or eat my vegetables? or stop sucking my thumb? or learn to read?—with simple assertions: Because it is *right* to do so, because *God* says so, or because *I* say so.

Often capital letters are used to create emphasis, as in this sentence from an article on Mick Jagger:

> ... through the murmurous hush of 18,000 craning minds, there sliced the hysterical cry, "THE ROLLING STONES!!!"

In the same article, the author uses another device, the reproduction of speech sounds in print:

> The audience, recoiling in audio-visual shock, not only screeeeeeeams, but starts climbing the furniture ...

You can find numerous examples of this kind of control, designed to remind the audience that these are important words, important sounds.

Another important device for providing emphasis is *word order,** perhaps the most subtle of the ways in which writers control their readers' perceptions. The same words, arranged in different orders, produce different effects. One example of this technique appeared earlier in this chapter:

> The old man looked pale but hearty.
> The old man looked hearty but pale.

The difference in meaning of these two sentences results from a basic principle of our language: the positions of strongest emphasis are the beginning and the end of the sentence. The last word in the sentence exerts a major control over the meaning. Furthermore, this principle applies as well to larger units of writing, so that frequently you can effectively scan an article or a book by reading only the first and last sentences of paragraphs; you can be fairly sure that you have covered the basic, most important features, even though you haven't read the whole thing.

The subtlety of this controlling technique lies, as you may have guessed, in the fact that we usually don't perceive word order—we are so engrossed with the words and their meanings that the order in which the words occur goes unnoticed, and we fail to perceive exactly how the writer has called certain words to our attention through their order. But it *is* an important device, as an example will illustrate. Look at this sentence, from General Douglas MacArthur's last speech at West Point:

> "Duty," "honor," "country"—those three hallowed words reverently dictate what you want to be, what you can be, what you will be.

Would this sentence have had the same effectiveness if it had been written in the following way?

> Three hallowed words—"duty," "honor," and "country"—reverently dictate what you want to be, can be, and will be.

The effectiveness of this sentence—its emotional power—derives from the placement of the three words *duty, honor, country* at the beginning, with the repetition *what you want to be, what you can be,* and *what you will be* placed at the end. Any other word order is less emotionally effective.

A similar controlling device is repetition—the repetition of words, phrases, even whole clauses. In the same speech, MacArthur used this device to describe the effect of the words "duty," "honor," and "courage" in the lives of the West Point cadets he was addressing:

> They teach you to be proud and unbending in honest failure, but humble and gentle in success; not to substitute words for action; not to seek the path of comfort, but to face the stress and spur of difficulty and challenge; to learn to stand up in the storm, but to have compassion on those who fail; to master yourself before you seek to master others; to have a heart that is clean, a goal that is high; to learn to laugh, yet never forget how to weep; to reach into the future, yet never neglect the past; to be serious, yet never take yourself too seriously; to be modest so that you will remember the simplicity of true greatness, the open mind of true wisdom, the meekness of true strength.

Can you count the number of repetitions (and repetitions within repetitions) that MacArthur has used here? Not only does the repetition make it easier for you to follow the speaker through this long sentence, but its rhythmic cadences impose themselves on your memory, so that you can almost predict what is to come. This kind of speaking and writing may involve you at a very deep psychological level, where you are scarcely aware of it, and may (as we observed in Unit 1) induce you to an agreement you do not fully understand.

Sometimes the repetition occurs on an even more subtle level than the repetition of words or phrases: it occurs in the repetition of sentence structures and patterns. Here is a sentence written by Lynn White, in a discussion of the need for ecological action:

> There are many calls to action, but specific proposals, however worthy as individual items, seem too partial, palliative, negative: ban the bomb, tear down the billboards, give the Hindus contraceptives and tell them to eat their sacred cows.

Here, White repeats three adjectives—*partial, palliative, negative*—each repetition adding stronger force to his statement. He also repeats four imperative commands: *ban the bomb, tear down the billboards, give the Hindus contraceptives and tell them to eat their sacred cows.* The repetition of the pattern, even though he has not repeated words, gives the sentence much more emotional force. By the time the sentence ends, it has achieved a marked emotional effectiveness.

In this same essay, White uses another device to create a particular emphasis: the device of sentence balance. He employs it in this case to stress a contrast between man and nature:

> Man's relation to the soil was profoundly changed. *Formerly man had been part of nature; now he was the exploiter of nature.*

The sentence balance (two independent clauses, one on each side of the semicolon) creates a context in which the opposition of man and nature is strengthened. White uses the same device to oppose science and technology:

> Science was traditionally aristocratic, speculative, intellectual in intent; technology was lower-class, empirical, action-oriented.

Whether you are aware of the process or not, your meaning-making mechanism is affected by such devices as word order, repetition, sentence balance. As with the selection of detail and the choice of words, writers use these techniques to create a context within which the reader is meant to respond as the writer intends. A reader who is alert to this possibility—a *participating* reader—can learn to evaluate the effectiveness of these devices by evaluating his or her own response. If you adopt this practice, you'll never confuse the map and the territory, and you'll always be aware of the contexts that control meaning for you.

practice 6

A WRITING TASK FOR READERS

Read the following newspaper articles carefully. Each represents a different map of a single territory: the murder of a young woman on a New York City street. Write an essay in which you explore the following questions: From what point of view is each article written? What devices (selection of detail, word choice, emphasis) has each writer used to achieve a particular effect? What effects do these articles achieve? How has the writer controlled the contexts to which the reader must respond?

Queens Woman Is Stabbed to Death in Front of Home

A 28-year-old Queens woman was stabbed to death early yesterday morning outside her apartment house in Kew Gardens.

Neighbors who were awakened by her screams found the woman, Miss Catherine Genovese of 82–70 Austin Street, shortly after 3 A.M. in front of a building three doors from her home.

The police said that Miss Genovese had been attacked in front of her building and had run to where she fell. She had parked her car in a nearby lot, the police said, after having driven it from the Hollis bar where she was day manager.

The police, who spent the day searching for the murder weapon, interviewing witnesses and checking automobiles that had been seen in the neighborhood, said last night they had no clues.

"Help" Cry Ignored, Girl Dies of Knifing

The neighbors had grandstand seats for the slaying of Kitty Genovese.

And yet, when the pretty diminutive 28-year-old brunette called for help, she called in vain.

It wasn't until she had been stabbed 12 times and had crawled into a vestibule, that somebody called police, and even then Kitty lay for 10 minutes, bleeding and unbefriended, before they arrived.

"I wonder how many lives could be saved in this City if people who ask for help were not ignored?" Magistrate Bernard J. Dubin mused yesterday in Queens Criminal Court. "How many people could have been saved from death if when they call for help other persons did not run away."

Karl Ross, 31, a poodle clipper, of 82–62 Austin St., Kew Gardens, a neighbor of Kitty's, finally did call police.

Mr. Ross had just testified that he recognized the girl, bleeding profusely after she had staggered into the vestibule of his apartment house. He returned to his apartment, he said, and called the police, and remained in the apartment until he heard them arrive, some ten minutes later.

A charge of breach of the peace was leveled against Mr. Ross later in the day by Detective Mitchell Sang, who said Mr. Ross tried to prevent him from questioning one of Miss Genovese's roommates, Mary Ann Zielonko.

Mr. Ross was sentenced to pay a $25 fine and serve five days on the breach of peace charge which was reduced from interference with an officer. The jail term was suspended.

Detectives on the case say that at least half a dozen neighbors heard Miss Genovese scream for help on Austin St. at about 3:30 A.M. yesterday. Several of the witnesses told police they saw a man bending over the girl straighten up and run away.

The girl, they said, then staggered around the corner onto 82nd St. Her slayer reappeared at that point, and then, not finding his victim, disappeared again. Finally, Miss Genovese returned to Austin St. and collapsed in the vestibule about 30 yards from her own apartment door.

Police, called by Mr. Ross, summoned an ambulance, and the girl was taken to Queens General Hospital, where she died a short time later. Assistant Queens Medical Examiner Dr. William Benninson said she had suffered 12 stab wounds in the chest, abdomen and back, inflicted by a very strong killer armed with a slender knife.

Police said Miss Genovese was manager of Ev's 11th Hour, a tavern at 193–14 Jamaica Ave., Hollis, and shared her apartment with Miss Zielonko and another waitress from the establishment.

Detectives are seeking to question a patron at the tavern with whom Miss Genovese had had dinner earlier in the evening. Although the girl's wallet was not found at the stabbing scene, investigators said they did not believe the motive was robbery.

Queens Barmaid Stabbed, Dies

An attractive 28-year-old brunette who had given up a more prosaic life for a career as a barmaid and residence in a tiny Bohemian section of Queens was stabbed to death early yesterday.

Catherine (Kitty) Genovese, 5 feet 1 and 105 pounds, was stabbed eight times in the chest and four times in the back and she had three cuts on her hands— probably inflicted as she tried to fight off her attacker near her apartment in an alley-way, at 82–70 Austin St., at Lefferts Blvd., Kew Gardens.

Late yesterday, police said the 30 detectives assigned to the case had not come up with any clues or a possible motive for the savage murder.

Had Teen Nuptial Annulled

Police of the Richmond Hill precinct said Kitty had had her teen-age marriage annulled two months after her wedding and, when her large family moved to Connecticut, she stayed in New York on her own.

She worked for an insurance firm, but gave that up for a barmaid's career. In August, 1961, her travels with a "fast crowd" contributed to her arrest on a bookmaking rap.

Police pieced together this account of her last hours: at 6 P.M. Thursday, she left Ev's Eleventh Hour Tavern, 193–14 Jamaica Ave., Hollis, where she had been a barmaid and co-manager for 1½ years.

She and a male patron went on a dinner date to Brooklyn, and returned to Ev's at midnight. Her escort left (he was questioned by cops yesterday and his alibi freed him of suspicion in the crime).

3 Girls Shared Apartment

Kitty left the bar at 3 A.M. and drove her Fiat sports car seven miles to her home. She parked in the Long Island Rail Road's parking lot next to the group of buildings where she and 2 other girls shared an apartment.

She walked along Austin St., instead of going more directly to her apartment via a walkway at the rear of the building. Police said she apparently walked out front to have the protection of the street lights.

Gasps "I've Been Stabbed!"

Neighbors suddenly heard screams and the roar of an auto driving off. Leaving a trail of blood, Kitty staggered back toward the parking lot, around the rear of the structures, and collapsed in the doorway of 82–60 Austin St., next to her home.

"I've been stabbed! I've been stabbed!" the brunette gasped.

Kitty died in an ambulance en route to Queens General Hospital, Jamaica.

UNIT 4

Metaphoric Language: Contexts and Comparisons

MIND

Mind in its purest play is like some bat
That beats about in caverns all alone,
Contriving by a kind of senseless wit
Not to conclude against a wall of stone.

It has no need to falter or explore;
Darkly it knows what obstacles are there,
And so may weave and flitter, dip and soar
In perfect courses through the blackest air.

And has this simile a like perfection?
The mind is like a bat. Precisely. Save
That in the very happiest intellection
A graceful error may correct the cave.

(Richard Wilbur)

Evaluating Your Learning

When you've finished reading this unit, you should be able to demonstrate your knowledge of what you've read by

- finding examples of metaphoric language in selected readings and in your own reading and explain (either orally or in writing) how the metaphoric process works
- finding examples of different types of metaphoric language—metaphor, simile, personification, allusion, analogy, and allegory—and describing the differences among them
- explaining whether or not a metaphor is appropriate or inappropriate in its context
- describing the effect of instances of metaphoric language on the context in which they appear

A Look Back and a Look Ahead

In the last unit, we studied two kinds of language use: the language of fact and the language of belief. We made the distinction between map and territory—between the word and the thing it stands for—and looked at ways in which maps and territories are often confused.

We also looked carefully at the ways in which the writer manipulates the context of a word or a phrase to control its meaning for the reader, and discussed some ways in which writers control readers' perceptions through techniques of slanting. By analyzing these techniques—the selection of detail, the choice of words, the emphasis of a given sentence or passage—the reader can evaluate the degree to which a writer has gone beyond the reporting of facts to affect the reader's opinions and beliefs. Now let's go on to an examination of metaphoric language, linking it to our earlier discussions of the language of fact and the language of belief.

The Metaphoric Process

In the first chapter we defined the metaphoric use of language as the extension of the meaning of a word *through comparison*. When writers use metaphor, they bring together two or more different things or concepts, uniting them as a single idea. In so doing, the writer seeks to extend the qualities or characteristics of one word to the other, thus enlarging the reader's understanding of the first word. This process makes the meaning of the first word more specific or concrete.

Here are several examples of metaphors, together with brief "translations" of them. (A translation of a metaphor is a discussion of the possible meanings "packed" into the metaphor.) All of these metaphors appeared on the same editorial page of the San Francisco *Chronicle*.

Metaphor

We do not have two national [political] parties; we have conglomerations of state parties whose delegates swim upstream every four years to spawn a candidate and a platform.

Translation

Like migrating salmon responding to an instinctual urge (and with as little careful planning and foresight), delegates produce candidates and platforms exactly like themselves. (There's a double metaphor here: what exactly is a "platform"? Is it, like *real* platforms, built out of "planks"?

Metaphor

Mayor-Elect Moscone's blanket invitation for all members of city boards and commissions to resign is a scatter-gun approach to a target-pistol problem.

Translation

Mayor-Elect Moscone should have been more selective in his requests for resignations—instead of discharging everyone, he should have discharged only certain people. (Is there another double metaphor in this statement? What is it?)

Metaphor

This [the politician's comments, quoted by the writer in his preceding paragraph] is high-octane stuff, but it is mostly gaseous diffusion. It is the stuff of which two-day seminars are made.

Translation

This politician's suggestions are powerful, but they aren't very practical.

Each of these metaphoric maps operates by the same process: the writer maps a territory by comparing it to another territory—politicians to salmon, "cleaning out City Hall" to target practice, political statement to high-octane gasoline *and* to hot air. As you can see, however, the metaphor and the translation are different. Which (the metaphor or the translation) seems to you more interesting? more lively? If you are like most readers, you will agree that *something* (although it's hard to say what) is lost in the translation, and that the metaphoric statement is much more attention-getting and seems to have more meaning packed into it. You're correct in your belief that the metaphor is somehow more *meaningful* than direct statement; as we will see, whether the metaphor is a simple simile ("the quarterback is as fast and as accurate as a well-oiled machine") or a more complicated allegory involving two stories going on at the same time, it combines two terms in one, creating the effect of "more meaning." In this unit we will study the metaphoric process in much greater detail, in an attempt to help you sharpen your critical abilities in two ways: first, to analyze the different parts of the comparison the writer has used in the metaphor; and second, to evaluate the purpose and effectiveness of the writer's use of metaphoric language.

Types of Metaphoric Language

Metaphoric language is probably the most difficult of all language use for readers. There are several reasons for this. First, metaphoric language does not have a direct relationship to the thing it refers to. (Factual and emotional language is much more direct.) Returning to our earlier example, we all know what the word "spawn" means. But how does a group of party delegates "spawn" a candidate and a platform? There is an indirect logical similarity here (or at least the writer thinks so), but it may take the reader a moment to figure it out. A much more direct, but less interesting way to say it would be the factual statement: "Every four years the delegates choose a candidate and write a statement of their beliefs and intentions." Metaphoric language is harder to read because of its indirectness, but readers are rewarded for their efforts by a livelier and more interesting idea.

The second reason for the difficulty of metaphoric language is related to the first. Metaphoric language requires the reader's full attention, full participation. In much of your reading activity, you can be rather passive (although never entirely passive, as we argued in Unit 1), processing facts and observations without much active involvement. When you read metaphoric language, however, *you* have to complete the metaphor in your own mind; you have to become involved in the reading in order to understand what's being said and suggested. Metaphoric language requires an active, attentive reader who is willing to make an effort to complete the comparison, and lazy or hurried readers will certainly miss much of what's happening on the page.

We can categorize the different types of metaphoric language by the quality and degree of their indirectness and the extent to which they require the reader's participation. To the five generally accepted categories of metaphor—simile, metaphor, personification, allusion, and analogy—we'll add allegory, a form of metaphoric language that requires the reader to decide which things or concepts outside the writing are being compared to those in it, often without any cues from the writer.

Simile and Metaphor

The two simplest forms of metaphoric language, *simile* * and *metaphor*,* provide a relatively direct likeness between two different things. Simile uses *like, as,* or *so* to make the comparison explicit. You may know T. S. Eliot's famous description, "The evening is spread out against the sky like a patient etherized upon a table...." Here is another example, from a description of an old man, written by Robert Penn Warren:

> Because it is Saturday he has on a wool coat.... His long wrist bones hang out from the sleeves of the coat, the tendons showing along the bone *like the dry twist of grapevine still corded on the stove-length of a hickory sapling....* The big hands, with the knotted, cracked joints and the square, horn-thick nails, hang loose off the wrist bone *like clumsy, home-made tools hung on the wall of a shed after work....* The color of the face is red, a dull red *like the red clay mud or clay dust which clings to the bottom of his pants and to the cast-iron-looking brogans on his feet,* or a red *like the color of a piece of hewed cedar which has been left in the weather.* (Italics added by text authors.)

In this passage three similes—all very concrete and detailed—add much life and realistic specificity to the description. Look at it without the similes:

> Because it is Saturday he has on a wool coat. His long wrist bones hang out from the sleeves of the coat, the tendons showing along the bone. The big hands, with the knotted, cracked joints and the square, horn-thick nails, hang loose off the wrist bone. The color is red, a dull red.

Do you agree that the passage is much less effective without the similes? Lost, of course, are the images of the old man's life that cling tenaciously to him; without those images—the stove-wood, the home-made tools, the red clay mud, the hewed cedar—he is somehow less complete, and our perception of him is less *real*.

Metaphor, strictly defined, conveys the same direct comparison. It omits the *like, as,* or *so* and implies that one thing is identical with another. An example of simple metaphor is Henry Miller's definition of modern culture: an "air-conditioned nightmare," or Mary McLaughlin's statement about her return to the city:

> I'm moving back to New York and I can't wait. Those fierce canyons hold no terrors for me: I've known the battle field of Suburbia and I'm not going to reenlist.

Because metaphoric language works indirectly, transferring the emotions we feel about one thing to another thing, it is able to awaken powerful emotional responses in us. For example, we may not have thought of our feelings about modern culture, but Miller's definition of culture as a *nightmare* is likely to awaken a strong response in us, and we are much more likely to respond strongly than if he had said, "Modern culture is bad."

In a very important way, *all* language is metaphoric, not just phrases that signal their metaphoric quality or are obviously metaphoric. We talk of table *legs* and *wing* nuts and *stony* expressions; we say that we are *too old to cut the mustard* or that we are *madder than a wet hen* or *sicker than a dog.* We say that she *held all the trumps,* that he has *lost*

EEK & MEEK   **by Howie Schneider**

Some cartoonists play with metaphors. Here is an example in which a cartoonist pictures a character who takes a metaphor literally—(reading one map when he should have read another). Can you find other cartoon instances of this kind of comic misreading? Can you find instances from your reading of persons who have taken metaphors literally? Try drawing your own cartoon or writing your own joke to illustrate this comic occurrence. (Reprinted by permission of Newspaper Enterprise Association, or NEA).

all his marbles, that they *ran the gamut* of the objections. A Swedish philosopher of language once remarked that our vocabularies are a "gallery of faded metaphors," and Ralph Waldo Emerson said that language is "fossil poetry." Our dictionaries are full of words that began as metaphors, and whose metaphoric quality is easily awakened within certain contexts (in poetry, for instance). Writers often establish contexts that help to emphasize the metaphoric quality of words and expressions, and readers who want to respond fully to the writer's message need to learn to decipher these.

Personification

Since our bodies and our emotions are the most familiar things in the world to us, we naturally tend to use them as reference points for describing other, less familiar things. This device—known as *personification* *—attributes human qualities or attitudes to nonhuman things or concepts. If a writer describes an ocean as *angry,* an owl as *wise,* or a house as having *small slits for eyes,* then he or she is using personfiication.

Look at this passage, an extended example of personification:

> There were the houses, too—a long, lurching row of discontented incurables, smirched with the age-long marks of ague, fevers, cancer, and consumption.... Even the sun shudders now when she touches a roof, for she feels some evil has chilled the glow of her garment.

The writer here compares the houses to "incurables"—people ill with flu, fever, cancer, tuberculosis—and the sun to a person who shrinks from physical contact with them. The comparison is even more indirect than most metaphors and similes, however, because when you read and interpret personification you recognize not only the two terms used ("houses" and "incurables," in this instance) but also a third term through which you associate part of the image with something not mentioned—your knowledge of human behavior (in this case, the behavior of incurably ill patients). For another example, consider a politician's reference to "the greedy appetite of inflation." You interpret this image instantly by considering the meaning of the term "greedy appetite," attaching this meaning to the inanimate concept "inflation," and then reflecting on the human sense of "greed" and "appetite." Personification is slightly more indirect than simile and metaphor.

practice 1

1. From your reading, make a list of about ten or a dozen similes, metaphors, and personifications. Provide a "translation" for each, like the translations provided at the beginning of this unit, explaining *literally* what comparison is being made.

2. One of the functions of metaphor, as we have said, is to awaken emotional response. Read each of the following short passages carefully and consider the basic metaphor in each. What kinds of emotional attitudes are the writers expressing? How do their metaphors help them to convey those attitudes? Are the metaphors useful in persuading you to share the writer's belief? Which do you think is most effective?

A. But if [man, the "paragon of animals"] allows himself to multiply unchecked, he is in danger of becoming the planet's cancer. After all, what is a cancer? It is a monstrous, or pathological, growth whose cells have ceased to be controlled in their proliferation, have embarked on a course of unlimited multiplication, and have lost some or all of their organization.

B. The world is aflame with man-made public disasters, artificial rains of brimstone and fire, planned earthquakes, cleverly staged famines and floods. The Prince of Creation is destroying himself. He is throwing down the cities he has built, the works of his own hand, the wealth of many thousand years in his frenzy of destruction, as a child knocks down its own handiwork, the whole day's achievement, in a tantrum of tears and rage.

C. Between the atmospheric roof of air above and the lithospheric cellar of rock below is our house and home, the biosphere. It is the only house mankind will ever have, interplanetary explorations notwithstanding. And today this house is in a frightful mess. Man, the master, sits amidst offal in the living-room, counting his short-term profits. Well, tomorrow's another day. We'll get to the housekeeping then. But in the United States, that kind of tomorrow never seems to happen. Some people are beginning to suspect that, due to a lack of interest, tomorrow has been cancelled.

3. In the following paragraphs, a writer provides two descriptions of ant life. What are the basic metaphors the writer is working from in each instance? What clues enabled you to decipher these comparisons? What similes, metaphors, and personifications help the writer to "fill out" his idea?

A. [The ants] farm fungi, raise aphids as livestock, launch armies into wars, use chemical sprays to alarm and confuse enemies, capture slaves. The families of weaver ants engage in child labor, holding their larvae like shuttles to spin out the thread that sews the leaves together for their fungus gardens. They exchange information ceaselessly. They do everything but watch television.

B. A solitary ant, afield, cannot be considered to have much of anything on his mind; indeed, with only a few neurons strung together by fibers, he can't be imagined to have a mind at all, much less a thought. He is more like a ganglion on legs. Four ants together, or ten, encircling a dead moth on a path, begin to look more like an idea. They fumble and shove, gradually moving the food toward the Hill, but as though by blind chance. It is only when you watch the dense mass of thousands of ants, crowded together around the Hill, blackening the ground, that you begin to see the whole beast, and now you observe it thinking, planning, calculating. It is an intelligence, a kind of live computer, with crawling bits for its wits.

4. Looking back at the two metaphors above, can you tell how they contradict one another—or, if not contradict, supplement one another? Explain how the two metaphors are connected to this sentence, from the same article:

. . . they, and the bees and termites and social wasps, seem to live two kinds of lives: they are individuals, going about the day's business without much evidence of thought for tomorrow, and they are at the same time component parts, cellular elements, in the huge, writhing, ruminating organism of the Hill, the nest, the hive.

Write a paragraph or two explaining how each metaphor supports one aspect of this statement.

5. Read the following paragraph closely and comment on its predominant types of language. Why, do you think, has the writer chosen to develop this idea as he has?

Wit is a lean creature with sharp inquiring nose, whereas humor has a kindly eye and comfortable girth. Wit, if it be necessary, uses malice to score a point—like a cat it is quick to jump—but humor keeps the peace in an easy chair. Wit has a better voice in a solo, but humor comes into the chorus best. Wit is as sharp as a stroke of lightning, whereas humor is diffuse like sunlight. Wit keeps the season's fashions and is precise in the phrases and judgments of the day, but humor is concerned with homely eternal things. Wit wears silk, but humor in homespun endures the wind. Wit sets a snare, whereas humor goes off whistling without a victim in its mind. Wit is sharper company at table, but humor serves better in mischance and in the rain. When it tumbles wit is sour, but humor goes uncomplaining without its dinner. Humor laughs at another's jest and holds its sides, while wit sits wrapped in study for a lively answer. But it is a workaday world in which we live, where we get mud upon our boots and come weary to the twilight—it is a world that grieves and suffers from many wounds in these years of war: and therefore as I think of my acquaintances, it is those who are humorous in its best and truest meaning rather than those who are witty who give the more profitable companionship.

practice 2

A WRITING TASK FOR READERS

Reread the passage in Practice 1.5 above, noticing how the writer has contrasted two very similar abstractions through the use of metaphoric language, making them very real and close to us. Try this same writing activity for yourself, choosing one of the following pairs of abstractions and using the passage above as a model. If you prefer, make up your own pair of abstractions.

fear and anxiety
love and infatuation
anger and irritation

Allusion

Your knowledge of the culture in which you live and the cultures that preceded it determines your ability to respond to *allusion.** Allusion expresses a relationship between some subject and a well-known (or supposedly well-known) person, event, or piece of writing. For example, during the siege of publicity over the national Watergate investigations, any political scandal was likely to be called "another Watergate." Of course, *we* have no difficulty deciphering this allusion—but what about the generations that follow us? Will it be as easy for your grandchildren or your children's grandchildren to recognize in the reference to Watergate a reference to political scandal and the betrayal of public trust? All writers use allusion, choosing their allusions out of their reading, out of their whole cultural experience; readers confronting those allusions must share the writer's recollections and cultural experiences—at least to the extent that they recognize each allusion and know what is being referred to.

Allusions (often mixed with other metaphors) pepper our reading. Here are four examples:

> The event-making man . . . finds a fork in the historical road, but he also helps, so to speak, to create it. . . . At the very least, *like Caesar and Cromwell and Napoleon,* he must free the path he has taken from opposition. . . .

> Churchill too loves pleasures, and he too lacks neither gaiety nor a capacity for exuberant self-expression, together with the habit of blithely *cutting Gordian knots* in a manner which often upsets his experts. . . .

> I would set out in my father's car for town, where my friends lived. I had, by moving ten miles away, at least acquired friends: an illustration of that strange law whereby, *like Orpheus leading Eurydice,* we achieve our desire by turning our back on it.

> The decade being tragic, should not our way of living correspond? The pillars of the twenty-thousand-year-old house are crumbling, the human experience totters. . . . Ought we not, at such a moment, to act *as Wagnerian heroes and heroines, who are raised above themselves by the conviction that all is lost or that all can be saved, and stride singing into the flames?*

Each allusion you encounter—whether it is a literary, historical, or mythological allusion—functions in the same way: to bring two contexts together so that the context in which the allusion originally appeared supplements the new context. It's easy to see that this kind of "context-doubling" also doubles the meanings the reader can make. In the first example above, the writer exploits the reader's knowledge of Caesar, Cromwell, and Napoleon and of their historical roles to add meaning to his description of the "event-making man." By *borrowing* the historical context in which each of these famous military and political men acted and applying it to the context of the "event-making man" he multiplies the possible layers of meaning at least three times! The allusions in this single sentence, combining the contexts of history and the present, give the writer the ability to pack a great deal of meaning into a small space.

Of course, the writer runs the risk of using an allusion that the reader isn't familiar with. In that case, the writer hasn't gained anything by the use of the allusion and may even alienate those readers who are frustrated by numerous allusions they can't easily understand. But those readers are missing a large part of the potential meaning of many writings by their inability to decipher the allusions and explore all the potential contexts opened up to them. What can you do if you don't see what the writer is getting at? Some allusions are so common that they appear in the dictionary. The term "Gordian knot," which appears in the second example above, refers to an intricate knot tied by King Gordius of Phrygia, cut by Alexander the Great; you'll find it in the dictionary as a synonym for a "perplexing problem." Other allusions may appear in encyclopedias—names like *Orpheus* and *Eurydice,* for instance, or *Caesar, Cromwell, Napoleon.* Still others, like the reference to Wagnerian heroes and heroines in the last example above, may be deciphered through a careful reading of the context. You can look up the name *Wagner* in any encyclopedia; once you know that he was a composer of opera, you can decipher the statement that his characters "stride singing into the flames," dying tragically. Your abitility to connect that allusion to the plight of modern man is a test of your ability to read metaphors in general.

The most frequent allusions that you'll encounter in your reading of most modern writing are to Shakespeare (*he had a Hamlet-like bearing*), to the Bible (*he was a Jeremiah with an apocalyptic voice*), to Greek mythology (*like Orpheus leading Eurydice*), to history (*Caesar, Cromwell, Napoleon*). An allusion pays a compliment to the reader. The writer is saying, in effect: "Dear Reader, you are a knowledgeable and widely read person whose reading experience includes the masterpieces of our culture and whose historical knowledge includes all of our cultural past. You'll be sure to understand and appreciate this reference I'm about to make." In a way, an allusion is rather like an "in joke"; it works only for those able to make the connection.

Your understanding of allusion is measured by the scope and variety of your reading and your familiarity with the "great books" of the culture —not by your ability to use a dictionary or an encyclopedia (although those tools may be important to help you gain some useful background knowledge of the context in which the reference originally appeared). As Richard Altick has pointed out, the only way to become really adept at reading and interpreting allusions is to "read and read and read— and then to remember."

practice 3

A WRITING TASK FOR READERS

Here are a number of passages that contain allusions. Using whatever tools are required (dictionary, encyclopedia, original source materials), find out the original context of each of these allusions and write a paragraph about each passage, explaining the allusion and describing how it adds meaning to the new context in which it has been placed. What has the author achieved through the use of the allusion? Which allusions are the most difficult to respond to? Why?

A. Irony properly suggests the *opposite* of what is explicitly stated, by means of peripheral clues—tone of voice, accompanying gestures, stylistic exaggeration, previous familiarity with the ironist's real opinions. Thus, for "Brutus is an honorable man," we understand "Brutus is a traitor."

B. From that sky like hot metal the sun blazed down on bare flats, bare yard, bare boards, tarpaper roof. . . . After one ruined crop, or two, or three, their watchfulness was a kind of cursing from a circle of Hell.

C. In the blooming mill's spacious gloom, ruby lights are sharp tiny watch gems under the clockwork of thin naked steel beams and the writhing of vermiform silver pipes. . . . Silver pipes—a deafening clack-a-clack-clack—the spilling of metallic avalanches—the groaning barks of Cerbera in labor.

D. Take five-and-twenty heaps of cinders dumped here and there in an outside city lot; imagine some of them magnified into mountains, and the vacant lot the sea; and you will have a fit idea of the general aspect of the Encantadas, or Enchanted Isles. A group rather of extinct volcanoes than of isles; looking much as the world at large might, after a penal conflagration. . . . But the special curse, as one may call it, of the Encantadas, that which exalts them in desolation above Idumea and the Pole, is, that to them change never comes; neither the change of seasons nor of sorrows. Cut by the Equator, they know not autumn, and they know not spring; while already reduced to the lees of fire, ruin itself can work little more upon them. The showers refresh the deserts; but in these isles, rain never falls. Like split Syrian gourds left withering in the sun, they are cracked by an everlasting drought beneath a torrid sky. "Have mercy on me," the wailing spirit of the Encantadas seems to cry, "and send Lazarus that he may dip the tip of his finger in water and cool my tongue, for I am tormented in this flame."

E. A hypercritical American once remarked publicly, after a long bout of watching old British comedies late at night on television, that the most typical English sport was obviously not hunting, but robbing banks. I have a feeling he was right. Every English gentleman cherishes in his bosom the thought of getting away with a perfect haul, of emptying the coffers in some way so perfect that no one will even know what has happened. What fascinates him is not so much the capture of the money, which he would be happy enough to distribute in the spirit of Robin Hood, but the mechanics of the thing.

F. The sports hero represents the masculine virtues, the Mars complex, as the popular motion picture actress or the bathing beauty contestant represents Venus.

Analogy

Analogy * carries the metaphoric process far beyond the narrower range of simile, metaphor, personification, or allusion—all of which usually depend on a single point of comparison between the two things or ideas being compared. Analogy is an *extended comparison* that relates the two things or ideas at a number of points, directly expressing several similarities between two distinctly different territories. A clear example of analogy appears in this description:

> The distinctions between Newton's and Einstein's ideas about gravitation have sometimes been illustrated by picturing a little boy playing marbles in a city lot. The ground is very uneven. An observer in an office ten stories above the street would not be able to see these irregularities in the ground. Noticing that the marbles appear to avoid some sections of the ground and move toward other sections, he might assume that a "force" was operating which repelled the marbles from certain spots and attracted them toward others. But another observer on the ground would instantly perceive that the path of the marbles was simply governed by the curvature of the field. In this little fable Newton is the upstairs observer who imagines that a "force" is at work, and Einstein is the observer on the ground, who has no reason to make such an assumption. Einstein's gravitational law, therefore, merely describes the field properties of the space-time continuum.

Analogy is particularly useful for clarifying difficult ideas (as it is used here) and for making unfamiliar abstractions concrete. In order to build an effective analogy, however, the writer must find a map that corresponds in several significant ways to whatever map he or she wants to explain—as the map of the marble game corresponds to the differences between two philosophers of science.

practice 4

From your everyday reading, find an example of an analogy to share with the class. Explain the comparison and indicate all the important points at which the two maps come together. Are there any significant differences that the writer should have pointed out?

practice 5

A WRITING TASK FOR READERS

1. Here is an analogy written by Fred Hoyle, describing the concept of the expansion of the universe. Can you think of another analogy that might be used to explain this difficult idea? Write a paragraph using a different example to clarify the concept of the expanding universe.

Observations indicate that the different clusters of galaxies are constantly moving apart from each other. To illustrate by a homely analogy, think of a raisin cake baking in an oven. Suppose the cake swells uniformly as it cooks, but the raisins themselves remain the same size. Let each raisin represent a cluster of galaxies, and imagine yourself inside one of them. As the cake swells, you will observe that all the other raisins move away from you. Moreover, the farther away the raisin, the faster it will seem to move. When the cake has swollen to twice its initial dimensions, the distance between all the raisins will have doubled itself—two raisins that were initially an inch apart will now be two inches apart; two raisins that were a foot apart will have have moved two feet apart. Since the entire action takes place within the same time interval, obviously the more distant raisins must move apart faster than those close at hand. So it happens with the clusters of galaxies.

2. Here is an analogy that includes several smaller analogies within it. Exactly what analogies does the author use? Is he successful, do you think, in creating this explanation through mixed analogy?

The thing to remember about the atmosphere is its size. A little air is so thin, so fluid; in small amounts it can slip about so rapidly, that conditions which give rise to a hurricane cannot be reproduced on a small scale. In trying to explain a hurricane, therefore, one must describe the large thing itself, not a model of it. . . .

It happens like this. The air above a warm patch of sea, somewhere near the Canaries, is warmed: so it will tend to be pushed up and replaced by the colder, weightier air around. In a warm room it would rise in a continuous gentle stream, and be replaced by a gentle draught under the door—no excitement. But on a large scale it cannot; that is what is different. It rises in a single lump, as if it were encased in a gigantic balloon—being actually encased in its own comparative sluggishness. Cold air rushes in underneath not as a gentle draught but as a great wind, owing to the bodily lifting of so great a bulk of air.

Air moving in from all round towards a central point: and in the middle, air rising: that is the beginning. Then two things happen. The turning of the earth starts the system turning: not fast at first, but in a gentle spiral. And the warm air which has risen, saturated with moisture from the surface of the sea, cools. Cooling, high up there, its moisture spouts out of it in rain. Now, when the water in air condenses, it releases the energy that held it there, just as truly as the explosion of petrol releases energy. Millions of horse-power up there loose. As in a petrol-motor, that energy is translated into motion; up rises the boundless balloon still higher, faster spins the vortex.

Thus the spin of the Earth is only the turn of the crank-handle which starts it; the hurricane itself is a vast motor, revolved by the energy generated by the condensation of water from the rising air.

And then consider this. Anything spinning fast enough tends to fly away from the centre—or at any rate, like a planet round the sun, reaches a state of balance where it cannot fly inwards. The wind soon spins round the centre of a hurricane so fast it can no longer fly into that centre, however vacuous it is. Mere motion has formed a hollow pipe, as impervious as if it were made of something solid.

That is why it is often calm at the center of a hurricane: the wind actually cannot get in.

So this extraordinary engine, fifty miles or more wide, built of speed-hardened air, its vast power generated by the sun and by the shedding of rain, spins west-ward across the floor of the Atlantic, often for weeks together, its power mounting as it goes. It is only when its bottom at last touches dry land (or very cold air) that the throttle is closed; no more moist air can be sucked in, and in a few days, or weeks at most, it spreads and dies.

Allegory

The most indirect form of metaphoric writing, *allegory,** never really *says* what it is about: its primary purpose is to suggest terms or ideas, not to express them fully. As we have seen, in the other forms of metaphor the writer is comparing two terms, both of which are expressed, however indirectly. In allegory, however, the writer uses only *one* term, relying on the reader to fill in the second out of his or her intuition and experience. Readers who want to read allegory have to be active, participating readers so that they can create for themselves the scene or idea that the author directs them to but never actually describes.

Allegory can best be defined with an example. Here is a humorous short fable by James Thurber. As you read, try to decide what kind of beliefs and behavior Thurber is *really* talking about—that is, what terms are absent from the allegory. What clues gave you this information?

THE RABBITS WHO CAUSED ALL THE TROUBLE

Within the memory of the youngest child there was a family of rabbits who lived near a pack of wolves. The wolves announced that they did not like the way the rabbits were living. (The wolves were crazy about the way they themselves were living, because it was the only way to live.) One night several wolves were killed in an earthquake and this was blamed on the rabbits, for it is well known that rabbits pound on the ground with their hind legs and cause earthquakes. On another night one of the wolves was killed by a bolt of lightning and this was also blamed on the rabbits, for it is well known that lettuce-eaters cause lightning. The wolves threatened to civilize the rabbits if they didn't behave, and the rabbits decided to run away to a desert island. But the other animals, who lived at a great distance, shamed them, saying, "You must stay where you are and be brave. This is no world for escapists. If the wolves attack you, we will come to your aid, in all probability." So the rabbits continued to live near the wolves and one day there was a terrible flood which drowned a great many wolves. This was blamed on the rabbits, for it is well known that carrot nibblers with long ears cause floods. The wolves descended on the rabbits, for their own good, and imprisoned them in a dark cave, for their own protection.

When nothing was heard about the rabbits for some weeks, the other animals demanded to know what had happened to them. The wolves replied that the rabbits had been eaten and since they had been eaten the affair was a purely internal matter. But the other animals warned that they might possibly unite against the wolves unless some reason was given for the destruction of the rabbits. So the wolves gave them one. "They were trying to escape," said the wolves, "and, as you know, this is no world for escapists."

When did you first realize that Thurber is writing about the behavior of people? Do you think he is describing a particular political situation, or is his description more general? Does it apply to people and situations you have known? If you can stretch the events in the fable to stand for experiences that you know directly or indirectly, then Thurber has communicated with you on a variety of levels. But what happens if you fail to read the "other" level of the allegory, the absent term? Have you missed the "meaning" of the writing? Obviously, if the writer intended the meaning to include both levels—the *literal level,**present on the page, and the *allegorical* * or symbolic level that is completed in the mind—and if you fail to read at both levels, you have missed some part of the *author's* meaning. Or if you make some connections at the allegorical level that the author doesn't intend for you to make, you may have "misread" the allegory. The problem lies, of course, in the fact that the allegorical meaning is *absent,* and that it is up to you as the reader to fill it in, responding to the signals given on the first level. As a reader, you are free to make whatever meaning you can—as long as you make sure that you are responding reasonably to the author's cues.

Allegory includes a wide variety of established literary forms, like fable and parable. It also includes almost any piece of writing, however, that you perceive as symbolizing some other, unstated concept, event, or idea. It is the most complex form of writing—it gives the reader the most freedom to make whatever meaning he or she believes to be best; at the same time, it makes the reader *responsible* for complete response. In that sense, it is the most demanding kind of reading you will do.

Readers often ask why writers go to such lengths to "obscure" their meanings. The answer isn't an easy one, and if you are out of patience with writers who don't state their meanings directly, you may not be satisfied with it. But here it is. Writers understand the creative role that the reader plays in the communication process—the reader's meaning-making activity. Some writers, however, for some purposes, want to confine that creativity. A writer who wants to communicate the workings of a machine, for example, wants to tie the reader down to a particular meaning; for that purpose, he or she uses factual language and precise terms. Readers who encounter such communications can feel fairly secure as they read, knowing that there is just *one* appropriate meaning, and feeling comfortable when they have achieved it.

Other writers, for other purposes, want to challenge their readers' imaginations, to encourage their creativity. These writers use appropriate forms of metaphor—from simile to allegory—for this purpose, giving their readers the freedom of exploring the maps and territories for themselves. If you are a reader who appreciates precision, this freedom may be unwelcome, and this attitude too permissive—perhaps even irresponsible. For that reason, you may prefer to confine your reading to scientific and technological writing. That's unfortunate, however, for you'll be missing out on much of what our culture has considered to be the "best" writing. Perhaps, with practice, this kind of reading will come more easily to you; perhaps, with practice, you'll feel more comfortable with it and more sure of your abilities. And perhaps with this comfort will come a greater interest in metaphoric language—language that doesn't specify exactly all of the things to which it refers, that works by *indirection,* rather than directly. Discussing this problem with your classmates and teacher and listening to their opinions may help you to explore your own attitudes toward the kind of reading you like best—and the kind of reading you don't enjoy.

Evaluating Metaphoric Language

In order to read metaphoric language with a careful, critical awareness, you must first be able to recognize it in any of its various forms—simile, metaphor, personification, allusion, analogy, and allegory. Then you must be able to identify the maps—either specified or implied—which the writer has placed together to form the metaphoric image. Finally, you must be able to judge the appropriateness of the comparison in order to gauge its effectiveness. We've looked at two of the activities involved in reading metaphoric language (recognizing and identifying); now let's look at the last: judging the appropriateness of the comparison.

Does the Comparison Fit?

The essential act of metaphoric language, comparing one thing with another, transfers the qualities of one part of the comparison to the other (Newton and Einstein are like two observers watching boys play marbles). Most of the time, this comparison only works one way; that is, only one of the things or concepts receives the characteristics of the other. (The writer isn't interested in showing that observing a marble game is like being Newton and Einstein, for instance.) But what happens if the metaphoric match-up is not quite right? if the choice of metaphors is not appropriate? Richard Altick provides us with a good example and an excellent discussion of an ill-fitting metaphor:

The following quotation from a newspaper report of a concert by the Pittsburgh Symphony Orchestra illustrates a writer's failure to observe the rules of appropriateness and consistency:

> Having opened the program with Moussorgsky's "A Night on Bald Mountain," a work which has been preserved for posterity by the brilliance of Rimsky-Korsakoff's orchestration, the orchestra launched into the main musical bill-of-fare for the evening, Brahms' second symphony. One could hardly have wished for more, for this Brahms masterpiece stands as a monument of musical architecture to the German master. From the opening, with its haunting principal theme, to the close, Mr. Reiner guided the big orchestra through the maze of sturdy contrapuntal fabric which is Johannes Brahms, with the skill of a harbor pilot steering a boat safely into port through familiar but treacherous waters.

Now the tone of the whole article (not reprinted here) is serious. The writer apparently wishes to present an accurate report of a concert, which is a delicate and complex imaginative experience. But does his choice of language and metaphor support this serious intent? Is it, indeed, at all consistent with the subject discussed? Scarcely. "Launch" has the connotation of impetuous, headlong, forceful, even somewhat disorderly action; one of its dictionary definitions is "to shove off." Can a symphony orchestra be said to "launch" into anything—unless (which is plainly not the case here) the writer wants to ridicule its performance? Is "bill-of-fare," with its connotation of restaurant food, appropriate in a report of an event in the concert hall? "Monument of musical architecture," although it cannot stand too much logical scrutiny and is, in any event, cliché, at least is more in keeping with the tone of the whole article. But above all, what about the metaphor by which the conductor is likened to a pilot and the Brahms symphony to an ocean liner, while the difficulties of the work are represented first as a maze (of fabric!) and then as the treacherous waters of a harbor? The continuity of tone is rudely disrupted as, against our expectation and our desire, we are forced to envision a grizzled pilot on the bridge of the *Queen Elizabeth* as she slowly makes her way among the tugboats and barges of New York harbor. What has happened to the Brahms symphony? The writer, it is quite plain, completely lacks a sense of fitness.

Many metaphors fail for precisely the reason Altick points out: because the writers have chosen inappropriate comparisons. If these comparisons are strong enough, they may lead the reader to associate the wrong image with the idea being explained. As Altick suggests, we don't want to see a Brahms symphony as the *Queen Elizabeth* or a football team as a ballet company: The offensive line moved through its drills with the grace and ease of a company of *prima donnas*.

Is It Fresh?

As we commented earlier, all language is metaphoric, in a sense, since it is the product of our human efforts to establish correspondences, to connect one thing with another. Phrases like *a wave of humanity, the standard-bearer of decency* indicate how thoroughly the language depends on metaphor—metaphor that has, for most purposes, become fossilized and nearly unrecognizable. Most good writers attempt to avoid fossilized language when they can, reaching past the *cliché* * for the fresh metaphor. Good readers, too, attempt to evaluate the writer's choice of terms as they read, looking for those comparisons which are novel and interesting. Like Sidney Harris, they would like to read or hear, just once,

> about tacks that aren't brass, questions that aren't moot, coasts that aren't clear, fates that aren't worse than death, and a mean that isn't golden.
> And, just once, a null without a void, a might without a main, a far without a wide, a six of one without a half-dozen of the other, tooth without a nail, and ways without means.

Writers who use clichéd metaphors are likely to be lazy writers—reaching for the first thing that comes to mind, the most convenient expression. Writers who use clichés invite their readers' contempt.

Is It Consistent?

We've all encountered "mixed" metaphors—different comparisons that somehow got tossed into the same sentence and muddled together. This paragraph is typical of such confused writing:

> These two student senators are as different as night and day: one has missed the boat completely on this issue while the other one has come up smelling like a rose. But they have one thing in common: in their committee work, both are way out in left field. One, particularly, just can't keep his foot out of his mouth.

If you're a little dizzy, it's no wonder. As you read, you automatically make connections among the images the writer presents you with; if the images are as mixed as these, however, you can't make very many coherent connections, and you end your reading in confused frustration.

The mixed metaphor provides such a conglomeration of images that its effect is usually comic. In fact, some writers of irony and humor deliberately use the mixed metaphor as a comic device. Here's a self-description by a character in Mark Twain's *Life on the Mississippi.*

I'm the old original iron-jawed, brass-mounted copper-bellied corpse-maker from the wilds of Arkansaw! Look at me! I'm the man they call Sudden Death and General Desolation! Sired by a hurricane, dam'd by an earthquake, half-brother to the cholera, nearly related to the small pox on my mother's side!

The humor of the description stems from the inappropriateness of the metaphors—their deliberate inappropriateness—to the description of a man: his father a hurricane, his mother an earthquake, his half-brother the cholera. Tossed into that exaggerated description are the inconsistent metaphors: "original iron-jawed, brass-mounted, copper-bellied corpse-maker." The exaggerations and inconsistencies here result in a funny description—which is exactly what the author intended.

practice 6

Here is a selection of metaphors, drawn from a variety of sources. Read each one carefully and evaluate it for its effectiveness, noting whether the comparison is appropriate, whether the metaphor is consistent, and whether it is fresh.

A. Invariably, whenever a coach or a manager fails, when it is said that the team "got away" from him, the fact of the matter is not that the boss was too hard or too soft but that he hadn't been able to bring the team's personnel into concert with himself, his personality. "Housecleanings," for this reason, are not so much seeking better players as they are the new wife getting rid of the old wife's furniture.

B. Eric Spilker, a New York–based film distributor and Technicolor fanatic, believes that Technicolor's standards began slipping in the '50's, and that an era officially ended last year when the company closed down its last dye-transfer plant and converted entirely to a cheaper and quicker process called "color positive." To purists, this amounted to decline and fall.
    "It's like what always happens with civilization," says Spilker.

C. Europe is lovely, but it looks like a poodle cut—the trees are numbered, the flat parts divided like a checkerboard, the rivers are as slim and well-behaved as the mercury in a thermometer. The towns, like dead men's bones on the line of a caravan, huddle white and dry, crowded behind defenses that have crumbled.

D. There are a thousand thousand strands in the American tapestry. The warp and woof is beyond a weaver's art. Is the sun beginning to set on the American dream? Are we following Victoria's empire into shadow and nostalgia? Did the system abort Nixon only to die of septic poisoning? Does a phalanx of missile-tipped American centurions wait in the wings?

E. One of the generalizations you hear in condemnation of the news media is that when it makes an error in presenting a story, the retraction never catches up with the original story. Like all generalizations, this one does not always hold, but all too often it does. A case in point could well be the story a United Press International reporter broke about ... [college] athletes being paid for work they did not do. . . . Had the story been pursued diligently enough by other news media, perhaps the whole picture would have been painted in then since it seemed likely that the UPI series only skimmed the surface and distorted the true facts. But the initial effort ran into roadblocks. The [officials] decided to clam up and let the school's president handle all comment. . . .

F. It is time to turn aside from our misplaced meditation on the privileged brain, the aristocratic heart. Let the proletariat arise. I give you . . . the liver! Let us celebrate that great maroon snail, whose smooth back nestles in the dome of the diaphragm, beneath the lattice of the rib cage, like some blind wise slave, crouching above its colleague viscera, secret, resourceful, instinctive.

G. The famous Stonewall peaches may be on the verge of getting their little buds in a jam. The buds, like so many other tender young things nowadays, think they're old enough to leave their mothers' arms and go out into the world on their own in a blaze of glory. . . . It's the same old problem. The buds have come under the influence of the sun too early in life, and nobody can talk them into changing their ways once they've started blooming. How can a peach tree convince her blooming young progeny, "Get yourself back in the limb where you belong before you are accosted by Jack Frost. You're liable to get killed. You'll wake up one of these mornings black and blue all over, and you'll never grow up to be a pretty peach. You may end up on the grass, and the fuzz will never find you." All the warnings simply will fall on deaf petals, just like they always do.

H. "The city isn't going to have a Santa Claus to save it," said Kenneth Axelson, the former J. C. Penney Co. executive installed by Mayor Abraham Beame as deputy mayor for finance of the City of New York. "The solution is obvious, and it means more than nibbling away. We have to have major surgery." **

I. How gaudy the good old days were depends on who is doing the gauging. As a mirror of lifestyles in general, sport is a finely calibrated measuring rule in the realm of retrospect.

practice 7

TWO WRITING TASKS FOR READERS

1. Read the following two passages, both describing Miami Beach, and analyze the differences between the kinds of language used. Write several paragraphs describing these differences, and evaluate the effectiveness of each description.

   A. Miami grew because some men had great imaginations, seeing in the sand and scrubby trees near Biscayne Bay resort hotels, shopping, streets, residential areas. These men turned their dreams into action by building bridges across the bay to Miami Beach, dredging the bay and pumping sand over tree stumps and roots. Cities with paved streets and public utilities were mapped out and the subdivision began to grow out of the sand.

   Businessmen "retired" to Florida to build new fortunes in land development. John S. Collins, a retired New Jersey nurseryman, began as a fruit grower and then turned to bridge-building; he built one of the first Miami Beach bridges.

Carl F. Fisher, another retired businessman, left his Indiana home to risk his fortune in the real estate business.

B. They snipped the ribbon in 1915, they popped the cork, Miami Beach was born. A modest burg they called a city, nine-tenths jungle. An island. It ran along a coastal barrier the other side of Biscayne Bay from young Miami—in 1868 when Henry Lum, a California 'forty-niner, first glimpsed the island from a schooner, you may be certain it was a jungle, cocoanut palms on the sand, mangrove swamp, and palmetto thicket ten feet off the beach. But by 1915 they were working the vein. John S. Collins, a New Jersey nurseryman (after whom Collins Avenue is kindly named) brought in bean fields and avocado groves; a gent named Fisher, Carl G., a Hoosier—he invented Prestolite, a millionaire—bought up acres from Collins, brought in a work-load of machinery, men, even two elephants, and jungle was cleared, swamps were filled, small residential islands were made out of baybottom mud, dredged, then relocated, somewhat larger natural islands adjacent to the barrier island found themselves improved, streets were paved, sidewalks put in with other amenities—by 1968, one hundred years after Lum first glommed the beach, large areas of the original coastal strip were covered over altogether with macadam, white condominium, white luxury hotel and white stucco flea-bag. Over hundreds, then thousands of acres, white sidewalks, streets and white buildings covered the earth where the jungle had been. Is it so dissimilar from covering your poor pubic hair with adhesive tape for fifty years? **

practice 8

A CASE HISTORY OF YOUR READING EXPERIENCE

Reading actually begins when you recognize words on a page, but it doesn't stop there. You may make several re-readings before you are satisfied that you fully understand the meaning of the words as they combine in your mind. If you are reading a road sign, for example, or a telephone bill, the progression from recognition to understanding may be a very short one. But if you are instead reading passages like the two that follow, you will find that their information is not exhausted by a single reading—that several readings will reward you with greater understanding. As you read and reconsider the following passages try to watch yourself engaged in this process of reading.

First, read the following two passages, which have been called "allegories," or "parables." Jot down briefly your understanding of the meaning of each passage, on both the *literal* and *allegorical* levels. Next, read the study problems carefully, making notes on your answers. How, specifically, did your responses to the stories change after you read the study problems? Do you now see any "new" meanings in these stories? Write several paragraphs describing your perception of each story.

Then discuss the stories with other students in the class. Are their readings similar to yours? Are they different? After the class meeting, write another

** Norman Mailer, from *Miami and the Siege of Chicago*. Reprinted by permission of the author and the author's agent, Scott Meredith Literary Agency, Inc., 845 Third Avenue, New York, New York 10022.

short paragraph describing your perceptions of the stories. Have your readings changed again? If so, what accounts for your new perceptions?

When you have finished compiling this "history" of your changing understanding of these stories, organize it into a coherent essay that describes how you read the passages at your first reading and how your readings may have changed during your later study and your discussion with the class. Describe as accurately as possible the factors that contributed to your changing understanding.

Passage 1

One evening a king of a far land was standing at his window, vaguely listening to some music drifting down the corridor from the reception room in the other wing of the palace. The king was wearied from the diplomatic reception he had just attended, and he looked out of the window pondering about the ways of the world in general and nothing in particular. His eye fell upon a man in the square below—apparently an average man, walking to the corner to take the tram home, who had taken that same route five nights a week for many years. The king followed this man in his imagination—pictured him arriving home, *perfunctorily* [1] kissing his wife, eating his late meal, inquiring whether everything was right with the children, reading the paper, going to bed, perhaps engaging in the love act with his wife or perhaps not, sleeping, and getting up and going off to work again the next day.

And a sudden curiosity seized the king which for a moment banished his fatigue, "I wonder what would happen if a man were kept in a cage, like the animals at the zoo?"

So the next day the king called in a psychologist, told him of his idea, and invited him to observe the experiment. Then the king caused a cage to be brought from the zoo, and the average man was brought and placed therein.

At first the man was simply bewildered, and he kept saying to the psychologist who stood outside the cage, "I have to catch the tram, I have to get to work, look what time it is, I'll be late for work!" But later on in the afternoon the man began soberly to realize what was up, and then he protested vehemently, "The king can't do this to me! It is unjust, and against the laws." His voice was strong, and his eyes full of anger.

During the rest of the week the man continued his vehement protests. Then the king would answer, "Look here, you get plenty of food, you have a good bed, and you don't have to work. We take good care of you—so why are you objecting?" Then after some days the man's protests lessened and then ceased. He was silent in his cage, refusing generally to talk, but the psychologist could see hatred glowing like a deep fire in his eyes.

But after several weeks the psychologist noticed that more and more it now seemed as if the man were pausing a moment after the king's daily reminder to him that he was being taken good care of—for a second the hatred was postponed from returning to his eyes—as though he were asking himself if what the king said were possibly true.

And after a few weeks more, the man began to discuss with the psychologist how it was a useful thing if a man were given food and shelter, and that man

---

[1] Routinely done without care or interest.

had to live by his fate in any case and the part of wisdom was to accept his fate. So when a group of professors and graduate students came in one day to observe the man in the cage, he was friendly toward them and explained to them that he had chosen this way of life, that there are great values in security and being taken care of, that they would of course see how sensible his course was, and so on. How strange! thought the psychologist, and how pathetic—why is it he struggles so hard to get them to approve of his way of life?

In the succeeding days when the king would walk through the courtyard, the man would *fawn* 2 upon him from behind the bars in his cage and thank him for the food and shelter. But when the king was not in the yard and the man was not aware that the psychologist was present, his expression was quite different— sullen and morose. When his food was handed to him through the bars by the keeper, the man would often drop the dishes or dump over the water and then be embarrassed because of his stupidity and clumsiness. His conversation became increasingly one-tracked; and instead of the involved philosophical theories about the value of being taken care of, he had gotten down to simple sentences like "It is fate," which he would say over and over again, or just mumble to himself, "It is."

It was hard to say just when the last phase set in. But the psychologist became aware that the man's face seemed to have no particular expression: his smile was no longer fawning, but simply empty and meaningless, like the grimace a baby makes when there is gas on its stomach. The man ate his food, and exchanged a few sentences with the psychologist from time to time; his eyes were distant and vague, and though he looked at the psychologist, it seemed that he never really *saw* him.

And now the man, in his desultory 3 *conversations, never used the word "I" any more.* He had accepted the cage. He had no anger, no hate, no rationalizations. But he was now insane.

That night the psychologist sat in his parlor trying to write a concluding report. But it was very difficult for him to summon up words, for he felt within himself a great emptiness. He kept trying to reassure himself with the words, "They say that nothing is ever lost, that matter is merely changed to energy and back again." But he couldn't help feeling something *had* been lost, something had been taken out of the universe in this experiment, and there was left only a void.

Study Problems

1. How many stages does the man in the cage go through? How is each one different? What is the allegorical meaning of this progression?

2. What is the role of the king? Why does he decide to begin this experiment? What do you think the king represents?

3. The psychologist seems to serve a "summing up" function, almost as though he is providing the moral of the story. What is his conclusion? Do you agree with him?

4. What is your response to this story, on its literal and allegorical levels? What difficulties did you have in reading it?

2 To demean oneself in order to flatter, as a dog might do.

3 Random or incidental.

Passage 2—*The Doer of Good*

It was night-time, and He was alone.

And He saw afar off the walls of a round city, and went towards the city.

And when He came near He heard within the city the tread of the feet of joy, and the laughter of the mouth of gladness, and the loud noise of many lutes. And He knocked at the gate and certain of the gate-keepers opened to Him.

And He beheld a house that was of marble, and had fair pillars of marble before it. The pillars were hung with garlands, and within and without there were torches of cedar. And He entered the house.

And when He had passed through the hall of chalcedony and the hall of jasper, and reached the long hall of feasting, He saw lying on a couch of sea-purple one whose hair was crowned with red roses and whose lips were red with wine.

And He went behind him and touched him on the shoulder, and said to him: "Why do you live like this?"

And the young man turned round and recognized Him, and made answer, and said: "But I was a leper once, and you healed me. How else should I live?"

And He passed out of the house and went again into the street.

And after a little while He saw one whose face and raiment were painted and whose feet were shod with pearls. And behind her came slowly, as a hunter, a young man who wore a cloak of two colours. Now the face of the woman was as the fair face of an idol, and the eyes of the young man were bright with lust.

And He followed swiftly and touched the hand of the young man, and said to him: "Why do you look at this woman and in such wise?"

And the young man turned round and recognized Him, and said: "But I was blind once, and you gave me sight. At what else should I look?"

And He ran forward and touched the painted raiment of the woman, and said to her: "Is there no other way in which to walk save the way of sin?"

And the woman turned round and recognized Him, and laughed, and said: "But you forgave me my sins, and the way is a pleasant way."

And He passed out of the city.

And when He had passed out of the city, He saw, seated by the roadside, a young man who was weeping.

And he went towards him and touched the long locks of his hair, and said to him: "Why are you weeping?"

And the young man looked up and recognized Him, and made answer: "But I was dead once, and you raised me from the dead. What else should I do but weep?"

Study Problems

1. How many questions does the "He" of the story ask? How is each one alike? How is the last one different from the others? Does the last response cause you to respond differently to the other three?

2. What is the role of the "He" of the story? Why is the pronoun capitalized? What does the title, "The Doer of Good," have to do with this "He"?

3. Is the city merely a place or is it also a state of mind? If so, how would you characterize it? Is there any significance in the fact that the last character, the young man who weeps, is *outside* the city?

4. The language of this story sounds very formal, almost ceremonial. Does it remind you of any other reading you have done? Is there any connection between this passage and that reading? Why has the author chosen to use this language?

READING
FOR
LANGUAGE
AND
MEANING

When *Did* "Civilization" Begin?

Marrying Absurd

How To Lie With Statistics

Ego: The Ali-Frazier Fight

When *Did* "Civilization" Begin?

1   If you had studied cultural history a decade or so ago, you would have learned that civilization was born in the Middle East some 8000 years ago, when man turned from a nomadic hunting-gathering economy and settled down in villages to cultivate the native wild wheat and barley, and to domesticate animals. By assuring the food supply, agriculture gave men leisure for other pursuits, leading to new cultural advances. Basketry was developed, and the weaving of cloth. The first pottery was made in Mesopotamia around 5000 B.C., you were informed, and copper smelting began in Chaldea a *millennium* [1] later. By 3000 B.C., brick cities and temples had arisen, and the Sumerians had developed the art of writing.

2   From the Middle Eastern heartland, the textbooks went on, knowledge of the new techniques diffused eastward to India and China, southward to Egypt—whose 4700-year-old pyramids were considered the oldest stone monuments on earth—and westward to Troy and Crete, reaching Mycenaean Greece by 1600 B.C.

3   This chronology was based on two principal dating methods. The relative ages of older objects and sites were determined by stratigraphy—measuring the depth of the strata in which they lay and estimating how long it had taken the layers of earth or rubble above to accumulate. For "historic" times (*i.e.*, after men learned to write), the dating scheme was more reliable. The Sumerians, Assyrians and, in particular, Egyptians had left records of dynasties back to a little before 3000 B.C., along with observations of star positions during important events. This enabled modern astronomers to date the incidents quite accurately.

4   Once the chronology of ancient Egypt had been determined, it was used to establish dates in lands with which the Egyptians traded. Thus, when stone vases known to have been made in Egypt in the third millennium B.C. were found in tombs on Crete, it established the possibility that the Minoan civilization of Crete was at least that old. But such early cross-dating could not be used for Western Europe, since artifacts of provable Egyptian or Aegean manufacture were not found there. So, on the reason-

By Ronald Schiller, reprinted with permission from the May 1975 Reader's Digest. *Copyright 1975 by The Reader's Digest Assn., Inc.*

[1] A period of one thousand years.

able assumption that illiterate peoples must be more primitive than those who could read, it was taken for granted that the European monuments were built later.

5   Thus, the *megaliths* [2] and massive stone tombs of Iberia, western France, Britain, Ireland and Scandinavia were considered crude imitations of the more sophisticated structures of the East. However, such a masterpiece as Stonehenge could have been erected only under the direction of Mycenaean architects, it was claimed. European prehistory, as one *savant* [3] summed it up, is the story of "the irradiation of Western barbarism by Eastern enlightenment."

6   *Tradition Upset.* This orderly sequence of civilization's march was logical, supported by seemingly irrefutable evidence—and taught as fact. Yet practically all of the assumptions on which it was based were wrong. Recent discoveries and more accurate scientific dating techniques now reveal, for instance, that domestication of plants and grain began independently in Thailand perhaps as early as in the Middle East, and only a short time later in Peru and Mexico; that the Japanese were making pottery before people in the Near East; and that the natives of Rumania may have invented a form of writing centuries before the Sumerians. Equally disconcerting has been the discovery that the earliest megalithic tomb of Western Europe is about 2000 years older than Egyptian pyramids, and that the Mycenaeans could never have built Stonehenge, since it was essentially completed centuries before Mycenaean civilization began.

7   The new findings have made a shambles of the traditional theory of pre-history. Although the Middle East–Aegean area is still recognized as a major cradle of the civilized arts, it no longer holds a monopoly on their invention. Indeed, in some respects civilization arrived there comparatively late. The intricate spiral carvings on the stone temples of Malta, once held to be imitations of those in Minoan palaces, are now known to be earlier, indicating that if there was any diffusion of architectural ideas, it was not from east to west, but the other way around.

8   This archeological upheaval began when nuclear scientist Willard F. Libby developed radiocarbon dating in 1949. He established that when nitrogen in the air is bombarded by neutrons (which are produced by cosmic rays from space), some of its atoms are transmuted into radioactive carbon-14, which combines with oxygen to form carbon dioxide in the atmosphere. This is absorbed by plants during photosynthesis. Animals eat plants, or other animals which eat plants, so that all living things contain the same tiny proportion of radioactive carbon-14 atoms as the atmosphere.

When a plant or animal dies, it stops taking in radiocarbon, and what is already in the tissues proceeds to break down at a known rate until it eventually disappears. Thus, by measuring the amount of radioactivity

[2] Huge stones used as monuments.

[3] A scholar or specialist.

still present, the age of any dead organic material—wood, ashes, grain, beeswax, cloth, antlers or bone—could be determined, give or take a few decades.

9   *Strange New "Clocks."* Archeologists were delighted by the first radiocarbon reports, for they appeared, for the most part, to confirm accepted *chronologies.*[4] This enthusiasm was short-lived, however. Radiocarbon analysis of the tree rings of the oldest living things on earth, the bristlecone pines of the White Mountains of California,** some of which have been growing for almost 5000 years, revealed that the planet had been subjected to much heavier doses of cosmic rays in ages past. Thus, plant and animal remains originally dated at 4000 B.C., for example, were actually 600 years older. With these new, corrected carbon dates, the traditional chronologies of prehistoric man and his works have collapsed.

10   Carbon dating has limitations, however. It cannot be applied to inorganic matter such as stone tools, pottery shards or metal artifacts; nor can it reliably date organic remains much beyond 40,000 years of age, because there is too little radiocarbon left to be measured. To meet these difficulties, several new radioactive "clocks" have been developed.

11   The age of pottery can now be determined by the thermoluminescent technique, which measures the intensity of the *photon*[5] glow emitted by ground-up *shards*[6] when rapidly heated to high temperatures. It was this technique that led archeologists at the University Museum in Philadelphia to the discovery that pottery found in Turkey had been made an incredible 9000 years ago.

12   The ages of bones can now be dated back as far as several hundred thousand years through a process called aspartic-acid racemization, which measures the ratio of D-amino acid to L-amino acid in their structure. The larger the proportion of D-amino acid, the older the bone. Racemization tests of ancient skeletons found in California, made by Jeffrey Bada of the Scripps Institution of Oceanography in California, suggest that man arrived in North America at least 50,000 years ago. For fossils, campsites and artifacts older than several hundred thousand years, dating can be done by measuring the extent to which radioactive potassium has decayed into argon gas in the volcanic strata in which they lie. Such tests now indicate that man may have appeared on earth more than three million years ago.

13   *Dazzling Illiterates.* How do historians explain the new and earlier dates for important inventions that have been popping up in such unexpected spots? In place of the traditional scenario of "cultural diffusion" from a central source, they speak of "independent inventions," meaning that tools, farming, villages, pottery, *metallurgy,*[7] cities, kings and states

** See "What the Ancient Pines Teach Us," The Reader's Digest, December '72.

4 The arrangement of events in order of their estimated occurrence.

5 A unit for measuring illumination.

6 Broken pieces of pottery.

7 The process of refining metals by separating them from their ores.

developed in different parts of the world independently of each other—and not necessarily in any standard order. Each culture developed in a manner dictated by its own needs, resources and ingenuity.

14   The first known potters on earth were Japanese fishermen, not Near Eastern farmers as theory insisted they should have been. Nor did agriculture necessarily tie men to sedentary village life. Mexicans remained nomadic for about 3000 years after they had learned to cultivate corn, and early European farmers used a slash-and-burn method of cultivation which forced them to move as the old fields wore out. The Maya of southern Mexico and Central America built great pyramids and developed a written script, but had no great cities, while the later Incas in Peru built grandiose cities, roads and a political empire without learning to write—and neither people discovered the wheel.

15   As an example of how risky it is to downgrade the capabilities of early man, consider the Stone Age Britons of the third millennium B.C., whom a respected archeologist a generation ago depicted as "disgusting savages." They were illiterate, sparsely scattered over the land, without towns, cities or kings. Yet the building of Stonehenge, their supreme accomplishment, would have dazzled the Sumerians and Egyptians of the time. Radiocarbon dating of charcoal, and of animal antlers which the Britons used as picks, indicates that construction began around 2700 B.C. and continued for over a millennium. Long, flat stones weighing up to 50 tons were cut and hauled 25 miles to the building site.

16   All told, building Stonehenge is calculated to have required more than 18 million man-hours of labor, occupying most of the working population for years at a time. We can only guess why people endured such exhausting toil. But it is likely that Stonehenge was used for religious ceremonies, in which the celestial bodies played a key role. For the structure is an astronomical observatory, laid out with geometric precision. When viewed from the heart of the circle, the rays of the sun on Midsummer Day—when the sun has reached its most northerly point—rise over the Heel Stone. Other massive stones of the monument's inner horseshoe framed the rising and setting of the moon and sun at the solstices. Thus, the early Britons were apparently master astronomers and mathematicians, as well as master builders. Some "savages"!

17   *Music and Mammoths.*   Nor was the life of early man as "nasty and brutish" as believed. The ceremonial burial of the dead, along with the supplies they would need in an afterlife, indicates a belief in immortality. Found in the Shanidar cave of Iraq was a 50,000-year-old skeleton of an arthritic Neanderthal male, one of whose arms had been amputated above the elbow in childhood and who was evidently blind in one eye. Unable to fend for himself, he had been cared for by his companions until his death at the then ripe age of 40. Hunters of mammoths at the Dolní Vestonice site in Czechoslovakia made music on bone flutes over 20,000 years ago. Particularly moving are the 9000-year-old child-size sandals which were found in a cave in North America. They were lined with rabbit fur to protect tender feet.

18   The archeological finds of the past ten years have been enormous, and

sophisticated new search devices have quickened the pace of discovery. Sonar sounders are locating ancient, previously unsuspected underwater structures and shipwrecks. Magnetometers have mapped the deeply buried ruins of buildings, such as in the 6th century B.C. Greek city of Sybaris in southern Italy. Aerial photography has disclosed traces of ancient earthworks, roads and villages beneath ripening grain in scores of fields.

19   Just how far back in time man and his culture may eventually be traced, no one can foretell. But the dates are retreating even further from the innocent days of the 17th century when Irish Archbishop Ussher and his followers, using the genealogies of the Book of Genesis as their source, calculated that the world had been created in the year 4004 B.C., on the 23rd day of October, at nine o'clock in the morning.

Study Questions: "When *Did* "Civilization" Begin?"

1. What kind of language—factual, emotional, metaphorical—does the author rely most heavily on in this article? On what evidence do you base your answer?
2. In paragraphs 1 to 5, the author describes an earlier map of the same territory he is about to describe: the beginnings of civilization. How was that older map constructed? By what techniques? How is the new map of this pre-historical territory different from the older map? By what techniques does it refute the older map?
3. What difficulties are encountered when we try to map a territory like this one? How can we be sure that this author is presenting a reliable map?

Marrying Absurd

1   To be married in Las Vegas, Clark County, Nevada, a bride must swear that she is eighteen or has parental permission and a bridegroom that he is twenty-one or has parental permission. Someone must put up five dollars for the license. (On Sundays and holidays, fifteen dollars. The Clark County Courthouse issues marriage licenses at any time of the day or night except between noon and one in the afternoon, between eight and nine in the evening, and between four and five in the morning.) Nothing else is required. The State of Nevada, alone among these United States, demands neither a premarital blood test nor a waiting period before or after the issuance of a marriage license. Driving in across the Mojave from Los Angeles, one sees the signs way out on the desert, looming up from that moonscape of rattlesnakes and mesquite, even before

the Las Vegas lights appear like a mirage on the horizon: "*Getting Married?* Free License Information First Strip Exit." Perhaps the Las Vegas wedding industry achieved its peak operational efficiency between 9:00 P.M. and midnight of August 26, 1965, an otherwise unremarkable Thursday which happened to be, by Presidential order, the last day on which anyone could improve his draft status merely by getting married. One hundred and seventy-one couples were pronounced man and wife in the name of Clark County and the State of Nevada that night, sixty-seven of them by a single justice of the peace, Mr. James A. Brennan. Mr. Brennan did one wedding at the Dunes and the other sixty-six in his office, and charged each couple eight dollars. One bride lent her veil to six others. "I got it down from five to three minutes," Mr. Brennan said later of his feat. "I could've married them *en masse*, but they're people, not cattle. People expect more when they get married."

2   What people who get married in Las Vegas actually do expect—what, in the largest sense, their "expectations" are—strikes one as a curious and self-contradictory business. Las Vegas is the most extreme and allegorical of American settlements, bizarre and beautiful in its *venality* [1] and in its devotion to immediate gratification, a place the tone of which is set by mobsters and call girls and ladies' room attendants with amyl nitrate poppers in their uniform pockets. Almost everyone notes that there is no "time" in Las Vegas, no night and no day and no past and no future (no Las Vegas casino, however, has taken the *obliteration* [2] of the ordinary time sense quite so far as Harold's Club in Reno, which for a while issued, at odd intervals in the day and night, mimeographed "bulletins" carrying news from the world outside); neither is there any logical sense of where one is. One is standing on a highway in the middle of a vast hostile desert looking at an eighty-foot sign which blinks "*Stardust*" or "*Caesar's Palace*." Yes, but what does that explain? This geographical *implausibility* [3] reinforces the sense that what happens there has no connection with "real" life; Nevada cities like Reno and Carson are ranch towns, Western towns, places behind which there is some historical *imperative*. [4] But Las Vegas seems to exist only in the eye of the beholder. All of which makes it an extraordinarily stimulating and interesting place, but an odd one in which to want to wear a candlelight satin Priscilla of Boston wedding dress with Chantilly lace insets, tapered sleeves and a detachable modified train.

3   And yet the Las Vegas wedding business seems to appeal to precisely that impulse. "Sincere and Dignified Since 1954," one wedding chapel advertises. There are nineteen such wedding chapels in Las Vegas, intensely competitive, each offering better, faster, and, by *implication*,[5]

[1] Willingness to be bought.

[2] Blotting out without a trace.

[3] Seemingly unbelievable fact.

[4] A binding rule, duty, or command.

[5] Something suggested or indicated indirectly.

more sincere services than the next: Our Photos Best Anywhere, Your Wedding on A Phonograph Record, Candlelight with Your Ceremony, Honeymoon Accommodations, Free Transportation from Your Motel to Courthouse to Chapel and Return to Motel, Religious or Civil Ceremonies, Dressing Rooms, Flowers, Rings, Announcements, Witnesses Available, and Ample Parking. All of these services, like most others in Las Vegas (sauna baths, payroll-check cashing, chinchilla coats for sale or rent) are offered twenty-four hours a day, seven days a week, presumably on the premise that marriage, like craps, is a game to be played when the table seems hot.

4 But what strikes one most about the Strip chapels, with their wishing wells and stained-glass paper windows and their artificial *bouvardia*,[6] is that so much of their business is by no means a matter of simple convenience, of late-night *liaisons* [7] between show girls and baby Crosbys. Of course there is some of that. (One night about eleven o'clock in Las Vegas I watched a bride in an orange minidress and masses of flame-colored hair stumble from a Strip chapel on the arm of her bridegroom, who looked the part of the expendable nephew in movies like *Miami Syndicate.* "I gotta get the kids," the bride whimpered. "I gotta pick up the sitter, I gotta get the midnight show." "What you gotta get," the bridegroom said, opening the door of a Cadillac Coupe de Ville and watching her crumple on the seat, "is sober.") But Las Vegas seems to offer something other than "convenience"; it is merchandising "niceness," the *facsimile* [8] of proper ritual, to children who do not know how else to find it, how to make the arrangements, how to do it "right." All day and evening long on the Strip, one sees actual wedding parties, waiting under the harsh lights at a crosswalk, standing uneasily in the parking lot of the Frontier while the photographer hired by The Little Church of the West ("Wedding Place of the Stars") *certifies* [9] the occasion, takes the picture: the bride in a veil and white satin pumps, the bridegroom usually in a white dinner jacket, and even an attendant or two, a sister or a best friend in hot-pink *peau de soie*, a flirtation veil, a carnation nosegay. "When I Fall in Love It Will Be Forever," the organist plays, and then a few bars of Lohengrin. The mother cries; the stepfather, awkward in his role, invites the chapel hostess to join them for a drink at the Sands. The hostess declines with a professional smile; she has already transferred her interest to the group waiting outside. One bride out, another in, and again the sign goes up on the chapel door: "One moment please— Wedding."

5 I sat next to one such wedding party in a Strip restaurant the last time I was in Las Vegas. The marriage had just taken place; the bride still wore her dress, the mother her corsage. A bored waiter poured out a few

---

[6] Showy flowers often used in brides' bouquets.

[7] Brief, illicit love affairs.

[8] A copy.

[9] Declares to be certain, true, or official.

swallows of pink champagne ("on the house") for everyone but the bride, who was too young to be served. "You'll need something with more kick than that," the bride's father said with heavy jocularity [10] to his new son-in-law; the ritual [11] jokes about the wedding night had a certain Panglossian [12] character, since the bride was clearly several months pregnant. Another round of pink champagne, this time not on the house, and the bride began to cry. "It was just as nice," she sobbed, "as I hoped and dreamed it would be."

Study Questions: "Marrying Absurd"

1. Joan Didion's essay provides a good example of the various slanting techniques: selection of detail, word choice, emphasis. Find several examples of each of these techniques in the essay and explain in several sentences how each one functions and what you think its effect is on the reader.

2. Slanting usually reveals the author's attitude toward his or her subject as well as controlling the reader's attitudes. Sum up as clearly as you can Didion's attitude toward Las Vegas weddings. On what evidence do you base your statement?

3. We said earlier that when a writer slants a written piece, he or she has controlled the contexts within which the reader can make meaning. In what ways has Didion controlled the contexts that cause you to view Las Vegas weddings in a particular way? You have already found several examples of contexts controlled by slanting. However, Didion seems also to rely on another, unstated context *outside* the essay, a context that she expects you to share with her. What is it? How does it function to control your perception of what's going on within the essay?

How to Lie with Statistics

The Sample with the Built-in Bias

1   "The average Yaleman, Class of '24," *Time* magazine noted once, commenting on something in the New York *Sun*, "makes $25,111 a year."

2   Well, good for him!

3   But wait a minute. What does this impressive figure mean? Is it, as it

Reprinted from How to Lie With Statistics *by Darrell Huff. By permission of W. W. Norton & Company, Inc. Copyright 1954 by Darrell Huff and Irving Geis.*

[10] Humor, joking.

[11] The standard procedure for a public ceremony.

[12] Absurdly observing traditional practices or beliefs even when those traditions no longer apply to the situation at hand. Pangloss is a naively optimistic character in Voltaire's novel *Candide*.

appears to be, evidence that if you send your boy to Yale you won't have to work in your old age and neither will he?

4   Two things about the figure stand out at first suspicious glance. It is surprisingly precise. It is quite improbably *salubrious*.[1]

5   There is small likelihood that the average income of any far-flung group is ever going to be known down to the dollar. It is not particularly probable that you know your own income for last year so precisely as that unless it was all derived from salary. And $25,000 incomes are not often all salary; people in that bracket are likely to have well-scattered investments.

6   Furthermore, this lovely average is undoubtedly calculated from the amounts the Yale men *said* they earned. Even if they had the honor system in New Haven in '24, we cannot be sure that it works so well after a quarter of a century that all these reports are honest ones. Some people when asked their incomes exaggerate out of vanity or optimism. Others minimize, especially, it is to be feared, on income-tax returns; and having done this may hesitate to contradict themselves on any other paper. Who knows what the revenuers may see? It is possible that these two tendencies, to boast and to understate, cancel each other out, but it is unlikely. One tendency may be far stronger than the other, and we do not know which one.

7   We have begun then to account for a figure that common sense tells us can hardly represent the truth. Now let us put our finger on the likely source of the biggest error, a source that can produce $25,111 as the "average income" of some men whose actual average may well be nearer half that amount.

8   This is the sampling procedure, which is the heart of the greater part of the statistics you meet on all sorts of subjects. Its basis is simple enough, although its refinements in practice have led into all sorts of by-ways, some less than respectable. If you have a barrel of beans, some red and some white, there is only one way to find out exactly how many of each color you have: Count 'em. However, you can find out approximately how many are red in much easier fashion by pulling out a handful of beans and counting just those, figuring that the proportion will be the same all through the barrel. If your sample is large enough and selected properly, it will represent the whole well enough for most purposes. If it is not, it may be far less accurate than an intelligent guess and have nothing to recommend it but a spurious[2] air of scientific precision. It is sad truth that conclusions from such samples, biased or too small or both, lie behind much of what we read or think we know.

9   The report on the Yale men comes from a sample. We can be pretty sure of that because reason tells us that no one can get hold of all the living members of that class of '24. There are bound to be many whose addresses are unknown twenty-five years later.

10   And, of those whose addresses are known, many will not reply to a

---

[1] Indicating health and well-being.

[2] False.

questionnaire, particularly a rather personal one. With some kinds of mail questionnaire, a five or ten per cent response is quite high. This one should have done better than that, but nothing like one hundred per cent.

11   So we find that the income figure is based on a sample composed of all class members whose addresses are known and who replied to the questionnaire. Is this a representative sample? That is, can this group be assumed to be equal in income to the unrepresented group, those who cannot be reached or who do not reply?

12   Who are the little lost sheep down in the Yale rolls as "address unknown"? Are they the big-income earners—the Wall Street men, the corporation directors, the manufacturing and utility executives? No; the addresses of the rich will not be hard to come by. Many of the most prosperous members of the class can be found through *Who's Who in America* and other reference volumes even if they have neglected to keep in touch with the alumni office. It is a good guess that the lost names are those of the men who, twenty-five years or so after becoming Yale bachelors of arts, have not fulfilled any shining promise. They are clerks, mechanics, tramps, unemployed alcoholics, barely surviving writers and artists ... people of whom it would take half a dozen or more to add up to an income of $25,111. These men do not so often register at class reunions, if only because they cannot afford the trip.

13   Who are those who chucked the questionnaire into the nearest wastebasket? We cannot be so sure about these, but it is at least a fair guess that many of them are just not making enough money to brag about.

14   It becomes pretty clear that the sample has omitted two groups most likely to depress the average. The $25,111 figure is beginning to explain itself. If it is a true figure for anything it is one merely for that special group of the class of '24 whose addresses are known and who are willing to stand up and tell how much they earn. Even that requires an assumption that the gentlemen are telling the truth.

15   Such an assumption is not to be made lightly. Experience from one breed of sampling study, that called market research, suggests that it can hardly ever be made at all. A house-to-house survey purporting [3] to study magazine readership was once made in which a key question was: What magazines does your household read? When the results were tabulated and analyzed it appeared that a great many people loved *Harper's* and not very many read *True Story*. Now there were publishers' figures around at the time that showed very clearly that *True Story* had more millions of circulation than *Harper's* had hundreds of thousands. Perhaps we asked the wrong kind of people, the designers of the survey said to themselves. But no, the questions had been asked in all sorts of neighborhoods all around the country. The only reasonable conclusion then was that a good many of the respondents, as people are called when they answer such questions, had not told the truth. About all the survey had uncovered was snobbery.

16   To be worth much, a report based on sampling must use a representa-

---

[3] Giving the appearance, claiming.

tive sample, which is one from which every source of bias has been removed. That is where our Yale figure shows its worthlessness. It is also where a great many of the things you can read in newspapers and magazines reveal their inherent lack of meaning.

17   A psychiatrist reported once that practically everybody is neurotic. Aside from the fact that such use destroys any meaning in the word "neurotic," take a look at the man's sample. That is, whom has the psychiatrist been observing? It turns out that he has reached this edifying conclusion from studying his patients, who are a long, long way from being a sample of the population. If a man were normal, our psychiatrist would never meet him.

18   Give that kind of second look to the things you read, and you can avoid learning a whole lot of things that are not so.

The Well-Chosen Average

19   You, I trust, are not a snob, and I certainly am not in the real-estate business. But let's say that you are and I am and that you are looking for property to buy along a road that is not far from the California valley in which I live.

20   Having sized you up, I take pains to tell you that the average income in this neighborhood is some $15,000 a year. Maybe that clinches your interest in living here; anyway, you buy and that handsome figure sticks in your mind. More than likely, since we have agreed that for the purposes of the moment you are a bit of a snob, you toss it in casually when telling your friends about where you live.

21   A year or so later we meet again. As a member of some taxpayers' committee I am circulating a petition to keep the tax rate down or assessments down or bus fare down. My plea is that we cannot afford the increase: After all, the average income in this neighborhood is only $3,500 a year. Perhaps you go along with me and my committee in this—you're not only a snob, you're stingy too—but you can't help being surprised to hear about that measly $3,500. Am I lying now, or was I lying last year?

22   You can't pin it on me either time. That is the essential beauty of doing your lying with statistics. Both those figures are legitimate averages, legally arrived at. Both represent the same data, the same people, the same incomes. All the same it is obvious that at least one of them must be so misleading as to rival an out-and-out lie.

23   My trick was to use a different kind of average each time, the word "average" having a very loose meaning. It is a trick commonly used, sometimes in innocence but often in guilt, by fellows wishing to influence public opinion or sell advertising space. When you are told that something is an average you still don't know very much about it unless you can find out which of the common kinds of average it is—*mean, median, or mode.*

24   The $15,000 figure I used when I wanted a big one is a mean, the arithmetic average of the incomes of all the families in the neighborhood.

You get it by adding up all the incomes and dividing by the number there are. The smaller figure is a median, and so it tells you that half the families in question have more than $3,500 a year and half have less. I might also have used the mode, which is the most frequently met-with figure in a series. If in this neighborhood there are more families with incomes of $5,000 a year than with any other amount, $5,000 a year is the modal income.

25   In this case, as usually is true with income figures, an unqualified "average" is virtually meaningless. One factor that adds to the confusion is that with some kinds of information all the averages fall so close together that, for casual purposes, it may not be vital to distinguish among them.

The Gee-Whiz Graph

26   There is terror in numbers. Humpty Dumpty's confidence in telling Alice that he was master of the words he used would not be extended by many people to numbers. Perhaps we suffer from a trauma induced by grade-school arithmetic.

27   Whatever the cause, it creates a real problem for the writer who yearns to be read, the advertising man who expects his copy to sell goods, the publisher who wants his books or magazines to be popular. When numbers in tabular form are taboo and words will not do the work well, as is often the case, there is one answer left: Draw a picture.

28   About the simplest kind of statistical picture, or graph, is the line variety. It is very useful for showing trends, something practically everybody is interested in showing or knowing about or spotting or deploring or fore-

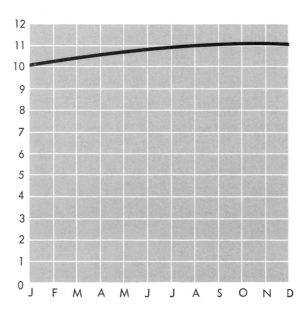

casting. We'll let our graph show how national income increased ten per cent in a year.

29   Begin with paper ruled into squares. Name the months along the bottom. Indicate billions of dollars up the side. Plot your points and draw your line, and your graph will look like the one on p. 109.

30   Now that's clear enough. It shows what happened during the year and it shows it month by month. He who runs may see and understand, because the whole graph is in proportion and there is a zero line at the bottom for comparison. Your ten per cent *looks* like ten per cent—an upward trend that is substantial but perhaps not overwhelming.

31   That is very well if all you want to do is convey information. But suppose you wish to win an argument, shock a reader, move him into action, sell him something. For that, this chart lacks schmaltz. Chop off the bottom.

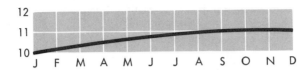

Now that's more like it. (You've saved paper too, something to point out if any carping fellow objects to your misleading graphics.) The figures are the same and so is the curve. It is the same graph. Nothing has been falsified—except the impression that it gives. But what the hasty reader sees now is a national-income line that has climbed halfway up the paper in twelve months, all because most of the chart isn't there any more. Like the missing parts of speech in sentences that you met in grammar classes, it is "understood." Of course, the eye doesn't "understand" what isn't there, and a small rise has become, visually, a big one.

32   Now that you have practiced to deceive, why stop with truncating? You have a further trick available that's worth a dozen of that. It will make your modest rise of ten per cent look livelier than one hundred per cent is entitled to look. Simply change the proportion between the ordinate [4] and the abscissa.[5] There's no rule against it, and it does give your graph a prettier shape. All you have to do is let each mark up the side stand for only one-tenth as many dollars as before [p. 111]. That *is* impressive, isn't it? Anyone looking at it can just feel prosperity throbbing in the arteries of the country. It is a subtler equivalent of editing "National income rose ten per cent" into ". . . climbed a whopping ten per cent." It is vastly more effective, however, because it contains no adjectives or adverbs to spoil the illusion of objectivity. There's nothing anyone can pin on you.

[4] The vertical measuring line in a graph.
[5] The horizontal measuring line in a graph.

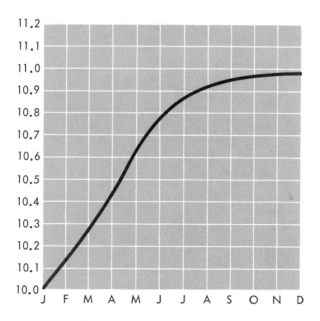

The One-Dimensional Picture

33   A decade or so ago you heard a good deal about the little people, meaning practically all of us. When this began to sound too condescending, we became the common man. Pretty soon that was forgotten too, which was probably just as well. But the little man is still with us. He is the character on the chart.

34   A chart on which a little man represents a million men, a moneybag or stack of coins a thousand or a billion dollars, an outline of a steer your beef supply for next year, is a pictorial graph. It is a useful device. It has what I am afraid is known as eye-appeal. And it is capable of becoming a fluent, devious, and successful liar.

35   The daddy of the pictorial chart, or pictograph, is the ordinary bar chart, a simple and popular method of representing quantities when two or more are to be compared. A bar chart is capable of deceit too. Look with suspicion on any version in which the bars change their widths as well as their lengths while representing a single factor or in which they picture three-dimensional objects the volumes of which are not easy to compare. A truncated [6] bar chart has, and deserves, exactly the same reputation as the truncated line graph we have been talking about. The habitat of the bar chart is the geography book, the corporation statement, and the news magazine. This is true also of its eye-appealing offspring.

36   Perhaps I wish to show a comparison of two figures—the average weekly wage of carpenters in the United States and Rotundia, let's say.

[6] Cut short.

111

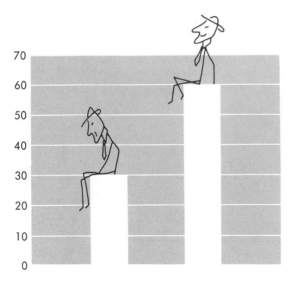

The sums might be $60 and $30. I wish to catch your eye with this, so I am not satisfied merely to print the numbers. I make a bar chart. (By the way, if that $60 figure doesn't square with the huge sum you laid out when your porch needed a new railing last summer, remember that your carpenter may not have done as well every week as he did while working for you. And anyway I didn't say what kind of average I have in mind or how I arrived at it, so it isn't going to get you anywhere to quibble. You see how easy it is to hide behind the most disreputable statistic if you don't include any other information with it? You probably guessed I just made this one up for purposes of illustration, but I'll bet you wouldn't have if I'd used $59.83 instead.)

37   There it is, with dollars-per-week indicated up the left side. It is a clear and honest picture. Twice as much money is twice as big on the chart and looks it [see above].

38   The chart lacks that eye-appeal though, doesn't it? I can easily supply that by using something that looks more like money than a bar does: moneybags. One moneybag for the unfortunate Rotundian's pittance, two for the American's wage. Or three for the Rotundian, six for the American. Either way, the chart remains honest and clear, and it will not deceive your hasty glance. That is the way an honest pictograph is made [p. 113].

39   That would satisfy me if all I wanted was to communicate information. But I want more. I want to say that the American workingman is vastly better off than the Rotundian, and the more I can dramatize the difference between thirty and sixty the better it will be for my argument. To tell the truth (which, of course, is what I am planning not to do), I want you to infer something, to come away with an exaggerated impression, but I don't want to be caught at my tricks. There is a way, and it is one that is being used every day to fool you.

40   I simply draw a moneybag to represent the Rotundian's thirty dollars,

and then I draw another one twice as tall to represent the American's sixty. That's in proportion, isn't it?

41   Now *that* gives the impression I'm after. The American's wage now dwarfs the foreigner's [*below*].

42   The catch, of course, is this. Because the second bag is twice as high as the first, it is also twice as wide. It occupies not twice but four times as much area on the page. The numbers still say two to one, but the visual impression, which is the dominating one most of the time, says the ratio is four to one. Or worse. Since these are pictures of objects having in reality three dimensions, the second must also be twice as thick as the first. As your geometry book put it, the volumes of similar solids vary as the cube of any like dimension. Two times two times two is eight. If one money bag holds $30, the other, having eight times the volume, must hold not $60 but $240.

43   And that indeed is the impression my ingenious little chart gives. While saying "twice," I have left the lasting impression of an overwhelming eight-to-one ratio.

44   You'll have trouble pinning any criminal intent on me, too. I am only doing what a great many other people do. *Newsweek* magazine has done it—with moneybags at that.

Post Hoc Rides Again

45   Somebody once went to a good deal of trouble to find out if cigarette smokers make lower college grades than non-smokers. It turned out that they did. This pleased a good many people and they have been making much of it ever since. The road to good grades, it would appear, lies in giving up smoking; and, to carry the conclusion one reasonable step further, smoking makes dull minds.

46   This particular study was, I believe, properly done: sample big enough and honestly and carefully chosen, correlation having a high significance, and so on.

47   The fallacy is an ancient one which, however, has a powerful tendency to crop up in statistical material, where it is disguised by a welter of impressive figures. It is the one that says that if B follows A, then A has caused B. An unwarranted assumption is being made that since smoking and low grades go together, smoking causes low grades. Couldn't it just as well be the other way around? Perhaps low marks drive students not to drink but to tobacco. When it comes right down to it, this conclusion is about as likely as the other and just as well supported by the evidence. But it is not nearly so satisfactory to propagandists.

48   It seems a good deal more probable, however, that neither of these things has produced the other, but both are a product of some third factor. Can it be that the sociable sort of fellow who takes his books less than seriously is also likely to smoke more? Or is there a clue in the fact that somebody once established a correlation between extroversion and low grades—a closer relationship apparently than the one between grades and intelligence? Maybe extroverts smoke more than introverts. The point is that when there are many reasonable explanations you are hardly entitled to pick one that suits your taste and insist on it. But many people do.

49   To avoid falling for the *post hoc* fallacy and thus wind up believing many things that are not so, you need to put any statement of relationship through a sharp inspection.

Study Questions: "How to Lie With Statistics"

1. If we can consider verbal language—words—to resemble maps, can we also consider charts and diagrams as maps? What about statistics? Do you think that they are more adequate maps than words? What type of language use do they most appear to resem-

ble? Why? In what ways can charts "map" the real world? Consider these questions and write several paragraphs in response.

2. In "How to Lie With Statistics" the author argues that charts and graphs can be used to construct faulty maps of reality. In your reading of magazines and newspapers, find one example of a graph or chart that you think *misrepresents* or "mismaps" its territory. After identifying your faulty map, write a thorough discussion of your findings. Include a copy of the graph or chart you have used.

3. In the first question, we asked you to determine what kind of language charts and graphs most resemble. With your response to question 2 in mind, would you make the same answer? Can a graph be used to provoke an emotional response from the reader? How?

The Ali-Frazier Fight

1   Sooner or later, fight metaphors, like fight managers, go sentimental. They go military. But there is no choice here. Frazier was the human equivalent of a war machine. He had tremendous firepower. He had a great left hook, a left hook frightening even to watch when it missed, for it seemed to whistle; he had a powerful right. He could knock a man out with either hand—not all fighters can, not even very good fighters. Usually, however, he clubbed opponents to death, took a punch, gave a punch, took three punches, gave two, took a punch, gave a punch, high speed all the way, always working, pushing his body and arms, short for a heavyweight, up through the middle, bombing through on force, reminiscent of Jimmy Brown knocking down tacklers, Frazier kept on coming, hard and fast, a hang-in, hang on, go-and-get-him, got-him, got-him, slip and punch, take a punch, wing a punch, whap a punch, never was Frazier happier than with his heart up on the line against some other man's heart, let the bullets fly—his heart was there to stand up at the last. Sooner or later, the others almost all fell down. Undefeated like Ali, winner of 23 out of 26 fights by knockout, he was a human force, certainly the greatest heavyweight force to come along since Rocky Marciano. (If those two men had ever met, it would have been like two Mack trucks hitting each other head-on, then backing up to hit each other again—they would have kept it up until the wheels were off the axels and the engines off the chassis.) But this would be a different kind of fight. Ali would run, Ali would keep hitting Frazier with long jabs, quick hooks and rights while backing up, backing up, staying out of reach unless Frazier could take the punishment and get in. That was where the military problem began. For getting in against the punishment he would take was a question of morale, and there

Excerpts from "Ego" by Norman Mailer, in Life *magazine, March, 1971. Reprinted by permission of the author and the author's agents, Scott Meredith Literary Agency, Inc., 845 Third Avenue, New York, New York 10022.*

was a unique situation in this fight—Frazier had become the white man's fighter, Mr. Charley was rooting for Frazier, and that meant blacks were boycotting him in their heart. That could be poison to Frazier's morale, for he was twice as black as Clay and half as handsome, he had the rugged decent life-worked face of a man who had labored in the pits all his life, he looked like the deserving modest son of one of those Negro cleaning women of a bygone age who worked from 6 in the morning to midnight every day, raised a family, endured and occasionally *elicited* [1] the exasperated admiration of white ladies who would kindly remark, "That woman deserves something better in her life." Frazier had the mien of the son, one of many, of such a woman, and he was the hardest-working fighter in training many a man had ever seen, he was conceivably the hardest-working man alive in the world, and as he went through his *regimen,* [2] first boxing four rounds with a sparring partner, Kenny Norton, a talented heavyweight from the coast with an almost unbeaten record, then working on the heavy bag, then the light bag, then skipping rope, 10 to 12 rounds of sparring and exercise on a light day, Frazier went on with the doggedness, the concentration, and the pumped-up fury of a man who has had so little in his life that he can endure torments to get everything, he pushed the total of his energy and force into an absolute abstract exercise of will so it did not matter if he fought a sparring partner or the heavy bag, he lunged at each equally as if the exhaustions of his own heart and the clangor of his lungs were his only enemies, and the head of a fighter or the leather of the bag as it rolled against his own head was nothing but some abstract thunk of material, not a thing, not a man, but thunk! thunk! something of an obstacle, thunk! thunk! thunk! to beat into thunk! oblivion. And his breath came in rips and sobs as he smashed into the bag as if it were real, just that heavy big torso-sized bag hanging from its chain but he attacked it as if it were a bear, as if it were a great fighter and they were in the mortal embrace of a killing set of exchanges of punches in the middle of the eighth round, and rounds of exercise later, skipping rope to an inhumanly fast beat for this late round in the training day, sweat pouring like jets of blood from an artery, he kept swinging his rope, muttering, "Two-million-dollars-and-change, two-million-dollars-and-change," railroad train chugging into the terminals of exhaustion. And it was obvious that Durham, jeweler to his diamond, was working to make the fight as abstract as he could for Frazier, to keep Clay out of it—for they would not call him Ali in their camp—yes, Frazier was fortifying his ego by depersonalizing his opponent, Clay was, thunk! the heavy bag, thunk! and thunk!—Frazier was looking to get no messages from that cavern of velvet when black people sent their good wishes to Ali at midnight, no, Frazier would insulate himself with prodigies of work, hardest-working man in the hell-hole of the world, and on and on he drove himself into the depressions each day of killing daily exhaustion.

[1] Brought out.

[2] A regulated system of diet or exercise.

2   That was one half of the strategy to isolate Frazier from Ali, hard work and thinking of thunking on *inanimate* [3] Clay; the other half was up to Durham who was running front relations with the blacks of North Philly who wandered into the gym, paid their dollar, and were ready to heckle on Frazier. In the four rounds he boxed with Norton, Frazier did not look too good for a while. It was 10 days before the fight and he was in a bad mood when he came in, for the word was through the gym that they had discovered one of his favorite sparring partners, just fired that morning, was a Black Muslim and had been calling Ali every night with reports, that was the rumor, and Frazier, sullen and cold at the start, was bopped and tapped, then walloped by Norton moving fast with the big training gloves in imitation of Ali, and Frazier looked very easy to hit until the middle of the third round when Norton, proud of his something like 20 wins and one loss, beginning to get some ideas himself about how to fight champions, came driving in to mix it with Frazier, have it out man to man and caught a right which dropped him, left him looking limp with that half-silly smile sparring partners get when they have been hit too hard to justify any experience or any money they are going to take away. Up till then the crowd had been with Norton. There at one end of the Cloverlay gym, a street-level store-front room which could have been used originally by an automobile dealer, there on that empty, immaculate Lysol-soaked floor, designed when Frazier was there for only Frazier and his partners to train (as opposed to Miami where Ali would rub elbows with the people) here the people were at one end, the end off the street, and they jeered whenever Norton hit Frazier, they laughed when Norton made him look silly, they called out, "Drop the mother," until Durham held up a gentlemanly but admonishing finger in request for silence. Afterward, however, training completed, Durham approached them to answer questions, rolled with their *sallies,*[4] jived the people back, subtly enlisted their sympathy for Frazier by saying, "When I fight Clay, I'm going to get him somewhere in the middle rounds," until the blacks quipping back said angrily, "You ain't fighting him, Frazier is."
        "Why you call him Clay?" another asked. "He Ali."
        "His name is Cassius Clay to me," said Durham.
        "What you say against his religion?"
        "I don't say nothing about his religion and he doesn't say anything about mine. I'm a Baptist."
        "You going to make money on this?"
        "Of course," said Durham, "I got to make money. You don't think I work up this sweat for nothing."

3   They loved him. He was happy with them. A short fat man in a purple suit wearing his revival of the wide-brim bebop hat said to Durham, "Why don't you get Norton to manage? He was beating up on *your* fighter," and the fat man cackled for he had scored and could elaborate the tale

---

[3] Not alive; considered to be an object rather than a person.

[4] Heckling cries.

for his ladies later how he had put down Yank who was working the daily rite on the edge of the black street for his fighter, while upstairs, dressed, and sucking an orange, sweat still pouring, gloom of excessive fatigue upon him, Frazier was sitting through his two-hundredth or two-thousandth interview for this fight, reluctant indeed to give it at all. "Some get it, some don't," he had said for refusal, but relented when a white friend who had done road work with him interceded, so he sat there now against a leather sofa, dark blue suit, dark T-shirt, mopping his brow with a pink-red towel, and spoke dispiritedly of being ready too early for the fight. He was waking up an hour too early for roadwork each morning now. "I'd go back to sleep but it doesn't feel good when I do run."

"I guess the air is better that hour of the morning."

He nodded sadly. "There's a limit to how good the air in Philly can get."

"Where'd you begin to sing?" was a question asked.

4   "I sang in church first," he replied, but it was not the day to talk about singing. The loneliness of hitting the bag still seemed upon him as if in his exhaustion now, and in the thoughts of that small insomnia which woke him an hour too early every day was something of the loneliness of all blacks who work very hard and are isolated from fun and must wonder in the just-awakened night how large and pervasive was the curse of a people. "The countdown's begun," said Frazier, "I get impatient about now." For the fight, Ali was wearing red velvet trunks, Frazier had green. Before they began, even before they were called together by the referee for instructions, Ali went dancing around the ring and glided past Frazier with a sweet little-boy smile, as if to say, "You're my new playmate. We're going to have fun." Ali was laughing. Frazier was having nothing of this and turned his neck to embargo him away. Ali, having alerted the crowd by this big first move, came prancing in again. When Frazier looked ready to block him, Ali went around, evading a contact, gave another sweet smile, shook his head at the lack of high spirit. "Poor Frazier," he seemed to say.

5   At the weigh-in early that afternoon Ali looked physically resplendent; the night before in Harlem, crowds had cheered him; he was coming to claim his victory on the confluence of two mighty tides—he was the mightiest victim of injustice in America and he was also—the 20th Century was nothing if not a tangle of opposition—he was also the mightiest *narcissist* [5] in the land. Every beard, dropout, homosexual, junkie, freak, swinger, and plain simple individualist adored him. Every *pedantic* [6] liberal soul who had once loved Patterson now paid homage to Ali. The mightiest of the black *psyches* [7] and the most filigreed of the white psyches were ready to roar him home, as well as every family-loving hard-working square American who genuinely hated the war in Vietnam. What a tangle of ribbons he carried on his lance, enough cross purposes to be the knight-

[5] Someone excessively interested in his or her appearance, abilities, and importance.

[6] Having an unnecessary emphasis on minor, trivial details.

[7] Soul or mind.

resplendent of television, the *fell* [8] hero of the medium, and he had a look of unique happiness on television when presenting his program for the course of the fight, and his inevitable victory. He would be as content then as an infant splashing the waters of the bathinette. If he was at once a saint and a monster to any mind which looked for category, any mind unwilling to encounter the thoroughly dread-filled fact that the 20th Century breed of man now in birth might be no longer half good and half evil—generous and greedy by turns—but a *mutation* [9] with Cassius Muhammad for the first son—then that mind was not ready to think about 20th Century Man. (And indeed Muhammad Ali had twin poodles he called Angel and Demon.) So now the *ambiguity* [10] of his presence filled the Garden before the fight was fairly begun, it was as if he had announced to that plural billion-footed crowd assembled under the shadow of the jet which would fly over them that the first *enigma* [11] of the fight would be the way he would win it, that he would initiate his triumph by getting the crowd to laugh at Frazier, yes, first premise tonight was that the poor black man in Frazier's soul would go berserk if made a figure of roll-off-your-seat amusement.

6   The referee gave his instructions. The bell rang. The first 15 seconds of a fight can be the fight. It is equivalent to the first kiss in a love affair. The fighters each missed the other. Ali blocked Frazier's first punches easily, but Ali then missed Frazier's head. That head was bobbing as fast as a third fist. Frazier would come rushing in, head moving like a fist, fists bobbing too, his head working above and below his forearm, he was trying to get through Ali's jab, get through fast and sear Ali early with the terror of a long fight and punches harder than he had ever taken to the stomach, and Ali in turn, backing up, and throwing fast punches, aimed just a trifle, and was therefore a trifle too slow, but it was obvious Ali was trying to shiver Frazier's *synapses* [12] from the start, set waves of depression stirring which would reach his heart in later rounds and make him slow, deaden nerve, deaden nerve went Ali's jab flicking a snake tongue, whoo-eet! whoo-eet! but Frazier's head was bobbing too fast, he was moving faster than he had ever moved before in that bobbing nonstop never-a-backward step of his, slogging and bouncing forward, that huge left hook flaunting the air with the confidence it was enough of a club to split a tree, and Ali, having missed his jabs, stepped nimbly inside the hook and wrestled Frazier in the clinch. Ali looked stronger here. So by the first 45 seconds of the fight, they had each surprised the other profoundly. Frazier was

[8] Fierce, deadly, terrible.

[9] A sudden change in chromosomes producing new inheritable characteristics in the children which did not belong to the parents; a change producing a new breed.

[10] Something understood in two or more seemingly contradictory ways; indefinitely understood.

[11] A seemingly unexplainable thing or person; a mystery or puzzle.

[12] Contact points between neurons in the brain, where nerve impulses are transmitted from one to another neuron.

fast enough to slip through Ali's punches and Ali was strong enough to handle him in the clinches. A pattern had begun. Because Ali was missing often, Frazier was in under his shots like a police dog's muzzle on your arm, Ali could not slide from side to side, he was boxed in, then obliged to go backward, and would end on the ropes again and again with Frazier belaboring him. Yet Frazier could not reach him. Like a *prestidigitator* [13] Ali would tie the other's punches into odd knots, not even blocking them yet on his elbows or his arms, rather throwing his own punches as defensive moves, for even as they missed, he would brush Frazier to the side with his forearm, or hold him off, or clinch and wrestle a little of the will out of Frazier's neck. Once or twice in the round a long left hook by Frazier just touched the surface of Ali's chin, and Ali waved his head in *placid* [14] contempt to the billions watching as if to say, "This man has not been able to hurt me at all."

7   The first round set a pattern for the fight. Ali won it and would win the next. His jab was landing from time to time and rights and lefts of no great consequence. Frazier was hardly reaching him at all. Yet it looked like Frazier had established that he was fast enough to get in on Ali and so drive him to the ropes and to the corners, and that spoke of a fight which would be determined by the man in better condition, in better physical condition rather than in better psychic condition, the kind of fight Ali could hardly want for his strength was in his pauses, his nature passed along the curve of every *dialectic*,[15] he liked, in short, to fight in flurries, and then move out, move away, assess, take his time, fight again. Frazier would not let him. Frazier moved in with the snarl of a wolf, his teeth seemed to show through his mouthpiece, he made Ali work, Ali won the first two rounds but it was obvious he could not continue to win if he had to work all the way. And in the third round Frazier began to get to him, caught Ali with a powerful blow to the face at the bell. That was the first moment where it was clear to all that Frazier had won a round. Then he won the next. Ali looked tired and a little depressed. He was moving less and less and calling upon a skill not seen since the fight with Chuvalo when he had showed his old ability, worked on all those years ago with Shotgun Sheldon, to lie on the ropes and take a beating to the stomach. He had exhausted Chuvalo by welcoming attacks on the stomach but Frazier was too *incommensurable* [16] a force to allow such total attack. So Ali lay on the ropes and wrestled him off, and moved his arms and waist, blocking punches, slipping punches, countering with punches—it began to look as if the fight would be written on the ropes, but Ali was getting very tired. At the beginning of the fifth round, he got up slowly from his stool,

---

[13] A performer of quick, skillful tricks by sleight of hand.

[14] Calm, quiet, undisturbed.

[15] A method of logical inquiry following a sequence in which an event or idea (thesis) generates its opposite (antithesis) and leads to a reconciliation of the two (synthesis).

[16] Having no equal, nothing against which it can be measured.

very slowly. Frazier was beginning to feel that the fight was his. He moved in on Ali jeering, his hands at his side in mimicry of Ali, a street fighter mocking his opponent, and Ali tapped him with long light jabs to which Frazier stuck out his mouthpiece, a jeer of derision as if to suggest that the mouthpiece was all Ali would reach all night.

8   There is an *extortion* [17] of the will beyond any of our measure in the exhaustion which comes upon a fighter in early rounds when he is already too tired to lift his arms or take advantage of openings there before him, yet the fight is not a third over, there are all those rounds to go, contractions of torture, the lungs screaming into the dungeons of the soul, washing the throat with a hot bile that once belonged to the liver, the legs are going dead, the arms move but their motion is limp, one is straining into another will, breathing into the breath of another will as agonized as one's own. As the fight moved through the fifth, the sixth and the seventh, then into the eighth, it was obvious that Ali was into the longest night of his career, and yet with that skill, that research into the pits of every miserable *contingency* [18] in boxing, he came up with odd *somnambulistic* [19] variations, holding Frazier off, riding around Frazier with his arm about his neck, almost entreating Frazier with his arms extended, and Frazier leaning on him, each of them slowed to a pit-a-pat of light punches back and forth until one of them was goaded up from exhaustion to whip and stick, then hook and hammer and into the belly and out, and out of the clinch and both looking exhausted, and then Frazier, mouth bared again like a wolf, going in and Ali waltzing him, trying him, tapping him lightly as if he were a speed bag, just little flicks, until Frazier, like an exhausted horse finally fleeing the crop, would push up into a trot and try to run up the hill. It was indeed as if they were both running up a hill. As if Frazier's offensive was so great and so great was Ali's defense that the fight could only be decided by who could take the steepest pitch of the hill. So Frazier, driving, driving, trying to drive the heart out of Ali, put the pitch of that hill up and up until they were ascending an unendurable slope. And moved like somnambulists slowly working and rubbing one another, almost embracing, next to locked in the slow moves of lovers after the act until, reaching into the stores of energy reaching them from cells never before so used, one man or the other would work up a contractive spasm of skills and throw punches at the other in the straining slow-motion hypnosis of a deepening act. And so the first eight rounds went by. The two judges scored six for Frazier, two for Ali. The referee had it even. Some of the Press had Ali ahead—it was not easy to score. For if it were an alley fight, Frazier would win. Clay was by now hardly more than the heavy bag to Frazier. Frazier was dealing with a man, not a demon. He was not respectful of that man. But still! It was Ali who was landing the majority of punches. They were light, they were usually weary, but some had snap,

[17] Getting money by threats or the misuse of authority.

[18] An unforeseen or unexpected accidental occurrence.

[19] Like a sleepwalker.

some were quick, he was landing two punches to Frazier's one. Yet Frazier's were hardest. And Ali often looked as tender as if he were making love. It was as if he could now feel the whole absence of that real second fight with Liston, that fight for which he had trained so long and so hard, the fight which might have rolled over his laurels from the greatest artist of *pugilism* [20] to the greatest brawler of them all—maybe he had been prepared on that night to beat Liston at his own, be more of a slugger, more of a man crude to crude than Liston. Yes, Ali had never been a street fighter and never a whorehouse knock-it-down stud, no, it was more as if a man with the exquisite reflexes of Nureyev had learned to throw a knockout punch with either hand and so had become champion of the world without knowing if he was the man of all men or the most delicate of the delicate with special privilege endowed by God. Now with Frazier, he was in a sweat bath (a mud-pile, a knee, elbow, and death-thumping chute of a pit) having in this late year the fight he had sorely needed for his true greatness as a fighter six and seven years ago, and so whether ahead, behind or even, terror sat in the rooting instinct of all those who were for Ali for it was obviously Frazier's fight to win, and what if Ali, weaknesses of character now flickering to the surface in a hundred little moves, should enter the vale of prizefighting's deepest humiliation, should fall out half conscious on the floor and not want to get up. What a death to his followers.

9   The ninth began. Frazier mounted his largest body attack of the night. It was preparations-for-Liston-with-Shotgun-Sheldon, it was the virtuosity of the gym all over again, and Ali, like a catcher handling a fast-ball pitcher, took Frazier's punches, one steamer, another steamer, wing! went a screamer, a steamer, warded them, blocked them, slithered them, winced from them, absorbed them, took them in and blew them out and came off the ropes and was Ali the Magnificent for the next minute and thirty seconds. The fight turned. The troops of Ali's second corps of energy had arrived, the energy for which he had been waiting long agonizing heart-sore vomit-mean rounds. Now he jabbed Frazier, he snake-licked his face with jabs faster than he had thrown before, he anticipated each attempt of Frazier at counterattack and threw it back, he danced on his toes for the first time in rounds, he popped in rights, he hurt him with hooks, it was his biggest round of the night, it was the best round yet of the fight, and Frazier full of energy and hordes of sudden punishment was begin-ning to move into that odd *petulant* [21] concentration on other rituals besides the punches, tappings of the gloves, stares of the eye, that species of mouthpiece-chewing which is the prelude to fun-strut in the knees, then Queer Street, then waggle on out, drop like a steer.

10   It looked like Ali had turned the fight, looked more like the same in the 10th, now reporters were writing another story in their mind where Ali was not the magical untried Prince who had come apart under the first real

[20] Boxing.

[21] Impatient or irritable.

pressure of his life but was rather the greatest Heavyweight Champion of all time for he had weathered the purgatory of Joe Frazier.

11   But in the 11th, that story also broke. Frazier caught him, caught him again and again, and Ali was near to knocked out and swayed and slid on Queer Street himself, then spent the rest of the 11th and the longest round of the 12th working another bottom of Hell, holding off Frazier who came on and on, sobbing, wild, a wild horror of a beast, man of will reduced to the common denominator of the will of all of us back in that land of the animal where the idea of man as a tool-wielding beast was first conceived. Frazier looked to get Ali forever in the 11th and 12th, and Ali, his legs slapped and slashed on the thighs between each round by Angelo Dundee, came out for the 13th and incredibly was dancing. Everybody's story switched again. For if Ali won this round, the 14th and the 15th, who could know if he could not win the fight? . . . He won the first half of the 13th, then spent the second half on the ropes with Frazier. They were now like crazy death-march-maddened mateys coming up the hill and on to home, and yet Ali won the 14th, Ali looked good, he came out dancing for the 15th, while Frazier, his own armies of energy finally caught up, his courage ready to spit into the eye of any devil black or white who would steal the work of his life, had equal madness to steal the bolt from Ali. So Frazier reached out to snatch the magic punch from the air, the punch with which Ali topped Bonavena, and found it and thunked Ali a hell and hit Ali a heaven of a shot which dumped Muhammad into 50,000 newspaper photographs—Ali on the floor! Great Ali on the floor was out there flat singing to the sirens in the mistiest fogs of Queer Street (same look of death and widowhood on his far-gone face as one had seen in the fifth blind round with Liston) yet Ali got up, Ali came sliding through the last two minutes and thirty-five seconds of this heathen holocaust in some last exercise of the will, some iron *fundament* [22] of the ego not to be knocked out, and it was then as if the spirit of Harlem finally spoke and came to rescue and the ghosts of the dead in Vietnam, something held him up before arm-weary triumphant near-crazy Frazier who had just hit him the hardest punch ever thrown in his life and they went down to the last few seconds of a great fight, Ali still standing and Frazier had won.

12   The world was talking instantly of a rematch. For Ali had shown America what we all had hoped was secretly true. He was a man. He could bear moral and physical torture and he could stand. And if he could beat Frazier in the rematch we would have at last a national hero who was hero of the world as well, and who could bear to wait for the next fight? Joe Frazier, still the champion, and a great champion, said to the press, "Fellows, have a heart—I got to live a little. I've been working for 10 long years." And Ali, through the agency of alter-ego Bundini, said—for Ali was now in the hospital to check on the possible fracture of a jaw—Ali was reported to have said, "Get the gun ready—we're going to set traps."

[22] Foundation.

Oh, wow. Could America wait for something so great as the Second Ali-Frazier?

Study Questions: "The Ali-Frazier Fight"

1. What does Mailer mean when he says (in the first line of the article) that fight metaphors, like fight managers, "go sentimental"? Is Mailer concerned to avoid the clichés that most sports writers use? Why? Why doesn't he just create a clear, factual map of this event?

2. Mailer compares the two fighters in an interesting way. Frazier, he says, "had the rugged decent life-worked face of a man who had labored in the pits all his life. . . ." Ali, on the other hand, was "the mightiest narcissist in the land. . . ." What kind of attitudes on the part of the writer does this comparison reveal? Why does he choose these two sets of images?

3. Pick out a metaphoric pattern in the description of the fight that you find unusual or interesting and describe its emotional qualities.

4. The fight took place in March 1971, and caused a great furor in American magazines and newspapers. Find several reports of the fight in magazines or newspapers of the time and compare them to the Mailer report. What differences do you find?

STYLE
AND
STRUCTURE

UNIT 5

Structure
and
Meaning:
Reading Sentences

Actually, thinking is most mysterious, and by far the greatest light upon it that we have is thrown by the study of language. This study shows that the forms of a person's thoughts are controlled by inexorable laws of pattern of which he is unconscious. These patterns are the unperceived intricate systematizations of his own language—shown readily enough by a candid comparison and contrast with other languages, especially those of a different linguistic family. His thinking itself is in a language—in English, in Sanskrit, in Chinese. And every language is a vast pattern-system, different from others, in which are culturally ordained the forms and categories by which the personality not only communicates, but also analyzes nature, notices or neglects types of relationships and phenomena, channels reasoning, and builds the house of his consciousness. *(Benjamin Lee Whorf)*

Evaluating Your Learning

When you've finished reading and studying this unit, you should be able to demonstrate your knowledge by

- describing how structure and meaning are related in reading
- explaining the ways in which sentence length is related to the reader's understanding
- defining cumulative and suspended sentences and finding examples of them in your reading
- describing sentence balance and identifying elements of balance in your reading
- describing repetition as an element of sentence structure and finding examples of it in your reading

A Look Back and a Look Ahead

In Units 1 to 4, we discussed the kinds of language understanding that skillful readers have acquired, and we examined in detail the kinds of language uses that we find in our everyday reading: the language of fact, an accurate, relatively objective map of the "real" world aimed primarily to inform us; the language of belief, a subjective map of the world designed to play on our emotions and to influence our understanding, as well as to express the beliefs of the writer; and the language of metaphor, the combination of two maps, encouraging us to make connections between different things and ideas. We talked, too, about the meaning-making process and the reader's active role in it; we discussed the role of the participating reader, the reader who understands how facts and ideas may be presented in slanted contexts and how those contexts are carefully controlled by the writer.

But understanding the uses of language is only one of the kinds of skills that critical readers use. Another important skill is the ability to understand the relationship of ideas—a relationship that is expressed in the *structure* of the sentences, paragraphs, and paragraph sequences of any reading material—in order to understand how the writer can use certain structures of language to control the meaning-making process of the reader. In fact, we can say that the writer controls the *structural context* * within which the reader makes meaning, just as he or she controls the word context. In the next few units, we'll look at structural devices analogous to the techniques of slanting: we'll look at the ways in which writers control sentences, ordering the reader's perception through sentence length, through sentence structure, through arrangements of phrases and clauses. Then we'll look at paragraphs and paragraph organization, and finally at sequences of paragraphs. On each of these structural levels, we will examine the principles of the relationships between *central* or *topic* ideas, *restating* and *specifying* ideas, and *qualifying* ideas. In this unit, we will begin to examine sentence structures: *suspended* and *cumulative* sentences, and sentence *balance* and *repetition*.

The Role of Structure in Meaning

As readers, we have a tendency to focus our attention on words, and to see the meaning-making process as primarily a product of the way the writer has used words. However, words are only one part of the total meaning-making process. The *structures* of language—that is, the patterns by which words are put together—play a very large role in the way the reader perceives any event or idea reported in writing. As readers, we are often influenced as much by the *way* a message is constructed as by the language the writer uses, although we may not recognize the immediate effect of the structure on our perception. In fact, our entire view of the universe is structured, language specialists tell us, by the way our language is patterned. That is, our perceptions are shaped by the structure of the language itself. In a very real sense, we cannot *see* anything we don't have a name for; in the same sense, we cannot combine words and ideas in any structures other than those provided for us by our language. It is not so difficult to see, then, why some students of language have suggested that the *structure* of our language thinks for us.

What is difficult to see, of course, is how this structure makes meaning, or how it helps us to make meaning, since the structure is almost invisible and since it becomes apparent only if we look closely enough. One purpose of this unit is to help you become more familiar with the basic structures of the sentence in order to make them *visible* to you, in order to make you more conscious of the ways they influence your understanding of the writer's ideas. Another purpose—a major purpose—is to help you cope with the two problems that confront most readers: sentence length and sentence complexity.

Two Reading Problems: Sentence Length and Sentence Complexity

For many readers, the most important factors in their ability to make meaning out of a sentence structure are sentence length and sentence complexity. Many readers (are you among them?) consistently complain that writers are deliberately trying to confuse them by writing sentences that are long and complicated; they prefer short sentences that say the same thing more directly. Let's examine this issue and see what it involves.

Sentence length, of course, is easy to measure. You can take any number of sentences, count the total words, and divide by the number of sentences. Sentence complexity, on the other hand, is related to the number of *phrases* * and *clauses* * a writer has *embedded* * within the sentence. A simple, uncomplicated sentence looks like this subject-verb pattern:

The invention of cars increased people's mobility.

A *complex sentence,* * however, has many modifiers, often phrases and clauses used to modify the basic subject-verb structure of the sentence. Look at this complex sentence of fifty-seven words, written by a political scientist:

The problem that most democratic theorists would regard as the most difficult and most important one arises because of the ever-present possibility under a democratic governmental structure that the right of the majority to rule will come into conflict with the right of individuals and minorities to assert and register in a formal way their political preferences.

The complexity of this sentence, as you can clearly see, depends upon the many component parts of it, components which restate, specify, and qualify the basic structure. That structure is relatively simple:

The problem arises because of the possibility that the right of the majority will come into conflict with the right of individuals and minorities.

It *is* a hard sentence to read. Unfortunately, however, its complexity is typical of many sentences you will be reading throughout your college career. The sooner you can learn strategies for dealing with this complexity, and the sooner you understand why writers resort to sentences like this, the better equipped you will be to understand what you read.

As you may already know from your own writing and reading

experience, young writers write short sentences without much complexity. You may also know that writers who write for young children usually use short sentences and simple sentence patterns in order to make reading easier—this style is often called *Dick and Jane style,* or *primer style.*⃰ Here is an example of writing aimed at sixth-grade readers:

> Effective communication is an important skill. People who communicate clearly get their jobs done quickly. They do not need to spend time trying to figure out what they are supposed to do.

These sentences are easy to read because they are short (an average of nine words per sentence) and because the writer has used only the most familiar sentence pattern: a subject-verb pattern that is the most common structure in the English language:

> Communication is . . . a skill. People . . . get . . . jobs done . . . They do not need. . . .

Here is another example, this one taken from a passage written for twelfth-graders. What differences do you see between these sentences and those above?

> Words are symbols which represent real things, real events, real feelings. They have no meaning in and of themselves unless we anchor them firmly to the things, events, feelings they are intended to represent. If we have no knowledge of Swahili and happen to hear two people talking fluently in that language, the only power their words are likely to have over us is to make us feel excluded, confused, or just plain frustrated.

The differences in these two passages, as you can easily see, have to do with the structure of the sentences—with their length (an average of twenty-five words per sentence in the twelfth-grade passage; an average of nine in the sixth-grade passage) and with their complexity, the way the writer has added phrases and clauses to the basic sentence frameworks.

What are the reasons for the various sentence lengths and levels of complexity in the sentences above? If it is true that the sixth-grade sentence is the easiest to read, why aren't all writers required to write that way? Wouldn't that help to eliminate misunderstandings and facilitate communication? In some sense, it is probably true that the simplest sentences are least likely to be misunderstood. But the answer is more complicated than that. Let's look at several different aspects of the question before we attempt to give a definitive answer.

We've already commented on the most obvious reason for the

variety of sentence lengths and complexity: the age of the audience and the amount of reading experience the audience may have had. The less you have read (as you may know from your own experience), the harder it may be for you to cope with long sentences, sentences that contain a variety of embedded clause and phrase patterns. Inexperienced readers simply find it difficult to process a great deal of complex information and writers who write for them oblige them by giving them more simple, easy-to-read sentences.

Most writers assume, however, that the more experienced readers become, the better able they are to process information. As you saw in the example above, writers of high school texts assume that their readers are able to handle sentences of sixteen to eighteen words, with several embedded clauses or phrases. In order to pack more ideas into the relatively short space of the sentence, and in order to achieve density and efficiency, the writer chooses a more complex sentence structure. It is up to the readers to gauge their reading strategies accordingly.

But, you may complain, why do writers indulge in such long sentences as the fifty-seven-word monster produced by the political scientist? *No* reader, you may argue, no matter what educational background he or she may have, can find that sentence easy to read! Your complaint—and in many cases it is a valid complaint—is difficult to answer, just as it was difficult to answer the related question, "Why do writers obscure meaning, rather than making their idea clear?" Let's try three different answers. The first is that some writers, with their minds on their ideas, simply don't take their readers into account. They build long, complicated sentences because they forget that—on the other end of the communications process—someone has to decode their messages. Related to this group is that group of poor writers—many of whom succeed in getting into print!—who write long, intricate sentences because they don't have the skill to write simply and directly. You'll encounter many of these writers in your reading life, and you'll often respond by putting their work aside and reading something else instead. Poor writers who unnecessarily confuse their readers just don't deserve to be read.

The second answer, however—which has to do with the content, rather than with the writer—is more complicated. There are many ideas that cannot be adequately expressed in simple terms. They are complicated, intricate, many-faceted notions that would lose their rounded complexity in a shorter, less involved form. As you begin to deal with these ideas, in college and in your professional life, you'll notice that writers have developed a variety of sentence strategies for presenting these difficult ideas to you. If you want to gain the knowledge that's contained in these sentences, you must master the forms in which the ideas are presented. At this point, you'll develop an evaluative sense that will help you answer the question, "Is the information here important enough to warrant the time and energy I'm going to spend digging it out of these sentences?" If the answer is *yes,* you'll plunge ahead, using all your resources to understand the structure. If the answer is *no,* you'll turn to something easier, less complex, less demanding—and perhaps less informative.

The third answer—like the first—has to do with writers themselves, but in a very different way. There are some writers (often "literary" writers fall into this category) who want to challenge their readers to a full participation in the reading act—who write long, complicated sentences because they believe that short sentences and simple structures put readers to sleep. And they want their readers awake! A good example of this kind of writing is the opening sentence from William Faulkner's novel *Absalom, Absalom!*

> From a little after two oclock until almost sundown of the long still hot weary dead September afternoon they sat in what Miss Coldfield still called the office because her father had called it that —a dim hot airless room with the blinds all closed and fastened for forty-three summers because when she was a girl someone had believed that light and moving air carried heat and that dark was always cooler, and which (as the sun shone fuller and fuller on that side of the house) became latticed with yellow slashes full of dust motes which Quentin thought of as being flecks of the dead old dried paint itself blown inward from the scaling blinds as wind might have blown them.

Reading like this is not for the faint-hearted or for those who (as we suggested earlier) are just along for the ride. This kind of writing is tough stuff, meant for mature adults with the skill and interest necessary to unravel the intricate patterns Faulkner is weaving here. It is meant for *participating* readers who believe (with the author) that part of the story happens inside them, as they read and decipher the narrative. In your reading of literature, you'll encounter many other writers who demand this kind of participation of you—and this demand is focused in the structural difficulty of their writing, in their sentences and paragraphs.

Now that we've surveyed the arguments for the use of long sentences (their ability to convey elaborate meanings, to demand the reader's full participation), it's time to say something—several things— about the short sentence and its effective use. Short sentences are used for emphasis, for dramatic effect. Here, for example, is the introduction from a short *Newsweek* essay on unemployment. Notice how the writer uses short sentences at the most important points in his argument—at the beginnings and ends of paragraphs.

> Danny is an educated man. He is a master of writing research papers, taking tests, talking and filling out forms. He can rattle off

his social-security number as easily as he can his name because it was also his student identification number. He can analyze Freud from a Marxian viewpoint and he can analyze Marx from a Freudian viewpoint.

In short, Danny is an unskilled worker and he has a sociology degree to prove it. He is of very little use to American industry.

This is nothing new. Colleges have been turning out unskilled workers for decades. Until five years ago, most of these unskilled workers took their degrees in sociology, philosophy, political science or history and marched right into the American middle class. Some filled executive positions in business and government but many, if not most, went into education, which is the only thing they knew anything about. Once there, they taught another generation the skills necessary to take tests and write papers.

But that cycle broke down. Teachers are overabundant these days, college applications are down, plumbers are making $12 an hour and liberal-arts graduates are faced with a choice—graduate school or the taxicab.[1]

In this essay, the short sentences do exactly the job they were designed to do—they provide short, punchy statements that sum up a main point or introduce a point that is going to be expanded and commented on in another sentence.

Occasionally, however, writers use short sentences to provide a different kind of emphasis: an emotional emphasis. You will find this use in passages where the writer wants to express a strong belief—or wants to persuade the reader to that belief. In the following *New Yorker* article, George Wald provides an example of this kind of use, as he argues for banning all nuclear weapons:

I think I know what is bothering the students. I think that what we are up against is a generation that is by no means sure that it has a future.

I am growing old, and my future, so to speak, is already behind me. But there are those students of mine, who are in my mind always; and there are my children, the youngest of them now seven and nine, whose future is infinitely more precious to me than my own. So it isn't just their generation; its mine, too. We're all in it together.

Are we to have a chance to live? We don't ask for prosperity, or security. Only for a reasonable chance to live, to work out our destiny in peace and decency. Not to go down in history as the apocalyptic generation. . . .

[1] Peter Carlson, "Danny is an educated man," copyright 1974, by Newsweek, Inc. All rights reserved. Reprinted by permission.

We have to get rid of those atomic weapons, here and every-where. We cannot live with them.

I think we've reached a point of great decision, not just for our nation, not only for all humanity, but for life upon the earth. . . . Three billion years ago, life arose upon the earth. It is the only life in the solar system.

About two million years ago, man appeared. He has become the dominant species on the earth. All other living things, animal and plant, live by his sufferance. He is the custodian of life on earth, and in the solar system. It's a big responsibility.[2]

Wald's statement is made even more emotional and powerful by the use of short, emphatic sentences that carry intense emotional force. Occasionally these short sentences are not even sentences at all—just fragments of sentences. These fragments, too, take on emphatic force and intensity and become a part—an effective part—of the whole emotional statement.

practice 1

1. One language researcher has studied the sentence length and its relationship to "reading ease." Here is a table that represents his measurement of reading difficulty:

AVERAGE SENTENCE LENGTH IN WORDS

Very Easy	8 words or less
Easy	11
Fairly Easy	14
Standard	17
Fairly Difficult	21
Difficult	25
Very Difficult	29 or more

With this information in mind, see if you can determine the reading difficulty of each of the following passages.

A. In the ancient world art was one important way of helping the people under-stand the idea of kingship. The average man usually knew his king only through art. He probably never actually saw him. It was the artist's job to show the people something about the all-powerfulness of the king. To do this, he depended on certain traditional symbols, so he could picture the king's majesty in a way the people could understand.

[2] From "Notes and Comment" in *The New Yorker*. Reprinted by permission; © 1969 The New Yorker Magazine, Inc.

B. In the ancient world, art was perhaps the most important way of enabling the public to comprehend the abstract concept of kingship. The average citizen of antiquity usually knew his rules only through artistic representations, rather than through actual presence. The artist was responsible for revealing to the people the god-like-ness and omnipotence of the king, usually by depending on certain traditional symbols, picturing the ruler in a way clearly decipherable by the people.

C. In the ancient world, art was perhaps the most significant means of making concrete for the public the abstract concepts of kingship, for the average citizen of antiquity usually knew his ruler only through artistic representation, rather than through actual presence. The burden of giving a physical presence to the divinity or omnipotence of the king fell to the artist, who relied primarily on certain prescribed and traditional symbolic forms to interpret kingly attributes in a way clearly decipherable by the people.

Which of these passages, do you think, was written for the youngest audience? Which for the oldest? How can you tell? What are the characteristics of the sentences that distinguish the most difficult from the least difficult passage?

2. The following passage has been chosen for the variety in sentence length. Read it carefully and decide why the writer tailored the sentences as he did. For what effect?

The day starts on a note of despair: the sorrowing dove, alone on its telephone wire, mourns the loss of night, weeps at the bright perils of the unfolding day. But soon the mockingbird wakes and begins an early rehearsal, setting the dove down by force of character, running through a few slick imitations, and trying a couple of original numbers into the bargain. The redbird takes it from there. Despair gives way to good humor. The Southern dawn is a pale affair, usually, quite different from our Northern daybreak. It is a triumph of gradualism; night turns to day imperceptibly, softly, with no theatrics. It is subtle and undisturbing. As the first light seeps in through the blinds I lie in bed half awake, despairing with the dove.... All seems lost, all seems sorrowful. Then a mullet jumps in the bayou outside the bedroom window. It falls back into the water with a smart smack. I have asked several people why the mullet incessantly jump and I have received a variety of answers. Some say the mullet jump to shake off a parasite that annoys them. Some say they jump for the love of jumping—as the girl on the horse seemed to ride for the love of riding (although she, too, like all artists, may have been shaking off some parasite that fastens itself to the creative spirit and can be got rid of only by fifty turns around a ring while standing on a horse).

Two Types of Sentence Constructions: Suspended and Cumulative

Sentence length and sentence complexity are only two of the important factors that influence readers in their efforts to make meaning out of sentences. Another important factor is sentence construction: the way the major meaning-components are arranged. If the subject, verb, and complement come late in the sentence, we call the sentence *suspended* (you may know this sentence construction by the name "periodic"). If the subject-verb-complement pattern is completed relatively early in the sentence, with clauses and phrases added around it, we call the sentence *cumulative.*

The Suspended Sentence

In the *suspended sentence,** the writer builds both suspense and forward momentum by withholding the *topic pattern* * (the complete subject-verb-complement) until the end of the sentence. At this point, the sentence makes finished sense. Here are two examples of the suspended sentence:

> For the child who cannot sleep in the dark, *there must be soft light.* For the child who is sensitive to sound, *there must be ways of muting noise.*

In these two suspended sentences, the climax occurs at the end. The reader must wait until completion of the sentence to complete the meaning; the waiting—particularly if it is of long duration—inevitably creates suspense. What's the meaning? What does the writer have in mind? What's going to happen? In relatively short suspended sentences, like those above, the wait is short and there is not much suspense; the reader's questions are answered almost as soon as they have been asked. But what about this long suspended sentence? What kinds of questions develop in your mind as you begin to read it?

> If too many Americans believe the police do not follow the law; that they do not really warn the ignorant of their rights and question unfairly and relentlessly; that they arrest and hold without significant evidence and bring an exhausted, confused, injured and frightened victim to witness a line-up and then urge an immediate identification of a suspect; that they stop and frisk on bare suspicion or to intimidate; that they tap phones and bug rooms and perhaps worse; that they care more for order than justice; that a pay-off is possible and the rich will never have serious problems with police; and if Americans harboring these beliefs live in mass urban society where police are always present and must be; where you see them every day; where you feel powerless against them and do not trust them—then *there is trouble.*

The two long *if*-clauses that begin this sentence (*If too many Americans* ...and *if Americans harboring these beliefs*...) create the inevitable question: *then what?* That question isn't answered until the very end of the sentence: *then there is trouble.* The writer has built *real* suspense— and at the same time has involved the reader by raising the question, forcing the reader to begin a search for the answer, and then postponing the answer almost to the point of frustration. If you are like most readers, your sense of suspense built as you read through the sentence, and it was with relief that you arrived at the end and discovered the complete topic pattern—the subject, verb, and complement—that gave the sentence meaning. Your curiosity, in a sense, propelled you forward, toward the topic pattern at the end of the sentence.

Because the clauses and phrases that make up the bulk of the suspended sentence are often arranged very carefully, in a balanced order, these sentences usually appear quite formal, and are frequently used on ritualistic and ceremonial occasions. Here's an example from Lincoln's *Gettysburg Address*, where the final word *ground* is required to make sense of the three verbs, *dedicate, consecrate, hallow:*

> S V S V
> But in a larger sense, *we cannot dedicate—we cannot consecrate—*
>
> S V COM
> *we cannot hallow—*this *ground.*

The repetition of the three verbs makes the sentence appear stately, ceremonial. Here is another example, the opening sentence of the Declaration of Independence, where a suspended sentence creates a very solemn mood.

> When in the Course of human events, it becomes necessary for one people to dissolve the political bands which have connected them with another, and to assume among the powers of the earth, the separate and equal station to which the Laws of Nature and of
> S
> Nature's God entitle them, a decent *respect* to the opinions of man-
> V COMPLEMENT
> kind *requires that they should declare the causes which impel them to the separation.*

Sentences like this may trouble you as a reader—precisely because you need to read through to the end to make sense of them, and because they require of you a high level of participation.

The suspended sentence lies at one end of a continuum, a range of possible choices the writer might make. The subject-verb-complement topic pattern might be completed late in the sentence, building suspense and forward momentum—or at the beginning of the sentence, or somewhere in the middle, adding additional details, examples, and analogies almost as after-thoughts. It is convenient to think of these as being separate sentence "types" (some grammar books treat them that way). It's more accurate, however, to say that they are at opposite ends of a single continuum: the possible positions of the topic pattern. In fact, in some cases it may even be misleading to categorize a sentence as one "type" or another, for many sentences fall at various points on this continuum —some toward the suspended sentence, some toward the cumulative sentence.

The Cumulative Sentence

In spite of its usefulness, the suspended sentence is not a very popular form in modern American prose. The construction you will encounter most frequently is the *cumulative sentence,** in which the topic pattern is completed near the beginning or in the middle of the sentence, followed by one or more additional phrases or clauses. This construction is called cumulative because the phrase and clause modifiers have been *added* to the topic pattern, so that the sentence seems to "ebb" and "flow" dynamically, *accumulating* descriptive and explanatory details, explanations, and qualifications. Here are some examples. Notice where the topic patterns (subject-verb-complement) are placed in relation to the phrases and clauses that comment on them:

> S   V   COM
> Another *means* of raising water *is* the *treadmill,* operated by stepping on a series of rotating pedals along the rim of a small wheel, to which is connected a larger one carrying a series of buckets or scoops.

> To maintain a permanent system of irrigation along a river with
> S   V
> seasonal high and low stages, the *water had to be raised,* at times over a dyke, at times to still higher ground.

>   S   V   COM
> From time to time during the game *I watched Unitas* on the sidelines, hands thrust into the pockets of his blue windbreaker, standing alone, occasionally turning and restlessly stubbing at the ground with the toe of his football shoe.

Reading a cumulative sentence, like those above, the reader has the sense that the writer is probing the idea, thinking it out, testing it. Reading a suspended sentence, the reader may have the impression that the writer has "prepackaged" the idea for its most effective delivery. As one writer has commented:

> The cumulative sentence is the opposite of the periodic suspended sentence. It does not represent the idea as conceived, pondered over, reshaped, packaged, and delivered cold. It is dynamic rather

than static, representing the mind thinking. The main clause ... exhausts the mere fact of the idea; logically, there is nothing more to say. The additions stay with the same idea, probing its bearings and implications, exemplifying it or seeking an analogy or metaphor for it, or reducing it to details. Thus the mere form of the sentence generates ideas. It serves the needs of both the writer and the reader, the writer by compelling him to examine his thought, the reader by letting him into the writer's thought.

For most readers, the most difficult thing about reading the suspended and cumulative sentences—both of them sometimes long—is using the topic pattern to organize the details that the writer presents, surrounding that base. Without a sure sense of the topic pattern on which the remainder of the sentence is built, you can't adequately understand the sentence. (That doesn't mean that you have to consciously look for the subject, verb, and complement of each sentence. It does mean, however, that you should have a *sense* of what the topic pattern is, and that you should be able to locate it in the sentence.) A suggestion: read a dozen long sentences aloud every day, reading each one several times, until you begin to get a sense of their organization. Oral reading—in a closet, to your roommate, out on a beach—will certainly help you to develop a better sense of sentence construction and a keener ear for meaning.

practice 2

A WRITING TASK FOR READERS

Here are several sentences, both cumulative and suspended. Read each one aloud several times, listening to the rhythms each construction develops. Then decide which sentences are cumulative and which are suspended by identifying the position of the subject-verb-complement topic pattern. Write a commentary on the effects of these sentences on the reader.

A. Today there are more automobiles—85 million—on the highways than there were people in 1900 and as many cluttering our environment, sitting on blocks in back yards, resting stripped and smashed upon city streets and alongside freeways and country roads.

B. While the student is interacting with adults who are less accountable to him than his parents are, his parents, seeing the college experience as pivotal to later success or failure for their child, are often trying their hardest to influence his life.

C. The utter wretchedness of central city slums, crammed with most of the sickness, poverty, ignorance, idleness, ugliness, vice and crime of the whole metropolis, its residents impotent, incapable, incommunicado and physically isolated by surrounding freeways without exits, slowly drains compassion from the human spirit and breeds crime.

D. The International Convention for the Regulation of Whaling, ratified in 1935, gave protection to right and bowhead whales, which already were commercially extinct, and prohibited the taking of females accompanied by calves.

E. Rising standards of academic performance in primary and secondary schools, the "baby boom" of the war, the slowness with which major American universities have expanded their size—all have resulted in increasing selectivity by the admissions offices of the most prestigious American colleges and universities.

F. Electronic brains which predict election results, lie-detectors which make you confess the truth, new drugs which make you testify to lies, radiations which produce biological monsters—all these developments of the last fifty years have created new vistas and new nightmares, which art and literature have not yet assimilated.

Sentence Balance and Repetition

Oral reading—once an everyday practice in schools and homes, now practiced only on rare occasions—will help you gain the skill of understanding complex structures. It will also help you to learn to recognize another subtle device—sentence balance and repetition.

A *balanced sentence* * has similar constructions on either side of a central point, often a colon or a semicolon:

> Travel is no cure for melancholia; space-ships and time-machines are no escape from the human condition.

Notice the way the writer has arranged the sentence parts to stress their equality: *travel* is equivalent to *space-ships* and *time-machines; cure* and *escape* are equivalent; *melancholia* and *the human condition* are equivalent. The balanced pattern allows this writer to underscore his meaning by repeating his statement.

A related pattern is *antithesis,* * the use of sentence balance to express contrasting ideas. Here is a series of such sentences written by the great nineteenth-century playwright, Bernard Shaw:

> Your friends are all the dullest dogs I know. They are not beautiful: they are only decorated. They are not clean: they are only shaved and starched. They are not dignified: they are only fashionably dressed. They are not educated: they are only college passmen. They are not religious: they are only pew renters. They are not moral: they are only conventional. They are not virtuous: they are only cowardly.

A series of such sentences is especially emphatic, like this paragraph. A passive reader, falling into the rhythms of these balanced, emphatically contrasting statements, can be lulled into witless agreement with the writer's opinions. When you find sentence balance, you should read very carefully, assessing each statement and attempting to be aware of just how the writer's use of structure is structuring *your* response.

Another related pattern is repetition—of words, of sentence structures, or of sounds. Look at this sentence, for example:

> The more you live and the more you look, the more aware you are of a consistent pattern—as universal as the stars, as the tides, as breathing, as night and day—underlying everything.

The writer of this sentence begins three phrases with the same words— *the more you ... the more you ... the more you;* and then adds four others beginning with as: *as universal as the stars, as the tides, as breathing, as night and day.* Perhaps you can see these repetitions more clearly in a diagrammatic presentation:

> The more you live
>   and
> the more you look,
> the more aware you are of a consistent pattern—as universal
>   as the stars,
>   as the tides,
>   as breathing,
>   as night and day
>   —underlying everything.

When you can see the structure clearly, it is easier to understand it; whether or not you saw it on the first reading, however, you probably responded unconsciously to it.

Readers usually appreciate repetition in sentence structure for a very practical reason: it makes reading much easier. The reader (probably only dimly aware of the repeated structure) begins to develop a pattern of expectations that are fulfilled by the repetition. See if you can become conscious of your expectations and the patterns you are anticipating as you read the following sentences. When do you become aware of the repetition?

> You may have been aware, inadvertently, that craftsmanship has become a dirty word these years because, again, it implies standards —something done well or done badly. The result of this convenient avoidance is a plentitude of actors who can't project their voices, singers who can't phrase their songs, poets who can't communicate emotion, and writers who have no vocabulary—not to speak of painters who can't draw.

Did you begin to be conscious of the pattern when you encountered the phrase *singers who* ...? or the phrase *poets who* ...? Most readers probably begin to respond (unconsciously) to the second repetition—by the third, they know what to expect. Some readers respond so well, in fact, that they can almost predict the phrases that will follow; they can read faster, more easily, because they know what's coming. Structural repetition can help readers make their way through very long and complex sentences. Study this sentence by Martin Luther King for an example of structural signals that help guide the reader:

> I have almost reached the regrettable conclusion that the Negroes' great stumbling block in the stride toward freedom is not the White Citizen's "Counciler" or the Ku Klux Klanner, but the white moderate who is more devoted to "order" than to justice; who prefers a negative peace which is the absence of tension to a positive peace which is the presence of justice; who constantly says "I agree with you in the goal you seek, but I can't agree with your methods of direct action"; who paternalistically feels that he can set the time-table for another man's freedom; who lives by the myth of time and who constantly advises the Negro to wait until a "more convenient season."

Can you find the point where you recognized that the "who" clauses (there are six of them) were helping you to organize the complexity of this long sentence? The reader is aided by the repetition to find a way through a very long sentence. Readers who can develop an ear for the repetitive rhythms of the sentence are better readers; they are more easily able to follow the writer's thought.

Occasionally, prose writers use another kind of structural repetition —the repetition of sound patterns. We're used to this kind of repetition in poetry, where we find not only *rhymes,** but *alliteration* * (the repetition of consonants, usually at the beginnings of words) and *assonance* * (the repetition of vowel sounds). One famous example that you undoubtedly have read is this stanza from Edgar Allan Poe's "The Raven":

> Once upon a midnight dreary, while I pondered, weak and weary,
> Over many a quaint and curious volume of forgotten lore—
> While I nodded, nearly napping, suddenly there came a tapping,
> As of some one gently rapping, rapping at my chamber door.
> "'Tis some visiter," I muttered, "tapping at my chamber door—
>   Only this and nothing more."

How many patterns of repeated sounds can you trace? They weave a very complicated pattern through the lines of verse. Prose writers, you may be surprised to learn, use some of these same devices—rhyme, alliteration, assonance—to bring music to their sentences, to establish mood, to call attention to certain ideas. See if you can find the end rhymes in this sentence:

> Of all the ills that our poor criticized, analyzed, sociologized society is heir to, the focal one, it seems to me, from which so much of our uneasiness and confusion derive, is the absence of standards.

If you pointed out that criti*ized*, analy*zed*, sociolog*ized* all end in the same sound, you've correctly identified the rhyme. But does it contribute anything to the meaning? If you consider the writer's main point to be that the society is *heaped over* with too much criticism, you can see that the repetition emphasizes that point with (in a sense) too much of the same sound.

Like sentence structure repetitions, the repetition of sound structures is usually found in emotional language, where the writer wants to persuade you to share a perception, an opinion, a belief. Look at these sentences from James Baldwin's description of the ghetto dwellers of Harlem:

> They patiently browbeat the landlord into fixing the heat, the plaster, the plumbing; this demands prodigious patience; nor is patience usually enough. In trying to make their hovels habitable, they are perpetually throwing good money after bad.

The repeated *p* sounds, and the repetition of the *h* sound in *h*ovels *h*abitable help Baldwin to make his argument seem forceful and urgent.

The music of English prose is not just an instrument of persuasion, of course. It is an instrument of delight—delight in our own sense-making, pleasure in our own abilities to take the form of our messages and make it into something beautiful in itself. Perhaps, if you are intent on getting to the "meaning" of a message, it is hard for you to linger to appreciate the pleasures of form and structure—but if you don't you'll be missing one of the most pleasurable aspects of our language. Participating readers—responsive readers—not only hear and understand the writer's message but hear and understand the formal patterns in which the message is cast.

practice 3

The following short passages have been selected because of the complex use of sentence balance, structural repetition, and sound repetition. Study each passage carefully, reading it aloud several times. What kinds of structural and sound patterns do you notice? What effect, do you think, is the writer trying to achieve with the repetitions? Is he or she successful?

A. Congress shall make no law respecting an establishment of religion, or prohibiting the free exercise thereof; or abridging the freedom of speech, or of the press; or the right of the people peaceably to assemble, and to petition the Government for a redress of grievances.

B. Freedom of speech is best conceived, therefore, by having in mind the picture of a place like the American Congress, an assembly where opposing views are represented, where ideas are not merely uttered but debated, or the British Parliament, where men who are free to speak are also compelled to answer. We may picture the true condition of freedom as existing in a place like a court of law, where witnesses testify and are cross-examined, where the lawyer argues against the opposing lawyer before the same judge and in the presence of one jury. We may picture freedom as existing in a forum where the speaker must respond to questions; in a gathering of scientists where the data, the hypothesis, and the conclusion are submitted to men competent to judge them; in a reputable newspaper which not only will publish the opinion of those who disagree but will reexamine its own opinion in the light of what they say.

C. There is, indeed, much wrong with cities—big and little—but the answer is not to abandon or completely to rebuild them on abstract principles. Only on paper can you disperse concentrations of population and create small urban stars with planned satellites around them. In the course of many years devoted to reclamation of waterfront, manufacturing of topsoil to cover thousands of acres of new parks, buying and preserving large areas of natural woodlands and shores in advance of the realtor and subdivider, planting thousands of trees along parkways and expressways, building hundreds of playgrounds, planning cultural centers in place of decaying tenements, tightening zoning and building laws, restricting billboards, opposing entrenched power companies and other utility corporations to keep the basic natural public resources inalienable, and stopping water pollution, I never caught a glimpse of the breast beaters who are now touted as pundits in this field.

D. The decline of the public square probably marks a turning point in our social and cultural history. It is a part of the larger movement toward the mass society, the less personal and less neighborly society. The automobile, the drive-in, the movie, the radio, TV, and the newspaper columnist have taken the place of the park bench, the curbstone, the soapbox, the animated group debate, the Punch and Judy show, the dancing bear, the organ-grinder with his perform- ing monkey, and the hawker of pretzels, hot tamales, sliced cocoanut, and candied melon rinds. Foreign immigration has slowed to a dribble, and the second and third generations of immigrant stock have become Americanized and conformist; they too have taken to the suburbs and become enamoured of creature comforts. There are fewer individualists and eccentrics today, fewer fringe movements in politics and religion, fewer extremes of right and left, fewer devotees of strange and esoteric cults and heresies. . . . Fewer people seem interested in the larger and deeper questions of the meaning of human existence, the true ends of life—and hence these questions are discussed and debated less. Even those persons who carry on the liberal and humanist tradition have them- selves become "intellectuals"—that is, specialists—and there seems to be a growing gap between them as intellectual elite and the folk.

E. Virtue is not the absence of vices or the avoidance of moral dangers; virtue is a vivid and separate thing, like pain or a particular smell. Mercy does not mean not being cruel or sparing people revenge or punishment; it means a plain and positive thing like the sun, which one has either seen or not seen. Chastity does not mean abstention from sexual wrong; it means something flaming, like Joan of Arc.

F. The unrenewable resources in greatest danger of depletion today are not the minerals that we gouge from the earth but our fellow-travelers on Spaceship Earth, those furred, finned, feathered and chlorophylled cousins of ours that evolved from our common colloidal soup.

practice 4

A WRITING TASK FOR READERS

Here are two passages taken from very similar moments in American history —the inauguration of a president. The first is from Thomas Jefferson's First Inaugural Address, March 4, 1801; the second from the Inaugural Address of John Fitzgerald Kennedy, January 20, 1961. Read each passage carefully, and decide what parallels you can find in the way each speaker has used sentence structure, repetition, and patterns of sound. Write an essay comparing the two.

A. During the contest of opinion through which we have passed, the animation of discussion and of exertions has sometimes worn an aspect which might impose on strangers unused to think freely and to speak and to write what they think; but this being now decided by the voice of the nation, announced according to the rules of the constitution, all will, of course, arrange themselves under the will of the law, and unite in common efforts for the common good. All, too, will bear in mind this sacred principle, that though the will of the majority is in all cases to prevail, that will, to be rightful, must be reasonable; that the minority possess their equal rights, which equal laws must protect, and to violate which would be oppression. Let us, then, fellow citizens, unite with one heart and one mind. Let us restore to social intercourse that harmony and affection without which liberty and even life itself are but dreary things. And let us reflect that having banished from our land that religious intolerance under which mankind so long bled and suffered, we have yet gained little if we countenance a political intolerance as despotic, as wicked, and capable of as bitter and bloody persecutions. During the throes and convulsions of the ancient world, during the agonizing spasms of infuriated man, seeking through blood and slaughter his long-lost liberty, it was not wonderful [that is, *surprising*] that the agitation of the billows should reach even this distant and peaceful shore; that this should be more felt and feared by some and less by others; that this should divide opinions as to measures of safety. But every difference of opinion is not a difference of principle. We have called by different names brethren of the same principle. We are all republicans—we are all federalists.

B. To those nations who would make themselves our adversary, we offer not a pledge but a request: that both sides begin anew the quest for peace, before the dark powers of destruction unleashed by science engulf all humanity in planned or accidental self-destruction.

We dare not tempt them with weakness. For only when our arms are sufficient beyond doubt can we be certain beyond doubt that they will never be employed.

But neither can two great and powerful groups of nations take comfort from our present course—both sides overburdened by the cost of modern weapons, both rightly alarmed by the steady spread of the deadly atom, yet both racing to alter that uncertain balance of terror that stays the hand of mankind's final war.

So let us begin anew—remembering on both sides that civility is not a sign of weakness, and sincerity is always subject to proof. Let us never negotiate out of fear. But let us never fear to negotiate.

Let both sides explore what problems unite us instead of belaboring those problems which divide us.

Let both sides, for the first time, formulate serious and precise proposals for the inspection and control of arms—and bring the absolute power to destroy other nations under the absolute control of all nations.

Let both sides seek to invoke the wonders of science instead of its terrors. Together let us explore the stars, conquer the deserts, eradicate disease, tap the ocean depths, and encourage the arts and commerce.

Let both sides unite to heed in all corners of the earth the command of Isaiah— to "undo the heavy burdens . . . and let the oppressed go free."

And if a beachhead of cooperation may push back the jungle of suspicion, let both sides join in creating a new endeavor, not a new balance of power, but a new world of law, where the strong are just and the weak secure and the peace preserved.

practice 5

In your own reading, find ten or a dozen examples of sentences and paragraphs which demonstrate the principles of sentence structure that you have been studying in this unit. Bring your findings to class for discussion.

UNIT 6

Understanding Sentence Patterns

The sentence is the most important unit of English speech. The sentence is more important even than the word. . . . The effective speaker and writer of prose is he who does not merely *catch* his sentence-patterns but who *grips* them and wields them with well-controlled purpose.   *(Simeon Potter)*

Words differently arranged have a different meaning, and meanings differently arranged have different effects.   *(Pascal)*

Evaluating Your Learning

When you've finished reading and studying this unit, you should be able to demonstrate your knowledge by

- defining active and passive topic patterns and finding examples of them in your assigned and free reading
- describing the possible reasons for the writer's choice of either pattern
- distinguishing between the simple sentence and the combined sentence
- defining each of the four combined sentence patterns and finding examples in your own reading
- describing the possible reasons for the writer's use of these patterns

A Look Back and A Look Ahead

We've been discussing sentence structure and its effect on your understanding of the meaning of a passage. The *suspended sentence,* we said, postponed the completion of the *topic pattern* (the subject-verb-complement components of a sentence) until the end of the sentence; the *cumulative sentence,* on the other hand, completed the topic pattern at the beginning or in the middle of the sentence and accumulated phrases and clauses around it, as though the writer were finishing his or her exploration of the idea right in front of the reader. We also discussed the principles of sentence balance and repetition and talked about ways in which these devices are used to control the reader's understanding and response.

In this unit, we're going to undertake a more difficult task: looking inside the sentence itself and examining *how* the topic pattern is formed, *how* phrases and clauses are added to the topic pattern; we'll also analyze the kinds of information these phrases and clauses bring to the topic pattern: restating information, specifying information, and qualifying information. We'll look, too, at the ways writers coordinate patterns by tying them together for special effects.

Let's begin by looking at the most elementary kind of sentence, the *simple sentence*.*

The Simple Sentence

We saw some examples of these very short, very readable sentences in our discussion of sentence length. Here, as an example, is a passage made up primarily of such sentences:

> Our scientists and engineers could make a kitchen table fly. Enough money could do it. That's America's competence—solving problems with money. Toss a social problem at us. We'll fumble it almost every time.

> We can't do it tomorrow. But we *can* change our cities. We can change the quality of life in the ghettos. We *can* change the slums. We can turn our cities into the pride of this nation.

You can see how easy these sentences are to read: they are not complicated by much *modification* * (words, phrases, and clauses that add additional information to the topic pattern). They consist primarily of that topic pattern (the subject-verb-complement) and perhaps a prepositional phrase or several single-word adjectives and adverbs. The topic pattern itself is not difficult to find—it is almost the entire sentence! Because the sentence is so short and compact, you don't have to wait long for the completion of the topic pattern, and the sentence makes immediate sense at one glance.

We'll return to a more complete discussion of the pros and cons of the simple sentence in a moment. However, let's interrupt this discussion to turn to another important issue: the nature of the topic pattern itself.

Active and Passive Topic Patterns

The simple sentence is always one of two types: it may be an *active topic pattern* * or a *passive topic pattern*.* The difference between these two may be confusing at first, but careful readers are able to distinguish between them; they find that it is helpful to know whether all the essential sentence information is before them (as it is in the active pattern) or whether some information has been rearranged or withheld altogether (as it is in the passive pattern).

All of the sentences except one ("That's America's competence") in the passage above are active patterns. The subject *acts* and the verb shows the action *performed* by the subjects. Let's represent the topic patterns of some of the sentences in this way:

subject	verb	complement
scientists and engineers	could make (fly)	a kitchen table
(You)	toss	a social problem
we	fumble	it
we	can change	the slums

In these active topic patterns, the relationship between the actor (the subject) and the object of the action (the complement) is clear and direct: the subject acts on the complement directly. In the passive topic pattern, however, the subject does not act; it is acted upon—by the *agent,* frequently named in a *prepositional phrase* * beginning with the word *by* (the boy was bitten *by the dog*). Let's translate the topic patterns of the sentences above into the passive pattern, so that we can see the difference:

> A kitchen table could be made to fly by our scientists and engineers—if they were given enough money by us. . . . A social problem could be tossed at us by you, and it would be fumbled by us every time. . . . The slums can be changed by us.

Now let's look at the topic patterns themselves:

subject	verb	agent
a kitchen table	could be made (to) fly	by our scientists and engineers
A social problem	could be tossed	by you
it	would be fumbled	by us
the slums	can be changed	by us

Can you see how this "transformation" (making the complement into the subject, the active verb into a passive verb, the subject into the agent) has been achieved? Of course, these passive sentences sound strange; most published writers don't write in this awkward way (although many novice writers do). Professional writers use the passive topic pattern much more gracefully and naturally—so naturally, in fact, that it is only the sharp-eyed reader who recognizes that the topic pattern is passive. Read this short paragraph carefully:

> The files were turned over to the attorney-general yesterday and were whisked to the place earlier designated for their safekeeping. It was rumored that the governor's auto was escorted away from the statehouse in the middle of the night, and there was speculation that the car was being driven to a secret hideaway. A summit meeting of state officials and high party officers was planned.

What's going on in this short news story? *Who* is responsible for turning over the files? for "whisking" them away? *Who* designated the hiding place? *Who* spread the rumor about the governor's car leaving? Was the governor actually *in* the car? *Who* drove the car? All of these questions are prompted by the fact that each topic pattern is passive, and that part of the information—an essential part—has been withheld, as it often is in the passive pattern. The subjects do not perform the action; instead, they are *acted upon*, but the agents are not named.

subject	verb	agent
files	were turned over and were whisked	by whom?
the governor's car	was escorted	by whom?
the car	was being driven	by whom?
a summit meeting	was planned	by whom?

Readers who want *all* the information are often frustrated by this kind of writing because it *pretends* to give us a report of what happened but instead only reports a part of the action. It shows what was done (the verb) and the target of the action (the subject), but it often doesn't tell "whodunit."

On the other hand, writers frequently find the passive topic pattern to be a very useful one. For example, suppose the writer doesn't *know* who performed the action:

The dikes were built sometime during the third century B.C.

The writer-historian obviously wouldn't have written:

Somebody built the dikes sometime during the third century B.C.

Many passive patterns are used because the writer chooses to conceal the fact of his or her lack of knowledge, rather than to call attention to it.

Or suppose that the real actor is so obvious that the writer doesn't want (or need) to call our attention to it:

The voting citizens of the state ratified the new constitution last week.
The new constitution was ratified last week.

Most of us would agree that we don't need all the information contained in the first sentence, and that the passive topic pattern contained in the second sentence is appropriate to our needs.

Yet a third reason is responsible for the use of the passive pattern in modern American prose. We saw earlier how writers manipulate sentence length, sentence complexity, and the placement of the topic pattern (in suspended or cumulative sentences)—to emphasize certain ideas and to control the structural contexts within which ideas take on importance for the reader. In the same way, writers choose between active and passive topic patterns in order to control the way in which you see the relative importance of the ideas. Look at these two versions of the same sentence, for instance:

passive topic pattern
> On the northern front, all resistance was wiped out by left-wing Angolan troops and their Cuban allies.

active topic pattern
> On the northern front, left-wing Angolan troops and their Cuban allies wiped out all resistance.

In the active pattern, the writer emphasizes the idea of *resistance;* in the passive pattern the writer emphasizes the terms "left-wing troops" and "their Cuban allies." You'll recall that in Unit 3 we talked about the ways contexts are controlled for emphasis. Notice here how the passive pattern *buries* the real subject in the middle of the sentence, the position of least emphasis. The active pattern puts the subject up front, where it receives the emphasis it deserves. The difference may sometimes be slight, but often it is crucial, for this structural choice shapes the reader's response to the scene being described.

One more important word about passive topic patterns. Some writing—in the sciences and social sciences, for example—relies heavily on the passive topic pattern because it lends objectivity or distance to the writing. Here, for example, is a paragraph written in scientific style—in the passive pattern:

> In nearly all forms of animal life, structural strength is provided by the bony skeleton of the body. The strength and rigidity of bone are produced by its composition and its architecture, unique among living tissues. About one-third of its mass is created by mineral crystals; the rest of the organic matrix is constituted by bone cells, small blood vessels, and variable amounts of fluid. The present knowledge of the nature of the mineral component of bone may be summarized in the following way....

In most of these sentences the writer appears to use the passive topic pattern habitually, because it is so natural a feature of scientific and technical writing. In the last sentence, the writer probably chooses the passive topic pattern deliberately, to avoid using the first person pronoun *I,* which almost never appears in any kind of scientific writing. Whether or not scientific and technical writers need to employ the passive pattern as often as they do is a matter of some debate. Many editors maintain that writers often misuse the passive pattern, creating wordy, indirect sentences where more concise, more direct sentences would be appropriate and effective. The fact is, however, that the passive pattern is a regular stylistic feature of most scientific writing, and readers should become aware of its use.

practice 1

A WRITING TASK FOR READERS

Here are some sentences that are fairly simple, without much modification. Identify the topic pattern (active? passive?) of each lettered part of the sentence and suggest why the writer might have chosen to construct the sentence in that way. If the agent in a passive pattern has been omitted, suggest the reason the writer might have left it out.

(a) Television reflects the virtues and faults of our time. (b) Its electronic principles were conceived by the prophets of technology about the same time (c) that practical radio was being demonstrated. (d) But in fifty years, television has grown from an idea to a fulfilled reality. (e) In that same time, man's other ideas have significantly changed his environment. (f) Earth is mined for minerals; (g) air is liquified; (h) the climate is altered. (i) Television records our environmental disasters daily, in our living rooms. (j) Television is blamed for many events, (k) even though it only reflects those events.

practice 2

In your own reading, find examples of active and passive topic patterns that seem to you to exemplify the principles we've described in this chapter. Look especially for examples of the passive pattern in which the writer seems to want to avoid naming the real actor.

The Combined Sentence

The structures of all sentences are not as simple as those we've been looking at, however, and in your college reading you will rarely encounter any passage as easy to read as those in the first pages of this chapter. Most sentences are what we'll call *combined sentences* *; they represent a number of simple sentences consolidated into a single sentence.

Let's look closely at the differences between simple and combined sentences. Study this passage carefully, noting your responses to it as you read:

Readers often read ineffectively. They fail to see the organization behind the writing. They read separate phrases. They read separate clauses. They do not distinguish important ideas in the sentence. They do not distinguish less important ideas.

Easy to read? Of course. The ideas are simple, straightforward, uncomplicated—and dull and repetitious, as well. But these simple sentences can be consolidated to produce this more difficult-to-read but more effective *combined* sentence:

Readers read ineffectively because they fail to see the organization behind the writing, reading separate phrases and clauses without distinguishing important ideas in the sentence from less important ideas.

The longer sentences with internal punctuation that you find in your reading are combined sentences, made up of different kinds of sentence patterns related to one another in fairly complicated ways. Readers, who have to make their way through these mazes of meaning-patterns, need to learn to recognize the combinations that writers have employed and use them as guides to decipher meaning.

There are four important combination patterns: the *coordinating pattern,** the *restatement pattern,** the *specifying pattern,** and *qualifying pattern.** Some of these combination patterns you already know and use in your everyday speech and informal writing; some are typical primarily of written speech—of *formal* written speech—and you may be less familiar with them. If you can learn to recognize these four patterns easily—if you can learn to hear their distinctive rhythms as you read and to spot the signals that identify them—you can then quickly and efficiently untangle any sentence that puzzles you.

The Coordinating Pattern

You are already very well acquainted with the *coordinating pattern;* it was one of the first that you learned when you started combining words and word groups. In fact, it has often been noticed that children use coordinating patterns much more frequently than adults do, both in their writing and in their speech. This is probably true because adults have other, more complicated combination patterns available to them, while young children have mastered just this simple combination.

Even though coordination is one of the earliest language skills we develop as we become more capable speakers, it is also one of the most crucial, for it is a basic logical process. In fact, coordination is one of the most important logical processes that speakers and writers possess, for it enables us to see the logical connections between ideas. Basically, we can say that coordination shows four different kinds of logic, through the use of several different kinds of *coordinators:*

kind of logic	coordinator
additive logic	*and*
contrastive logic	*but, yet*
alternative logic	*or, nor*
cause-effect logic	*for, so*

The comma, the semicolon, and occasionally the colon are punctuation marks that also indicate coordination; used alone, they simply indicate the fact of coordination, however, without providing any indication of what kind of logical relationship ties the coordinated parts together.

To see how coordination works, look carefully at this passage. How many coordinators do you see? (Let's look just for coordinating words, and leave punctuation marks for a later examination)

> Some of my misery was loneliness and some of it fear of old William Pollexfen, my grandfather. He was never unkind and I cannot remember that he ever spoke harshly to me, but it was the custom to fear and admire him. He had won the freedom of some Spanish city, . . . but was so silent that his wife never knew it till he was near eighty, and then from the chance visit of an old sailor. . . . We knew that he had been in many parts of the world, for there was a great scar on his hand made by a whaling-hook, and in the dining-room was a cabinet with bits of coral in it and a jar of water from the Jordan for the baptizing of his children and Chinese pictures upon ricepaper and an ivory walking-stick from India that came to me after his death.

If you saw ten coordinators in this passage (seven *ands,* two *buts,* and one *for*) you have counted accurately. In this 164-word passage, the author has used more coordinators than we would usually expect—one for approximately every 16 words. (Find a passage of similar length in another reading and count the coordinators. Are there more or fewer per word than in the passage above?) In fact, the author has used so many coordinators that he seems to want to create a special effect. He is writing from the point of view of a child, speaking of a grandfather the child loved and feared. Remembering what we said a moment ago about children's use of coordination, can you make any comment on the kind of effect he may be trying to create?

Usually, readers don't have any special difficulty responding to the logic (additive, contrastive, alternative, cause-effect) indicated by the coordinators in the sentence; they are so familiar that the reader immediately perceives the logic and reads through them without trouble. However, you may find yourself puzzled by the coordination that is indicated by punctuation alone. Let's look now at the most frequent difficulty you may encounter in understanding more complex forms of coordination: the use of the semicolon.

We've already seen how semicolons can be used to create sentence balance by joining, or coordinating, similar ideas in similar sentence structures:

> The word "new"—in our country especially—has magical connotations. *What is new must be good(;) what is old is probably bad. In creating, the artist commits himself(;) in appreciating, you have a commitment of your own.*

In each sentence, the writer has coordinated two complete sentences (two complete topic patterns) with a semicolon. However, in neither sentence is the logic of the coordination clearly stated. The writer *implies* a certain logical relationship and the reader is left to *infer* what that relationship might be. In the first pair of coordinated sentences, the writer seems to imply a contrastive relationship, opposing what is new and what is old. In the second pair of sentences, the writer seems to be adding two similar ideas: the artist's commitment and the audience's commitment. Because the logic isn't clearly specified, the reader is required to fill it out, to complete it, using whatever structure and meaning clues he or she can collect from the sentences themselves. Active readers, who are participating fully in the meaning-making process, can usually make the inference; passive readers, on the other hand, may be unable to complete the meaning or to make an appropriate inference because they haven't been actively participating in the reading process. Look at this passage, in which the writer has coordinated several sentences. What kind of logic does the writer appear to be using? What is its effect on the reader?

> No one seemed to be able to write about [Marilyn Monroe] without reassuring us that despite her instability and the graveness of her emotional problems, she was still vital and eager, still, however precariously, a going concern. Marilyn Monroe was an earnest, ambitious actress, determined to improve her skill; Marilyn Monroe had failed in several marriages but she was still in pursuit of fulfillment in love; Marilyn Monroe had several times miscarried but she still looked forward to having children; Marilyn Monroe was seriously engaged in psychoanalysis; Marilyn Monroe's figure was better than ever; she was learning to be prompter; she was coping, or was struggling to cope, with whatever it was that had intervened in the

making of her last picture—so, on the well-worn track, ran all the news stories.

Most careful readers would probably agree that this writer is using *additive* logic, piling up evidence in support of the statement that the news stories pictured Marilyn Monroe as "vital and eager," a "going concern." Did this accumulation of detail have the effect of persuading you that she was indeed still in charge of herself? Or did it have just the opposite effect—which the writer appears to have intended—of persuading you that in spite of all this frantic activity, Marilyn Monroe was on the edge of disaster, as indeed she was. This effective use of additive logic is an instance of exaggeration, which any careful reader, any *participating* reader, will recognize.

Additive and contrastive are the kinds of logic most frequently implied by the use of the semicolon. You many encounter a cause-effect statement, however:

> The ancient Egyptian did not draw the vowels when writing his words; he knew what sounds to expect and how to pronounce the words, so that showing them in the writing was unnecessary.

You could almost add a *because* somewhere in the vicinity of the semicolon. In fact, in order to understand the connection between the two sentences here, you *must* provide the causal connection that the author implies.

Often, the logical relationship established isn't additive, contrastive, alternative, or causal. Instead, the writer uses the semicolon or the colon as a way of tying together a general statement and a more specific statement. Look at the way the writer of these sentences, for example, uses both the colon and the semicolon, providing two statements of the same idea—the first one abstract and general, the rest concrete and specific:

> We must cease to talk in abstractions: we must see *concretely*. Communists talk abstractly of "liquidating" their "class enemies"—which sounds as harmless as pouring cyanide on the pages of a telephone directory. But the poet or the plain man sees the concrete reality: he sees the pistol placed behind the right ear; he hears the muffled bang; he watches the gray cerebral matter spurt out of the shattered skull.

The writer achieves a vivid point in an emotional argument through the very carefully calculated use of structure. (As a reader, you may be responding to the ugliness of the imagery; you may ignore the structure. However, the structure is the means by which the writer achieves the emotional response.) In the first sentence, the writer has created a balanced structure—balanced on the colon. In the third pair of sentences, the writer uses the colon again—with the general sentence first (*But the poet or the plain man sees the concrete reality*), followed by three sentences which translate that generalization into three specific instances. The reader is left with the most specific, the most vivid of these.

practice 3

A WRITING PRACTICE FOR READERS

The following sentences make use of the coordinating pattern in some significant way. Study each one carefully and then write a brief commentary on the kind of coordination that has been used and the kind of inferences readers are left to draw from it.

A. The car was going a wild forty-five miles an hour across the open and as Macomber watched, the buffalo got bigger and bigger until he could see the gray, hairless, scabby look of one huge bull and how his neck was a part of his shoulders and the shiny black of his horns as he galloped a little behind the others . . . ; and then, the car swaying as though it had just jumped a road, they drew up close and he could see the plunging hugeness of the bull, and the dust in his sparsely haired hide, the wide boss of horn and his out-stretched, wide-nostrilled muzzle. . . .

B. Later, as the idea of change became embodied . . . in many cultures, the young could learn from their elders that they should go beyond them—achieve more and do different things. But this beyond was always within the informed imagination of their elders; the son might be expected to cross the seas his father never crossed, study nuclear physics when his father had only an elementary school education, fly in the plane which his father watched from the ground. The peasant's son became a scholar; the poor man's son crossed the ocean his father had never seen; the teacher's son became a scientist.

C. The contemporary "liberal" does not merit the name: he is, and will hereafter be designated as, a *state* liberal, or a *total* liberal, or a *collectivist* liberal. The *true* liberal subordinates security to opportunity; he accepts struggle and danger as the price that a man must pay for being a free moral agent. He seeks, before all, to set man free from dictation by the group.

D. Ironically, as man has shrunk the world to a seemingly manageable size, his abilities to deal with it appear to be equally shriveled: affluence has produced the mass-media man, the unraised man, the bureaucratized man—in short, the alienated man.

E. Students who are interested in films often acquire the best in-depth introduction to the art through an intensive study of films which were particularly meaningful to them, but college and university film societies seldom provide film notes, seminars with film-makers and critics, or opportunities to make their own films; far less do they make a conscious effort to stimulate students to participate in such serious intellectual exploration.

F. The functional purpose of university education is manipulative; its purpose is to increase man's power over men and machines; there is every possibility in the present system that the increase will not be balanced by the appropriate controls.

G. Because [woman] is the emblem of spending ability and the chief spender, she is also the most effective seller of this world's goods. Every survey ever held has shown that the image of an attractive woman is the most effective advertising gimmick. She may sit astride the mudguard of a new car, or step into it ablaze with jewels; she may lie at a man's feet stroking his new socks; she may hold the petrol pump in a challenging pose, or dance through woodland glades in slow motion in all the glory of a new shampoo; whatever she does her image sells. . . . Seeing that the world despoils itself for this creature's benefit, she must be happy; the entire structure would topple if she were not.

practice 4

In your own reading, find five or six examples of the use of the coordination pattern which seem to you particularly interesting. Bring these examples to class with you and be prepared to describe how they work and what their special interest is.

The Restatement Pattern

The *restatement pattern* (sometimes called the appositive pattern) is found more frequently in written speech than in spoken speech; for that reason, it may cause some readers difficulty. If they do not recognize its function in the sentence, they may have trouble with its meaning.

The restatement pattern is a noun or noun word group (sometimes a whole noun *clause* * or a sentence) that adds information to the sentence by restating, more specifically, one of the major nouns in the sentence. Here is an example of a very simple restatement pattern:

Sometime this month over one million American young men will place sixty cents on a counter somewhere and walk away with a copy of *Playboy, one of the most spectacular successes in the entire history of American journalism.*

The italicized noun word-group restates, in much greater detail, the word *Playboy.* If you recognized that the phrase performs that function, you won't get lost in the sentence. Otherwise, however, you may have to go back to the beginning and try again to make sense of the phrase. Usually the need to reread is caused by just this problem: the failure to make sense of a difficult phrase on the first try and the necessity to reread (or reconstruct) the sentence once more, in an effort to force it to make sense.

Readers can easily spot restatement patterns by recognizing that the main word in the pattern is a pronoun (as it is in the example above) or—more likely—a noun. The restatement pattern is usually set off by commas or dashes from the rest of the sentence. Here are some examples of the kinds of restatement patterns you'll encounter in your reading. Each restatement pattern has been italicized, the main noun in each restatement has been circled, and the noun to which it refers (often called the *antecedent noun* *) has been boxed. Read each of these sentences aloud several times until you can begin to hear the rhythms of the restatement pattern. Notice, as you read, where it is located in relation to the noun it refers to.

a. Sophisticated instruments developed by physical scientists— *computers , nuclear sensors and even cameras aboard earth satellites*—are helping archeologists to identify and explore promising sites and to interpret the artifacts they excavate there.

b. *The pitcher's windup , the anticipatory crouch of the infielders, the quick waggle of the bat as it poises for the pitch*—these subtle miniature movements are as meaningful as the homeruns and the strikeouts.

c. *Rising standards of academic performance in primary and secondary schools, the "baby boom" of the war, the slowness with which major American universities have expanded their size*— all have resulted in increasing selectivity by the admissions offices of the most prestigious American colleges and universities.

d. There has been more change between the birth of a father and the birth of his son than in the preceding millennium—*atomic energy, supersonic flight, television and Telstar , Apollo 8, Hiroshima and Vietnam , and 1 billion more people.*

e. We've just made our way through inconclusive revolutions . . . trying to make up our minds how we feel about nature. . . . The oldest, easiest-to-swallow idea was that the earth was man's

personal ⬚property⬚ , *a* ⬭combination⬮ *of garden, zoo, bank vault*

and energy source, placed at our disposal to be consumed, ornamented, or pulled apart as we wished.

f. The small ⬚tribe⬚ of Iks, *formerly nomadic* ⬭hunters and

gatherers in the mountain valleys of northern Uganda, have

become ⬚celebrities⬚ , *literary* ⬭symbols⬮ *for the ultimate fate of*

disheartened, heartless mankind at large.

You can see that the placement of these restatement patterns varies: you may find them at the beginning of the sentence (*b* and *c*); in the middle (*a, e, f*); at the end (*d, f*). You may even find two (or more) restatement patterns used in one sentence (*f*). You can also see that there is a pattern to their organization: the noun antecedent makes a general statement, which is defined more specifically by the main restatement nouns and the phrases that add information to them. This is especially true when the antecedent noun is restated by a *series* of restatement patterns:

a. instruments   computers . . . sensors . . . cameras
b. movements   windup . . . crouch . . . waggle
c. all   standards . . . baby boom . . . slowness
d. change   energy, flight, television and Telstar,
                  Apollo 8, Hiroshima and Vietnam, billion

Each of the restatement nouns further specifies the more general antecedent noun.

Sometimes very long word-groups, even whole sentences, can be arranged in restatement patterns. These sentences are usually very long and cause readers much grief; however, they are a useful filing system that can hold a great deal of information, and writers will probably continue to use them. Let's look at one of these sentences and see if we can find an easy way to understand its organization.

Most of the known pheromones [pronounced *fer-e-mons*: defined as chemical substances that produce slight odors] are small, simple molecules, active in extremely small concentrations. Eight or ten carbon atoms in a chain are all that are needed to generate precise, unequivocal directions about all kinds of matters—*when and where to cluster in crowds, when to disperse, how to behave to the opposite*

> *sex, how to ascertain what is the opposite sex, how to organize members of a society in the proper ranking orders of dominance, how to mark our exact boundaries of real estate, and how to establish that one is, beyond argument, one's self.*

In this very long sentence, the writer has filed all kinds of useful information about pheromones—all of it under the general noun "matters." In fact, he has set up seven functions of pheromones in this single sentence, describing each in some detail. Were you able to follow the restatement patterns? Each one is a single noun pattern (a noun clause), built on the recurring phrases "when to," "how to," and "where to." Go back and reread the sentence aloud three or four times, until you've begun to feel the rhythms of it. Then try reading this sentence aloud. What parts of it cause you trouble?

> From the founding of Harvard College in 1636 through the mid-nineteenth century, one college was much like another: colleges were few in number and private, with physical facilities limited to housing and a few classrooms; the curriculum was limited to ancient languages and literature, philosophy and religion, and mathematics —about twenty classic courses, rigidly taught and required of all; the faculty and the administration were interchangeable; the students would be lawyers, statesmen, doctors, ministers, and sometimes leading businessmen, and almost all were from America's small upper class.

Now go back and count the restatement patterns you see. How many do you find? Four? That's good; "colleges," "curriculum," "faculty and administration," "students" are the main nouns in each of the four restatement patterns. But what is the general noun to which they all refer? You can't find it, as you can see after a careful search, because it isn't there: all of these patterns restate the general idea that the colleges were all *alike*, outlining specific ways in which this generalization (never stated in a single noun) is true. Now read the sentence aloud again, two or three times, noticing the punctuation. How is the restatement series separated from the main sentence? How is each single restatement separated from its neighbor? Check the preceding sentence example. How is that series separated from the main sentence? How are the items separated from one another?

The restatement pattern often results in long, complex sentences— the kind of sentences that make readers sigh as they contemplate the page ahead. Some suggestions: if you get lost in a sentence that looks as if it might be built on a restatement pattern or a series of restatement patterns, first check for a general noun in the main sentence and for specific restatement nouns. Then read the sentence aloud, making a mental note of the punctuation and listening for the rhythms of the passage. Don't stop with one reading; each time you reread and understand more clearly you are becoming more skilled in the recognition of patterns. This recognition will help you to untangle not only the sentence you are working on at the moment, but others like it that you will encounter in the future.

practice 5

A WRITING TASK FOR READERS

Here are a number of passages, each of which contains one or more restatement patterns. Find each restatement pattern and underline it; circle each restatement noun; put a box around each main or antecedent noun in the main sentence. Read each sentence aloud several times, listening for the rhythms of the passage. (If you have difficulty reading a sentence aloud, ask your instructor or your roommate to read it for you, and then see if you can read with greater understanding.) Which are the easiest sentences to read? Why are they easier than others? Which are most difficult? Does your ranking of easy/difficult match that of your classmates?

A. Bids on drilling sites off southern California—the first sale in that area since the 1969 oil spill in the Santa Barbara Channel—fell far short of expectations.

B. On the flats off some of the Keys, I have opened small loggerheads and heard the warning snapping of claws as the resident shrimps, small, amber-colored beings, hurried into the deeper cavities.

C. Christmas toys broken before New Year's, wash-n-wear suits that neither wash well nor wear well, appliances that expire a month after the guarantee, Barbie dolls, frozen pizza—these are but a few of the shoddy goods whose main contribution to our civilization, apart from a momentary satisfaction to the purchaser, is to swell the sanitary-fill schlock heaps that are the feces of our Gross (and how!) National Product. [You may have to look up the word "schlock" in a current dictionary of slang.]

D. Fundamentalist, revolutionary, ecclesiastical bureaucrat, counterculture hippie, porno film maker—all are busily engaged in making Jesus into their own images and likenesses. ... Indeed, if one wants a picture of Jesus most in keeping with what we know about him, one might turn to the Pantocrator of the Monreale mosaic which portrays Jesus as a strong, fierce, vigorously attractive male—an appealing but very tough customer indeed; certainly no one to mess with.

E. Soldiers have an unnervingly keen feeling for each other. ... This uncanny facility—to read men the way one reads a book—has marked great military leaders for centuries.

F. Among these [social evils] are the pathologies of American life that have been ushered in by the need for mass production in a highly populated society ... : the widespread destruction of creatures of forest, field, and stream, sometimes deliberate as in hunting, sometimes indirect through our agricultural and industrial practices; the whole realm of injustices to the American consumer, in price, food quality, and health risk, as well as the poor performance of highly advertised, consumer durables; the corruption of ... government and industrial management; and the poor quality of our lives, culturally, spiritually, intellectually, and creatively.

practice 6

In your own reading, find three or four examples of restatement patterns that you think exemplify some of the principles we've been discussing in this section. Bring them to class and be ready to share them with the other students.

The Specifying Pattern

The *specifying pattern,* an adjective word-group used to add new information to nouns, brings greater specificity and vividness to the sentence through the use of descriptive words. (You'll remember that the restatement pattern is a *noun* word-group used to fill the same function.) Writers use two kinds of adjective word groups, *adjective phrases* * and *adjective clauses.**

The adjective phrase. Most college readers recognize single-word adjectives without difficulty:

> We rode all night, and when dawn came were dismounting on the crest of the hills ... with a *wonderful* view westwards over the *green* and *gold* Guweira plain, and beyond it to the *ruddy* mountains hiding Akaba and the sea.

You may not know, however, that *adjective phrases*—groups of words built on adjectives, are also used to modify—or *specify*—nouns. Here is an example:

> The tall stalk had fallen, but there on the ground lay the mat of basal leaves, *gray-green ... and only somewhat crisped and browned at the edges.*

Often, however, adjective phrases are built on *verbal adjectives,** words that have been converted from verbs to serve as adjectives, specifying and describing nouns.

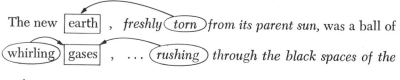

The new ⌐earthe⌐ , *freshly* ⟨*torn*⟩ *from its parent sun,* was a ball of ⟨*whirling*⟩ ⌐gases⌐ , ... ⟨*rushing*⟩ *through the black spaces of the universe....*

The three verbal adjectives have been circled; the phrases built on two of them have been italicized. You can see in these words the signals of the verbal adjective: the endings -n (*torn*) and -ing (*whirling, rushing*). Other endings are -en, -ed, -d, and -t. (You may have learned in an earlier grammar study that these verbal adjectives are called *present* and *past participles* *; the present participle always ends in -ing; the past participle has the other endings.) You'll notice that adjective phrases built on these verbal adjectives are often (but not always) set off from the rest of the sentence by a comma or a pair of commas.

> [The hawk] could sail for hours, searching the blanched grasses below him with his telescopic eye, gaining height against the wind, descending in mile-long, gently declining swoops when he curved and rode back, never beating a wing.

> He was very nattily dressed in a dark pinstriped suit, *moving*
>
> *through the locker room somewhat nervously and with an* abstracted *air, as if he had put an expensive pair of cuff links down and could not remember exactly where.*

Although they are not critical to the sense of the sentence, these adjective phrase specifying patterns bring in much additional information, adding color and *action* to the sentence. (They add action because they used to be verbs, and they still carry much of the verbal force.)

The adjective clause. The second specifying pattern is called the adjective clause. Like the adjective phrase, it allows the writer to add specific descriptive information to the noun. It is signalled by *adjective relators* * —*who* (*whose, whom*), *which, that*—and *adverb relators* *—*when, where, why*. Each relator refers to, or specifies, an antecedent noun earlier in the sentence, and in order to get the meaning straight, the reader must correctly identify exactly which noun **the adjective** clause pattern specifies. Look at these examples. (The clause has been underlined, the relator circled, and the noun antecedent boxed.)

> Life on an air-conditioned mountaintop—for instance, the most
>
> luxurious skyscraper penthouse , *where man is limited to*
>
> *large, dramatic, distant views, where he hears only loudspeaker*
>
> *sounds, where he cannot risk exposure to the weather*—is severely
>
> monotonous.

The result of this convenient avoidance [of craftsmanship] is a plentitude of │actors│ ⟨*who*⟩ *can't project their voices,* │singers│ ⟨*who*⟩ *can't phrase their songs,* │poets│⟨*who*⟩ *can't communicate emotion,* and │writers│⟨*who*⟩ *have no vocabulary*—not to speak of │painters│⟨*who*⟩ *can't draw.*

Frequently, adjective clauses are used in *parallel structures* * like the one above and this one, in which the rhythmic cadences of the repeated adjective clauses set up a melancholy cadence:

I have almost reached the regrettable conclusion that the Negroes' great stumbling block in the stride toward freedom is not the White Citizen's "Counciler" or the Ku Klux Klanner, but the │white moderate│⟨*who*⟩*is more devoted to "order" than to justice;* ⟨*who*⟩*prefers a negative* │peace│⟨*which*⟩*is the absence of tension to a positive* │peace│⟨*which*⟩*is the presence of justice;*⟨*who*⟩*constantly says "I agree with you in the goal you seek, but I can't agree with your methods of direct action";* ⟨*who*⟩*paternalistically feels that he can set the time-table for another man's freedom;* ⟨*who*⟩ *lives by the myth of time* and⟨*who*⟩*constantly advises the Negro to wait until a "more convenient season."*

You can see, too, that one of the adjective clauses has within it two others, a sentence strategy which further strengthens the rhythmic pattern that is being established.

Reading these last two sentences aloud several times will give you a clear idea of the sound pattern that the adjective clause establishes.

practice 7

The following short passages all make use of several different kinds of adjective specification. How many specifying patterns can you identify? Read each sentence aloud several times, marking the position of the specifying pattern, the noun to which it refers, and the punctuation. Would the sentence be as effective if the specifying pattern were omitted? Is the sense changed if some are removed?

A. The combination of fast feet and a flat, wide tail serving as rudder gives the roadrunner a double advantage over lizards and low-flying insects. He simply darts and twists after his prey, screeching into ninety-degree turns, careening around sagebrush and spurting into a straightaway as he catches his meals on the run.

B. Moths that fly by day are not properly to be called moths; they do not excite that pleasant sense of dark autumn nights and ivy-blossom which the commonest yellow-underwing asleep in the shadow of the curtain never fails to rouse in us. They are hybrid creatures, neither gay like butterfies nor sombre like their own species. Nevertheless, the present specimen, with his narrow hay-coloured wings, fringed with a tassel of the same colour, seemed to be content with life.

C. Cowboys could perform terrible labors and endure bone-grinding hardships. . . . They were riders, first and last. I have known cowboys broken in body and twisted in spirit, bruised by debt, failure, loneliness, disease and most of the other afflictions of man, but I have seldom known one who did not consider himself phenomenally blessed to have been a cowboy, or one who could not cancel half the miseries of existence by dwelling on the horses he had ridden, the comrades he had ridden them with, and the manly times he had had. If the cowboy is a tragic figure, he is certainly one who will not accept the tragic view.

D. There is one reasonable and systematic explanation of witchcraft which does not assume that the witches or the public were mad. It is that witchcraft was simply a religion—a non-Christian religion, an anti-Christian religion, which was practiced in Europe and elsewhere before the introduction of Christianity, which survived as it were "underground," and which is fundamentally opposed to Christianity, as to Judaism and Islam also. . . . You and I probably do not believe in the Haitian god Ogoun, or in Baron Saturday and The Siren and Marinette-Congo and such elementals; but we can easily believe that there are powerful subliminal psychical forces which Christianity and other reasonable spiritual religions help us to keep under control, and which a really irrational cult, calling on the historic forces of sex, and blood, and the night, and the animal ancestors, would set free within us.

The Qualifying Pattern

Next to the coordinating pattern, the qualifying pattern probably occurs more frequently than any other in written speech—and if you listen carefully, you will hear it often in spoken speech. The function of this sentence pattern is to *qualify*—to modify, limit, or impose restrictions upon—the verb of the main statement of the sentence. For an example, look at this topic pattern:

We can calculate what the earth's temperature would have been four billion years ago.

Without support, this assertive statement would challenge most readers to a disbelieving "Oh, yeah? How?" Now look at the sentence after it has been qualified by an *if*-statement that establishes a condition:

> *If we assume that the earth four billion years ago had the same distribution of land and water, clouds and polar ice, so that it absorbed the same relative amount of sunlight that it does today,* we can calculate what its temperature would have been.

The assertion is much more acceptable now because we understand under what conditions the calculation might be achieved. If we add one more qualification, we can see the sentence as the author originally wrote it:

> (1) *If we assume that the earth four billion years ago had the same distribution of land and water, clouds and polar ice, so that it absorbed the same relative amount of sunlight that it does today,* and (2) *if we also assume that it had the same atmosphere it has today,* we can calculate what its temperature would have been.

These qualifications are crucial to the meaning of the sentence, as you can see, for they establish the two conditions (that the earth absorbed the same amount of sunlight and that it had the same atmosphere) under which the writer can calculate what its temperature might have been.

Qualifying patterns, like specifying patterns, may be *phrases* * or *clauses.* * Qualifying phrases often add useful statements about time:

> *During the more or less stable portion of the lifetime of the star,* the hot interior region, converting hydrogen into helium, gradually eats its way outward from the very center.

Or a qualifying phrase may state a condition:

> *Under the pressure of rising wages,* the United States has traveled far down the road of reducing menial labor, which currently engages somewhere between 10 and 15 percent of the working population.

Or a qualifying phrase may tell a place:

> *In some cities* it's already hard to keep menial jobs filled. *In the booming Dallas region,* with its unemployment rate of only 2.1 percent, jobs for waitresses, private guards, trash collectors, and busboys were recently going begging.

These qualifying phrases, as you've probably already noticed, are prepositional phrases used as *adverbs.* * They add important information to the sentence.

Qualifying clauses operate in the same way: to tell time, place, manner, purpose, condition, cause-effect, comparison, or contrast. Let's look at a few examples. The qualifying clause has been italicized and the *qualifying subordinator* * (the word that links the qualifying clause with the rest of the sentence) has been circled.

a. (When) *there is considerable evidence to support a thesis but*

the evidence remains inconclusive, all you can do is conjecture. (time. Because *when* is also used to signal a specifying clause, the two are sometimes confused. If you'll remember that the qualifying *when* can be replaced with *whenever,* you'll be able to tell the difference. In this sentence, you could say "Whenever there is. . . .")

b. The main camps and forts were always built (where) *there were*

springs or wells, on the theory that whoever controlled the water supply controlled the country for miles around. (place. *Where,* you'll remember, also signals a specifying clause. If you can replace the *where* with *wherever,* the clause qualifies the verb instead of specifying a noun. In this sentence, you could say "wherever there were springs. . . .")

c. (If) *most of us realized early enough the fact that we have only*

one life to lead, and that every moment of it that escapes reflection is irretrievable, we should live it differently. (condition)

d. (Since) *historians do not often make fully explicit the values*

behind their choices, we usually must infer these from the purpose and the organization of the books themselves. (cause)

e. Many people feel unsure of their abilities to read and write

competently, *even* (though) *communication is a survival skill in*

our culture. (contrast)

You'll notice that the qualifying patterns in these sentences are movable: they may appear at the beginning of the sentence, at the end, or even in the middle. The writer chooses the position of the qualifying pattern in order to emphasize the idea in various ways. Qualifying patterns are usually, although not always, set off from the rest of the sentence by commas.

You may also have noticed that sometimes (often, in fact), writers put the most important idea into the qualifying pattern. Look at sentence *c*, for instance, where the qualifying pattern seems to make a statement that has much more importance—certainly much more sentence weight— than the statement of the topic pattern. In sentence *a*, as well, the sentence would make almost no sense at all without the qualification. The qualifying pattern is of such importance that readers who fail to read it carefully and understand it thoroughly run the risk of missing the meaning of the whole sentence.

practice 8

A WRITING TASK FOR READERS

Here are several short passages containing qualifying patterns, both phrases and clauses. Mark each qualifying pattern by underlining the pattern and circling the qualifying subordinator. What kind of logic does the qualification state? Does it indicate time, place, manner, condition, cause, comparison, contrast, or purpose? Is the qualification of less importance than the idea it qualifies, or of equal importance? Would the emphasis be changed if the position of the qualifying pattern were changed?

A. The paradox of the human condition is expressed more in education than elsewhere in human culture, because learning to learn has been and continues to be *Homo sapiens'* most formidable evolutionary task. Although it is true that mammals ... have to learn so much that it is difficult to say ... which behavior is inborn and which is learned, the learning task has become so enormous for man that today, education, along with survival, constitutes a major preoccupation.

B. Parents leave their children in front of the TV as baby sitter, because many assume that it is infinitely safer to watch the Sesame world of television than to walk in the world outside of their home. But is it?

Unlike television, the child grows older. One day he walks out of the TV room. A child who for years has been trained to control the little world by changing the channels when he didn't like it, and was accustomed to maintaining the same distance between himself and the world televised for his amusement, is naturally threatened by the presense of real people he cannot control. When others push him around, make faces at him, he cannot control them. He begins to feel that this real world unjustly limits him because it seldom offers alternative channels to turn to.

C. When social animals are gathered together in groups, they become qualitatively different creatures from what they were when alone or in pairs. Single locusts are quiet, meditative, sessile things, but when locusts are added to other locusts, they become excited, change color, undergo spectacular endocrine revisions, and intensify their activity, until, when there are enough of them packed shoulder to shoulder, they vibrate and hum with the energy of a jet airliner and take off.

D. I fish because I love to; because I love the environs where trout are found, which are invariably beautiful, and hate the environs where crowds of people are found, which are invariably ugly; because of all the television commercials, cocktail parties, and assorted social posturing I thus escape; because, in a world where most men seem to spend their lives doing things they hate, my fishing is at once an endless source of delight and an act of small rebellion; because trout do not lie or cheat and cannot be bought or bribed or impressed by power, but respond only to quietude and humility and endless patience; because I suspect that men are going along this way for the last time, and I for one don't want to waste the trip; because mercifully there are no telephones on trout waters; because only in the woods can I find solitude without loneliness; because bourbon out of an old tin cup always tastes better out there; because maybe one day I will catch a mermaid; and, finally, not because I regard fishing as being so terribly important but because I suspect that so many of the other concerns of men are equally unimportant—and not nearly so much fun.

UNIT **7**

Sentences in Sequence: The Art of Making Connections

The essential principle of all ... design is that *what comes first should prepare for what follows and what follows should strengthen and clarify what has come before.* (I. A. Richards)

Evaluating Your Learning

When you've finished reading and studying this unit, you should be able to demonstrate your knowledge of what you've read by

- recognizing the topic sentences that have been explicitly provided in some paragraphs and describing the topic sentences that have been only implicitly provided in others
- identifying sentences used to restate, specify, and qualify topic sentences within paragraphs and accurately describing their functions in the development of the paragraph
- identifying the restatement paragraph in given readings and finding examples of it in your own reading
- identifying descriptive, narrative, and associative paragraphs and describing their function
- tracing a restatement-specification sequence of paragraphs in a given essay

A Look Back and A Look Ahead

For the last several units, we've been considering the ways in which sentence structures control our perception of the writer's ideas—whether those ideas are cast in short or long sentences, in suspended or cumulative or balanced sentences, or whether the writer has used sentence repetition or active or passive patterns or simple or combined sentences. We looked carefully at the coordinating pattern, the restatement pattern, the specifying pattern, and the qualifying pattern, finding examples of each of these patterns in professionally written sentences. However, sentences are not the only structures that shape our understanding and responses; sentences come in larger sequences called paragraphs. The reader, faced with paragraphs of connected sentences, must learn the fine art of following the connections the writer seems to be making—and of making connections for himself or herself. In fact, much of the task of reading beyond the sentence lies in just this: the ability to clearly see and understand the complex patterns of connections that writers make.

The Paragraph

Paragraphs are complex matters, for there are many strategies that writers adopt consciously to control their ideas and other strategies that they seem to adopt unconsciously. In the development of a series of interconnected ideas, the writer uses each paragraph as a kind of "platform" for the development of one part of that series. In the paragraph he or she states the main idea in a topic sentence (a controlling sentence that functions much like the topic pattern in a cumulative or suspended sentence), and then uses additional sentences to restate the idea, or specify it, or qualify it. Like sentence writers, the paragraph writer develops the main idea by patterns of restatement, specification, and qualification. The same logical operations, then, are used for sentence-writing and for paragraph-writing.

As a structure that can serve to control the reader's understanding, the paragraph marks the limits of the exploration of the idea that the writer intends to make, or intends the reader to make. But readers can't afford to stop there, within the limits of what the writer has presented to them; they must understand the structure of the presentation, in order to see which ideas have been emphasized, which suppressed—and with that knowledge, to form their own evaluation of the presentation and of the ideas themselves. Critical readers go beyond the boundaries suggested by the writer to attempt to understand analytically how the writer has organized the material and why he or she has presented it in this way.

The Topic Sentence

The organizing idea of the paragraph is stated in the *topic sentence,** just as the controlling idea of most sentences appears in the topic pattern—the subject-verb-complement component—of the sentence itself. Topic sentences usually operate at a fairly general level, and the writer uses the rest of the paragraph to tie down his idea by restating it in other words, by specifying it through illustration and detail, or by qualifying it. Topic sentences, then, are "umbrella" sentences which are broad enough to cover all of the ideas introduced in the paragraph and yet narrow enough to exclude irrelevant ideas. Often paragraphs are governed by only one of these sentences, and the rest of the paragraph depends on that one general statement; however, just as a whole sentence may be made up of two (or more) sentences joined together, so a paragraph may be organized around two (or more!) topic sentences, each one controlling a part of the paragraph.

Most topic sentences do not wear a sign announcing I AM A TOPIC SENTENCE. Instead, it is left to the reader to decide which is the governing idea of the paragraph. Usually a topic sentence is signalled by its level of generality. Look at the following paragraph, for example:

(1) Man uses the spoken or written word to express the meaning of what he wants to convey. (2) His language is full of symbols, but also often employs signs or images that are not strictly descriptive. (3) Some are mere abbreviations or strings of initials, such as UN, UNICEF, or UNESCO; others are familiar trademarks, the names of patent medicines, badges, or insignia. (4) Although these are meaningless in themselves, they have acquired a recognizable meaning through common usage or deliberate intent. Such things are not symbols. (5) They are signs, and they do no more than denote the objects to which they are attached.

The first sentence of this paragraph is clearly the most general and inclusive; it *contains* all the other sentences. To understand this important concept, let's represent the paragraph more schematically, abstracting its statements and organizing them in a hierarchy or "ladder" of inclusion:

Sentence 1   spoken or written word (language) expresses
                meaning

  Sentence 2   language is full of symbols and signs

    Sentences 3–6   signs are patterns of letters or designs
                            that have acquired meaning through use

As we said earlier, however, some paragraphs have more than one topic sentence; the idea moves from its first inclusive statement to another inclusive statement or to a restatement. Study this paragraph closely:

(1) The world is a flux of more or less identifiable things and events in which the solitary animal may, with luck, pick his way and preserve his life. (2) But the "world" in which we live is quite different. (3) It is made up of separate and identifiable components, it is rich in meanings, and much of it can be manipulated for other purposes. (4) It is not just a world into which we were born, but a world we inherited. (5) Its parts have been characterized and distinguished from each other, its relations noted and interpreted, its meanings expressed and analyzed, by our forebears. (6) Thus society has, to some extent, created the world we perceive, its shapes, its meanings, its beauties and uglinesses. (7) We inherit, by being born in society, an intelligible world and a system of symbols, and we cannot have one without the other.

The most inclusive statements in this paragraph occur at the beginning and the end. In the first sentence, the writer defines the term "world" very broadly; in the last sentence, he redefines world as a social world. The sentences in between serve as "rungs" on a ladder or hierarchy of inclusion, related to these two sentences. Let's represent the paragraph schematically:

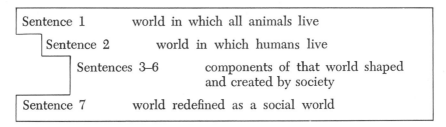

Sentence 1   world in which all animals live

Sentence 2   world in which humans live

Sentences 3–6   components of that world shaped and created by society

Sentence 7   world redefined as a social world

Not all writers organize their paragraphs around explicitly organized topic sentences, although every paragraph of analytic or expository writing, whether it is well or poorly organized, has as its basis an *implicit* organizing statement. Paragraphs without topic sentences usually cause readers difficulty; they may be judged to be incoherent or badly written —and that may in fact be true. However, if you can create the implicit topic sentence that organizes the apparently random sentences, you will be able to make sense out of even the most incoherent paragraph. Look at this paragraph, for instance:

(1) Although current communes originated in agrarian settlements, principally in California and the West, urban communes have become more common as people have banded together, in most cases merely to counteract the anonymity and loneliness of city life. (2) In some instances mutuality of interest, such as women's liberation, shared professional goals, political activism, or religious practice, provides the underlying basis for communal living; in others spiralling rentals and rising cost of living are the major motives. (3) All household goods are commonly shared as well as household expenses. (4) There are indications that communal living has made some inroads on marriage statistics within the last few years. (5) Commune dwellers feel that their life-style provides the companionship of marriage without the "dead-end" commitment it entails. (6) In all communes most members have had some experience in sensitivity training or group encounters.

What do you think is the organizing statement implicit in this paragraph? Would something like the following sentence help to hold together all of these ideas?

Commune dwellers have a number of shared interests, not only in the goods and property they hold together, but in attitudes and life-styles.

Whether or not the writer provides such a sentence explicitly, as the topic sentence of the paragraph, the reader who hopes to make sense out of the multiple ideas contained within the paragraph will have to create some organizing statement. Only active readers, of course, can order such a meaning-making statement; a passive reader can only accept what the writer has chosen to present, in the order it is presented.

practice 1

Identify the topic sentences in each of the following paragraphs; if there is none, recreate the implicit organizing sentence you think must be behind the writer's sentences. If there is a topic sentence, do you think it is too specific? too general? If so, try to create a new one, more appropriate to the sentences within the paragraph. Discuss your conclusions with the other students in your class. Did everyone agree on the same topic sentence? Did everyone recreate the same implicit topic sentence? What accounts for the other choices that were made? Do all readers make exactly the same kind of meaning from a paragraph? Under what conditions would they be more likely to agree? to disagree?

A. The rains, the eroding away of the earth, the rush of sediment-laden waters have continued, with varying pulse and tempo, throughout all of geologic time. In addition to the silt load of every river that finds its way to the sea, there are other materials that compose the sediments. Volcanic dust, blown perhaps halfway around the earth in the upper atmosphere, comes eventually to rest on the ocean, drifts in the currents, becomes waterlogged, and sinks. Sands from coastal deserts are carried seaward on offshore winds, fall to the sea, and sink. Gravel, pebbles, small boulders, and shells are carried by icebergs and drift ice, to be released to the water when the ice melts. Fragments of iron, nickel, and other meteoric debris that enter the earth's atmosphere over the sea—these, too, become flakes of the great snowfall [of sediment]. But most widely distributed of all are the billions upon billions of tiny shells and skeletons, the limy or silicious remains of all the minute creatures that once lived in the upper waters.

B. Despite the confusion, however, there can be detected an elusive likeness among most of the works of early art recently brought to light. Remembering that some of the wider cultures have been described as primitive merely because their modes of ornament and representation lack the high polish and refined naturalism of European traditional practice, and that these will ultimately be judged as different, but not elementary, cultures—such as, for instance, the Mayan and the West African Benin—one may note a distinctive first aspect, a recognizable character, in most of the works called primitive. It arises, perhaps, from a preserved simplicity, an uninvolved directness of statement, and an intuitive grasp of decorative unity. The link is one of feeling, or approach, of unidentifiable nuances of formal expression, rather than a material or a stylistic likeness. There is a stamp of special vividness or direct vigor in art not yet civilized, which marks it off as a product of unlettered, not yet mature men.

C. How far ahead are you thinking? As the demands for immediate changes in women's lives become more strident and angry, this is a question every woman must ask herself and try to answer honestly. For the time span within which change is projected will make a great difference, I believe. Concentration on the very near future—a decade or two—will certainly bring about some very necessary reforms, but it will also obscure the basic issue—how women will face living in a world in which homemaking and childbearing are no longer the central focus of their lives. Change in our time can be only a step toward preparing our daughters and our daughters' daughters to think and act in new ways.

D. The *direct* ending of a life, with or without the patient's consent, is euthanasia in its simple, unsophisticated, and ethically candid form. This is opposed by many teachers, Roman Catholics, and others. They claim to see a moral difference between deciding to end a life by deliberately doing something and deciding to end a life by deliberately *not* doing something. To many others this seems a very cloudy distinction. What, morally, is the difference between doing nothing to keep the patient alive and giving a fatal dose of a pain-killing or other lethal drug? The intention is the same, either way. A decision *not* to keep a patient alive is as morally deliberate as a decision to *end* a life. As Kant said, if we will the end we will the means. Although differences persist in its application, the *principle* of mercy-death is today definitely accepted, even in religious circles where the pressures of death-fear have been strongest. Disagreements concern only the "operational" or practical question—who does what under which circumstances?

The Restatement-Specification Paragraph

You'll remember that in our discussion of sentence structure, we talked about the restatement pattern, a sentence pattern that enables the writer to file several informative, specific details under a rather general topic pattern. Here's one of the examples we looked at, graphically rearranged to emphasize the form and function of each of the restatements:

Eight or ten carbon atoms in a chain are all that are needed to generate precise, unequivocal directions about all kinds of matters—
> when and where to cluster in crowds,
> when to disperse,
> how to behave to the opposite sex,
> how to ascertain what *is* the opposite sex,
> how to organize members of a society in the proper ranking orders of .dominance,
> how to mark our exact boundaries of real estate, and
> how to establish that one is, beyond argument, one's self.

When the sentence is arranged in this way, you can easily see that the topic pattern (the main subject-verb-complement framework of the sentence) makes a general statement, while the restatements add a number of specific details in support of the topic pattern.

We also looked at another sentence, a specifying pattern that was developed by the addition of adjective clause specification to a rather general main sentence. Let's represent that sentence graphically, in a *frame,** in order to see its development:

I have almost reached the regrettable conclusion that the Negroes' great stumbling block in the stride toward freedom is . . . the white moderate

who is more devoted to "order" than to justice;

who prefers a negative peace which is the absence of tension to a positive peace which is the presence of justice;

who constantly says "I agree with you in the goal you seek, but I can't agree with your methods of direct action";

who paternalistically feels that he can set the time-table for another man's freedom;

who lives by the myth of time and

who constantly advises the Negro to wait until a "more convenient season."

This specification pattern develops just as the restatement pattern develops—through a series of phrases or clauses, each containing a specific detail, added to the rather general statement in the main topic pattern of the sentence.

One important paragraph pattern, the restatement-specification pattern, works in precisely the same way as the sentences above. The writer sets down his central idea rather generally in the topic sentence, and then goes on to restate it or specify it, in a number of ways. Here's an example of this kind of paragraph, "framed" so that you can see its structure clearly:

(1) Almost anything that an animal can employ to make a sound is put to use.

(2) Drumming, created by beating the feet, is used by prairie hens, rabbits, and mice; the head is banged by woodpeckers and certain other birds; the males of deathwatch beetles make a rapid ticking sound by percussion of a protuberance on the abdomen against the ground; a faint but audible ticking is made by the tiny beetle *Lepinotus inquilinus*, which is less than two millimeters in length.

(3) Fish make sounds by clicking their teeth, blowing air, and drumming with special muscles against tuned inflated air bladders.

(4) Solid structures are set to vibrating by toothed bows in crustaceans and insects.

(5) The proboscis of the death's-head hawk moth is used as a kind of reed instrument, blown through to make high-pitched, reedy notes.

The main idea of the topic sentence (that *animals make sounds*) is *restated* in four sentences; one of those sentences (the first one) is made up of several sentences joined together by semicolons.

Here's another example of this kind of paragraph pattern. Notice how the writer helps you anticipate the paragraph pattern by giving you clues to the relationship of these sentences to one another and to the topic sentence. What kind of clues can you find as you read?

> (1) Similarly, in the United States there is both a deep commitment to developmental change, which is interpreted as progress, and a continuing resort to absolutism, which takes many forms. (2) First, there are the religious sects and minor political groups, the principal appeal of which is their dogmatism with regard to right and wrong. (3) There are also the Utopian communities, that have been a constant feature of our social, political, and intellectual development. (4) And there is in addition the tacit acceptance of a color caste system that exists in violation of our declared belief in the fundamental equality of all men.

Let's frame this restatement-specification paragraph and point out the word-cues (circled) and the sentence-structure cues (parallel constructions, sentence repetition, italicized) that simplify your reading task.

---

(1) Similarly, in the United States *there is* both a deep commitment to developmental change, *which is interpreted as progress,* and a continuing resort to absolutism, *which takes many forms.*

> (2) ⟨First⟩, *there are* the religious sects and minor political groups, *the principal appeal of which is their dogmatism with regard to right and wrong.*

> (3) *There are* ⟨also⟩ the Utopian communities, *that have been a constant feature of our social, political, and intellectual development.*

> (4) And *there is* ⟨in addition⟩ the tacit acceptance of a color caste system *that exists in violation of our declared belief in the fundamental equality of all men.*

You'll notice that the writer has used three word-cues that indicate that each sentence in the restatement-specification series (sentences 2 to 4) provides additional detail to the topic sentence: *first, also, in addition.* You can also see that each restatement-specification sentence (and the topic sentence as well) is built on a similar pattern: a *there is/there are* topic pattern, to which an adjective clause specifying pattern has been added. Each of these restatement-specification sentences operates at the *same* level of generality; it is more specific than the topic sentence, but no more (or less) specific than any other sentence in the restatement-specification pattern.

From these two examples you can see that the restatement-specification paragraph is based upon a distinct pattern of reference: each of the sentences in the restatement-specification series refers directly to, or directly supports, the topic sentence, rather than referring to or supporting any other sentence in the paragraph. No sentence is firmly connected to the one before it or the one after it, and the sentences of both paragraphs could even be rearranged without any disruption in the logical flow of the paragraph. (Try rearranging the sentences in each of the paragraphs above. Do you see any difference in the meaning when the sentences are reordered?) Because series restatement-specification sentences all operate at the same level of generality, and because they all refer to the topic sentence only, they can be organized to suit whatever emphasis the writer wishes to develop.

Restatement-specification paragraphs are relatively simple paragraphs, as you can see, and are usually used when the writer wants to state several points for later discussion (in an introduction, for instance, or in a paragraph that introduces a series of following paragraphs) or when he or she wants to review several points that have already been made (in a conclusion, or in a paragraph that concludes a series of preceding paragraphs). The restatement paragraph is not a useful means of developing an argument, however, because it cannot present complex ideas with various kinds of logical relationships—as we'll see later, in greater detail. However, this paragraph form does appear frequently in all kinds of writing—in textbooks, in magazine articles, in essays and nonfiction works—and readers should learn to recognize it. Because it doesn't develop argument, it is the kind of paragraph that a reader can skim quickly, noting the major supporting details. Readers who can anticipate this paragraph pattern can read it very quickly without sacrificing comprehension.

practice 2

Each of the following paragraphs is built on the restatement-specification pattern: the topic sentence is followed by a series of sentences, all of which refer directly to (or support) the topic sentence, operating at the same level of generality. First, skim each paragraph quickly, noting the way the writer has supported the topic sentence. Then study each paragraph more carefully. What is the general statement of each topic sentence? How does each restatement-specification sentence support the topic sentence? Has the writer used any word-cues or any structural cues that help you to anticipate the paragraph pattern? (You might look for such words as *and, besides, moreover, similarly, in addition, finally, as well*—and the familiar *first, second, third.*) Underline the structural cues you are able to find and circle the word-cues. Could the restatement sentences be rearranged without disturbing the logic of the paragraph?

A. (1) The paradoxes are many in the shift of higher education from a minority to a majority phenomenon. (2) At the same time that college is more important to youth in the sense of being required as an opening to a career, it is less important in the sense that going to college by itself does not automatically convey high status. (3) At the same time that knowledge about the world is vastly increasing, many students continue to view college as a purposeful path to a vocation rather than as an intellectually enriching experience. (4) At the same time that students need greater intellectual guidance, and perhaps moral guidance as well, from their teachers because the students are poorly prepared by previous family and school background, teachers are less attracted to spend time with the students beyond the classroom and the office hour. (5) At the same time that there seemingly are many diverse kinds of institutions among which the applicant may choose the one that fits him best, he is constrained from a rich choice by individual circumstances (previous school record, cost, and imperfect knowledge of possible options) and by the tendency of colleges and universities to grow more like one another.

B. (1) The recency of much knowledge is astonishing when one stops to consider it. (2) Millions of men are still living who could have seen Darwin. (3) The man who discovered that germs cause disease died in 1910. (4) The father of antiseptic surgery lived until 1912. Pavlov was living in 1936, Freud in 1939. (5) It was not until 1875 that the essential nature of the act of fertilization was understood, and not until the 1920's that the various hormones were isolated. (6) Only in the past two decades has the study of animal behavior been put on a scientific basis. (7) Our knowledge of prehistoric man is almost entirely a twentieth-century affair, and an awareness of how much that knowledge affects our knowledge of ourselves seems destined to wait until the twenty-first or later.

C. (1) Nothing about the racoon is rare, delicate, or specialized. (2) He is as common as dirt and as hardy as weeds. (3) When wild chestnuts disappear he switches to acorns and hazelnuts; when his den trees are cut down he moves into fox burrows, culverts, caves and old barns; in the deep South he is active all year, but he sleeps through Northern winters; where the sea provides shellfish he abandons his nocturnal habits and fishes in broad daylight, following the ebb tide. (4) He lives in suburbs, sleeping in attics and raiding garbage cans. (5) He develops a rich, heavy coat for Canadian winters and a thin, almost white one for the hot brilliance of the Florida Keys. (6) He eats crayfish in Ohio swamplands, and on Cape Sable he must dig wells down to fresh water. (7) In Michigan he is an important cash crop and in Florida he is a pest.

practice 3

In your other reading, find one or two examples of restatement paragraphs and bring them to class for discussion. Write a short commentary on each paragraph, noting the way the writer has used each restatement sentence to refer to the topic sentence and pointing out any word-cues and structural cues that enable the reader to clearly see the paragraph development. Also note where your paragraph came from—at what point in the discussion the writer used this paragraph pattern. What function does it serve in the overall development of the writer's argument?

practice 4

In order to make your understanding of the restatement paragraph more concrete, try writing one. Develop a topic sentence that makes a general statement and add three or four sentences of restatement, supporting the topic idea at a more specific level.

Combined Paragraph Development Patterns

The restatement-specification paragraph is only one of a great variety of paragraph strategies writers use. More frequently, they write paragraphs in which the sentences are related logically to one another not just in one way (as in the restatement-specification paragraph), but in a variety of ways. In addition to *specifying* * and *restating* * sentences, which illustrate or add detail, they may also use *qualifying* * sentences, which modify the idea by comparing or contrasting another idea to it, by imposing a condition on it, by indicating its cause or its effect, or by telling the time, place, or manner in which the action took place. (If the logical qualifications we're describing here sound familiar to you, you're right—they are the same kinds of qualifications that adverb phrases and clauses impose on the main topic pattern of the sentence; you may review these sentence patterns in Unit 6.) The interweaving of these three kinds of sentences, some of them performing more than one logical function in the paragraph, creates a very complex idea structure. One of your most difficult tasks as a reader is to trace out the development of that idea structure as it's revealed in the relationship between the sentences of the paragraph. A first step toward understanding those logical relationships is to understand the pattern of reference.

Patterns of Reference

For readers, one of the complicating factors in most paragraphs is the *pattern of reference.* * In the restatement-specification paragraph, as we saw, the reference pattern provides little difficulty, for all of the sentences refer only to the topic sentence. In most paragraphs, however, the pattern of reference is much more complex, for many sentences do not refer to the topic sentence; instead, they may refer to one another preceding sentence.

Read the following paragraph carefully, noting that sentences 2 and 4 refer to the topic sentence, while sentences 3 and 5 refer to the preceding sentences. The paragraph has been framed for you to make your study easier.

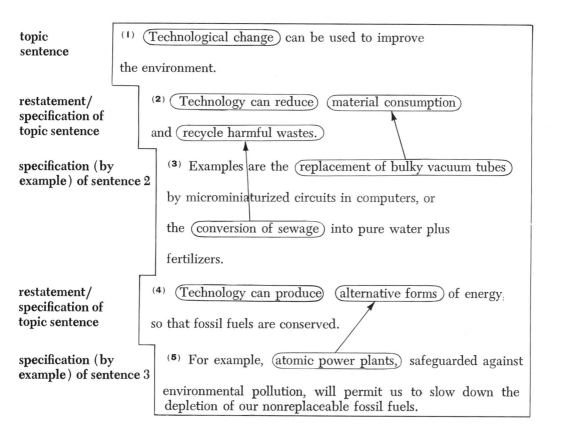

topic sentence

(1) Technological change can be used to improve the environment.

restatement/ specification of topic sentence

(2) Technology can reduce material consumption and recycle harmful wastes.

specification (by example) of sentence 2

(3) Examples are the replacement of bulky vacuum tubes by microminiaturized circuits in computers, or the conversion of sewage into pure water plus fertilizers.

restatement/ specification of topic sentence

(4) Technology can produce alternative forms of energy. so that fossil fuels are conserved.

specification (by example) of sentence 3

(5) For example, atomic power plants, safeguarded against environmental pollution, will permit us to slow down the depletion of our nonreplaceable fossil fuels.

Can you see that sentences 3 and 5 are not directly related to the topic sentence? They are directly related to sentences 2 and 4, and only indirectly to the topic sentence. You can also see by what logical means the sentences are related to one another: sentences 3 and 5 specify by providing examples; sentences 2 and 4 are restatement-specification sentences, each one restating the idea of technological change and specifying one kind of change (reduction . . . production).

Let's look now at a paragraph that is built through a series of qualifying sentences that show time, cause, result, and place.

topic sentence	(1) Heavy silt and mud in rivers and streams is a major cause of the death of many fresh-water fish.
qualification of topic sentence: shows *when*	(2) During rains, heavy drainage runoff from bare slopes where trees have been logged carries tons of mud and silt into once-clear mountain streams.
qualification of sentence 2, shows result	(3) Because of the heavy load of sand and silty mud, the streams become brown and murky, and the water carries less oxygen.
qualification of sentence 3, shows result	(4) As a result, fish in the stream suffer from oxygen deprivation and gradually suffocate.
qualification of sentence 4, shows result, place where result may be found	(5) Downstream from the logging operations, you can see the carcasses of dead fish piled up on shores and sandbanks.

In this tightly developed paragraph, each of the sentences refers to the one immediately preceding it, qualifying it by telling when and under what conditions silt enters the stream; by describing the result of the silt deposits; by describing the result of the lowered oxygen levels; and by showing the final effect and the place where it may be found.

Let's look at one more paragraph, a more complex one, with several patterns of reference. As you study this paragraph frame, note the way the writer has developed several ideas at once: an analysis of the desires and purposes of two inventors (Marconi and Edison), and an assertion that they failed to see in their inventions any potential for entertainment. This paragraph has essentially one controlling idea: the inventors of the radio and the phonograph were interested in communicating information across distances and through time; they weren't interested in the entertainment value of these media. As you can see, the writer develops the idea in two parts: first through a description of Marconi and the radio, then through a description of Edison and the phonograph. Notice, however, the way the writer has carefully united these two separate parts: by the repetition in sentences 2, 3, 4, 7, and 8 of verbs of seeing (*envision, see, foresee*); and by the use of similar patterns of reference (sentences 5, 6, and 7 are related to one another in the same way that sentences 2, 3, and 4 are related. Did the writer carry out all this complicated patterning deliberately? Probably not—however, since this writer is aiming to convey information, he is concerned to write clearly and logically so that the reader is not confused, so that the reader *gets* the information. His insistence on clarity and logic and his obvious knowledge of the subject matter led him to create these patterns, and in revision, to further

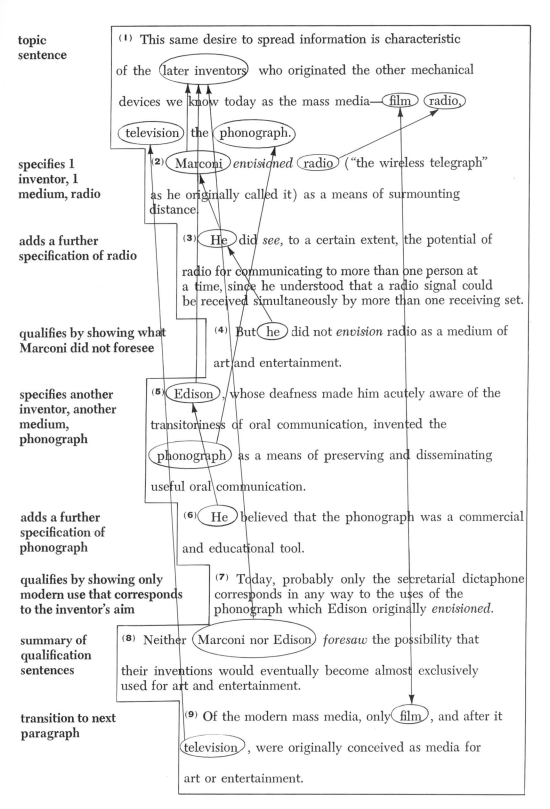

topic sentence

(1) This same desire to spread information is characteristic of the later inventors who originated the other mechanical devices we know today as the mass media—film radio, television the phonograph.

specifies 1 inventor, 1 medium, radio

(2) Marconi envisioned radio ("the wireless telegraph" as he originally called it) as a means of surmounting distance.

adds a further specification of radio

(3) He did see, to a certain extent, the potential of radio for communicating to more than one person at a time, since he understood that a radio signal could be received simultaneously by more than one receiving set.

qualifies by showing what Marconi did not foresee

(4) But he did not envision radio as a medium of art and entertainment.

specifies another inventor, another medium, phonograph

(5) Edison, whose deafness made him acutely aware of the transitoriness of oral communication, invented the phonograph as a means of preserving and disseminating useful oral communication.

adds a further specification of phonograph

(6) He believed that the phonograph was a commercial and educational tool.

qualifies by showing only modern use that corresponds to the inventor's aim

(7) Today, probably only the secretarial dictaphone corresponds in any way to the uses of the phonograph which Edison originally *envisioned*.

summary of qualification sentences

(8) Neither Marconi nor Edison *foresaw* the possibility that their inventions would eventually become almost exclusively used for art and entertainment.

transition to next paragraph

(9) Of the modern mass media, only film, and after it television, were originally conceived as media for art or entertainment.

187

emphasize them for the reader. Writers like this one make the reader's task much easier.

Tracing the pattern of reference—the logical connections of sentences within paragraphs—requires close attention on the part of readers, but they will find that they are rewarded with a much clearer understanding of both the content of the paragraph and the organization of the writer's ideas. Readers who can follow the pattern of reference are also able to see how the writer has arranged the ideas to produce a certain special effect in the reader's mind, shifting focus to avoid drawing attention to ideas the writer may find uncomfortable but necessary to mention, specifying at length ideas he or she may want to emphasize.

practice 5

Following are two framed paragraphs with the patterns of reference already indicated by the frame. Study each one carefully and then provide—in the margins of the paragraph—details of the relationship of one sentence to another. Is the sentence related to the preceding sentence through specification? through restatement? through qualification? What words demonstrate that relationship? Circle and underline any repeated words or phrases or structures that emphasize the pattern of reference. What effects does the writer achieve through the reference patterns?

(1) Though we like to tell ourselves that our purpose is to solve the social problem by ministering to men's needs, in practice we have a conception of human nature, and derived from it an educational system and a commercial and political propaganda, which treat all needs as unlimited.

(2) No income can therefore be sufficient to satisfy men's needs.

(3) For the appetite merely grows from feeding it.

(4) No standard of living is a standard.

(5) For there is always a more luxurious standard.

(6) No prosperity is rich enough.

(7) For the statistical curves on the charts might always go higher still.

(8) No nation can be big enough and no state can be powerful enough.

(9) For until someone has conquered the whole world, it is always possible to be bigger and greater than you are.

(1) Drug use is no different from any other form of human behavior, in that a great variety of distinct motives can cooperate to produce it.

(2) The particular weight of each of these motives and the way they are combined differs in each individual.

(3) Furthermore, drug use is affected not only by motives and forces *within* the individual, but by what is happening *outside* of him in his interpersonal environment.

(4) Thus, any effort to delineate "types" of motivations that enter into drug use is bound to be an oversimplification.

(5) For example, there are many individuals who share common characteristics with drug users but who do not use drugs because drugs are not available on their particular campus.

(6) Similarly, there are individuals who have little in common with other drug users, but who nonetheless use drugs.

practice 6

A WRITING TASK FOR READERS

Here are several paragraphs for your reading practice. Study each one carefully, noting the patterns of reference that you can see, and then frame each one. Add in the left margin your own commentary on the way the sentences are logically related—through specification, restatement, qualification. Note the words, phrases, and repeated structures that emphasize those relationships. Then write a brief statement describing the effect the writer has achieved through the paragraph structure. Is the language primarily informative? or does the writer seem to want to persuade you to a particular belief? Do you think the writer has effectively conveyed the idea? Compare your paragraph frames with those prepared by others in the class. Have you agreed? If not, what is the source of your disagreement? Why have you read the paragraph differently?

A. Riots are not new to our nation. We were born in revolution. Mob violence threatened the Constitutional Convention in Philadelphia in 1787, causing that convention to provide in the Constitution itself for a federal place of government and other places as needed to safely conduct the activities of the new republic. We witnessed mass violence over various issues in most parts of the country before the Civil War. Riots resulting from draft and racial protests caused five times more deaths in New York City in July 1863, one week after the battle of Gettysburg, than all the deaths in all the riots of the 1960's throughout the nation. In 1919 and 1943, the nation suffered major race riots. Few decades in our history are unscarred by riots.

B. The Great Stupa at Sanchi, in central India, consists of a hemispherical mound set upon a circular base, with a railed enclosure. At the mound's summit is an enclosed pavilion above which rises a tiered mast, or parasols. Inside the base and center of the stupa is a sealed chamber for the sacred relic. The sources of the stupa's form and meaning go back into the earlier history of India and of the Near and Far East. The stupa is derived from the burial mound, which may have originated in central Siberia at some early, as yet unknown date. The burial mound, or barrow, passed eastward into China and then Japan, where it took the form of the tumulus mound. Southwest from its probable point of origin, the barrow reappeared in India for the burial of rulers and holy men as well as the preservation of sacred relics. It was in use at the time of Buddha in the sixth century B.C. Buddha's dying injunction to his followers to build edifices containing his ashes and relics as reminders of his teachings led to the erection of the original eight stupas, now lost. These stupas were built on the sites of the great events in Buddha's life: his birthplace at Kapilavastu; the Bo tree at Bodhgaya, where he achieved Enlightenment; Sarnath, where he preached his first sermon; and the place of his death, Kusinagra. Others protected his footprints and the stone slabs from which he taught. These stupas were the focus of pilgrimages to recall and share in Buddha's triumph over evil and ignorance.

C. Men who live in democratic communities not only seldom indulge in meditation, but they naturally entertain very little esteem for it. A democratic state of society and democratic institutions keep the greater part of men in constant activity; and the habits of mind that are suited to an active life are not always suited to a contemplative one. The man of action is frequently obliged to content himself with the best he can get because he would never accomplish his purpose if he chose to carry every detail to perfection. He has occasion perpetually to rely on ideas that he has not had leisure to search to the bottom; for he is much more frequently aided by the seasonableness of an idea than by its strict accuracy; and in the long run he risks less in making use of some false principles than in spending his time in establishing all his principles on the basis of truth. The world is not led by long or learned demonstrations; a rapid glance at particular incidents, the daily study of the fleeting passions of the multitude, the accidents of the moment, and the art of turning them to account decide all its affairs.

D. The university, as it emerged out of medieval Italy, France, and England, and developed over the centuries, had three clear functions. The first was to train young men for essential professions: the church, the law, and medicine, and perhaps teaching. The second was to preserve the heritage of the past, and pass it on to future generations intact. The third—first clarified by Gottingen and her sister universities in Germany in the eighteenth and nineteenth centuries—was to expand the boundaries of knowledge through research. The two ancient universities of England added a fourth which was never quite clear: to train a social elite to the tasks of governance.

E. There is another paradox in man's relationship with other creatures: namely, that those very qualities he calls animalian—"brutal," "bestial," "inhuman"—are peculiarly his own. No other animal is so deliberately cruel as man. No other creature intentionally imprisons its own kind, or invents special instruments of torture such as racks and thumbscrews for the sole purpose of punishment. No other animal keeps its own brethren in slavery; so far as we know, the lower animals do not commit anything like the acts of pure sadism that figure rather largely in our newspapers. There is no torment, spite, or cruelty for its own sake among beasts, as there is among men. A cat plays with its prey, but does not conquer and torture smaller cats. But man, who knows good and evil, is cruel for cruelty's sake; he who has a moral law is more brutal than the brutes, who have none; he alone inflicts suffering on his fellows with malice aforethought.

Other Kinds of Paragraph Organizations

The paragraphs you've been reading here are built on patterns of restatement, specification, and qualification. They are *analytic* paragraphs, taken from essays, nonfiction works, textbooks, in which writers are concerned to convey information, to work through difficult, often abstract ideas, to persuade. There are several other important paragraph forms, however, that you will frequently encounter in your reading: *narrative,** *descriptive,** *journalistic,** and what we'll call *"associative"* *paragraphs.**

Narrative paragraphs tell a story. Their patterns of reference are easy to follow because they are usually built on time order: the events are usually recounted in the order in which they occurred. Here is an example, from "The Secret Life of Walter Mitty":

Walter Mitty stopped the car in front of the building where his wife went to have her hair done. "Remember to get those overshoes while I'm having my hair done," she said. "I don't need overshoes," said Mitty. She put her mirror back into her bag. "We've been through that," she said, getting out of the car. "You're not a young man any longer." He raced the engine a little. "Why don't you wear your gloves? Have you lost your gloves?" Walter Mitty reached in a pocket and brought out the gloves. He put them on, but after she had turned and gone into the building and he had driven on to a red light, he took them off again. "Pick it up, brother!" snapped a cop as the light changed, and Mitty hastily pulled on his gloves and lurched ahead. He drove around the streets aimlessly for a time, and then he drove past the hospital on his way to the parking lot.

Easy reading? Most narrative paragraphs are not difficult, because the logical order of events is a temporal order, and we have few problems following this pattern of reference. While other complicating factors make literary narrative often hard to read, this difficulty is not related to organization.

Descriptive paragraphs are usually built on a spatial pattern of reference, with the described elements related in the paragraph in the same way they are related in space. Here's an example:

Like so much of this country, Banyan suggests something curious and unnatural. The lemon groves are sunken, down a three- or four-foot retaining wall, so that one looks directly into their dense foliage, too lush, unsettlingly glossy, the greenery of nightmare; the fallen eucalyptus bark is too dusty, a place for snakes to breed. The stones look not like natural stones but like the rubble of some unmentioned upheaval. There are smudge pots, and a closed cistern. To one side of Banyan there is the flat valley, and to the other the San Bernardino Mountains, a dark mass looming too high, too fast, nine, ten, eleven thousand feet, right there above the lemon groves. At midnight on Banyan Street there is no light at all, and no sound except the wind in the eucalyptus and a muffled barking of dogs. There may be a kennel somewhere, or the dogs may be coyotes.

Frequently, writers combine narrative and descriptive sentences in their paragraphs, but again, readers have little difficulty following these patterns of reference: time and space reference is, under most conditions, a very easy reference pattern to understand.

A much more difficult form is the "associative" paragraph, which functions almost like metaphoric language by making connections indirectly, rather than directly. This kind of paragraph follows no logical rules, but lays down its own logic; it is not designed to *tell* its readers something, but to *challenge* them to discover it for themselves; it does not develop along *linear* patterns of reference, like analytic paragraphs, but through complex, often implicit patterns of *association*, some of which are never directly stated. For example, look at this paragraph from the writing of a student who is practicing "freewriting," writing without planning, just jotting down the ideas as they come. (Sometimes this kind of writing is called "automatic writing," because you do it without thinking about it.) The writer is feeling his way through his thoughts, associating one idea with another, but not in a very disciplined, logical way:

I think I'll write what's on my mind, but the only thing on my mind right now is what to write about for ten minutes. I've never done this before and I'm not prepared in any way—the sky is cloudy today, how's that? now I'm afraid I won't be able to think of what to write when I get to the end of the sentence—well, here I am at the end of the sentence—here I am again, again, again, again, at least I'm still writing—Now I ask is there some reason to be happy that I'm still writing—ah yes! Here comes the question again—What am I getting out of this? What point is there in it? It's almost obscene to always ask it but I seem to question everything that way and I was gonna say something else pertaining to that but I got so busy writing down the first part that I forgot what I was leading into. This is kind of fun oh don't stop writing—cars and trucks speeding by somewhere out the window, pens clittering across peoples' papers. The sky is still cloudy—is it symbolic that I should be mentioning it? Huh? I dunno. Maybe I should try colors, blue, red, dirty words—wait a minute, no can't do that, orange, yellow, arm tired, green pink violet magenta lavender red brown black green—now that I can't think of any more colors—just about done—relief? maybe.

Associative paragraphs are often difficult to translate into logical, analytic prose, just as metaphors are difficult to translate into informative language. And just as metaphoric language may sometimes be found in a straightforward, informative piece of writing, so associative sentences (sometimes a whole series of them) may be found in an analytic paragraph. When you encounter associative paragraphs, or when you find associative sentences within other paragraphs, your best approach is to relax, let your mind *play* with the ideas the writer is offering, make as many creative connections, as many meanings, as you can. Recognize that the author is not trying to impose meaning on you, but to challenge you to make your own freely, with few constraints. Demanding linear logic and confined meaning from an associative paragraph is like trying to put round pegs in square holes: you can only end in frustration.

practice 7

The following paragraphs have been built on several patterns of reference—narrative, descriptive, and associative, as well as the more familiar patterns of restatement, specification, and qualification. Some of them may be more or less "pure" paragraphs, in which only one pattern of reference is followed; others may be built on combinations of reference patterns. Some sentences may fulfill more than one of the patterns we've described in this unit (a specification sentence, for example, may be descriptive). Study each paragraph carefully, frame it (if that seems useful), and decide as precisely as you can what patterns of reference connect the sentences to one another. Compare your finds with those of other students in your class. On what points did you agree? disagree? What are the sources of your disagreement? Which paragraphs are easiest to understand? Which most difficult? Why?

A. There is a housing project standing now where the house in which we grew up once stood, and one of those stunted city trees is snarling where our doorway used to be. This is on the rehabilitated side of the avenue. The other side of the avenue—for progress takes time—has not been rehabilitated yet and it looks exactly as it looked in the days when we sat with our noses pressed against the windowpane, longing to be allowed to go "across the street." The grocery store which gave us credit is still there, and there can be no doubt that it is still giving credit. The people in the project certainly need it—far more, indeed, than they ever needed the project. The last time I passed by, the Jewish proprietor was still standing among his shelves, looking sadder and heavier but scarcely any older. Farther down the block stands the shoe-repair store in which our shoes were repaired until reparation became impossible and in which, then, we bought all our "new" ones. The Negro proprietor is still in the window, head down, working at the leather.

B. [Jimmy] Breslin made a revolutionary discovery. He made the discovery that it was feasible for a columnist to leave the building, go outside and do reporting on his own, actual legwork. Breslin would go up to the city editor and ask what stories and assignments were coming up, choose one, go out, leave the building, cover the story as a reporter, and write about it in his column. If the story were big enough, his column would start on page one instead of inside. As obvious as this system may sound, it was unheard of among newspaper columnists, whether local or national. If possible, local columnists are even more pathetic. They usually start out full of juice, sounding like terrific boulevardiers and raconteurs, retailing in print all the marvelous *mots* and anecdotes they have been dribbling away over lunch for the past few years. After eight or ten weeks, however, they start to dry up. You can see the poor bastards floundering and gasping. They're dying of thirst. They're out of material. They start writing about funny things that happened around the house the other day, homey one-liners that the Better Half or the Avon lady got off, or some fascinating book or article that started them thinking, or else something they saw on the TV. Thank God for the TV! Without television shows to cannibalize, half of these people would be lost, utterly catatonic. Pretty soon you can almost see it, the tubercular blue of the 23-inch screen, radiating from their prose. Anytime you see a columnist trying to squeeze material out of his house, articles, books, or the television set, you've got a starving soul on your hands. . . . You should send him a basket. . . .

C. Kimono. It covers her from throat to ankles; with a gesture as feminine as the placing of a flower or as female as the cradling of a child, the hands themselves can be concealed into the sleeves until there remains one unbroken chalice-shape of modesty proclaiming her femininity where nudity would merely parade her mammalian femaleness. A modesty which flaunts its own immodestness like the crimson rose tossed by no more than one white flick of hand, from the balcony window—modest, than which there is nothing more immodest and which therefore is a woman's dearest possession; she should defend it with her life.

D. There were in the Roman provinces two kinds of roads, both built by the legion, one type considered civil, the other military. The civil roads were main highways, wide and well paved, used for public transport and the swift movement of the post. The military roads were narrower and more direct and usually cut straight across country from fort to fort. In their usual methodical manner the legion erected a stone signpost every mile—or, more precisely, every 1,480 metres—of the way along their vast network of main roads. Well over 2,000 of these milestones have been found and recorded. One can imagine how many more lie under the sand and rubble of North Africa.

E. In the old days the Pit River Indians did not live in individual houses. In summertime they camped around in the hills and the valleys, moving about in small groups somewhat like our own families, here and there, fishing, hunting, gathering crops of roots and seeds, and practicing conscientiously a lot of good healthy loafing. In the fall, when the nights were getting sharp and the mule-deer were turning red, all these wandering small families returned home, converging from the hills, from the higher valleys and swales, down the canyons through the juniper, through the forests of tall pine, down to the sagebrush flats, all trekking home to some wintering ground, at Astaghiwa where there is a spring of hot water, at Tapaslu where the valley ends in a cul-de-sac, at Dalmo'ma where there are lots of wild turnips, to all the wintering grounds, there to dig themselves in for the coming winter and snow and blizzards and days of calm with the sun shining bright and the air cracking with frost.

F. It was in Burma, a sodden morning of the rains. A sickly light, like yellow tinfoil, was slanting over the high walls into the jail yard. We were waiting outside the condemned cells, a row of sheds fronted with double bars, like small animal cages. Each cell measured about ten feet by ten and was quite bare within except for a plank bed and a pot of drinking water. In some of them brown silent men were squatting at the inner bars, with their blankets draped round them. These were the condemned men, due to be hanged within the next week or two.

Reading Paragraphs in Sequence

So far, we've been looking at the way sentences are arranged in paragraphs, and at the logical relationships that connect those sentences to one another and to the topic sentence of the paragraph. In much the same way, however, we can look at the way paragraphs are arranged in essays, and describe the logical relationships that connect them to one another and to the topic statement that organizes the paragraph sequence.

The Restatement-Specification Sequence

In many analytic essays, writers use the restatement-specification pattern of reference to connect three or more paragraphs in a series. This kind of sequence usually begins with an *introductory* or *topic paragraph* * (or sometimes just a topic sentence in the first paragraph of the sequence). This introductory paragraph is followed by a series of *restatement-specification paragraphs,** often beginning with phrases repeated from the topic paragraph. Consider carefully this five-paragraph sequence from an article on drugs by Dr. Graham Blaine:

(1) A great deal has been written about the risks involved in drug-taking. Nevertheless, before delving into the motives behind the use of drugs, I should like to review those risks and compare them with the physiological and psychological effects which make each of these substances attractive to some of our young people.

(2) Here are the risks. Heroine is an addictive drug. A few injections may lead to a lifetime of alternation between a trancelike state and a frenetic search for the drug to forestall or offset painful withdrawal symptoms. A single dose of LSD may cause a paranoid psychosis in a person with no history of previous emotional instability. Such a psychosis can recur even though the drug is not ingested again. Rarely, LSD causes excitement leading to violent action which may be destructive to others or to oneself. Sometimes this results from paranoid delusions which stimulate a compulsion

to destroy before being destroyed, and sometimes from a sense of grandiosity which leads the drugtaker to demonstrate his indestructibility by leaping from a cliff or from a window. Chromosomal or brain cell damage may result from LSD. This possibility has not been conclusively proved, but the evidence is steadily mounting.

(3) The risks of marijuana smoking are less clear-cut and dramatic, but nonetheless real. They are: first, arrest and possible imprisonment, with damage to reputation in either case; and second, the possibility that the substance smoked is not marijuana but is another substance entirely or is marijuana laced with a much more dangerous hallucinogen such as DMT. A third risk comes from associations with pushers who are anxious to move users on to addictive and more expensive drugs. In addition, chronic pot smokers usually are trying to solve emotional problems of some sort by this futile means, and are avoiding sources of help which could be effective. Finally, one runs the risk of suffering an acute panic attack after using marijuana. For unknown reasons, some individuals are abnormally sensitive to the drug and may react to a single 'joint' in this way.

(4) Methadrine, a stimulant which has a chemical formula like that of benzedrine and is known in the lingo of the drugtakers as 'speed,' can cause a toxic psychosis characterized by paranoia and hallucinations. Once taken, it can produce a compulsion to continue injections for a number of days on end, resulting in loss of sleep and appetite. The consequent exhaustion and malnutrition account for many of the ill effects of this drug. The depression which often follows 'coming down off' the drug may last for months.

(5) The risk from glue sniffing, inhaling lighter fluid or the aerosol contained in glass-chilling devices, is the probability of destructive organic damage to various vital organs such as the brain, kidneys, and liver. In addition, a number of the compounds contained in these substances cause depression of the respiratory center and can bring about a fatal cessation of breathing.

In the topic paragraph of this sequence (1) the writer makes a general statement about the risks of drug taking. In paragraphs 2, 3, 4, and 5 he specifies each of these risks by describing a different drug: heroin, LSD, marijuana, methadrine, and glue and aerosol. If you have been able to identify this specification pattern (perhaps as early as the first or second paragraph) you can skim it quickly and then return when you have finished the sequence to clarify any points you may have missed or may not have understood.

Often, writers use cue words in the topic paragraph or topic sentence to signal the coming sequence. Here is a brief two-paragraph sequence that has only a topic sentence. The topic sentence has been italicized and the cue words circled. Can you restate the two main points being made in this paragraph sequence?

> But that is not all there is to the new music. *Outside of the sales charts and the big names and mass distribution and communica-*
>
> *tions business that have grown up around them are* (*two other*
>
> *facets of the musical scene.*) The first is the army of local amateur

and semi-professional young musicians who play the new music live at teenage night spots, college action spots, weekend dances, and shopping center moonlight sales. Their competence varies from embarrassing to as good and original as anything you can purchase at your town's 'music city.' A very few of these will get some measure of fame, the fleeting fame of one successful record and one big season in most cases. In almost every instance they simply make music for themselves and others and pick up a bit of money to help keep them in instruments, pot, and candy bars. A few reach such notoriety in their own locales that they are favored over most of the big national names in the new and emerging music. San Francisco's Jefferson Airplane has long been known in that area, and at this writing [mid-nineteen-sixties] they are gaining momentum on national charts. This group, and a few others like them on the West Coast, such as The Seeds and the Mothers of Invention in Los Angeles, manage to pick up more than pure pocket money, but, consistent with the ethic, they are usually content without cross-country glory and all the hassels inevitably bound up with fame.

Secondly, there is a smaller, less known world of musicians and fans which exists outside the sales charts and TV shows, but which is an important part of the happenings among the avant-garde and the action capitals. It helps to set the tone and color the lives of the more far out groups in much the same way that literary magazines influence the more commercially successful literary world. Here new styles are experimented with, worked out, and improved upon. Tastes in this fringe world of music, in which each little 'group' often has its own balladeer, may run months or sometimes years ahead of what one hears on popular radio. Bob Dylan, for example, was appreciated by thousands of people and scores of other musicians, some of them eminent, before the average American knew his name as part of the breakfast table chatter. Other artists manage to have long careers with only the support of such an informal and underground audience, and they never make it in the bigtime music world—a fact of life which really pleases many of them. The life of such artists is often checkered and gruelling and they live like vagabonds floating on a sometimes smooth, sometimes choppy sea of existence. But there are usually friends to give them a drink or a joint, friends to offer them a bed, and even a girl with whom they can share it. If they are rootless, they are also getting to do what they want (and that's something, isn't it?).

The topic sentence statement "two other facets of the musical scene" would give you a clue to what's coming: a sequence of two main points specifying these "facets." An experienced reader may skim quickly ahead to note both points, and then return to fill in the details; if the details don't seem important, or if the reader is reading for the main ideas, he or she may go on directly to the next paragraph.

The important thing to remember about the restatement-specification sequence is the pattern of reference: all the paragraphs in the sequence refer directly to the topic statement, just as all the sentences in a restatement-specification paragraph refer directly to the topic sentence. The writer is enumerating a series of major points, none of which are related directly to one another but are all related to the more general topic statement and specify it in some way.

For practice in analyzing the structure of paragraph sequences, turn to the two essays in the readings that follow this unit: "Why the American Press Is in Trouble" and "How Drastically Has Television Changed Our Politics?"

READING
FOR
STYLE
AND
STRUCTURE

A Style Primer

The Art of the Paragraph

Why the American Press Is in Trouble

How Drastically Has Television Changed Our Politics?

A Style Primer

Read each passage aloud several times before you begin to answer the questions below. Listen especially for sentence rhythm, for balance and repetition, for sound patterns—for the "music" of the writing. How do these structures affect your perception of the writer's idea? How is each passage different from the others? Can you describe these differences precisely? Which is most difficult to read? Why, specifically? Is the difficulty in vocabulary or in sentence structures? After you have read the passages aloud two or three times, ask yourself again about the reading difficulty. Do you still find the passage hard to read?

A NEW STYLE

(1) Most of the people who eventually wrote about my style, however, tended to concentrate on certain mannerisms, the lavish use of dots, dashes, exclamation points, italics, and ocassionally punctuation that never existed before ::::::::::: and of interjections, shouts, nonsense words, onomatopoeia,[1] mimesis,[2] pleonasm,[3] the continual use of the historical present, and so on. (2) This was natural enough, because many of these devices stood out even before one had read a word. (3) The typography [4] actually looked different. (4) Referring to my use of italics and exclamation points, one critic observed, with scorn, that my work looked like something out of Queen Victoria's childhood diary. (5) Queen Victoria's childhood diaries are, in fact, quite readable; even charming. (6) One has only to compare them with the miles of official prose she laid on Palmerston, Wellington, Gladstone in letters and communiqués and on the English

From "The Birth of the New Journalism" by Tom Wolfe. © 1972 by the NYM Corp. Reprinted with the permission of New York Magazine.

1 Words whose sounds imitate the sound they are used to represent.

2 Imitation.

3 Using more words than necessary to express an idea; redundancy.

4 Pieces of type. Wolfe's style is characterized by the use of & * ( ) + : ; and so forth.

people in her proclamations to see the point I'm making. **(7)** I found a great many pieces of punctuation and typography lying around *dormant* [5] when I came along—and I must say I had a good time using them. **(8)** I figured it was time someone violated what Orwell called "the Geneva conventions of the mind" ... a *protocol* [6] that had kept journalism and non-fiction generally (and novels) in such a tedious bind for so long. **(9)** I found that things like exclamation points, italics, and abrupt shifts (dashes) and syncopations (dots) helped to give the illusion not only of a person talking but of a person thinking. **(10)** I used to enjoy using dots where they would be least expected, not at the end of a sentence but in the middle, creating the effect ... of a skipped beat. **(11)** It seemed to me the mind reacted—*first!* ... in dots, dashes, and exclamation points, then *rationalized*,[7] drew up a brief, with periods.

Study Questions: "A New Style"

1. What is the relationship between what Wolfe is saying about his style and what he does in this passage?
2. Wolfe's sentences are written almost entirely in the active pattern. What effect does this choice have on you as a reader? How does this pattern fit into what seems to be Wolfe's philosophy about writing? (You might refer to a comment by Wolfe quoted earlier in this book: "Why should the reader be expected to just lie flat and let these people come tromping through as if his mind were a subway turnstile?") What does Wolfe expect of his reader?

A WELSH TOWN

(1) I was born in a large Welsh town at the beginning of the Great War—an ugly, lovely town (or so it was and is to me), crawling, sprawling by a long and splendid curving shore where truant boys and sandfield boys and old men from nowhere, beach-combed, idled and paddled, watched the dockbound ships or the ships steaming away into wonder and India, magic and China, countries bright with oranges and loud with lions; threw stones into the sea for the barking outcast dogs; made castles and forts and harbours and race tracks in the same; and on Saturday summer afternoons listened to the brass band, watched the *Punch and Judy*,[1] or hung about on the fringes of the crowd to hear the fierce religious speakers who shouted at the sea, as though it were wicked and wrong to roll in and out like that, whitehorsed and full of fishes. ...

Reprinted by permission of Harold Ober Associates Inc. © 1955 by the Trustees for the Estate of Dylan Thomas.

[5] Sleeping or inactive.

[6] A traditionally accepted form used on official or ceremonial occasions.

[7] Began to think logically and rationally.

[1] A puppet show featuring this comic, quarreling couple.

(2) This sea-town was my world; outside a strange Wales, coal-pitted, mountained, river-run, full, so far as I knew, of choirs and football teams and sheep and storybook tall hats and red flannel petticoats, moved about its business which was none of mine.

(3) Beyond that unknown Wales with its wild names like peals of bells in the darkness, and its mountain men clothed in the skins of animals perhaps and always singing, lay England which was London and the country called *the Front*,[2] from which many of our neighbours never came back. (4) It was a country to which only young men traveled.

Study Questions: "A Welsh Town"

1. Thomas relies heavily on the coordination pattern as a way of building his sentences. The first paragraph, as you can see, is one long sentence. Identify as many of the coordinated parts as you can. Why do you think the writer uses so much coordination? What effect is he trying to achieve?

2. In the last two paragraphs (sentences 2 to 4) the writer begins to describe an outside world. Describe specifically any changes you see in the structure of these sentences. Why do you think they are different from sentence 1?

3. Part of Thomas' effect in this passage is achieved by the use of an allusion to a land beyond the sea-town. What does he mean by the "Front, from which many of our neighbours never came back"? What effect does that allusion have on the reader?

SCHOOLDAYS

(1) All my early life lies open to my eye within five city blocks. (2) When I passed the school, I went sick with all my old fear of it.... (3) It was never learning I associated with that school: only the necessity to succeed, to get ahead of the others in the daily struggle to "make a good impression" on our teachers, who grimly, wearily, and often with ill-concealed distaste watched against our relapsing in the natural savagery they expected of Brownsville boys. (4) The white, cool, thinly ruled record book sat over us from their desks all day long, and had remorselessly entered into it each day—in blue ink if we had passed, in red ink if we had not—our attendance, our conduct, our "effort," our merits and demerits; and to the last possible decimal point in calculation, our standing in an unending series of "tests"—surprise tests, daily tests, weekly tests, formal midterm tests, final tests. (5) They never stopped trying to dig out of us whatever small morsel of fact we had managed to get down the

From A Walker In the City, © *1951, by Alfred Kazin. Reprinted by permission of Harcourt Brace Jovanovich, Inc.*

2 An abbreviated name for the front lines in a war, in this case, the grueling trench warfare along the lines in Europe during World War I.

night before. We had to prove that we were really alert, ready for anything, always in the race. (6) That white thinly ruled record book figured in my mind as the judgment seat; the very thinness and remote blue lightness of its lines instantly showed its cold authority over me; so much space had been left on each page, columns and columns in which to note down everything about us, *implacably* [1] and forever. (7) As it lay there on a teacher's desk, I stared at it all day long with such fear and anxious propriety that I had no trouble believing that God, too, did nothing but keep such record books, and that on the final day He would face me with an account in Hebrew letters whose phonetic dots and dashes looked strangely like decimal points counting up my every sinful thought on earth.

Study Questions: "Schooldays"

1. In this selection Kazin uses a great deal of adjectival specification to give an almost impressionistic effect, as though he were painting a picture of his feelings about the things he sees. How does the specification pattern help him to do this? Find a sentence that depends heavily on adjectival specification and describe it in detail.

2. Does Kazin use cumulative or suspended sentences? Are his sentences long or short? Comment on the length and structure of the sentences and the effect of this on your perception of his subject.

3. Kazin uses much repetition, both in words and in structures. Find several sentences that are built by repeated patterns and read them aloud several times. What is the effect of the repetition?

THE STEREOTYPE

(1) In that mysterious dimension where the body meets the soul the stereotype is born and has her being. (2) She is more body than soul, more soul than mind. (3) To her belongs all that is beautiful, even the very word beauty itself. (4) All that exists, exists to beautify her.

(5) The sun shines only to *burnish* [2] her skin and gild her hair; the wind blows only to whip up the color in her cheeks; the sea strives to bathe her; flowers die gladly so that her skin may luxuriate in their essence. (6) She is the crown of creation, the masterpiece. (7) The depths of the sea are ransacked for pearl and coral to deck her; the bowels of the earth are laid open that she might wear gold, sapphires, diamonds and

From Germaine Greer, The Female Eunuch. © *1971 McGraw-Hill. Reprinted by permission of the publisher.*

[1] Relentlessly refusing to be appeased.

[2] To make shiny or glossy.

rubies. (8) Baby seals are battered with staves, unborn lambs ripped from their mothers' wombs, millions of moles, muskrats, squirrels, minks, ermines, foxes, beavers, chinchillas, ocelots, lynxes, and other small and lovely creatures die untimely deaths that she might have furs. (9) Egrets, ostriches and peacocks, butterflies and beetles yield her their plumage. (10) Men risk their lives hunting leopards for her coats, and crocodiles for her handbags and shoes. (11) Millions of silkworms offer her their yellow labors; even the seamstresses roll seams and whip lace by hand, so that she might be clad in the best that money can buy.

Study Questions: "The Stereotype"

1. Greer, like Thomas, makes heavy use of coordination patterns, and yet the styles of the two writers are very different. Describe the structural differences between them. How does Greer make use of coordination? How does sentence length contribute to the difference in the effect?
2. Read aloud sentence 8. What do you hear? What is Greer trying to do in this sentence?

The Art of the Paragraph

FREEDOM AND THE UNIVERSITY

1   (1) Let us begin with the academy itself, and then consider the nature of the freedom which it enjoys. (2) What is a university, and what are its functions?

2   (1) A university is a place where young and old are joined together in the acquisition of knowledge and the search for truth.

3   (1) Its functions are three-fold. (2) First, to transmit knowledge imaginatively from one generation to the next. (3) Second, to provide society with a body of trained professionals—originally priests, doctors, lawyers, and scholars—which is why Old World universities still have only four faculties. (4) In modern times, and particularly in the United States, the university is expected to train for many other professions as well—architecture, journalism, teaching, forestry, engineering, and so forth, but the purpose is the same. (5) The third function of the university is rapidly becoming the most important: to expand the boundaries of knowledge through research and to discover new truths.

4   (1) Now, these functions imposed on the university by history and by circumstances mean that the university is to be a special kind of institution. (2) It is the only institution in Western society whose business it is to search for and transmit truth regardless of all competing or conflicting pressures and demands: pressures for immediate usefulness, for social

From Henry Steele Commager, "The Nature of Academic Freedom," The Saturday Review, August 27, 1966. Reprinted by permission of the publisher.

approval, pressures to serve the special interests of a government, a class, a professional group, a race, a faith, even a nation. (3) If the university performs its duty it will, of course, serve all of these interests, for we must believe that the search for truth is useful to all groups, but this is a by-product of the larger achievement of the training of the young to wisdom and the search for truth.

5   (1) The university is the chief instrument whereby society provides itself with independent criticism and advice, and with a continuous flow of ideas. (2) It maintains the university as it maintains scientists, doctors, judges, and priests, not to minister to its passions but to serve its deeper and more permanent needs. (3) Society does not impose its will on scientists because it wants to discover the secrets of the universe; it refrains from bringing pressure on judges because it wants to see justice done; it leaves doctors alone because it wants to discover the causes of and the cure for diseases; it permits religious freedom because it wants spiritual solace.[1] (4) Society provides freedom for scholars and for the university as an institution for the same elementary reason, because it wants to discover truth about as many things as possible.

Study Questions: "Freedom and the University"

1. In these paragraphs, Commager has two primary purposes: to define the function of the university and to explain why society protects the freedom of scholars. Read each of the five paragraphs carefully. How has the writer divided his major ideas? How do the paragraph divisions reflect that?

2. What are the purposes of the two short paragraphs at the beginning of this sequence?

3. Paragraph 3 follows the restatement pattern very closely. Which sentence deviates from that pattern? What does this sentence do?

4. Trace out the pattern of reference in paragraph 4 and decide what function (restatement, specification, qualification) each sentence plays. The second sentence of this paragraph contains a restatement series. What noun do the restatement nouns refer to? How many restatements do you find in the series? Is this sentence confusing in any way?

5. The last paragraph describes the reasons why society maintains the university. What are they? How are sentences 3 and 4 related? How else might Commager have written these sentences? Would another form have been more or less effective?

6. Read the paragraph sequence over again when you have finished the study questions. The paragraph should be easier to understand now. If it is, why is that true? If it isn't, what difficulties are you still having? Compare your reading problems with those of other students.

[1] Comfort or consolation.

Why the American Press Is in Trouble

1   The American press is in trouble. The trouble is partly owing to causes we can't do much about; and the trouble is partly our own fault. We ought to talk about these things.

2   Let me define a term, like Humpty-Dumpty, so that it means what I want it to mean and neither more nor less. By press, for the purpose of these observations, I mean the country's daily newspapers. This indicates no indifference to problems of magazines or of the people who produce news for radio and TV. They have their troubles, too, and of course they also are part of the press or, in the suit-and-tie word, part of the media. It is only that I started in newspapering as a 12-year-old copy-boy for the "Oklahoma City Times"—that was a fairly considerable time ago—and daily newspapers are my first love.

3   We are in trouble. Almost everything else in the country is growing. The press is standing still. In 1974, as a matter of fact, we went backward. Daily circulation fell from 63.1 million to 61.8 million; the number of daily papers slipped from 1,774 to 1,768. I haven't yet seen the figures for 1975, but they won't be significantly brighter. They're probably worse. Most of the papers are still earning a profit, but the profits aren't remarkably high; and some papers, like my own "Washington Star," have suffered such bleeding losses that they teeter on the edge of collapse.

4   What has gone wrong? Some of the factors are economic, some technological, some competitive. A part of the melancholy picture arises from the changing nature of our people: When it comes to communication, we are no longer a nation predominantly of readers, but of viewers and hearers. There is one factor more, of greater concern than the others: The press has failed, by and large, in its first responsibility for its own growth and survival. We have not sold the people on the meaning and necessity of a free press in a free society. Accordingly, we have lost the confidence —or failed to gain the confidence in the first place—of many readers we sorely need.

5   Newspapering's economics are crazy; it is like no other business on earth. It permits no inventories and no stockpile; you can no more sell yesterday's newspaper than you can sell last week's matinee. There is a similarity to show biz: The end product of entertainment is entertainment, which is its own *ephemeral* [1] reason for existing. The end product of newspapering is a newspaper, which has no *intrinsic* [2] function. You can use a newspaper to start a fire, or wrap a fish, or line a shelf, or swat the cat; but our product, basically, is information. You cannot wear it, drive it, eat it, drink it, or live in it. It isn't the product itself—the physical

James J. Kilpatrick, *"Why the American Press Is in Trouble,"* Nation's Business, *February, 1976, pp. 11–12. Reprinted by permission of the author and the publisher.*

[1] Lasting only a short time.

[2] Essential inborn quality of a thing.

newspaper—that earns a profit; it's the advertising that pays our way. The high cost of newsprint and the high cost of labor have made it all touch and go.

6   The technology is changing. Until quite recently we were printing papers essentially as Mr. Gutenberg printed Bibles 500 years ago. Now, we are caught in a revolutionary transition from hot metal to cold type. The costly new machines ultimately will produce economies; meanwhile, they produce headaches, earlier deadlines, and grief from the unions.

7   Competition changes also. Most people say that they get most of their news from television, and, in a superficial sense, this may be so. What they get is headlines, tidbits, capsules—and they get even this meager diet fleetingly by eye and ear. The broadcast media, whose fare is primarily entertainment, anyhow, never can offer more than a small fraction of the information that a newspaper offers its readers in permanent form, at their own selection, at their own convenience. The significant competition is for the advertising dollar. Here we struggle.

8   We are struggling in relation to another phenomenon: the changing nature of literacy, or what passes for literacy. Something of enormous importance is happening here; we cannot yet comprehend it fully. The median age in the United States is 28. Half of our people were born before 1947, half after; and this is to say, half before TV, half after TV. It is an oversimplification, but not a gross oversimplification, to contrast an old and declining generation of readers and a new and rising generation of nonreaders. For those of us whose lives are bound to the printed word, the implications inevitably are sobering.

9   In fact, all of these considerations are sobering, but matters of economics, technology, competition, and literacy would not trouble us so greatly if it were not for the final concern. This is the relatively low regard in which the press is held. Periodically, the Gallup and Harris pollsters attempt to measure the confidence of the American people in various American institutions. Like other subjective data, not subject to *empirical* [3] confirmation, the figures do not have to be accepted as precisely true; but if the figures are only generally true, the people have little more confidence in the press than they have in the United States Congress. It is a terrible prospect to ponder.

10   Assuming, *arguendo*,[4] that this is so, we of the press ought to inquire why this is so. One explanation—I think it a feeble explanation—is that no one loves the messenger who brings bad news. In recent years, the press has dealt mostly in bad news; therefore, no one loves the press. But what we are dealing in is the raw stuff of history, and always and inevitably, as Gibbon said, history is largely a record of the crimes, follies, and misfortunes of mankind. Newspapers have been bringing bad news for years; and once, the press flourished.

11   I suspect the declining level of confidence may be traced to other causes. Three come especially to mind: We make too many errors and do

[3] Based upon experience and observation rather than theory.

[4] Let us argue (Italian).

not correct enough of them; we too often blur the line between straight news and editorial opinion; and we have acquired a reputation of being rather too big for our britches.

12   To produce a daily paper is to produce a daily miracle. It is a never-ending wonder, even to those who have spent their lives in the process, that all of the copy gets written, set, printed, and into the trucks on time. In such a crash operation, errors are inevitable—errors of fact, errors of understanding. An increasing number of newspapers regularly run correction boxes. The practice ought to be universal; it would be one way to regain public confidence.

13   Also, it seems to me, we should observe rigorously the rule that news is news, and opinion is opinion, and the two ought never to be confused. Once, it was different. Most newspapers were partisan organs. The customer who bought the "Richmond Whig" knew what he was getting, and if he didn't like it he could buy the "Enquirer" or "Times" instead. Only a handful of major cities today offer competing papers with opposing editorial philosophies. This makes it all the more important for editors to make certain—as certain as they can—that news is presented fairly and cleanly, without trace of partisanship or bias. Opinion should be plainly labeled as such. I would warn the unsophisticated reader with a kind of highway sign: "This article is not presented as 'news,' but rather as analysis and interpretation; it reflects the opinion of the writer whose byline appears below." On every issue of serious controversy, I would try to carry opposing opinions. A newspaper can state its own position in its own editorials.

14   On the third point: I have a notion that newspapers would do well to pull in their horns for a while. The impression still is widely held that the press hounded Richard Nixon out of office. The charge, in my view, is not true. Granted, a spirit of mutual animus existed between the President and the Washington press corps. The Watergate scandals were reported with a furious intensity not observed in previous administrations. But it was the courts and the Congress that exposed the story and impelled the resignation.

15   Nevertheless, an impression persists that the press—and here I would include TV also—is abusing its power. We are thought to be throwing our weight around. Instead of reporting the news, we are said to be shaping the news; we are not spectators, but actors. Reporters have an obligation to persist in their efforts to dig out the news, but there is a fine line between persisting and bullying, between aggressive journalism and insulting conduct. The Lord did not mean reporters to be celebrities or prima donnas. A little less high-and-mightiness would be marvelously welcome.

16   Our most serious mistake—our failure to sell the concept of a free press—has its ironical aspects. Here we are in the business of communication, and we do not communicate the one idea on which our very existence depends. Newspapermen rarely write about newspapers. I am no exception. I have been writing these pieces for *Nation's Business* for two years, and this is the first time I have written a line about the press. We ought to untie our tongues.

17   A free press is vital to a free people. Unhappily, this fundamental conviction is not universally held. To believe in freedom—really, truly to believe in freedom—is the most difficult of all political theologies. It demands tolerance, and tolerance is among the rarest of human virtues. To put up with the other guy's misguided ideas requires patience; and when the other guy's ideas are not merely misguided, but rude, distasteful, blasphemous, or evil, it's difficult to pay even lip service to the First Amendment. My guess is that not ten percent of our people believe absolutely in a free press.

18   Sad to say, this also seems to be increasingly true of judges. The most insidious of all threats to a free press—the threat of "prior restraint"—is creeping through the bench. This notion holds that judges have the power to issue orders, enforceable by prison sentences for contempt, to prevent newspapers from publishing certain material. Such orders, whether issued in the name of fair trial or national security, are becoming more frequent. This is the path that leads ultimately, far down the road, to despotism.

19   I do not mean to cry gloom and doom. Our press is still the freest in the world. Legions of young people still hunger for newspaper jobs. We still sell an awful lot of papers. But the troubles are there, and we who love the craft and believe in its survival had better get off our rumps. It is not enough to talk to each other at professional meetings; we must talk to the country, too.

Study Questions: "Why the American Press Is in Trouble"

1. What are the five factors Kilpatrick cites to explain why the American press is "in trouble"? What paragraph describes these factors? How is the organization of this paragraph a miniature of the organization of the whole essay? Explain how the sentences in the paragraph correspond to the paragraphs in the essay.

2. What difference do you notice between the order of ideas in the paragraph and the order of the same ideas in the essay? Why do you think the change was made in the essay structure?

3. What is the reference pattern of paragraphs 5 to 8?

4. What is the reference pattern of paragraphs 12 to 15? How does paragraph 11 function in relation to these paragraphs? How do paragraphs 9 and 10 serve to organize this part of the essay?

How Drastically Has Television Changed Our Politics?

1   The time has come for a preliminary assessment of the impact of television on our politics. More and more Americans, it appears, are forming their impressions of the world on the basis of the things they see on the

"How Drastically Has Television Changed Our Politics?" by Arthur Schlesinger, Jr. Reprinted with permission from TV Guide.® Copyright © 1966 by Triangle Publications, Inc., Radnor, Pennsylvania.

tiny screen. Recent surveys report television as the main source of news for more than 50 percent of our voters, and *Broadcasting* magazine could plausibly argue in 1964 that television had become the "Nation's primary news medium." This widening influence of televison over American life raises the question how TV is affecting the basic character of our political system and whether it is strengthening or weakening the workings of our democracy.

2   Some observers, for example, claim that television is producing a more alert and better-informed electorate; others that it is reducing our politics to a mixture of high-pressure salesmanship and beauty contests. The assessment is bound to be preliminary because the evidence is inadequate, contradictory and inconclusive. But I wish to offer an historian's *tentative* [1] thoughts on a complex problem.

3   Television touches politics in a number of ways. For purposes of convenience, one may perhaps distinguish four types of coverage: (1) news programs, (2) *pseudo* [2]-news programs, (3) interpretation, and (4) party programs. It may be well to discuss each category and then attempt a general appraisal.

News

4   Probably the greatest influence in shaping political judgment is still the reality of events themselves. A depression, a war, a debate over national policy, constitutional rights protected or denied, economic securities enlarged or imperiled, bills passed or defeated. Such facts remain the great *determinants* [3] of political opinion. And it is in communicating these facts that television has had its most impressive success.

5   A notable recent example was the coverage of the hearings on Vietnam before the Senate Foreign Relations Committee. I have no doubt that future historians will conclude that these hearings opened a new phase in the Vietnam debate. Before the hearings, most people had suppressed any disquietude they may have felt over the deepening national involvement in Vietnam on the assumption that the President had more information and no doubt knew best. But the hearings had the clear effect, for better or worse, of legitimatizing dissent. If eminent generals, diplomats, and senators were unhappy about our actions in Vietnam, then the ordinary citizen felt free to indulge in his own doubts. And the hearings not only opened up debate over Vietnam; they also ended the taboo which had so long prevented discussion of American relations with Communist China. Would these hearings have had the same effect had they not been on television? I think plainly not—and all the more credit therefore to the NBC network which carried them in full.

6   Television, through the vivid reporting of actual events, can thus incite new thoughts and emotions in the electorate. It also has the effect in many

[1] Proposed experimentally or provisionally; not definite or final.

[2] False or pretended; deceptively similar to something else.

[3] Factors that cause or influence outcomes.

cases of heightening the sense of popular participation in public matters. Thus the McCarthy-Army hearings undoubtedly made many viewers feel, as they had not before, that the Wisconsin senator was a threat not just to other people but to themselves. When sustained over a long time, this increased sense of popular participation can alter somewhat the workings of political institutions. It seems already, for example, to have reshaped so basic a device in our politics as the Presidential nominating convention.

7   For most of our history, the convention was a relatively closed powwow for professional politicians, who got chummily together, discussed their candidates, made their deals and presented the results to a passive public. People might have exclaimed, "Who is James Polk?" when they heard (via telegraph) the outcome of the Democratic Convention of 1884; but they did not feel indignant over the fact that the name of the nominee meant so little to them.

8   Television has changed all that. The dark-horse candidate, emerging unknown out of smoke-filled rooms for nomination on the 46th ballot, is probably a thing of the past. The tiny screen has made the public an active partner. The feedback is too quick and intense to encourage any convention to risk ditching the favorite of the national audience in favor of a crony of the party professionals. In addition, television has had the happy effect of making conventions shorter. It is safe to assume that the nation will never again have to endure 103 ballots, as it did during the Democratic Convention of 1924.

9   Conventions, of course, with their inherent drama and suspense, are particularly well adapted to the inquisitive camera. But even television's day-by-day reporting of politics has undoubtedly given the electorate a larger knowledge of public personalities and a greater acquaintance with public issues. News coverage, I think, represents television's best contribution to democratic responsibility.

Pseudo-News

10   By "pseudo-news"—a subclassification of Daniel Boorstin's general category of "pseudo-event" (in his book *The Image*)—I mean the creation of news on the *initiative* [4] of the medium. Perhaps the term is unnecessarily invidious; for often the news thus elicited is entirely legitimate. Lawrence Spivak's *Meet the Press* and its various imitators, for example, have greatly advanced public enlightenment through the years by their interrogations of national figures.

11   On the other hand, some pseudo-news is mischievous and irresponsible. When President Johnson issued his challenge to the intellectual community a year or so ago, a news television crew descended on my office in the evident hope that I could be stimulated to denounce the President. This seems a *factitious* [5] attempt to manufacture conflict (though, in justice

[4] Responsibility for beginning new actions or originating new procedures or ideas.

[5] Artificial or contrived; not spontaneous.

to the program, when I said that I considered the President's remarks appropriate, they filmed the interview anyway and put it on the air).

12   My feeling is that organized shows in a press-conference format serve a useful purpose but that television interviews designed to lure or trap people into sensational statements they would not otherwise make can be dispensed with. It is necessary to add, though, that television did not invent this technique; it is another bad habit it picked up from the press.

Interpretation

13   Editorialization on television has taken the form of thoughtful personal comment (Howard K. Smith, Eric Sevareid) or, with the recent encouragement of the FCC, of editorials by local stations. Neither form has thus far had very striking results. I do not know whether television has an inhibiting effect on comment but certainly no television commentator has spoken with the pungency or authority of Elmer Davis on radio, and men like Smith and Sevareid often look more constrained on the screen than they used to sound over the loudspeaker.

14   In the past, networks have attempted panel discussions, like the NBC series *The Big Issue* a few years back. This is still done a good deal locally and on educational television. Unquestionably these programs have improved the level of political discussion, in part because they permit the suggestion of subtleties and complexities in public problems. But, possibly for this reason, such programs do not seem to have been pursued very diligently by the networks.

15   What television has done most successfully in the field of interpretation is the analytical documentary—the kind of thing that Murrow and Friendly used to do for CBS, the *NBC White Papers*, the Bell & Howell shows. At their best, such programs have dealt with problems at a reasonable level of complexity and have been a highly effective form of public education.

Party Programs

16   By this I mean time purchased by political parties and leaders, or otherwise made available to them. This, I would say, has been the area of television's most conspicuous failure; and the trouble here begins with the nature of the medium itself. For the effect of television has been to cheapen political discourse, steadily reducing its length, its substance, and its rationality.

17   Sixty years ago an audience which traveled many miles to hear William Jennings Bryan or Robert M. La Follette hold forth on railroad regulation or the tariff would have felt cheated if the oration lasted less than a couple of hours. The coming of radio set in motion the shrinkage of the political speech, first to forty-five minutes, than to half an hour. Then came television. I can recall the insistence of the TV men in Adlai Stevenson's headquarters in 1956 that half an hour was far too long; unless it were a national crisis, fifteen minutes, they said, represented the outer limit of the attention span of an American audience.

18   Now the fifteen-minute speech is itself almost a thing of the past. The most sinister statistic in political telecasting is the one which records the ominous rise of the spot announcement. Hyman H. Goldin, a former FCC aide, has estimated that 60 percent of the money spent by candidates on television in recent general elections has gone for spots; the proportion of funds invested in program time has been steadily declining.

19   This development can only have the worst possible effect in degrading the level and character of our political discourse. If it continues, the result will be the vulgarization of issues, the exaltation of the immediately *ingratiating*[6] personality and, in general, an orgy of electronic *demagoguery*.[7] You cannot merchandise political candidates like soap and hope to preserve a rational democracy.

20   While this drift to spot announcements is in great part the preference of the candidates themselves, the industry cannot be held wholly guiltless, for it would much rather sell spots than program time. Both the candidates and the industry, however, prefer to blame the condition on the audience, which, both claim, will simply not sit still for thoughtful disquisitions on public policy. No doubt a large part of the mass audience could not care less about an intelligent discussion of issues. But there remain a substantial number of viewers, even if less than a majority, who do care. Does not television have an obligation to this important minority, too, as well as to the service of democracy in general?

21   The ultimate answer to this question lies in the movement which must some day come toward the diversification of the viewing public; UHF and pay-TV will no doubt make it easier for the medium to reach specialized audiences. In the meantime, one wonders whether more free time should not be made available to candidates, especially in Presidential elections. If democracy depends on rational communication, if television is now the dominant communications medium and if television licenses are granted, according to the Communications Act, with a view to the "public interest, convenience and necessity," then it would seem that one of the richest industries in the country might make systematic provision for free time for public debate, at least during Presidential elections.

22   I recognize that informally the industry has done a considerable amount of this. But I wonder whether it is doing enough to discharge the obligations which come with its highly profitable licenses. Is it not really pretty important to give the electorate a chance to hear a man who wants to be President, even if this outrages people who would prefer to see *The Beverly Hillbillies*? ** In addition to lowering the level of the party

---

** I would not exclude the possibility of achieving this result in part through a graduated system of federal subsidies, as proposed by broadcaster Stimson Bullitt, or through tax deductions for a portion of lost revenues, as proposed by former FCC Chairman E. William Henry; and I would support researcher Herbert Alexander's suggestion that Section 315 of the Communications Act be amended to permit a policy of "differential equality of access."

[6] Working too consciously to bring oneself into someone else's favor.

[7] An attempt to win quickly popular support or power by appealing to the emotions and prejudices of the people.

debate, television may give an initial advantage to the poised, photo-genic, other-directed, manipulable candidate.

23   The rush of professional actors into politics is an obvious consequence of the television age. One shudders a little to think what would have happened, for example, to the Adamses or Jackson or Lincoln if tele-vision had existed in the early years of the republic. On the other hand, television is a relatively unsparing medium; it consumes material *voraciously*,[8] in politics as well as in comedy and drama; and while it may lend itself to slick first impressions, it probably is not hospitable to sustained phonies and fakery. In the long run, I think, genuine qualities—intelligence, integrity, humor, firmness of purpose—will win out over calculated effects. The Kennedy-Nixon debates of 1960 was a case in point.

The Balance Sheet

24   Where do we end up? I do not think that television has *wrought*[9] a revolution in our political system. American democracy will adapt itself to the tiny box as it has to a series of technological changes from the start of the republic. The effects of television—apart from the nominating convention—have been mostly marginal. It would seem that, through news programs and, to some extent, through pseudo-news programs, television has somewhat widened public acquaintance with issues and personalities; but that, aside from documentaries, its efforts at intepreting the significance of news tends to be superficial; and that its party political programs have encouraged the oversimplification of issues and favored the smooth and bland over the rough-hewn candidate. If voters had to depend on television alone for the information on which they base political judgments, the results would undoubtedly be poor for American democracy.

25   Yet, so long as television is considered a supplement to newspapers, magazines, political meetings, and solitary midnight brooding by indi-vidual citizens, and not a substitute for them, it has in certain respects enriched our politics. And it could do so much more. Its power to convey the quality of political leadership is vast; the agony of grief which ran around the world when John F. Kennedy died after a short thousand days as President was obviously in part a result of the way television had made him a cherished figure in remote lands. If television would recognize an affirmative obligation to elevate the level of our politics, and applied as much thought and talent to this as it does to selling detergents, it might play a great role in helping to make our democracy more rational and responsible.

8 Greedily, even gluttonously, pursuing a desire or goal.

9 Older form of the past participle of "work," meaning to have made or brought into being.

Study Questions: "How Drastically Has Television Changed Our Politics?"

1. Describe the organization of the Schlesinger essay in general terms by answering the following questions: What two questions is Schlesinger attempting to answer in the essay? How is the subject divided? How is that division indicated?

2. How does this essay fit the restatement pattern we discussed in unit 7? How does it differ from that pattern?

3. How are the two essential questions in the essay answered in each major division? How can a division into parts be helpful in making a careful evaluation of television's general influence on politics?

4. How is the organization of the paragraphs in the section entitled "party programs" (paragraphs 16 to 23) different from the middle sections? How is it similar?

5. In what order are the pieces of the essay brought together in the last section (paragraphs 24 to 25)? How is the order of the preceding sections related to that order?

6. In making an evaluation, a writer will offer contrast and weigh the positive and negative features of his subject. What examples of this contrastive yet balanced structure—in sentences, paragraphs, and sections—do you find in the essay? (For an example of this kind of contrastive structure, see sentence 1 in paragraph 2).

7. Do you think Schlesinger successfully answers the question he begins with?

IV

LANGUAGE AND CONCEPTUAL STRUCTURES

UNIT 8

On Defining Definition: Ordering the World in Words

Definitions, contrary to popular opinion, tell us nothing about things. They only describe people's linguistic habits; that is, they tell us what noises people make under what conditions. Definitions should be understood as *statements about language.*   (S. I. Hayakawa)

Philosophers very often talk about investigating, analysing, the meaning of words. But let's not forget that a word hasn't got a meaning given to it, as it were, by a power independent of us, so that there could be a kind of scientific investigation into what the word *really* means. A word has the meaning someone has given to it.   (Ludwig Wittgenstein)

Evaluating Your Learning

When you've completed this unit, you should be able to demonstrate your understanding by

- describing the difference between surface structure and conceptual structure
- describing the relationship between words and things and telling why, given that relationship, definition is important
- defining three major kinds of definition—the "point-to" definition, the definition in other words, and the operational definition—and finding examples of them
- defining the problem of circularity, identifying examples of it, and telling how the formal definition and the descriptive definition avoid the problem
- evaluating examples of definition in other words and operational definitions and showing the differences between them

AS SOON AS I CAN DEFINE REALITY THEN I THINK I CAN COPE WITH IT!

Reprinted by permission of the Washington Star Syndicate, Inc.

- defining the term "undefinable term" and providing some examples of it from your reading
- evaluating given definitions in terms of the conceptual structure that underlies them
- pointing out implicit definitions

A Look Back and A Look Ahead

We've been discussing the ways readers make sense out of written language: how they respond to the language of fact, the language of belief, and the language of metaphor. We've also talked about how readers decipher the relationship of sentence components to one another, how they understand the ways in which whole sentences are related to other whole sentences within paragraphs, and how they make sense of the relationships of whole paragraphs to one another within paragraph sequences and within whole writings. Let us sum up all of what we've said about this meaning-making process by describing it as an *interactive process* *: under the direction and control of the writer, you as reader begin to make connections, constructing meaning out of the signals provided in the text itself, out of your own background, your own life experiences, and your own experiences with other written texts and with writing itself. Writing becomes meaningful, we've suggested, only as you give it meaning, meaning that is created through your interaction with the printed page. And that is why it is important for readers to be *active* readers, actively participating in the reading process. It is easy to see why passive readers, who simply let the words pass under their eyes, are not able to make their reading meaningful.

Up to this point in our study we've described in detail how you go about collecting meaning-signals through the language and through the structure of a written work—that is, through the *surface structure:* * what you can see on the page itself. However, that activity is not the whole of reading; if it were, we could turn the task of reading over to machines and let them collect and combine those surface structure details for us. As a matter of fact, that part of the reading activity— perceiving and responding to the surface structure—is a relatively simple activity to describe. What we must now turn to is much more difficult: a description of the ways in which we perceive and respond to the writer's *conceptual structure,** the underlying ideas and assumptions and beliefs that enable the writer to organize everything included in the writing. In a very real sense, the conceptual structure is the *generating force* that motivates the writing, for writers (like the rest of us) are impelled to write by their ideas. In order to fully understand the process of reading, then, and in order to be fully aware of all of the dimensions of meaning, readers must "read through" the surface structure—the words, the organizational structures—to the conceptual structure that informs the whole.

In some ways, of course, we've been dealing with aspects of the conceptual structure all during our discussion. In our review of language, for example, we observed that the choice and arrangement of words reveal the writer's attitudes and beliefs; when we talked about sentence structure we said that the organization of sentences and paragraphs depends on the writer's determination of which details are important, which should receive more or less emphasis. The choice of words and their organization into larger patterns of sentences and paragraphs give us important clues to the writer's conceptual structure: the framework of attitudes and beliefs that underlies *everything* written.

However, there are some aspects of writing that reveal the conceptual structure more clearly than others—or which, to put it another way, are more likely to influence the reader's responses. In the next two units we are going to look more closely at these aspects and at the way they reveal the conceptualizing processes that shape the writing. Our first problem will be to identify these conceptual structures as they are revealed in the examples we will be looking at—revealed in the way the writer defines the terms that are used and revealed in the argument that is assembled. Our second problem will be to understand how these conceptual structures shape the writing and then to attempt to evaluate them. We'll begin by discussing the importance of definition as a clue to the conceptual structures of the writer.

Definition

As we said in our discussion of territories and verbal maps, human beings live in a world of words—words that they use to describe, or map, the physical world around them and to report to other human beings their feelings about that world. But the word, we pointed out, has no direct relationship to the thing it refers to; it is only a map for a territory: an abstract representation that a number of speakers have agreed to accept as a "stand-in" for the thing itself. Because words and things are *arbitrarily related* in this way, a great part of the time we spend talking to one another is spent in the important business of checking our maps. We must make sure that the meaning we give to a certain term is shared by the person with whom we are speaking, and define the terms we use so that we are both using the same maps to refer to the same territories.

But not only are we engaged, as readers, in the business of checking to make sure that we understand the terms the writer is using; we are also engaged in the more difficult business of checking the writer's conceptual structure against our own conceptual structure. That is what we mean when we say "I agree with you" or "I disagree with you." Understanding definition plays a large role in our ability to understand underlying conceptual structures and to determine basic agreements and disagreements, not just in meaning, but in beliefs and values. Let's begin with the relatively simple problem of checking maps for meaning.

Kinds of Definitions

The Point-To Definition

Is it possible to agree exactly on the meanings of terms? It's fairly easy to define some words and to agree on those definitions: *chair* or *table*, for example, or *octopus*. To define terms like these, which have actual referents, which are real physical territories, all I have to do is *point to* two or three examples of the thing itself: :"That's what I mean by the word *chair*, and there's another, and there's still another." Or, if the thing is absent and I am able to find or draw a picture of it, I can point to the picture and say "Here's an octopus—that's what I mean when I say the word." For you to check your definition of any of these terms against mine is very simple: all you have to do is look where I'm pointing and say, "Yes, that's a chair," or "No, you're crazy! That's not an octopus—here's a picture of a *real* octopus!"

We can fairly easily define a physical territory with the "point-to" method. Some things, in fact, can be defined only in this way. How, for example, can you *tell* someone, in words, what the term "fuchsia" means? Or, to make the problem more specific, how can you tell a person who has been blind from birth what the word "chartreuse" refers to? Without

being able to point to one or more examples of the thing itself, you cannot communicate its meaning or define it precisely.

However, not all "point-to" definitions are precise enough to satisfy us. To illustrate this problem, here is an amusing story written by an anthropologist who was studying the language of a Congo tribe:

> I remember on one occasion wanting the word for Table. There were five or six boys standing round, and tapping the table with my forefinger, I asked "What is this?" One boy said it was a *dodela*, another that it was *etanda*, a third stated that it was *bokali*, a fourth that it was *elamba*, and the fifth said it was *meza*. These various words we wrote in our notebook, and congratulated ourselves that we were working among a people who possessed so rich a language that they had five words for one article.

However, the researcher soon discovered that the "point-to" definitions he had collected were not all definitions of the object he intended:

> One lad thought we wanted the word for tapping; another understood that we were seeking the word for the material of which the table was made; another had an idea that we required the word for hardness; another thought we wished a name for that which covered the table; the last, not being able, perhaps, to think of anything else, gave us the word *meza*, table—the very word we were seeking.

As the anthropologist's story suggests, if we point to something and hope for a clear definition of it we may be disappointed, for our gestures are often not clear enough to avoid misinterpretation.

Definition in Other Words

Definition by synonym. Useful as the "point-to" method is, it can't be used for most terms—either because they represent absent things for which we have no pictures or because they represent abstract concepts or feelings that cannot be pointed to. Writers then turn to the technique of defining *in other words*, using *synonyms* * to explain the terms they define. This strategy works well in many cases. The term "boulder," for example, can be defined clearly as "a large rock," or the term "finger" can be defined as "a digit." Strictly speaking, however, there are no synonyms, for no word means exactly what another word means. "Digit" and "finger," for instance, are often thought to be synonymous, but they mean different things, and no native American speaker would find the two completely interchangeable. (Would a minister performing a wedding ceremony be likely to say to the groom, "Place this ring on the third digit of your bride's left hand"?)

Nevertheless, most of us, when we attempt to define a term, must fall back on other words, whose meaning, in turn, can only be defined by *still other words*. Louis B. Salomon describes this circular difficulty that is inherent in all languages:

> Take the word *distance*. The key word in my dictionary's definition of it is *space;* the key words in its definition of *space* are *extension, position, direction*. Cross reference following the line of key words from *extension* takes me along the route: *extend—lengthen—long —extent—space* and *extend* (once around the track, you see). *Position* brings me back to the starting point without delay: the key word in its definition is *space*. *Direction* sends me to *move* and *point; move* returns me to *position*, and *point* completes the circle with *position* and *direction*. In pursuit of the meaning of *distance* I have covered a certain amount of distance, all right, but where am I?

What Salomon is describing is often called *circular definition,** a problem that occurs when we try to define words with other words. In fact, defining words through the use of synonyms is often a very confusing process, for as Salomon suggests, we often find ourselves wandering in circles. Consider the following definition from a pamphlet describing aviation equipment, for instance:

> REACTION ENGINE: An engine in which thrust is generated by expelling a stream of moving particles rearward.

This definition is perfectly clear—unless you are not sure what the word "thrust" means. Then (let's suppose) you turn back to the pamphlet, looking for the definition of the word. What do you find?

> THRUST: The propelling force exerted in a reaction engine by its exhaust.

As Monroe Beardsley observes in his comments on this circular definition, you would have to know the meaning of "thrust" before you could understand what a reaction engine is and how it works—but before you could understand "thrust," you would have to know what a reaction engine is. The reader is trapped in a circular definition made of words that never allows him or her to discover the real meaning.

Ambrose Bierce ironically illustrates this tendency to define in circles in his *Devil's Dictionary*, a collection of tongue-in-cheek definitions:

> MAGNET, *n*. Something acted upon by magnetism.
> MAGNETISM, *n*. Something acting upon a magnet.

The two definitions immediately foregoing are condensed from the works of one thousand eminent scientists, who have illuminated the subject with a great white light, to the inexpressible advancement of human knowledge.

Formal definition and descriptive definition. One way for writers to avoid circular definition (always a potential problem whenever we define in other words) is to make sure that the definition includes two parts: a *category term* that places the object in a particular class and a *limiting term* that distinguishes the object from other members of that class. A carrot, for example, is defined by the dictionary as a "biennial plant of the parsley family, with fernlike leaves, umbels of white flowers, and a fleshy, orange-red root." The definition establishes a class (a biennial plant of the parsley family) and then clearly distinguishes the carrot from all other members of the same family. Even though this is a definition in other words, it avoids the problems of circularity by establishing both a general category and a set of limiting specifics.

As a means of definition, this method (often called *formal definition* *) works very well. It can be used to define animals, plants, even concepts that can be defined precisely. However, as *Webster's New World Dictionary* observes, formal definition is not as useful for the average reader as it is for the scientist.

> The average city dweller, passing a field of large quadrupeds, might not know which horns would eventually prove to be deciduous, or which creatures possessed gall bladders and polycotyledonary placentas.

The formal definition so useful to scientists and dictionary-makers is of only limited service to most nonscientific writers and readers. As a result, many writers use another supporting kind of definition: a *descriptive definition,* * which provides enough distinguishing detail to allow the reader to "see" the object or event. (In this sense, a descriptive definition is rather like a "point-to" definition, except that it is expressed in words.) This descriptive definition, the dictionary says, can be used to further specify a formal definition, making it much more understandable for ordinary readers:

> The present dictionary, although it identifies the so-called American buffalo as *Bison bison,* a bovine mammal, adds that it has a "shaggy mane, short curved horns, and a humped back" and that it stands from five and a half to six feet high.

The descriptive definition is perhaps the most widely used way of providing a clear picture of the object or event the writer wants to dis-

cuss. It may appear in a variety of forms, with or without formal definition. Here, for example, is a fuller definition of the term "buffalo,"
describing the various buffalo in the herd:

> The calves would be light in color, sandy red or even yellow; packs
> of wolves and coyotes would be trailing them but the bulls would
> be on guard. Yearlings would be darker and "spike bulls," the four-
> year-olds whose horns had smooth, clean points, would begin to
> show the colors of maturity. There was much individual variation,
> but a typical bull would shade from a bright blond at the fore-
> quarters and hump to dark brown or even black at the hindquarters
> and under the belly. At calf-time the thick wooly hair would be
> shedding toward the near-nudity of mid-summer and the resulting
> patchiness would make a full-grown bull look even more ferocious
> and demoniac. . . . Such a bull, say eight or ten years old, would
> weigh just short of a ton, seventeen hundred or eighteen hundred
> pounds. He would stand six feet at the shoulders. From muzzle to
> rump he might be ten feet long.

The descriptive definition, at its most effective, is used to define a
physical phenomenon that can be relayed, using words, to the senses.
The descriptive terms that are used, as in the definition above, must be
as clear and precise as possible, since their purpose is to enable the
reader to "see" the object itself, almost as if the writer were pointing to it.

However, descriptive definitions are often used to pinpoint terms
that are not so readily available to the senses, and cannot be made as
clear and precise as we might wish. Look at the following descriptive
definition, for example. Do you see any problems that might arise from
it?

> America . . . is becoming a "technetronic" society: a society that is
> shaped culturally, psychologically, socially and economically by
> the impact of technology and electronics, particularly computers
> and communications.

This writer appears to define the word he has coined ("technetronic")
by describing the components that make it up—technology and electronics. But does the definition specify clearly enough what the "impact
of technology and electronics" really is? Or is this descriptive definition
as circular as the one we examined earlier? Does it merely say something
like this: a "technical-electronic society is a society shaped by technology
and electronics"? In this case, of course, a single definition—formal or
descriptive—is not equal to the task of completing the definition, and
the writer goes on for several pages in an attempt to define the term he
has used and to persuade us to accept his definition.

The extended definition: definition by analysis. Like the definition of "technetronic" above, many descriptive definitions require much more development. That development, in fact, can structure a whole essay or article, or can provide a major portion of the argument. Here, for example, are the first four paragraphs from an article on marital problems, defining the term by breaking it apart—*analyzing* it—into its major components:

> Marital complaints today are somewhat different from those of 10 or 15 years ago. Marriage counselors still hear about lack of communication, unfulfilled emotional needs, problems with the kids, sexual problems, infidelity, money, in-laws, alcoholism, and physical abuse.
>
> But three new problems have become common. The first is unequal growth patterns. This issue used to be called the "executive syndrome." The man was moving upward into more stimulating environments, while the woman, confined to the role of mother and homemaker, remained static. Now the reverse is often true. The woman, in a burst of anger, breaks out of her cocoon, demanding to exercise her wings. Because his wife takes this position suddenly, instead of evolving into it, the husband is unprepared to deal with the new flamboyant creature his wife has become.
>
> A second, related problem is sex-role stereotyping. Many men do not know how to summon the tenderness, warmth and sharing that women are beginning to expect. Women feel ambivalent or guilty about putting their needs on par with those of the rest of the family, but neither are they satisfied with their traditional role as self-effacing emotional support for the other members of the family.
>
> Finally, there's the personal response that used to be almost automatic, but now sticks like a bone in the throat—sacrifice. Marriage and parenthood require that people put aside certain needs and postpone some satisfactions. . . . Many younger people today, however, find any postponement or infringement of their personal fulfillment a source of serious conflict.**

The three-part definition of the term "marital complaints" generates definitions of three other terms: "unequal growth patterns," "sex-role stereotyping," and "sacrifice." Each of these definitions, in turn, generates a full paragraph of descriptive detail, defining each term as completely as possible. Many writers adopt this strategy: breaking up a larger, more difficult term into its component parts and defining the parts separately, in order to provide a definition of the larger term.

** Joanne and Lew Koch, "A Consumer's Guide to Therapy for Couples," reprinted by permission of *Psychology Today* Magazine. Copyright © 1976 Ziff-Davis Publishing Company.

practice 1

A WRITING TASK FOR READERS

Here is an excerpt from Norman O. Brown's book, *Life Against Death,* in which Brown attempts to define two of Sigmund Freud's important terms: "repression" and "unconscious." Study these paragraphs carefully, tracing out the other terms that Brown must define in order to define the two central terms. What methods of definition does he use? Why is it necessary for both Brown and Freud to define these phenomena in other words? Why can't they simply point to examples of them? What makes the definition of terms like these difficult? The problem is complicated by the fact that Brown is creating a map of Freud's map of a very imprecisely-marked-out territory. What kind of difficulties can be caused by this technique of building a map of a map? What other examples of this kind of double mapping activity can you think of? How reliable are these twice-removed maps? How is *your* map related to Brown's and to Freud's? Write an essay in which you consider these questions. (You need not refer to them; simply use them as idea-generators to get you started.)

There is one word which, if we only understand it, is the key to Freud's thought. That word is "repression." The whole edifice of psychoanalysis, Freud said, is based upon the theory of repression. Freud's entire life was devoted to the study of the phenomenon he called repression. The Freudian revolution is that radical revision of traditional theories of human nature and human society which becomes necessary if repression is recognized as a fact. In the new Freudian perspective, the essence of society is repression of the individual, and the essence of the individual is repression of himself.

The best way to explore the notion of repression is to review the path which led Freud to his hypothesis. Freud's breakthrough was the discovery of meaningfulness in a set of phenomena theretofore regarded, at least in scientific circles, as meaningless: first, the "mad" symptoms of the mentally deranged; second, dreams; and third, the various phenomena gathered together under the title of the psychopathology of everyday life, including slips of the tongue, errors, and random thoughts.

Now in what sense does Freud find meaningfulness in neurotic symptoms, dreams, and errors? He means, of course, that these phenomena are determined and can be given a causal explanation. He is rigorously insisting on unequivocal allegiance to the principle of psychic determinism, but he means much more than that. For if it were possible to explain these phenomena on behavioristic principles, as the result of superficial associations of ideas, then they would have a cause but no meaning. Meaningfulness means expression of a purpose or an intention. The crux of Freud's discovery is that neurotic symptoms, as well as the dreams and errors of everyday life, do have meaning, and that the meaning of "meaning" has to be radically revised because they have meaning. Since the purport of these purposive expressions is generally unknown to the person whose purpose they express, Freud is driven to embrace the paradox that there are in a human being purposes of which he knows nothing, involuntary purposes, or, in more technical Freudian language, "unconscious ideas." From this point of view a new world of psychic reality is opened up, of whose inner nature we are every bit as ignorant as we are of the reality of the external world, and of which our ordinary conscious observation tells us no more than our sense organs are able to report to us of the external world. Freud can thus define psychoanalysis as "nothing more than the discovery of the unconscious in mental life."

But the Freudian revolution is not limited to the hypothesis of an unconscious psychic life in the human being in addition to his conscious life. The other crucial hypothesis is that some unconscious ideas in a human being are incapable of becoming conscious to him in the ordinary way, because they are strenuously disowned and resisted by the conscious self. From this point of view Freud can say that "the whole of psychoanalytic theory is in fact built up on the perception of the resistance exerted by the patient when we try to make him conscious of his unconscious." The dynamic relation between the unconscious and the conscious life is one of conflict, and psychoanalysis is from top to bottom a science of mental conflict.

Definition in Action

We have seen that we cannot define all terms by the "point-to" method of definition. We've also seen that defining words by other words often takes us further from the thing we want to define, into a cloudy confusion of synonyms, or takes us around in circles, back to the point where we began. We've seen, too, that formal definition is most effective for scientific purposes and that descriptive definition is effective only for those terms that can be made apparent to the senses: physical objects and events. But as you know, a very large number of terms are neither scientific nor sensory—what kind of defining strategies *can* we use to make our definitions clear?

One answer, it would seem, is to define a word not in terms of other words, but in terms of *operations* or actions that can translate the abstract concept into a concept we can see and measure—into a concept we can *experience*. In order to define the term "distance" operationally, then, we could speak of the number of measuring units (one-foot rules or yardsticks or kilometers or light years) that we could lay end to end in the distance we want to define. Our *operational definition* * is more precise, more reliable, and easier to agree on than a definition in other words, and more convenient than a "point-to" definition.

To see the differences between an operational definition and a "point-to" definition or a definition in other words, consider the following discussion of the term "recession," taken from an article in *Time Magazine*. It's easy to see that in this case, the "point-to" definition won't work—in fact, other kinds of definition are necessary *because* we can't point to a certain set of economic conditions and assert "this is a recession."

One reason that economists can differ sharply over whether the U.S. is in a "recession" is that there is no simple, numerical definition of the term. Herbert Stein, chairman of the Council of Economic Advisors, offers a qualitative description: "An extended, substantial, and widespread decline in aggregate economic activity, but one less severe than earlier 'depressions.' " The job of determining just which downturns belong in that category has fallen to the National Bureau of Economic Research, whose word on the subject is practically law in the profession.

The NBER has classified five post–World War II business contractions as recessions. No single standard determines that judgment, but the five drops do have some common denominators. Each lasted at least nine months, during which real Gross National Product fell at least 1.5% and industrial production dropped a minimum of 8.1%. Also, the jobless rate rose at least 2.3 percentage points, to 6.1% or more, and employment declined in more than 80% of the 30 major non-farm industries that NBER statisticians watch closely.

So far, the current downturn has lasted roughly three months, and no figures are yet available on what has happened to the real G.N.P. Industrial production has dropped 1.4%, the jobless rate has risen six-tenths of a percentage point, to 5.2%, and employment has declined in about 20% of the nonfarm industries. So, by NBER standards, the U.S. is not yet in a recession—though it could enter one later.

In paragraph 1, you can see Herbert Stein's rather fuzzy attempt to define the word "recession" in other words: a recession is "an extended, substantial, and widespread decline in aggregate economic activity, but one less severe than earlier 'depressions.' " This definition gives us a vague idea of what a recession is, but it depends in turn upon the definition of other hard-to-pin-down words—"extended," "substantial," "widespread," "decline"—and by saying that a recession is *not* a depression, another term that must be defined if we are to understand clearly what a recession *is*. Defining the word "recession" by using other words leads us further away from the word itself and into a haze of abstractions.

In paragraph 2, you can see the operational definition provided by the National Bureau of Economic Research. This definition shows us a recession *in action*, giving criteria (the "yardstick") we could use to measure an economic condition and determine whether or not we could call it a recession. While not all economists would agree that this operational definition provides a reliable map of the territory "recession," most would agree that it is more *precise* than the definition in other words. Even if we can't come to a mutual agreement on an operational definition, however, it is much easier to see exactly where our disagreements lie, and we can begin to adjust our understanding.

Operational definitions, or definitions in action, are very helpful for readers, assisting them in the difficult task of translating abstract ideas into specific, perceivable terms. This kind of defining strategy is clearly illustrated in these paragraphs from an article on personal freedom. As you read, determine what constitutes the operational definition and what constitutes the term or terms being defined:

> The pipe under your kitchen sink springs a leak and you call in a plumber. A few days later you get a bill for $40. At the bottom is a note saying that if you don't pay within 30 days, there'll be a 10 percent service charge of $4. You feel trapped, with no desirable alternative. You pay $40 now or $44 later.
>
> Now make two small changes in the script. The plumber sends you a bill for $44, but the note says that if you pay within 30 days you'll get a special $4 discount. Now you feel pretty good. You have two alternatives, one of which will save you $4.
>
> In fact, your choices are the same in both cases—pay $40 now or $44 later—but your feelings about them are different. This illustrates a subject we've been studying for several years: What makes people feel free and why does feeling free make them happy? One factor we've studied is that individuals feel freer when they can choose between positive alternatives (delaying payment or saving $4) rather than between negative ones (paying immediately or paying $4 more).**

In this passage, the writers are attempting to define for their readers the concept of personal freedom, a very abstract notion, and yet one that is basic to most of our feelings about ourselves. To define what makes us feel "free," the writers give us an operational definition, a definition in action. This definition describes two instances—an example of what would make us feel confined or bound to a particular action and an example of what would make us feel as though we had exercised personal choice. The use of the operational definition makes the concept much more understandable.

practice 2

Here are some examples of the three kinds of definition we have studied. Read each one carefully and decide what terms have been defined (some of the passages contain more than one definition). Are these definitions effective?

** Jerold Jillison and John Harver, "Why We Like Hard, Positive Choices," reprinted by permission of *Psychology Today* Magazine. Copyright © 1976 Ziff-Davis Publishing Company.

A. There are medical leaders who are saying that irreversible coma is a sound reason for declaring a human being dead, even though his heart, lungs and other organs can be maintained with artificial aids. . . . One such leader is Dr. Henry K. Beecher, of the Harvard University Medical School. Dr. Beecher recently headed the 13-member Ad Hoc Committee from the Harvard faculty which examined the problem of defining death and suggested that brain death become the new criterion. Modern techniques, said the committee, "can now restore 'life' as judged by the ancient standards, even when there is not the remotest possibility of an individual recovering consciousness."

How can coma be diagnosed as irreversible? A number of doctors are devising tests. They generally focus on the electrical activity of the patient's brain, as measured by an electroencephalograph, a machine which records "brain waves." In a live human, an electroencephalogram (EEG) is recorded as a wavy line. But doctors have found that if it flattens out, becomes "isoelectric" (electrically neutral), death soon follows.

Between 1957 and 1967, three doctors at the University of Iowa studied 25 patients with isoelectric EEG's and found that all died (their hearts and breathing ceased) within one to five days after the first "flat" reading. They also studied eight other flat EEG cases where the patients' breathing was being sustained by mechanical respirators. All of these patients died within one to 38 days after the respirator was applied. The researchers then surveyed the world's medical literature and found no evidence of a patient surviving an EEG that had remained truly isoelectric for a number of hours. The doctors concluded that when brain death is diagnosed, "it is useless and inhuman to maintain the patient on a mechanical respirator."

B. LIME JELL-O LIVES! The switch was thrown, the needle twitched and yet another science-fiction nightmare had come true: by the most delicate of medical measurements, the quivering mass of lime Jell-O in the lab was unmistakably alive.

The experiment, at McMaster University in Hamilton, Ontario, was something of a joke—but Dr. Adrian R. M. Upton was making a serious point in the debate over how to determine the moment of death. As it stands, the final judgment is often made with the help of an electroencephalogram, or EEG; if other neurological responses can't be found, a flat pattern on an EEG is fairly conclusive evidence that a patient on a respirator is really dead. But as Upton demonstrated by inserting the EEG electrodes into a mold of lime Jell-O (the flavor his wife happened to have on hand) atop the plaster model of a human head, even that inert mass of colloids can be made to show signs of life.

What happened, as Upton explained it, was that the EEG picked up and recorded stray electrical impulses from nearby respirators, an intravenous feeding device and even from doctors and nurses walking around. The moral: if such interferences can be eliminated, there might be fewer tragic mistakes of diagnosis.**

C. Ours is a visual age. We are bombarded with pictures from morning till night. Opening our newspaper at breakfast, we see photographs of men and women in the news, and raising our eyes from the paper, we encounter the picture on the cereal package. The mail arrives and one envelope after the other discloses glossy folders with pictures of alluring landscapes and sunbathing girls to entice us to take a holiday cruise, or of elegant menswear to tempt us to have a suit made to measure. Leaving our house, we pass billboards along the road that try to catch our eye and play on our desire to smoke, drink or eat. At work it is more than likely that we have to deal with some kind of pictorial information: photographs, sketches, catalogues, blueprints, maps, or at least graphs. Relaxing in the evening, we sit in front of the television set, the new window on the world, and watch moving images of pleasures and horrors flit by. Even the images created in times gone by or in distant lands are more easily accessible to us than they ever were to the public for which they were created. Picture books, picture postcards and color slides accumulate in our homes as souvenirs of travel, as do the private mementos of our family snapshots.

D. A rigorous definition of a communication terminal is somewhat elusive. A typical communication system, whether biological or man-made, consists of a chain of several terminals and channels; a typical terminal converts the signal appropriate to one channel to another signal appropriate to the next channel, while preserving the signal's information content. For example, a message may originate in a human brain, be transmitted to the fingers, pass into a tele-typewriter, then travel over a wire line to a radio transmitter, journey through space to a radio receiver, be typed out onto a sheet of paper, be scanned by a pair of eyes and finally enter another human brain. The communication engineer is likely to regard as a terminal any apparatus at either end of a discrete electromagnetic channel, but perhaps more commonly a terminal is viewed as an apparatus designed to convert a visual, acoustic or tactile signal into an electrical signal, or vice versa.

E. PLOVERS (Family *Charadriidae*, Subfamily *Charadriinae*) are medium-sized to small shorebirds. The bill is rather short and has a noticeable swelling near the tip. The neck is short; so is the tail, which is carried horizontally, not drooping. The wings are pointed, almost narrow; flight is direct and fast. Plovers are active feeders, walking or running swiftly on shore or grassland, foraging for insects or small marine animals. The nests are on the ground. Typical plovers fall into two groups: the medium-sized unbanded plovers and the smaller ringed plovers.

F. Now, what is a bughouse square? A bughouse square is a public street-intersection or mall or park in a large city where gregarious, imaginative, exhibitionistic, and autocompulsive "ism" peddlers, agitators, soapboxers, folk evangelists, teachers, show-men, faddists, cultists, cranks, crackpots, dreamers and self-proclaimed messiahs congregate to impress one another and to display their wares. These performers attract a large number of disciples, camp-followers, hecklers, "wise-guys," honest inquirers, and humble seekers. There is always present a large number of the skeptical and the disputatious. And there is invariably a sprinkling of unemployed, hobos, punks, pimps, faggots, fey proletariat, strumpets, beatniks, and the more robustious and less fastidious of the Bohemians. In short, a really first-class bughouse square is a bit of skid row, carnival, evangelistic revival, poor man's town hall, and people's university rolled into one.

practice 3

In your own reading, find four or five examples of interesting definitions and bring them to class for discussion. What kind of defining strategy has the writer used? Is the definition effective?

Problems in Defining

Defining Emotional Responses

The operational definition is probably the best way of defining terms, but it's clear that there are some things that can't be easily defined in this way. Think about the word "noise," for instance, which the dictionary defines as "any loud, discordant, or disagreeable sound." This dictionary definition is not very helpful, however, for what you may consider a loud, discordant, or disagreeable sound may be very different from someone else's idea of loudness, discordance, or disagreeableness. For example, the director of Carnegie Hall (one of the most famous centers for the performing arts in the United States) has recently ruled that rock music is too loud to be played in the Hall; by his definition, then, rock music is not music but noise.

But the Carnegie Hall director's definition of noise (or someone else's definition of music, for that matter) is a very personal one, arising from sensory and emotional responses within the individual; it cannot be checked or measured in the same way that distance can be measured, or in the same way that a recession can be measured; it is not easily or precisely translated into other words, either. (Of course, you might argue, noise can be operationally defined in terms of decibels, units used to measure sound; however, this specialized definition developed by acoustical engineers is not of much help to the average person, who continues to experience noise whether or not he or she understands anything about decibels.)

The same problem of definition arises when we try to define feelings or emotional states. What do you mean when you say you're "happy"? Is your definition of happiness the same as everyone else's? Perhaps you could define happiness operationally: "When I'm happy I smile, I laugh, sometimes I even sing." Or maybe you would say this: "I'm happiest when I'm listening to my records" (or sewing, or talking with friends, or whatever). But these behaviors don't really make up that emotional state we call happiness; they are only evidences of it, and not very reliable ones, at that. (Is a smile or a laugh *always* evidence of happiness? Are you *always* happy when you're listening to records, or sewing, or talking with friends?) Our emotions exist inside ourselves and it is very difficult to make them public through language.

The knotty problem of defining emotional responses extends to the definition of many terms: democracy, justice, intolerance, and so forth. Much of the reading you'll be doing in your college work involves terms like these, and writers appear to spend a great deal of effort providing precise, carefully delimited maps of these very imprecisely marked

Defining Depends On Where You Are (B. C. by permission of Johnny Hart and Field Enterprises, Inc.)

territories. Often, the definitions you will read may even appear to be precise and may be supported not only by description but by examples.

However, readers need to be aware that definitions of such abstract terms, precise as they may seem, are frequently as much a statement of the writer's feelings and beliefs about a territory as they are a statement about the territory itself. In that sense, if we read carefully, we can discover as much about the writer's values and assumptions—his or her conceptual structures—as we can about the thing or idea that is being described. We can say that definitions like these are like mirrors: they reflect the one who's making the definition as well as the thing that is being defined.

For an example of the way a writer's conceptual structure can be revealed in the reflecting mirror of the definition, look at the following two passages, both of which are definitions of the term "the American Dream."

> The phrase "the American Dream" is a complex cluster of ideas, ideals, and attitudes which make up the "American way." It is not a phrase with precise meaning identical for all citizens; but for more than 200 years it has been a shorthand way of identifying those basic beliefs, attitudes, and aspirations which best define the American character, motivate our major decisions, and animate our conduct. It stands for a faith rather than a fact, the substance of things hoped for rather than a condition fully realized.... And I shall be thinking of it as embracing ... the following components: government by consent of the people ...; belief in the equal worth and dignity of every individual of whatever ethnic origin, religious, or political persuasion ...; the rights and worth of individuals ...; diversity ...; the right to be different ...; the inalienable right of private judgment ...; the belief that all should be provided an opportunity for maximum realization of individual potential ...; the right to pursue happiness....

In this paragraph the writer undertakes an analytic definition of the term "the American Dream," dividing the term into seven components, all of them intangible spiritual qualities that he believes to be characteristic of American ideals.

But is this the *only* way to describe the American Dream? Compare the following short passage to the one above:

> The American Dream? What is it but a greedy, materialistic desire to get rich quicker than the guy next door, a graceless, consuming, self-indulgent appetite for possessions and status that characterizes not only individual citizens but the state itself, in its dealings with other states? The American Dream is personal happiness pursued unendingly—past all reason, past all sanity, past all hope of building a secure and tolerant acceptance of all of our citizens.

Have these two writers been successful in defining the term "the American Dream"? Yes, to an extent: the first definition, especially, with its careful delineation of component parts, appears to precisely define the phrase—even though this term, like many others, is an abstraction, a concept that is created out of words, that has no physical reality.

However, both definitions are more successful in revealing to the careful reader the system of beliefs and values—the underlying conceptual structure—that generates them. Reading *through* the definitions to the concepts on which they are based, we can say that the first writer is a traditionalist and an optimist who believes firmly in the values expressed in the Bill of Rights (did you catch the similarity of his style to the style of the Bill of Rights?) and assumes that most Americans believe in them too. The second writer, on the other hand, appears to be much more cynical and pessimistic, with a rather dark view of what motivates twentieth-century Americans. Each writer succeeds in defining his own view more clearly than defining the phenomenon he presents to us. What *we* respond to, as readers, then, is not the territory itself, but the writer's conceptualization of it, which shapes and controls the definitions presented to us. If we are not careful readers, our evaluation of the definition will depend, in large measure, upon whether the writer's conceptualization of the territory matches our own. If it does, we are in agreement, and we are likely to say approvingly, "That's a very good, very accurate map." If it doesn't, we are likely to shake our heads and complain that the map doesn't match the real territory.

Implicit Definitions

Related to the problem of building maps that define the map-maker more accurately than the actual territory is the problem of building *implicit (or hidden) definitions* * into statements that do not immediately appear to be definitions. Look at this example, for instance:

> The war of the generations has been going on a long time, and it is unlikely that anything really new can be contributed to it. . . . But it is high time . . . to ask for understanding of the adult world and to argue against victory by the young in their warfare with the old.

This assertion is based on an implicit definition that is hidden away in the sentence. Made explicit, stated openly, the definition might look something like this:

> The relationship between the generations is a state of war.

When the definition that underlies this assertion is made explicit (making the underlying conceptual structure explicit as well), the difficulty with the statement is apparent. In order to substantiate his definition, the writer must provide evidence to convince the reader that the relationship between the younger generation and the older generation is indeed a warlike relationship. Without substantiating evidence, a reader is justified in questioning the validity of this writer's definition.

The "is" of identity.* When we define, we almost always use the verb *to be*, most frequently in its present-tense form "is":

> A decathlon *is* an athletic contest consisting of ten events.

> A holograph *is* a document handwritten by the author.

When we use the verb *to be* in definition, we are really building an equation, similar to a mathematical equation, but of course not as precise. What is on one side of the *is* is equal or identical to what's on the other side. For that reason, the *is* used in definition is often called the *is of identity*. In other words, when we define, we *identify* one thing as another.

A major problem in definition occurs, however, when we too quickly identify a thing as "being" something when it only momentarily behaves like something. Edward Sagarin untangles this problem for us:

> The little verb "to be" has caused a great deal of pain. . . . When we speak about a person who behaves in eccentric ways—who does eccentric things and commits eccentric acts—we tend to say that he "is" an eccentric. . . . It's the same when we say that a person "is" a thief, a cheat, a philanthropist or a jaywalker. "Being" any of these things may mean that the actions are committed once, sporadically, or commonly. But they are still actions, and we wouldn't necessarily say that they concerned a person's identity.
>
> The problems crop up when we start talking about other types of deviant behavior. We say of a person who drinks too much that he "is" an alcoholic, and we say of people who think bizarre.

thoughts that they "are" schizophrenic. This person is a drug addict and that person is a homosexual. Others are sadomasochists, pedophiliacs, juvenile delinquents. The English language is constructed in such a way that we speak of people *being* certain things when all we know is that they *do* certain things.**

As Sagarin goes on to point out, this *labeling* activity doesn't allow us to recognize that people and things change, and that particular behavior at a particular moment doesn't create a permanent definition. Writers are usually careful about making this kind of misleading statement (at least partly because they are both legally and morally responsible for what they say in print). However, you'll frequently see the "is" of identity misused in an election year, when candidates are speaking freely about one another:

He's a liberal, and you know what that will get you: higher taxes, more government interference in local affairs, and more inflation.

She's irresponsible—she made a couple of contradictory statements in a single speech.

You'll also find the "is" of identity used in advertisements, with a different intention. In these instances, the writer wants you to establish a particular label in your mind, and keep it there. Here are four examples of this use of definition, all from a recent issue of *Time*. Not one of these advertisements provides any support for the definition it offers:

Bourbon is I. W. Harper.

True luxury is more car to the foot. Not more foot to the car. Volvo.

The New Fiat 131. It's not a dream car. It's a reality car.

What's More? It's longer. It's leaner. It's slower. It's easy drawing. It's a cigarette. It's a new experience. It's a cooling blast.

The "is" of identity, used to establish a label that equates a product or a person with a performance or with an idea, without any substantiating evidence, is an ad-writer's strategy that critical readers need to look out for. A careful reader, confronted with a *be* verb that equates or identifies one thing with another, will question the identification and demand evidence that the label has been appropriately applied, on the basis of *real* identity.

** Edward Sagarin, "Thieves, Homosexuals, and Other Deviants," reprinted by permission of *Psychology Today* Magazine. Copyright © 1976 Ziff-Davis Publishing Company.

The playful definition. Most of the definitions we've been discussing have been serious attempts to create a reliable map for a territory— although some of the definitions turn out to be more reliable as maps of the map-maker's attitudes and beliefs! Not all definitions, however, represent such serious efforts to define; some "play" with the act of definition, often by building metaphoric definition. Here are a few examples:

> A conference is just an admission that you want somebody to join you in your troubles.

> The only things worth learning are the things you learn after you know it all.

> Worry is today's mouse eating tomorrow's cheese.

> Rumor is one thing that gets thicker as you spread it.

Sometimes this playfulness can be extended into a longer joke. This new definition of Kentucky's "progress" appeared in *Reader's Digest.*

> A salesman traveling along a new four-lane highway in Kentucky was impressed by signs extolling the "Beauty, Progress, and Industry" of the Blue Grass State. Then he came to a place where the road was partially blocked by a landslide caused by recent heavy rains. Easing by the flagman who was detouring traffic around the slide, he asked the obvious question: "Landslide?"
> "Nope," said the smiling flagman. "Just Kentucky on the move."

While definitions like these are usually not appropriate to a serious effort to explore a problem, they are often used to provide clarity and insight by surprising the reader with an unexpected analogy or a witty comment. The problem arises, of course, when the writer uses this definition alone, without any other definition or without any substantiating evidence, to prove a point in argument.

practice 4

A WRITING TASK FOR READERS

> Here is a section of Ambrose Bierce's *Devil's Dictionary.* Read it carefully and comment on the effectiveness and appropriateness of each definition. When you've finished, try your own hand at constructing a few of these "devilish definitions."

> > harangue, n. A speech by an opponent, who is known as an harangue-outang.
> > harbor, n. A place where ships taking shelter from storms are exposed to the fury of the customs.

hash, x. There is no definition for this word—nobody knows what it is.

idleness, n. A model farm where the devil experiments with seeds of new sins and promotes the growth of staple vices.

impiety, n. Your irreverence toward my deity.

infancy, n. The period of our lives when according to Wordsworth, "Heaven lies about us." The world begins lying about us pretty soon afterward.

kill, v.t. To create a vacancy without nominating a successor.

mine, adj. Belonging to me if I can hold or seize it.

practice 5

In Unit 1, you read Samuel Johnson's comments about the fine art of defining. Go back to pp. 18–19 and reread that paragraph. The last sentence, for our purposes here, is the most important. See if you can paraphrase Johnson's statement. What does his complaint in the last sentence have to do with what we've been talking about here? Is this paragraph any easier to read now than it was when you first began to study this text?

practice 6

A WRITING TASK FOR READERS

The following paragraphs contain several important definitions and a number of substantiating statements, supported by statistics. Read the paragraphs carefully and consider the problems in definition presented here. Write an essay discussing these problems.

Overpopulated America

I define as most seriously overpopulated that nation whose people by virtue of their numbers and activities are most rapidly decreasing the ability of the land to support human life. With our large population, our affluence and our technological monstrosities the United States wins first place by a substantial margin.

Let's compare the US to India, for example. We have 203 million people, whereas she has 540 million on much less land. But look at the impact of people on the land.

The average Indian eats his daily few cups of rice (or perhaps wheat, whose production on American farms contributed to our one percent per year drain in quality of our active farmland), draws his bucket of water from the communal well and sleeps in a mud hut. In his daily rounds to gather cow dung to burn to cook his rice and warm his feet, his footsteps, along with those of millions of his countrymen, help bring about a slow deterioration of the ability of the land to support people. His contribution to the destruction of the land is minimal.

An American, on the other hand, can be expected to destroy a piece of land on which he builds a home, garage and driveway. He will contribute his share to the 142 million tons of smoke and fumes, seven million junked cars, 20 million tons of paper, 48 billion cans, and 26 billion bottles the overburdened environment must absorb each year. To run his air conditioner he will strip-mine a

Kentucky hillside, push the dirt and slate down into the stream, and burn coal in a power generator, whose smokestack contributes to a plume of smoke massive enough to cause cloud seeding and premature precipitation from Gulf winds which should be irrigating the wheat farms of Minnesota.

In his lifetime he will personally pollute three million gallons of water, and industry and agriculture will use ten times this much water in his behalf. To provide these needs the US Army Corps of Engineers will build dams and flood farmland. He will also use 21,000 gallons of leaded gasoline containing boron, drink 28,000 pounds of milk and eat 10,000 pounds of meat. The latter is produced and squandered in a life pattern unknown to Asians. A steer on a Western range eats plants containing minerals necessary for plant life. Some of these are incorporated into the body of the steer which is later shipped for slaughter. After being eaten by man these nutrients are flushed down the toilet into the ocean or buried in the cemetery, the surface of which is cluttered with boulders called tombstones and has been removed from productivity. The result is a continual drain on the productivity of range land. Add to this the erosion of overgrazed lands, and the effects of the falling water table as we mine Pleistocene deposits of groundwater to irrigate to produce food for more people, and we can see why our land is dying far more rapidly than did the great civilizations of the Middle East, which experienced the same cycle. The average Indian citizen, whose fecal material goes back to the land, has but a minute fraction of the destructive effect on the land that the affluent American does.

Thus I want to introduce a new term, which I suggest be used in future discussions of human population and ecology. We should speak of our numbers in "Indian equivalents." An Indian equivalent I define as the average number of Indian citizens required to have the same detrimental effect on the land's ability to support human life as would the average American. This value is difficult to determine, but let's take an extremely conservative working figure of 25. To see how conservative this is, imagine the addition of 1000 citizens to your town and 25,000 to an Indian village. Not only would the Americans destroy much more land for homes, highways and a shopping center, but they would contribute far more to environmental deterioration in hundreds of other ways as well. For example, their demand for steel for new autos might increase the daily pollution equivalent of 130,000 junk autos which *Life* tells us that US Steel Corp. dumps into Lake Michigan. Their demand for textiles would help the cotton industry destroy the life in the Black Warrier River in Alabama with endrin. And they would contribute to the massive industrial pollution of our oceans (we provide one third to one half the world's share) which has caused the precipitous downward trend in our commercial fisheries landings during the past seven years.

The per capita gross national product of the United States is 38 times that of India. Most of our goods and services contribute to the decline in the ability of the environment to support life. Thus it is clear that a figure of 25 for an Indian equivalent is conservative. It has been suggested to me that a more realistic figure would be 500.

In Indian equivalents, therefore, the population of the United States is at least four billion. And the rate of growth is even more alarming. We are growing at one percent per year, a rate which would double our numbers in 70 years. India is growing at 2.5 percent. Using the Indian equivalent of 25, our population growth becomes 10 times as serious as that of India. According to the Reinows in their recent book *Moment in the Sun,* just one year's crop of American babies can be expected to use up 25 billion pounds of beef, 200 million pounds of steel and 9.1 billion gallons of gasoline during their collective lifetime. And the demands on water and land for our growing population are expected to be far greater than the supply available in the year 2000. We are destroying our land at a rate of over a million acres a year. We now have only 2.6 agricultural acres per person. By 1975 this will be cut to 2.2, the critical point for the maintenance of what we consider a decent diet, and by the year 2000 we might expect to have 1.2.

UNIT 9

Understanding the Patterns of Belief and Argument

"A name is a prison, God is free," once observed the Greek poet
Nikos Kazantzakis. He meant, I think, that valuable though language is to man,
it is by very necessity limiting, and creates for man an invisible prison.
Language implies boundaries. A word spoken creates a dog, a rabbit, a man.
It fixes their nature before our eyes; henceforth their shapes are, in a sense, our
own creation. They are no longer part of the unnamed shifting architecture
of the universe. They have been transfixed as if by sorcery, frozen into a concept,
a word. Powerful though the spell of human language has proved itself to be,
it has laid boundaries upon the cosmos.   *(Loren Eisley)*

"The general form of propositions is: This is how things are."—That is the kind of
proposition that one repeats to oneself countless times. One thinks that one is
tracing the outline of the thing's nature over and over again, and one is merely
tracing round the frame through which we look at it.   *(Ludwig Wittgenstein)*

Evaluating Your Learning

When you've finished studying this unit, you should be able to demonstrate your understanding by

- defining the terms "visual and verbal concepts" and "conceptual structure" and describing their relationships
- identifying the three kinds of inductive argument and describing how they function
- using the criteria for valid induction to evaluate given examples of inductive argument
- finding the conceptual structures that organize a given argument and evaluating the argument and the assumptions behind it
- evaluating your beliefs and values against those of the writer

A Look Back and a Look Ahead

In the last unit we talked about the way our definitions reflect the concepts and beliefs that underlie them. Definition, we said, often tells us more about the person who makes the definition than about the thing that is being defined. Our definitions depend on where we are and who we are and what we believe about the world at the moment we define an object, an event, an idea.

In this last unit, we'll turn to a more detailed discussion of how our values and beliefs—our *conceptual structure* *—influence what we see and how we report those perceptions in writing. We'll look carefully at the way these conceptual structures organize argument, and how readers can evaluate both the argument and the assumptions behind it. We'll also talk about the reader's own conceptual structure and how it shapes what he or she chooses to read and how he or she responds to it.

The Psychology of Perception

In Unit 1 we commented that experienced readers are able to predict the writer's language patterns a split second before they actually recognize the shapes of the words on the page. These readers *anticipate* what's coming not only because of their experience with probable combinations of letters but also because of their experience with larger language patterns, particularly with sentence patterns. This ability to make informed guesses about what's coming makes reading much easier: readers are able to organize the signals they receive from the text much more quickly and efficiently and with less effort. With experience in reading this ability increases, for the more you read, the more likely you are to make accurate predictions about what's ahead of you on the page. This ability, we said, is part of the whole meaning-making process.

Visual Concepts

The ability we're describing here—the ability to predict what's coming and to organize it very quickly into meaningful patterns—is very much like the predicting mechanism that structures all of our perceptions. This mechanism enables us to "read" the world around us easily and to make sense out of what we see and experience. Without this predicting mechanism, it would be impossible to make meaning out of the disordered randomness of the signals we receive from the physical world.

We can say, then, that our expectations are responsible for part, perhaps most, of what we see. For an example of the way this works, look quickly at Figure 1. What do you see? Would you describe the figure as a collection of variously shaped black blots arranged randomly against a white background? Or would you say that you see a dog? Now look more closely. If you see a dog, what enables you to read the marks on the page in such a way that the dog-shape becomes visible? Your familiarity with drawings of dogs in similar poses enables you to "see" something that isn't actually there on the page, to organize the random blots into a meaningful pattern so that your nervous system— your eye and your brain—can cope with the experience. This is true, psychologists tell us, because we can really only deal with what we understand and are familiar with. If we see something without an immediately perceivable structure—like the black blots in Figure 1—we tend to organize it quickly into something we can understand, something familiar, something meaningful.

What allows us to make meaning out of random experience? Perceptual psychologists, studying the visual habits of humans, describe a phenomenon they call a *visual concept*.* We are able to see a thing in the real world, they suggest, because we already *expect* to see it; we hold in our minds a *visual concept*—an idea of the way it looks—that allows us to perceive it. We check the incoming visual signals against our stock of visual concepts, or mental pictures; when the signal matches the concept we "see" the thing out there and "recognize" it, largely

Figure 1. (From Brent D. Ruben and Richard W. Budd, Human Communication Handbook, © 1975 by Hayden Book Co. Reprinted by permission of the publisher.)

because we already knew what it looked like and could, in some sense of the word, look *for* it.

Perhaps this idea will be clearer if we consider another aspect of the same problem: *visual ambiguity.** Glance at Figure 2 quickly and then look away again. What did you see? Actually, there are two possible readings of this famous figure: you may have seen a white vase against

Figure 2. Gestalt psychologists have used this drawing to illustrate figure-ground relationships for many years.

a black background or a pair of black faces against a white background. Which did you see first? Were you able to see both the faces and the vase *before* they were described for you? If you were able to see just one of these, what happened when you learned that this single drawing was built on two visual organizations? Were you able to read it differently once you knew what to look for?

This drawing illustrates another important principle of human perception. Once we have organized a configuration of visual signals into a meaningful pattern by matching it against a visual concept, our perception becomes "stable," and we are not likely to change it unless some serious difficulty forces us to reevaluate what we've seen. Reorganizing our perceptions, looking for another way to read the signals, is a job that requires some effort, and we tend to be comfortable and satisfied with what we see first.

practice 1

1. Another well-known drawing operates on the same principle of visual ambiguity we've been discussing. Look at Figure 3. What two readings can you give to this picture? How are they organized? Is it possible to see both pictures at once? (If you're having trouble finding two pictures in this drawing, look for the rabbit—the creature with its ears sticking out to the left— and the duck—with its bill where the rabbit's ears are.)

2. Now try an experiment. Choose two people who have never seen this drawing before. Say to one, "I want to show you a picture of a rabbit. Now tell me what you see." Then say to the other, "I want to show you a picture of a duck. Now tell me what you see." Can both of your subjects easily see what you've suggested to them? Can they read the other picture (the rabbit or the duck) in the drawing? What do they say when you point it out? The verbal clue that you give to your subjects when you show them the picture is supposed to establish a *perceptual set* * that biases them toward a particular reading. Did the perceptual set operate in the case of your subjects?

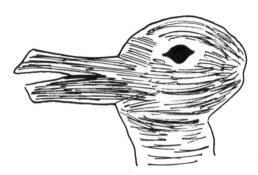

Figure 3. The rabbit-duck drawing was used in 1900 by psychologist Joseph Jastrow as an example of visual ambiguity.

If not, why not? Try out this experiment on more subjects if you are not satisfied with your first findings. Then write a brief report of what you've discovered and discuss your conclusions.

The Organization of Conceptual Structures

Where do visual concepts come from? Are we born with the ability to organize what we see into meaningful perceptions? Or is this ability (like so many other of our human abilities) learned? And if it is learned, who—or what—teaches us? The complete answer to this question is extremely complex, and you'll probably spend a major portion of your college study sorting through various answers to it—in history, in philosophy, in art. We can provide only the barest sketch of an answer here, but it will be sufficient to our purposes and it will enable us to turn our attention to the even more complicated problem of conceptual structures that we raised briefly in Unit 1 and in Unit 8.

The visual concepts that enable us to organize our perceptions in a meaningful way are *not* innate—that is, they are not like the reflexes and instincts we are born with (breathing, eating, and so on). Instead, they are given to us by our culture, which teaches us *which* phenomena, out of all the myriad phenomena in the world, are worth paying attention to.

These visual concepts, however, do not operate simply on the level of perception. They come to us as part of a larger value system. Kenneth Boulding comments on this in his book, *The Image*:

> Even at the level of simple or supposedly simple sense perception we are increasingly discovering that the message which comes through the senses is itself mediated through a value system. We do not perceive our sense data raw; they are mediated through a highly learned process of interpretation and acceptance. When an object apparently increases in size on the retina of the eye, we interpret this not as an increase in size but as movement. Indeed, we only get along in the world because we consistently and persistently disbelieve the plain evidence of our senses. The stick in water is not bent; the movie is not a succession of still pictures; and so on. *What this means is that for any individual organism or organization, there are no such things as "facts." There are only messages filtered through a changeable value system.* (italics added)

The values that Boulding is talking about here, which in turn structure our perception of the world, come to us as we learn our language and as we learn to communicate with those around us who share the same language (and hence the same values). We learn what names to give to things—that is, how to define and classify the objects and events in the world; we learn how to see the relationships among those objects and events.

practice 2

A DRAWING AND WRITING TASK FOR READERS

Visual concepts also come to us through pictorial representations, which give us conventional, stylized forms and patterns in which the "real" world is represented. In this sense, art teaches us to see certain things in certain ways. The following drawing comments on our tendency to reproduce the world through the "filter" of our culture's habits and styles. Can you think of other examples of this same phenomenon in art? Is all art a realistic portrayal of the world around us? If it isn't, who teaches us what forms to use when we draw? Now: make a sketch of some simple figures—a box, for example, and a tree, a mountain, a receding railroad track—that you learned to draw as a child. What details of your drawing work to make a collection of lines on a flat piece of paper look like a three-dimensional object? Look again at the drawing in the text. The "real world" in that drawing is composed of a box, two conventional-looking trees, some assorted curved lines. Do any parts of

your sketches look like parts of this drawing? Look outside at some trees and houses. Do any of them look like the picture, or like your sketches? How could the drawing be considered more a copy of other drawings than a copy of the natural world? How could the drawing being drawn by the artist in the picture be considered more a copy of other drawings than a copy of the "real" world? What is the artist copying, if he isn't copying the world? Write an essay considering these questions, illustrating it, if you like, with your own drawings.

Visual Concepts, Verbal Concepts, and Conceptual Structures

Because visual concepts are defined for us in language, they become almost completely identified with verbal concepts, or definitions, by the time we have entered school. As we grow older, we think more and more in words, as well as in images, and our verbal concepts, like our visual concepts, begin to shape what we see. A clear example of this tendency can be demonstrated by the experiment you performed earlier, in which you established a perceptual set (a predisposition to see a thing in a certain way) by telling your subject what he or she would see in the drawing. In this case, the verbal concept (or definition) *duck* and *rabbit* established a bias toward a particular perception: the verbal concept controlled what the subject saw. Verbal concepts, then, have the same power to enable us to read the world that visual concepts do: we can perceive certain phenomena *because* we have words that define them. Like visual concepts, verbal concepts are also extremely stable, and probably won't be reorganized unless some serious difficulty—what psychologists call "cognitive dissonance"—forces us to reexamine our definitions.

The problem is even more complicated than this, however, for visual and verbal concepts are organized together within a complex network of beliefs, values, and assumptions—what we earlier called our *conceptual structure*. These structures are extremely stable patterns of beliefs about the world around us that serve to organize what we see, how we use language, and how we behave. For instance, within a conceptual structure held in earlier centuries, the earth was seen as the actual, physical center of the universe, and all descriptions of the universe, all drawings, reflected that belief. Human beings, too, were seen as the center of things, with the rest of the creatures on this planet arranged in order beneath them. In a more modern conceptual structure, however, the earth is viewed as a single planet revolving around a single star, in a galaxy of countless other stars. It has been reduced in importance; it is no longer at the center of the universe. Human beings, too, have been reduced in importance: in some views, at least, they are seen to be equal to all of the other creatures on the planet—equal in the sense that no other species must be deprived of existence in order to make man's existence more comfortable.

Conceptual structures, which come to us through our culture—through our spoken language, through our reading, through art, architecture, science—include these central beliefs that organize our understanding of the world and our place in it. But they may also include such beliefs as political and ideological preferences, religious beliefs, belief in the supremacy of one race over another, sexual orientation. These beliefs, perhaps not so central as those which organize reality for us, structure our day-to-day behavior and enable us to make choices and decisions. They also establish the perspective through which we report, in language, our perceptions of the physical and social world.

Psychologists and scholars of language say that the minute we begin to verbalize what we see, the minute we transform our visual concepts into verbal concepts, we begin to refashion what we see—*in the direction of our beliefs and values.* We have a tendency to simplify what we've seen by omitting details. We often reshape what actually occurred by transforming it into more familiar terms. We may sharpen a feature that has some special emotional significance for us, and give it more prominence than it actually had. Describing this problem as it relates to the making of reliable reports, Gordon Allport reports a rumor that took place in a Maine community in the summer of 1945, just before Japan surrendered.

> A Chinese teacher on a solitary vacation drove his car into the community and asked his way to a hilltop from which he could obtain the pleasant view pictured in a tourist guide issued by the Chamber of Commerce in a neighboring town. Someone showed him the way, but within an hour the community was buzzing with the story that *a Japanese spy had ascended the hill to take pictures of the region.*

Allport comments that this incident was distorted because the people of the community reacted out of their biases and preconceptions—out of their beliefs about what Oriental people would do. They simplified the episode by leaving out all contradictory details: the fact that the visitor had courteously asked to be directed to his destination; the fact that no one had seen him carrying a camera. With these troublesome details omitted, they transformed the Oriental into a Japanese (a race they had read about but had probably seen only in movies) and the teacher into a spy, a term familiar to them through wartime news stories. Allport comments:

> A Chinese-teacher-on-a-holiday was a concept that could not arise in the minds of most farmers, for they did not know that some American universities employ Chinese scholars on their staffs and

that these scholars, like other teachers, are entitled to summer holidays.

Together with this transformation, they dwelt on features that seemed of special significance to them. The tourist's desire to find the top of a hill became, Allport says, the "much sharper, sinister purpose of espionage." The fact that the visitor was holding a picture in a guide book was sharpened into the act of picture-taking.

This incident provides an excellent example of a process that goes on every day, for all of us. When we report an event or an idea, in speech or in writing, we can't report all of it: we have to simplify our report and reduce the idea or event to its basic structure in order to communicate it. Because we can't communicate everything, we give only the details that are most significant for us; and because what is familiar is easier to communicate than what is strange, we generally report what our audience is prepared to hear or to read. The language of our report, a product of our conceptual structure, refashions the event itself and our perception of it. As Allport says: "Words sculpture our thoughts and commit us to ideas which are uncertain until uttered."

practice 3

A WRITING TASK FOR READERS

Arthur Ponsonby, in a book entitled *Falsehood in Wartime,* reports a series of newspaper accounts that deal with the fall of Antwerp, Belgium, to the German army in 1914. Read this series of short passages carefully, noting the differences among them.

> When the fall of Antwerp became known, the church bells were rung in Germany. (*Kölnische Zeitung*—Cologne, Germany)
>
> According to the *Kölnische Zeitung,* the clergy of Antwerp were compelled to ring the church bells when the fortress was taken. (*Le Matin*—Paris, France)
>
> According to what *Le Matin* heard from Cologne, the Belgian priests who refused to ring the church bells when Antwerp was taken have been driven away from their positions. (*The Times*—London, England)
>
> According to what *The Times* has heard from Cologne via Paris, the unfortunate priests who refused to ring the church bells when Antwerp was taken have been sentenced to hard labor. (*Corriere della Sera*—Rome, Italy)
>
> According to information to the *Corriere della Sera* from Cologne via London, it is confirmed that the barbaric conquerors of Antwerp punished the unfortunate Belgian priests for their heroic refusal to ring the church bells by hanging them as living clappers to the bells with their heads down. (*Le Matin*)

Write an essay describing how the conceptual structure held by each of these writers shapes the way he relays the story he has received. Can you pick out any evidence of details omitted, events transformed into more familiar terms, or features sharpened because of their special emotional significance?

practice 4

A WRITING TASK FOR READERS

The following comments appeared in *Saturday Review/World*, in response to an article on the distortion of perception. Read it carefully and then write an essay in which you use this passage to comment on the relationship between the visual concepts our culture teaches us to use and the "real" world around us.

How Real Is Our Reality?

I am haunted by one of the experiments described in Roger Lewin's article, "Observing the Brain Through a Cat's Eyes" (*Saturday Review/World*, October 5, 1974). Two groups of kittens are trained in separate, carefully controlled environments. One group can perceive only horizontal lines while the other sees only vertical. When both groups move out into the real world, we are treated to the disquieting spectacle of two sets of intelligent animals, both of the same species (they could even be siblings), both perfectly normal (within the definition of their upbringing); each sharing the same reality, yet experiencing that reality in a radically different manner—each, in fact, quite blind to important segments of the other's universe.

One can easily imagine a society where the horizontal-oriented cats were in the overwhelming majority and in unequivocal political ascendancy. Their view of the world would of course represent the norm. Those few cats who perceived vertically would be "hallucinating." They might be adjudged insane and put away in the crazy-cage. Verticality might even be considered subversive or heretical. . . .

The most pertinent questions that the horizontal and vertical cats give rise to are: how much of our reality is imprinted on us by our culture? And how much is denied us? We are taught what we are taught when we are at our most pliant, long before we have anything to say about it. In the process, what worlds are lost to us? Many creative people in the contemporary human-potential movements are convinced that (just as Don Juan is supposed to have demonstrated to Carlos Castaneda) other realities exist beyond our usual perceptions—realities we could have access to if only we could learn to open ourselves up to them.

Like the horizontally deprived cats, do we blunder around the world, never seeing beautiful places where we might stretch out and ease our souls? Like the missing verticals, do we keep knocking ourselves silly against obstacles we can't see are there?

Conceptual Structures in Written Argument: The Reflection of Ourselves

The point we want to make here is a simple but very emphatic one. Writers "see" through a conceptual structure of stable, well-established assumptions that enable them—even require them—to view the world in a certain way. Their conceptual structures organize their worlds, and what they "see," when they look outside themselves, is the reflection of their own ideas and assumptions. They record that reflection *as though it were the world,* and pass it along to you in their writing. They are recording their perceptions for the purpose of encouraging you to share in them: to adopt their conceptual structures as your own. In that sense, all writing—whether it is an article on the development of the laser in *Scientific American* or a review of American Indians in a history textbook or a newspaper editorial passionately pleading for your support in a local fund drive—is argument.

Where Writing Begins

All writing begins with assumptions about the physical or social or psychological worlds. These beliefs, which are part of the writer's conceptual structure, may have been acquired through the spoken language or through reading; or they may have been developed out of the writer's own personal experience; or even through well-controlled, carefully monitored experiment.

Assumptions that have been acquired scientifically, by experimental observation, occupy a special status in writing. They are used as the basis of formal argument, in what is called *deductive argument.** This form of argument is a complex affair that involves a carefully ordered set of specific relationships among assumptions, or *premises,** ending—if the argument is organized properly—in a valid *conclusion.** Deductive argument is like a geometric proof: given one set of terms and postulating another set of terms, we can draw a conclusion. You may be familiar with the classic form of the deductive argument, the *syllogism* *:

> All men are mortal.
> Socrates is a man.
> Therefore, Socrates is mortal.

Because the deductive argument and its proof, the syllogism, is a subject that deserves more than the sketchy treatment we could give it here, and because readers generally are not required to test an argument through the syllogism, we won't discuss it further. Instead, we'll go on to a discussion of how assumptions are used informally as premises in argument, and how readers can evaluate them.

Evaluating Argument

It's frequently a very difficult matter to determine the assumptions and beliefs that underlie writers' statements, for they do not often tell you exactly what they believe and they are not usually *able* to tell you how their conceptual structures have helped them reshape the world. As a reader, you must evaluate their conceptual structures through an evaluation of their arguments.

The most frequent kind of argument you will encounter in your reading is the *inductive argument.** If you want to make a general statement about a whole group of things (say, a whole group of students or a whole group of automobiles or a whole group of tennis courts), and if you can't measure every single thing or person in the group, what do you do? You look at *some* of the things and then generalize about *all* of the things on the basis of your observation. That is, you argue *inductively* by observing a number of instances or examples and establishing a general conclusion on the basis of those examples.

There are three kinds of inductive argument. Writers may sample several or a large number of specific instances, and may build an argument on these *samples.** Or they may observe that a certain event usually causes another event, establishing an inductive conclusion based on *cause and effect.** Finally, they may observe several similar events and build an inductive argument by *analogy.** Inductive argument is *valid* * when sufficient, acceptable evidence is offered to support it.

Induction by Sample

When writers collect examples, or *samples,* from a larger population of cases, and then establish conclusions based on those samples, they are building an inductive argument by sampling. Whenever a writer employs this method of argument, the reader is faced with the task of evaluating the samples that have been used, the procedures by which they have been collected, and the inductive conclusion that is based on them.

A reader may not always be aware that the writer has used induction by sample. Look at the following statement, for example:

> Last month, in the state of Arkansas, half of the state's cattle population was afflicted with hoof and mouth disease and faced destruction.

How does the writer *know* that half of the cattle in the state are sick? Is he personally acquainted with every report of every ailing cow in the state? No, the writer has probably sampled a portion of the total cattle population in the state and has drawn the conclusion (based on his count) that "half" the cattle in the state are sick. His sampling procedures, however, were probably not direct; his figures are likely to have been drawn from other sources, such as these:

1. The agriculture association in County X reports that 50 percent of the cattle in the county show symptoms of hoof and mouth disease.
2. Ten percent of the cattle in County Y are afflicted, the County Y *Star* says.
3. Three veterinarians in County Z say that they have treated 15 percent of the total population of cattle in the county for the disease.

Given the sampling procedures the writer used, was he justified in his statement that half the cattle in the state have hoof and mouth disease? Are the reports that he relies on all equally reliable? Is it clear that the percentages quoted in the sources add up to "half" the total population?

The criteria for valid induction by sample are relatively simple, and all readers should be able to use them to measure arguments they may find. The sample on which the conclusion is based should be *representative* * (or typical) of the total population. Surprisingly, not all writers observe this rule. Look at the following example, for instance:

YOUNG PEOPLE ARE BECOMING MORE RADICAL

Based on a survey of students enrolled at Boston University, researchers have concluded that young American adults between the ages of 18 and 25 have become more radical in their political beliefs over the past ten years.

Would you say that this conclusion is a valid one? Are students at Boston University representative or typical of all American young people? Your answer, most likely, is "no"; students at Boston University, for many reasons, are probably more "radical" than many community college students and certainly more "radical" than young adults who do not attend college. The researchers on whose report this summary is based have not paid careful attention to their sampling procedures; the group they surveyed is not representative of the larger group about which they wish to make a conclusion.

Representative samples have two characteristics. First, they are usually chosen randomly, from the entire population, and not just from a part of it. For instance, a writer making a statement about *all* young Americans' political beliefs should make sure that the sample has been chosen from both rural and urban populations, from the upper, middle, and lower classes, from educated and uneducated groups, and so on. You are probably familiar with the careful organization of the Gallup polls, which employ telephone directories, voter registration, and street directories as pools of names from which the samples are chosen, ensuring that they will be representative.

Second, a representative sample must be large enough to support the conclusion the writer wants to make. A student, for instance, filed this lab report:

> Over the last three weeks I have observed the growth of three tomato plants, all grown under identical conditions of light and heat. One plant was grown in silence; a second plant was grown to the steady accompaniment of classical music; and a third plant was grown to the steady accompaniment of rock music. Because the plant grown with rock music is now three inches taller and is much bushier than the other two, I conclude that plants grown with rock music will grow faster and better than other plants.

The writer's conclusion is interesting, but invalid, because it is not based on a large enough population. The three plants the writer tested do not offer enough evidence to support a generalization about all plants. The writer has committed the common fallacy, or error, of *hasty generalization.**

Inductive argument based on sampling is a popular form of argument. However, as Darrell Huff argues in the article on the misuse of statistics (pp. 105–14), inductive arguments built in this way are only as valid as the sample that supports them. To test induction by sample, the reader needs to ask whether the sample on which the writer has based his or her argument is representative of the total population and whether it is large enough to cover the variety of individuals within the population.

Cause and Effect Induction

A *Time Magazine* writer recently made the following prediction:

> Measured by the rate at which earlier levels of production have risen after a recession, the U.S. economy's recovery from its worst slump since the 1930's will be swift.

The *Time* writer's prediction is really an inductive argument based on cause and effect. His conclusion that the American economy will recover swiftly is based upon an earlier observation of the rate of business recovery from prior recessions. The conclusion is based upon the writer's observation that, in the past, certain causes were followed by certain effects. Is his inductive conclusion a valid one? If you answer "It all depends," you are probably right—for the validity of his prediction depends on two important factors: whether the writer's earlier observations of the economy are valid; and whether there is a sufficient similarity between the economic situation in the mid-seventies and the economic situations of the past to warrant the conclusion. His prediction is problematic, and careful readers will probably read the article with some cautious skepticism, testing what they know from their own experience and from their other reading against the predictions the writer has made.

This cause-effect inductive argument, like all other cause-effect arguments, is based upon a logical operation that can be represented this way:

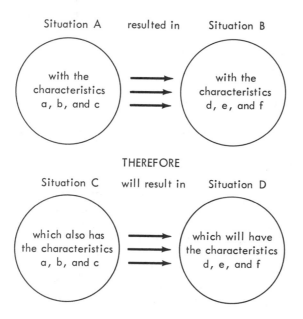

The cause-effect induction, as you can see, is only as valid as the report of the cause-effect relationship. One of the easiest ways to invalidate this kind of argument is to commit a *fallacy*, or error in reasoning, known as the *post hoc fallacy*.* (The term comes from the Latin phrase, *post hoc, ergo propter hoc*—after this, therefore because of this.) This fallacy occurs when the writer connects two events through cause and effect when they are only connected through time. For instance, let's say that a writer studying British economic cycles observes that on several occasions a rise in the birthrate has been followed within five years by a slump in the economy. He writes:

> Research indicates that rising birthrates in England produce economic depressions on a five-year cycle. On this basis we can predict a severe depression in 1978.

The writer's conclusion is not clearly supported by the evidence, however. The mere fact that situation B (the economic slump) *follows* situation A (the rise in birthrate) does not by itself guarantee that situation A *causes* situation B. There might be several other causes of the economic depressions, for instance, that the writer hasn't yet discovered. To support an argument that the events are related through cause and effect, the writer must provide some other convincing evidence of that relationship—evidence other than his or her assertion that they are related and evidence other than a mere connection in time.

Cause-effect induction is useful. It produces such folk sayings as "Red sky at night, sailor's delight; red sky in the morning, sailors take warning"—and prompts such scientific discoveries as the relationship between smoking and lung cancer. Misused, however, it can create faulty predictions that give the appearance of truth because they are based on "logic."

Induction by Analogy

Establishing a conclusion through the observation of analogous, or similar situations, is a third frequently used method of induction. Look at this report, for instance:

> The United States should be more fully aware of its commitments to the Republic of Korea, South Korean officials warned last week. Because of the recent events in Southeast Asia, the Korean government has recently become more insistent upon U.S. observance of its promises.

This statement reports an inductive conclusion drawn by Korean officials and built upon the process of analogy—an inductive argument that goes something like this:

1. The U.S. failed to honor its military and economic commitments in Southeast Asia.
2. The situations in Southeast Asia and in Korea are similar.
3. The U.S. will not honor its commitments in Korea.

Even more abstractly, we might represent the pattern of these analogous relationships like this:

Situation A
has the
characteristics
a, b, c, and d

Situation B
has the
characteristics
a, b, and c.
THEREFORE
It will soon have d.

"Figments" by Dale Hale is reprinted by permission.

Is the conclusion valid? Again, the answer is "It depends"—upon the degree of similarity and difference between situation A and situation B. While induction based upon the observation of analogous situations may allow a writer to make some interesting comparisons, building predictions upon it is still a risky business, and readers need to be aware of that risk. You can evaluate induction by analogy easily, for the conclusion is valid only as long as the comparison can be supported with adequate, relevant evidence, showing that the two situations are indeed comparable *and* that there are no unexpected differences which would invalidate the comparison. The conclusion is invalid if the comparison is insufficiently supported, or if it is founded on a questionable comparison.

Implicit Conclusions *

Sometimes, the writer does not state the conclusion explicitly, but simply leaves it implicit—leaves it for the reader to *infer,* or guess. You'll often find this kind of inductive pattern in cartoons. Look at the cartoon above, for instance. What are the elements of the inductive statement it makes? What conclusion can you infer from this evidence?

The implicit conclusion is effective because it forces the reader to participate, to make sense of the apparently random collection of details or pieces of evidence by creating a general conclusion that fits all of the evidence. (Remember your perception of the dog, in Figure 1, at the beginning of this unit?) If the writer has planned carefully, the conclusion the reader draws will be exactly the one the writer intended.

practice 5

Readers find inductive arguments everywhere—in textbooks, in magazine articles, in editorials. They must first of all learn to recognize the method of inductive argument that the writer is using and they must learn to evaluate it against the criteria for valid induction outlined in the discussion above. Here are a number of examples of inductive argument, some with implicit conclusions. Study each one carefully, identify the inductive method being used, and evaluate the validity of the argument. If the conclusion is implicit, make a note of the conclusion you have drawn from the evidence offered and compare it with the conclusions drawn by students in your class.

A. In Mark Twain's *Huckleberry Finn*, Huck is trying to explain to Jim why it is that French and American speakers speak a different language. Jim is having trouble understanding why he *can't* understand French:

"Looky here, Jim; does a cat talk like we do?"

"No, a cat don't."

"Well, does a cow?"

"No, a cow don't nuther."

"Does a cat talk like a cow, or a cow talk like a cat?"

"No, day don't."

"It's natural and right for 'em to talk different from each other, ain't it?"

"Course."

"And ain't it natural and right for a cat and a cow to talk different from us? You answer me that."

"Is a cat a man, Huck?"

"No."

"Well, den, dey ain't no sense in a cat talkin' like a man. Is a cow a man?—or is a cow a cat?"

"No, she ain't neither of them."

"Well, den, she ain't got no business to talk like either one er the yuther of 'em. Is a Frenchman a man?"

"Yes."

"Well, den! Dad blame it, why doan' he talk like a man? You answer me dat!"

B. In four cities requiring registration of all firearms, murders increased anywhere from 6 percent (New York City) to 102 percent (San Francisco). In the four cities covered by handgun controls only, the murder increase varied from two percent (Baltimore) to 53 percent (Cleveland). In the three cities without firearms restrictions, murders went up 14 percent in one instance (Los Angeles) and down in the other two (Houston—5 percent, Milwaukee, 18 percent).

C. We may observe a very great similitude between this earth which we inhabit and the other planets, Saturn, Jupiter, Mars, Venus, and Mercury. They all revolve around the sun, as the earth does, although at different distances and in different periods. They borrow all their light from the sun, as the earth does. Several of them are known to revolve round their axes like the earth, and, by that means, must have a like succession of day and night. Some of them have moons, that serve to give them light in the absence of the sun, as our moon does to us. They are all, in their motions, subject to the same law of gravitation, as the earth is. From all this similitude, it is not unreasonable to think, that those planets may, like our earth, be the habitation of various order [sic] of living creatures.

D. Late in 1959 the American Cancer Society enrolled 1,078,000 American volunteers in a project designed to produce enough statistics to convince anyone. . . . at the American Medical Association's clinical meetings in Portland, Ore., the Cancer Society's chief statistician, Dr. E. Cuyler Hammond, gave the first of a long series of reports on the million-subject study. . . . Dr. Hammond limited the first report to

422,094 of his volunteers—men aged 40 to 89. . . . Hammond's computer wizards found 36,975 pairs of men who were matched in every conceivable respect except their smoking habits. . . . In the 34 months of the study, the members of these closely matched pairs had very different health experiences. Of the nonsmokers, 662 died. Only twelve died of lung cancer, one from emphysema, 304 of coronary artery disease and eight from aortic aneurysm—leaving 329 for other causes. But among the smokers, 1,385 died—110 of lung cancer, 15 of emphysema, 30 of aortic aneurysm and 654 of coronary disease.

E. Youthful crime is less violent than adult crime. In 1967 9 percent of all persons arrested for murder were under eighteen, compared to 64 percent of the same age arrested for car theft. Only 37 percent of the persons arrested for murder were under twenty-five. Persons under twenty-one accounted for 30 percent of all arrests for aggravated assault, while the proportion of the same age group arrested for burglary, larceny and theft was two and a half times greater. . . . Fifty-four percent of all persons arrested for robbery were under twenty-one in 1967. . . .

F. In a study of 5,000 school-age children in London, Cyril Burt found that the incidence of left-handedness was 4.8 percent among normal children, 7.8 percent among the backward, and 11.9 percent among the retarded. He proved that there is a marked correlation between mental inferiority and left-handedness.

G. This is a big year for major wage settlements. Some 4.5 million workers in companies employing 1,000 or more workers will be getting new contracts, quite a few of them in the double-digit range. If that rate carries into the rest of industry, it will be inflationary. In 1975, wage rate adjustments under major collective bargaining settlements averaged 10.2 percent for the first year of the contract. . . . The economic climate is quite different now; the upswing is slated to continue all year. A rapid advance in corporate earnings is going to whet unions' appetites for fat wage contracts.

H. Another great renewable resource that is disappearing in the U.S. is the land itself. New concrete is poured over nearly one and a half million acres of it every year. By 1975, the U.S. will be building 2.5 million new housing units annually, and half of them will be single-family homes on lots calculated by archaic zoning regulations to waste land. New residential living space alone will annually require a land area nearly half the size of Rhode Island. And new interior roads, not the big expressways but the little neighborhood streets that lead to the front door, will stretch out over 22,000 linear miles—every year. In a little more than a decade, developers will have poured enough concrete over New Suburbia to build a Walnut Street to the moon.

Evaluating Conceptual Structures in Argument

Assumptions in Inductive Argument

At the beginning of this section, we said that all writing begins with assumptions that determine what the writer sees and how that perception is organized for presentation to the reader. If that is true, we can see that writers cannot discover anything new in the world—anything they don't already know. They can see only as far as their conceptual structures—their beliefs and values and assumptions—will let them see.

They can (as a famous scientist once commented) ask only the questions they already have answers for. "The problems are solved," the philosopher Ludwig Wittgenstein said, "not by giving new information, but by arranging what we have always known." In that sense, induction is not the "discovery logic" it is often said to be. The writer begins with a belief about something and then sets out to prove that the assumption is valid. The argument, even if it is arranged so that the conclusion seems to arise out of the evidence, is really built *the other way around*: the conclusion (the assumption) comes first, and the writer searches for appropriate supporting arguments to substantiate it.

That is why it is so important for readers to be able to evaluate not only the visible assumptions that structure the writer's arguments but the invisible assumptions as well—the assumptions that the reader can only infer from the text itself. For an example of this kind of inference-making and careful, critical evaluation, here is a short passage from an essay by Loren Eisley, a scientist and a writer:

> Scarcely had the moon flight been achieved before one U.S. Senator boldly announced: "We are the masters of the universe. We can go anywhere we choose." This statement was widely and editorially acclaimed.

On the face of it, the statement may seem justified by the fact of man's journey to the moon. Eisley, however, sees more clearly the invisible assumptions that structure the Senator's statement: a belief in man's ability to extend himself over all he can see; a faith in progress; a human ethnocentricity that fails to see its own limitations. He comments:

> [The Senator's statement] is a striking example of the comfort of words, also of the covert substitutions and mental projections to which they are subject. The cosmic prison is not made less so by a successful journey of some two hundred and forty thousand miles in a cramped and primitive vehicle. . . . Stars and the great island galaxies in which they cluster are more numerous than the blades of grass upon a plain. To speak of man as "mastering" such a cosmos is about the equivalent of installing a grasshopper as Secretary General of the United Nations. Worse, in fact, for no matter what system of propulsion man may invent in the future, the galaxies on the outer rim of visibility are fleeing faster than he can approach them.

What can we infer about Eisley's beliefs from his criticism of the Senator's words? We can see that he has a different view of man, that he emphasizes not man's power but his limitations, that he stresses not the length of the lunar journey but the tininess of that voyage when it is compared to the expanding universe. The senator, with his experience and interest in politics and government, where man can exert power and feel the results of his exertions, speaks out of a conceptual framework in which man is complete master of the world, where all things are possible. Eisley, the scientist, speaks out of his own first-hand knowledge of the restraints that confine men to their own planet—and even there, make them less than master.

Which of these conceptual structures is "right"? There is no answer to that question. We may believe, with Eisley, that the senator is talking about something that he doesn't know much about—that his view is limited by his lack of knowledge about the vastness of the universe. On the other hand, we may believe, with the senator, that human beings are capable of immense achievements that we cannot now even begin to predict. We may believe that one or another of these views is short-sighted and inadequate. But whatever we believe, we should know that our response to these statements, our evaluation of them, is conditioned by our own conceptual structure and our own tendency to accept statements that are similar to our beliefs and reject those that are significantly different.

How then can we *evaluate* a writer's assumptions? If we can measure a writer's belief only against our own, what kind of objective evaluation can we hope to produce? If we, like the writers we have been describing, can see only the reflection of our own ideas projected onto whatever we are reading and judging, how can we come to any reliable conclusions about the value of any writer's beliefs and assumptions?

Only participating readers can provide an answer to this question. They use their reading as a way of opening new views on the world, accepting the writer's invitation to share actively his or her conceptual framework for the moments they spend reading. During the time they are participating in the writer's world-view, they try to understand it: to feel how it feels to think in this way. For them, reading is the privilege of being a part of someone else's consciousness, getting inside another skin, seeing through another pair of eyes. When they've finished reading, they consciously and critically evaluate that perspective against their own—and evaluate their own perspective as well. If theirs is too narrow, they may broaden it; if it is too broad and undiscriminating, they may construct finer distinctions. They are flexible in their responses and willing to reshape parts of their conceptual structures when they find an intriguing, exciting new view.

In that sense, then, participating readers are reading themselves as well as the page.

READING FOR LANGUAGE AND CONCEPTUAL STRUCTURES

The Implications of Definition

Anti-Intellectualism in Our Time

Images of the Consumer's Mind On and Off Madison Avenue

Behavioral Study of Obedience

Eyewitness Testimony

The Implications of Definition

A FISH VS. A DAM: CAN NATURE WIN?

ATLANTA, Ga.—Can a tiny fish cancel a huge dam project?

Discovery of a rare, three-inch "snail darter" is threatening a $100-million dam being constructed with federal funds by the Tennessee Valley Authority (TVA).

The fish was discovered by a University of Tennessee professor while snorkeling in the Little Tennessee River near Lenoir City, some 20 miles southwest of Knoxville.

Federal wildlife officials are worried that operation of TVA's Tellico Dam now under construction near the site of the discovery would destroy the snail darter's only known habitat.

Environmentalists regard the snail darter's plight as a classic case of "progress" versus nature. It also shapes up as a difficult test for the Endangered Species Act of 1973.

TVA officials are resisting efforts to list the snail darter as a "rare and endangered" species. Such a listing could automatically trigger provisions of the Endangered Species Act and force cancellation of the Tellico project within two months.

TVA officials express doubt that the snail darter is actually a distinct species; and they hint that the fish is being used as a ploy by ecologists to kill the long-fought Tellico project.

Already $55 million has been spent on the dam and reservoir, which would provide additional electrical power and flood control for the eastern Tennessee area.

Dr. David A. Etnier, an ichthyologist and discoverer of the snail darter, describes it as a perch-like fish, greenish-brown, with rough scales. It feeds primarily on snails. To survive it requires swift-flowng waters over a clean riverbed. Tellico Dam would inundate the entire region of the river where the darter is known to exist.

Federal wildlife officials have reviewed the scientific studies that Dr.

By John Dillin, TCSM May 2, 1975. Reprinted by permission from The Christian Science Monitor. © 1975 The Christian Science Publishing Society. All rights reserved.

Etnier has prepared on the snail darter, and they say the research appears to be sound.

Dr. James D. Williams, fishery biologist for the U. S. Office of Endangered Species, says his department is preparing documents to formally list the darter as an endangered species.

If the listing is approved by the Secretary of the Interior, it would automatically prohibit a federal agency (including TVA) from taking any action that threatens the snail darter.

RULING EQUATES NEW "PRINGLES" TO OLD CHIPS

WASHINGTON (UPI)—The Food and Drug Administration Monday turned down objections from the makers of traditional potato chips and ruled that restructured chips of the "Pringles" variety also may be called potato chips.

The only proviso is that the label of such products must also state "Made from dried potatoes."

Makers of the slice-and-fry type of chip, who have been waging a fight against the restructured chips for the last two years, wanted the FDA to force the new products to call themselves "potato snacks" or a similar phrase. The new product has chipped into old-style chips, replacing them in up to 25 per cent of sales.

The traditional potato chip forces had contended consumers were being deceived by the phrase "potato chips" since the new varieties are made of chopped-up potatoes reshaped into a "perfect" size and stacked in cans.

But the FDA said the addition of the phrase "Made from dried potatoes" should take care of that, and the new chips otherwise meet the dictionary definition of a potato chip.

The regulation is effective on December 31, 1977.

In related actions the agency also ruled that onion rings made from chipped onions, rather than actual rings, shall be called "onion rings made from dried, diced onions," and that seafood products made from chopped fish, clams or shrimp shall be labeled "Made from minced fish."

THE SEX SHOPPE

Opening a massage parlor in Austin isn't easy. Just ask Claude Branton.

Branton is trying to open "The Sex Shoppe" at 507 W. Seventh St. (near several city historical landmarks), but an establishment offering steam baths, sex films and the like must meet certain specifications, according to city building inspection, health and planning departments.

Armand Ablando, assistant director of building inspection, said Branton came to the department Thursday morning and was informed of the requirements which must be met to open a massage parlor.

By Mark Browning, Texan Staff Writer, for The Daily Texan, *University of Texas, March 17, 1976.*

Proper zoning for "The Sex Shoppe" is another area of contention with city departments.

"Massage parlors are considered physical therapy and therefore are allowed office zoning," Ablando said, "but the sale of certain items isn't allowed." For example, he said, if movies were to be shown on the premises for commercial purposes, commercial zoning would be required, as it would for any other theater.

"Running an entertainment show is different from running a personal service business," Ablando said.

Steam baths would present another problem, Lawrence DeRoche of the health department said.

"The definition of massage parlors would include not only the giving of massages, but also steam baths," he said. "That requires a permit."

To get a health department permit, an application must be filled out in quadruplicate, DeRoche said. Copies are sent to the building inspection department, fire department and police department.

WHEN FAMILIES GO TO COURT

A widespread legal trend to overturn rules defining who can sue whom not only has made companies more liable for their products, but also has intruded into family relations. The old prohibition that husband and wife may not sue each other for injuries is falling in state after state, and some legal scholars argue for discarding the similar ban on children suing their parents. But Indiana, in the most recent ruling on the subject, declines to go that far. Although it abolished "interspousal immunity" two years ago, the state refuses to put an end to parent-child immunity because "the tendencies of unrestrained youth" that were cited when the rule was first imposed in 1924 still demand "the continuance of parental control."

Study Questions: "The Implications of Definition"

1. Each of the four examples in this reading presents a problem in defining. Identify the term(s) being defined and outline the definitions offered. Classify the definition according to the categories you learned in Unit 8. Evaluate the definition. What are the special problems in defining each term?

2. Why is the definition important in each of these instances? What factors besides a desire for accuracy determine how the term will be defined? Are there important social, political, or legal implications of any of these problems?

3. After you have examined each of these examples individually, what general conclusion can you draw about (a) the importance of definition in our society and (b) the motives or factors that influence how a term will be defined?

From Business Week, *February 16, 1976, p. 54. Reprinted by permission.*

Anti-Intellectualism in Our Time

1   Before giving some examples of what I mean by anti-intellectualism, I may perhaps explain what I do *not* mean. I am not dealing, except incidentally, with the internal feuds or contentions of the American intellectual community. American intellectuals, like intellectuals elsewhere, are often uneasy in their role; they are given to moments of self-doubt, and even of self-hatred, and at times they make *acidulous*[1] and sweeping comments on the whole tribe to which they belong. This internal criticism is revealing and interesting, but it is not my main concern. Neither is the ill-mannered or ill-considered criticism that one intellectual may make of another. No one, for example, ever poured more scorn on the American professoriat than H. L. Mencken, and no one has portrayed other writers in fiction with more venom than Mary McCarthy; but we would not on this account dream of classing Mencken with William F. Buckley as an enemy of the professors nor Miss McCarthy with the late senator of the same name.[I] The criticism of other intellectuals is, after all, one of the most

From Anti-Intellectualism in American Life, *by Richard Hofstadter.* © *1962, 1963 by Richard Hofstadter. Reprinted by permission of Alfred A. Knopf, Inc.*

[1] Critical, with an acid quality.

[I] These considerations serve as a forcible reminder that there is in America, as elsewhere, a kind of intellectual establishment that embraces a wide range of views. It is generally understood (although there are marginal cases) whether a particular person is inside or outside this establishment. The establishment has a double standard for evaluating the criticism of the intellectuals: criticism from within is commonly accepted as having a basically benign intent and is more likely to be heard solely on its merits; but criticism from outside— even the same criticism—will be resented as hostile and stigmatized as anti-intellectual and potentially dangerous. For example, some years ago many intellectuals were critical of the great foundations for devoting too much of their research money to the support of large-budget "projects," as opposed to individual scholarship. But when the Reece Committee was hot on the trail of the foundations, the same intellectuals were not happy to see the same criticism (among others more specious) pressed by such an agency. It was not that they had ceased to believe in the criticism but that they neither liked nor trusted the source.

Of course, not only intellectuals do this; it is a common phenomenon of group life. Members of a political party or a minority group may invoke a similar double standard against criticism, depending on whether it originates from inside or outside the ranks. There is, moreover, some justification for such double standards, in historical fact if not in logic, because the intent that lies behind criticism unfortunately becomes an ingredient in its applicability. The intellectuals who criticized the foundations were doing so in the hope (as they saw it) of constructively modifying foundation policies, whereas the line of inquiry pursued by the Reece Committee might have led to crippling or destroying them. Again, everyone understands that a joke, say, about Jews or Negroes has different overtones when it is told within the group and when it is told by outsiders.

important functions of the intellectual, and he customarily performs it with *vivacity*.[2] We may hope, but we can hardly expect, that he will also do it with charity, grace, and precision. Because it is the business of intellectuals to be diverse and contrary-minded, we must accept the risk that at times they will be merely quarrelsome.

2   It is important, finally, if we are to avoid hopeless confusion, to be clear that anti-intellectualism is not here identified with a type of philosophical doctrine which I prefer to call anti-rationalism. The ideas of thinkers like Nietzsche, Sorel, or Bergson, Emerson, Whitman, or William James, or of writers like William Blake, D. H. Lawrence, or Ernest Hemingway may be called anti-rationalist; but these men were not characteristically anti-intellectual in the sociological and political sense in which I use the term. It is of course true that anti-intellectualist movements often invoke the ideas of such anti-rationalist thinkers (Emerson alone has provided them with a great many texts); but only when they do, and only marginally, is highbrow anti-rationalism a part of my story. In these pages I am centrally concerned with widespread social attitudes, with political behavior, and with middle-brow and low-brow responses, only incidentally with *articulate*[3] theories. The attitudes that interest me most are those which would, to the extent that they become effective in our affairs, gravely inhibit or impoverish intellectual and cultural life. Some examples, taken from our recent history, may put flesh on the bones of definition. We might begin with some definitions supplied by those most acutely dissatisfied with American intellectuals.

3   *Exhibit A.* During the campaign of 1952, the country seemed to be in need of some term to express that disdain for intellectuals which had by then become a self-conscious *motif*[4] in American politics. The word *egghead* was originally used without invidious associations,[2] but quickly assumed them, and acquired a much sharper overtone than the traditional *highbrow.* Shortly after the campaign was over, Louis Bromfield, a popular novelist of right-wing political persuasion, suggested that the word might someday find its way into dictionaries as follows:[3]

> *Egghead:* A person of spurious intellectual pretensions, often a professor or the protégé of a professor. Fundamentally superficial. Overemotional and

[2] Liveliness, spirited energy.

[3] Well-formulated and clearly presented.

[4] Theme or main idea to be elaborated.

[2] The term was taken up as a consequence of a column by Stewart Alsop, in which that reporter recorded a conversation with his brother John. The columnist remarked that many intelligent people who were normally Republicans obviously admired Stevenson. "Sure," said his brother, "all the egg-heads love Stevenson. But how many egg-heads do you think there are?" Joseph and Stewart Alsop: *The Reporter's Trade* (New York, 1958), p. 188.

[3] Louis Bromfield: "The Triumph of the Egghead." *The Freeman.* Vol. III (December 1, 1952), p. 158.

feminine in reactions to any problem. *Supercilious* [5] and *surfeited* [6] with conceit and contempt for the experience of more sound and able men. Essentially confused in thought and immersed in mixture of sentimentality and violent evangelism. A *doctrinaire* [7] supporter of Middle-European socialism as opposed to Greco-French-American ideas of democracy and liberalism. Subject to the old-fashioned philosophical morality of Nietzsche which frequently leads him into jail or disgrace. A self-conscious prig, so given to examining all sides of a question that he becomes thoroughly addled while remaining always in the same spot. An anemic bleeding heart.

4   "The recent election," Bromfield remarked, "demonstrated a number of things, not the least of them being the extreme remoteness of the 'egghead' from the thought and feeling of the whole of the people."

5   *Exhibit B.* Almost two years later President Eisenhower appeared to give official sanction to a similarly disdainful view of intellectuals. Speaking at a Republican meeting in Los Angeles in 1954, he reported a view, expressed to him by a trade-union leader, that the people, presented with the whole truth, will always support the right cause. The President added: [4]

> It was a rather comforting thought to have this labor leader saying this, when we had so many wisecracking so-called intellectuals going around and showing how wrong was everybody who don't happen to agree with them.

> By the way, I heard a definition of an intellectual that I thought was very interesting: *a man who takes more words than are necessary to tell more than he knows.*

6   *Exhibit C.* One of the issues at stake in the controversies of the 1950's was the old one about the place of expertise in political life. Perhaps the high moment in the case against the expert and for the amateur occurred in 1957 when a chain-store president, Maxwell H. Gluck, was nominated to be ambassador to Ceylon. Mr. Gluck had contributed, by his own estimate, $20,000 or $30,000 to the Republican campaign of 1956, but, like many such appointees before him, was not known for having any experience in politics or diplomacy. Questioned by Senator Fulbright about his qualifications for the post, Mr. Gluck had some difficulty: [5]

---

[5] Contemptuous, haughty.

[6] Overindulged, filled.

[7] Dogmatically insisting on applying a theory to a situation regardless of the practical problems involved.

4 White House Press Release, "Remarks of the President at the Breakfast Given by Various Republican Groups of Southern California, Statler Hotel, Los Angeles ... September 24, 1954," p. 4; italics added. It is possible that the President had heard something of the kind from his Secretary of Defense, Charles E. Wilson, who was quoted elsewhere as saying: "An egghead is a man who doesn't understand everything he knows." Richard and Gladys Harkness: "The Wit and Wisdom of Charlie Wilson," *Reader's Digest,* Vol. LXXI (August, 1957), p. 197.

5 *The New York Times,* August 1, 1957.

Fulbright: What are the problems in Ceylon you think you can deal with?

   Gluck: One of the problems are the people there. I believe I can—I think I can establish, unless we—again, unless I run into something that I have not run into before—a good relationship and good feeling toward the United States. . . .

Fulbright: Do you know our Ambassador to India?

   Gluck: I know John Sherman Cooper, the previous Ambassador.

Fulbright: Do you know who the Prime Minister of India is?

   Gluck: Yes, but I can't pronounce his name.

Fulbright: Do you know who the Prime Minister of Ceylon is?

   Gluck: His name is unfamiliar now, I cannot call it off.

Doubts about Mr. Gluck's preparation for the post he was to occupy led to the suggestion that he had been named because of his contribution to the Republican campaign. In a press conference held July 31, 1957, a reporter raised the question, whereupon President Eisenhower remarked that an appointment in return for campaign contributions was unthinkable. About his nominee's competence, he observed: [6]

> Now, as to the man's ignorance, this is the way he was appointed: he was selected from a group of men that were recommended highly by a number of people I respect. His business career was examined, the F.B.I. reports on him were all good. Of course, we knew he had never been to Ceylon, he wasn't thoroughly familiar with it; but certainly he can learn if he is the kind of character and kind of man we believe him to be.

It is important to add that Mr. Gluck's service in Ceylon was terminated after a year by his resignation.

7   *Exhibit D.*   One of the grievances of American scientists was their awareness that America's disdain for pure science was a handicap not only to investigation but also to the progress of research and development in the Department of Defense. Examining Secretary of Defense Charles E. Wilson in 1954 before the Senate Committee on Armed Services, Senator Stuart Symington of Missouri quoted earlier testimony in which the Secretary had said, among other things, that if there was to be pure research it should be subsidized by some agency other than the Department of Defense. "I am not much interested," Secretary Wilson had testified, "as a military project in why potatoes turn brown when they are fried." Pressing Secretary Wilson, Senator Symington pointed to testimony that had been given about the lack of sufficient money for research not on potatoes but on bombers, nuclear propulsion, electronics, missiles, radar, and other subjects. The Secretary replied: [7]

> Important research and development is going on in all those areas. . . .
>
> On the other side, it is very difficult to get these men who are trying to think

[6] Ibid.

[7] U.S. Congress, 84th Congress, 2nd session, Senate Committee on Armed Services: *Hearings*, Vol. XVI, pp. 1742, 1744 (July 2, 1956): italics added.

out ahead all the time to come down to brass tacks and list the projects and what they expect to get. . . .

They would just like to have a pot of money without too much supervision that they could reach into. . . .

In the first place, *if you know what you are doing, why it is not pure research.* That complicates it.

8   *Exhibit E.*   The kind of anti-intellectualism expressed in official circles during the 1950's was mainly the traditional businessman's suspicion of experts working in any area outside his control, whether in scientific laboratories, universities, or diplomatic corps. Far more acute and sweeping was the hostility to intellectuals expressed on the far-right wing, a categorical folkish dislike of the educated classes and of anything respectable, established, pedigreed, or cultivated. The right-wing crusade of the 1950's was full of heated rhetoric about "Harvard professors, twisted-thinking intellectuals . . . in the State Department"; those who are "burdened with Phi Beta Kappa keys and academic honors" but not "equally loaded with honesty and common sense"; "the American respectables, the socially pedigreed, the culturally acceptable, the certified gentlemen and scholars of the day, dripping with college degrees . . . the 'best people' who were for Alger Hiss"; "the pompous diplomat in striped pants with phony British accent"; those who try to fight Communism "with kid gloves in perfumed drawing rooms"; Easterners who "insult the people of the great Midwest and West, the *heart* of America"; those who can "trace their ancestry back to the eighteenth century—or even further" but whose loyalty is still not above suspicion; those who understand "the Groton vocabulary of the Hiss-Acheson group." [8] The spirit of this rhetorical *jacquerie* [8] was caught by an editorial writer for the *Freeman:* [9]

> The truly appalling phenomenon is the irrationality of the college-educated mob that has descended upon Joseph R. McCarthy. . . . Suppose Mr. McCarthy were indeed the cad the "respectable" press makes him out to be; would this . . . justify the cataclysmic eruptions that, for almost a year now, have emanated from all the better appointed editorial offices of New York and Washington, D.C.? . . . It must be something in McCarthy's personal makeup. He possesses, it seems, a sort of animal negative-pole magnetism which repels alumni of Harvard, Princeton and Yale. And we think we know what it is: This young man is constitutionally incapable of deference to social status.

McCarthy himself found the central reasons for America's difficulties in areas where social status was most secure. The trouble, he said in the published version of his famous Wheeling speech, lay in [10]

[8] A peasants' revolt (specifically, the French peasants' revolt of 1358).

[8] This mélange of images is taken from the more extended account of the scapegoats of the 1950's in Immanuel Wallerstein's unpublished M.A. essay: "McCarthyism and the Conservative," Columbia University, 1954, pp. 46 ff.

[9] *Freeman,* Vol. XI (November 5, 1951), p. 72.

[10] *Congressional Record,* 81st Congress, 2nd session, p. 1954 (February 20, 1950).

the traitorous actions of those who have been treated so well by this Nation. It has not been the less fortunate or members of minority groups who have been selling this Nation out, but rather those who have had all the benefits that the wealthiest nation on earth has had to offer—the finest homes, the finest college education, and the finest jobs in Government we can give. This is glaringly true in the State Department. There the bright young men who are born with silver spoons in their mouths are the ones who have been worst.

9   *Exhibit F.* The universities, particularly the better-known universities, were constantly marked out as targets by right-wing critics; but according to one writer in the *Freeman* there appears to have been only an arbitrary reason for this discrimination against the Ivy League, since he considered that Communism is spreading in all our colleges: [11]

Our universities are the training grounds for the barbarians of the future, those who, in the guise of learning, shall come forth loaded with pitchforks of ignorance and cynicism, and stab and destroy the remnants of human civilization. It will not be the subway peasants who will tear down the walls: they will merely do the bidding of our learned brethren . . . who will erase individual Freedom from the ledgers of human thought. . . .

If you send your son to the colleges of today, you will create the Executioner of tomorrow. The rebirth of idealism must come from the scattered monasteries of non-collegiate thought.

10   *Exhibit G.* Right-wing hostility to universities was in part a question of deference and social status, but in part also a reflection of the old Jacksonian dislike of specialists and experts. Here is a characteristic assertion about the equal competence of the common man (in this case the common woman) and the supposed experts, written by the amateur economist, Frank Chodorov, author of *The Income Tax: The Root of All Evil,* and one of the most engaging of the right-wing spokesmen: [12]

A parcel of eminent economists, called into consultation by the Rockefeller Brothers Fund to diagnose the national ailment known as recession, came up with a prescription that, though slightly condensed, covered the better part of two pages in *The New York Times.* The prominence of these doctors makes it presumptuous for one who has not "majored" in economics to examine the ingredients of their curative concoction. Yet the fact is that all of us are economists by necessity, since all of us are engaged in making a living, which is what economics is all about. Any literate housewife, endowed with a modicum of common sense, should be able to evaluate the specfiics in the prescription, provided these are extracted from the verbiage in which they are clothed.

11   *Exhibit H.* Although the following may well be considered by discriminating readers as anti-cultural rather than anti-intellectual, I cannot omit some remarks by Congressman George Dondero of Michigan, long a vigilant crusader against Communism in the schools and against cubism,

[11] Jack Schwartzman: "Natural Law and the Campus," *Freeman,* Vol. II (December 3, 1951), pp. 149, 152.

[12] "Shake Well before Using," *National Review,* Vol. V (June 7, 1958), p. 544.

expressionism, surrealism, dadaism, futurism, and other movements in art: [13]

> The art of the isms, the weapon of the Russian Revolution, is the art which has been transplanted to America, and today, having infiltrated and saturated many of our art centers, threatens to overawe, override and overpower the fine art of our tradition and inheritance. So-called modern or contemporary art in our own beloved country contains all the isms of depravity, decadence, and destruction. . . .
>
> All these isms are of foreign origin, and truly should have no place in American art . . . All are instruments and weapons of destruction.

12   *Exhibit I.* Since I shall have much to say in these pages about anti-intellectualism in the evangelical tradition, it seems important to cite at least one survival of this tradition. These brief quotations are taken from the most successful evangelist of our time, Billy Graham, voted by the American public in a Gallup Poll of 1958 only after Eisenhower, Churchill and Albert Schweitzer as "the most admired man in the world": [14]

> Moral standards of yesterday to many individuals are no standard for today unless supported by the so-called "intellectuals."
>
> I sincerely believe that partial education throughout the world is far worse than none at all, if we only educate the mind without the soul. . . . Turn that man loose upon the world [who has] no power higher than his own, he is a monstrosity, he is but halfway educated, and is more dangerous than though he were not educated at all.
>
> You can stick a public school and a university in the middle of every block of every city in America and you will never keep America from rotting morally by mere intellectual education.
>
> During the past few years the intellectual props have been knocked out from under the theories of men. Even the average university professor is willing to listen to the voice of the preacher
>
> [In place of the Bible] we substituted reason, rationalism, mind culture, science worship, the working power of government, Freudianism, naturalism, humanism, behaviorism, positivism, materialism, and idealism. . . . [This is the work of] so-called intellectuals. Thousands of these "intellectuals" have publicly stated that morality is relative—that there is no norm or absolute standard. . . .

13   *Exhibit J.* In the post-Sputnik furor over American education, one of the most criticized school systems was that of California, which had been notable for its experimentation with curricula. When the San Francisco

---

[13] *Congressional Record,* 81st Congress, 1st session, p. 11584 (August 16, 1949); see also Dondero's address on "Communism in Our Schools," *Congressional Record,* 79th Congress, 2nd session, pp. A. 3516–18 (June 14, 1946), and his speech, "Communist Conspiracy in Art Threatens American Museums," *Congressional Record,* 82nd Congress, 2nd session, pp. 2423–7 (March 17, 1952).

[14] William G. McLoughlin, Jr.: *Billy Graham: Revivalist in a Secular Age* (New York, 1960), pp. 89, 212, 213; on the Gallup Poll, see p. 5.

School District commissioned a number of professional scholars to examine their schools, the committee constituted for this purpose urged a return to firmer academic standards. Six educational organizations produced a sharp counterattack in which they criticized the authors of the San Francisco report for "academic pettiness and snobbery" and for going beyond their competence in limiting the purposes of education to "informing the mind and developing the intelligence," and reasserted the value of "other goals of education, such as preparation for citizenship, occupational competence, successful family life, self-realization in ethical, moral, aesthetic and spiritual dimensions, and the enjoyment of physical health." The educationists argued that an especially praiseworthy feature of American education had been [15]

> the attempt to avoid a highly rigid system of education. To do so does not mean that academic competence is not regarded as highly important to any society, but it does recognize that historically, *education systems which stress absorption of accumulated knowledge for its own sake have tended to produce decadence.* Those who would "fix" the curriculum and freeze educational purpose misunderstand the unique function of education in American democracy.

14   *Exhibit K.*   The following is an excerpt from a parent's report, originally written in answer to a teacher's complaint about the lax standards in contemporary education. The entire piece is worth reading as a vivid statement by a parent who identifies wholly with the non-academic child and the newer education. As we shall see, the stereotype of the school-teacher expressed here has deep historical roots. [16]

> But kindergarten teachers understand children. Theirs is a child-centered program. School days were one continuous joy of games and music and colors and friendliness. Life rolled merrily along through the first grade, the second grade, the third grade ... then came arithmetic! Failure like a spectre arose to haunt our days and harass our nights. Father and mother began to attend lectures on psychology and to read about inferiority complexes. We dragged through the fourth grade and into the fifth. Something had to be done. Even father couldn't solve all the problems. I decided to have a talk with the teacher.
>
> There was no welcome on the mat of that school. No one greeted the stranger or made note of his coming. A somber hallway presented itself, punctuated at regular intervals by closed doors. Unfamiliar sounds came from within. I inquired my way of a hurrying youngster and then knocked at the forbidding threshold. To the teacher I announced my name, smiling as pleasantly as I could. "Oh, yes," she said, as if my business were already known to her and reached for her classbook, quick on the draw like a movie gangster clutching for his gun.

[15] *Judging and Improving the Schools: Current Issues* (Burlingame, California, 1960), pp. 4, 5, 7, 8; italics added. The document under fire was William C. Bark et al.: *Report of the San Francisco Curriculum Survey Committee* (San Francisco, 1960).
[16] Robert E. Brownlee: "A Parent Speaks Out," *Progressive Education,* Vol. XVII (October, 1940), pp. 420–41.

The names of the pupils appeared on a ruled page in neat and alphabetical precision. The teacher moved a bloodless finger down the margin of the page to my daughter's name. After each name were little squares. In the squares were little marks, symbols that I did not understand. Her finger moved across the page. My child's marks were not the same as those of the other children. She looked up triumphantly as if there were nothing more to be said. I was thinking of the small compass into which she had compressed the total activities of a very lively youngster. I was interested in a whole life, a whole personality; the teacher, merely in arithmetical ability. I wished I had not come. I left uninformed and uncomforted.

15   *Exhibit L.*   The following remarks have already been made famous by Arthur Bestor, but they will bear repetition. After delivering and publishing the address excerpted here, the author, a junior high-school principal in Illinois, did not lose caste in his trade but was engaged for a similar position in Great Neck, Long Island, a post which surely ranks high in desirability among the nation's secondary schools, and was subsequently invited to be a visiting member of the faculty of the school of education of a Midwestern university.[17]

Through the years we've built a sort of halo around reading, writing, and arithmetic. We've said they were for everybody ... rich and poor, brilliant and not-so mentally-endowed, ones who liked them and those who failed to go for them. Teacher has said that these were something "everyone should learn." The principal has remarked, "All educated people know how to write, spell, and read." When some child declared a dislike for a sacred subject, he was warned that, if he failed to master it, he would grow up to be a so-and-so.

The Three R's for All Children, and All Children for the Three R's! That was it.

We've made some progress in getting rid of that slogan. But every now and then some mother with a Phi Beta Kappa award or some employer who has hired a girl who can't spell stirs up a fuss about the schools ... and ground is lost. ...

When we come to the realization that not every child has to read, figure, write and spell ... that many of them either cannot or will not master these chores ... then we shall be on the road to improving the junior high curriculum.

Between this day and that a lot of selling must take place. But it's coming. We shall some day accept the thought that it is just as illogical to assume that every boy must be able to read as it is that each one must be able to perform on a violin, that it is no more reasonable to require that each girl shall spell well than it is that each one shall bake a good cherry pie.

We cannot all do the same things. We do not like to do the same things. And we won't. When adults finally realize that fact, every one will be happier ... and schools will be nicer places in which to live. ...

[17] A. H. Lauchner: "How Can the Junior High School Curriculum Be Improved?" *Bulletin of the National Association of Secondary-School Principals,* Vol. XXXV (March, 1951), pp. 299–301. The three dots of elision here do not indicate omissions but are the author's punctuation. The address was delivered at a meeting of this association. See Arthur Bestor's comments in *The Restoration of Learning* (New York, 1955), p. 54.

If and when we are able to convince a few folks that mastery of reading, writing, and arithmetic is not the one road leading to happy, successful living, the next step is to cut down the amount of time and attention devoted to these areas in general junior high-school courses. . . .

One junior high in the East has, after long and careful study, accepted the fact that some twenty percent of their students will not be up to standard in reading . . . and they are doing other things for these boys and girls. That's straight thinking. Contrast that with the junior high which says, "Every student must know the multiplication tables before graduation."

16   These exhibits, though their sources and intentions are various, collectively display the ideal assumptions of anti-intellectualism. Intellectuals, it may be held, are pretentious, conceited, effeminate, and snobbish; and very likely immoral, dangerous, and subversive. The plain sense of the common man, especially if tested by success in some demanding line of practical work, is an altogether adequate substitute for, if not actually much superior to, formal knowledge and expertise acquired in the schools. Not surprisingly, institutions in which intellectuals tend to be influential, like universities and colleges, are rotten to the core. In any case, the discipline of the heart, and the old-fashioned principles of religion and morality, are more reliable guides to life than an education which aims to produce minds responsive to new trends in thought and art. Even at the level of elementary education, a schooling that puts too much stress on the acquisition of mere knowledge, as opposed to the vigorous development of physical and emotional life, is heartless in its mode of conduct and threatens to produce social decadence.

Study Questions: "Anti-Intellectualism in Our Time"

1. Explain in detail the form of definition Hofstadter uses in his essay. Consider paragraphs 1 to 2, 3 to 15, and 16 as units. How does the method of definition differ in each of these units?
2. What method of induction does the author use? What is your evaluation of the validity of this method?
3. When Hofstadter formulates his definition of anti-intellectualism and attempts to substantiate his definition through argument, is he only interested in making our language more useful by clarifying the meaning of one of its terms, or does he have another purpose? What might it be? Substantiate your answer with references to the text.
4. Many people agree with the anti-intellectual attitudes Hofstadter is criticizing. How does he manage to discredit the anti-intellectuals' position without actually arguing against it? Recall what you learned about slanting by association in Unit 2 and about sampling in Unit 9.
5. Evaluate the emotional language in the statements the writer quotes from anti-intellectuals. What purpose does Hofstadter appear to have had when he selected these quotations?

6. Characterize the values and attitudes of the anti-intellectual position. Hofstadter characterizes them in paragraph 16. Do you agree or disagree with his conclusion?
7. Characterize the author's position by determining what he values and what stand he is likely to take on the issues raised by anti-intellectuals.
8. Compare your conceptual structure, your value system, with that of each of the opposed views of intellectuals offered in this essay. Which one most closely matches your own? Why?
9. Recalling the ideas you held on these issues before you read the essay, consider whether or not your ideas are different now. If they are, characterize the change you have experienced. If not, suggest why.

Images of the Consumer's Mind
On and Off Madison Avenue

1   The advertising man is not the only person who seeks to shape and change other people's beliefs, attitudes, and behavior. There are many kinds of people in our society, professional and non-professional, working for pay and for free, who for various combinations of *altruistic* [1] and selfish reasons are vitally interested in the theory and in the practice of shaping and changing other people's values, beliefs, attitudes, and behavior. Let me point, by way of illustration, to the psychotherapist, to the teacher, the missionary, the politician, and the lobbyist. All these have in common, with the advertising man, the desire to influence and to persuade others to believe and to act in certain ways in which they would not otherwise believe and act.

2   This does not mean that the advertising man wants to change the same sort of beliefs which, say, the therapist or the politician wants to change. Every human being has many different kinds of beliefs, and every advanced society seems to have encouraged the growth of different kinds of persuaders who specialize in trying to change some kinds of belief and not other kinds.

3   What, then, are the different kinds of beliefs which all men have and what kinds of beliefs does the advertising man wish most to influence? What are the properties of the different kinds of beliefs, and how easily is one kind changed compared with another kind? And what are the special problems which arise to plague the advertising man because of the fact that he specializes in trying to change certain kinds of beliefs and not other kinds, and what can he do about these problems?

4   To answer these questions, I would like to tell you about five kinds of beliefs which we have thus far isolated in our work at Michigan State University. This work is part of a larger, on-going program of research

By Milton Rokeach. Reprinted from Etc., *Vol. XXI, no. 3 by permission of the International Society for General Semantics.*

[1] Unselfish.

extending over the past decade on the nature of man's systems of belief: how such systems of belief are formed, organized, and modified, and how such systems differ from one person to the next.

5   To begin with, all persons are assumed to have belief systems, and each belief system contains tens of thousands of beliefs. These beliefs can not all be equally important to the person possessing them. It is necessary to assume that beliefs vary along a continuum of importance or centrality. Further, we must assume that the more important a belief the more it will resist change and the more trivial a belief the more easily it can be changed. And, finally, we must assume that the more important a belief which is changed, the more widespread the repercussions in the rest of the person's belief system, because many of the beliefs "hooked up" with it will change too.

6   The five kinds of beliefs which I will describe may be represented by five concentric circles, with the key beliefs at the center, and the more inconsequential beliefs along the outside circle. To help keep track of them let me call the innermost beliefs Type A, which is then followed by Type B, and so on, until we get to Type E along the outside circle.

7   At the core are Type A beliefs which I call primitive beliefs. These are beliefs we all share with one another about the nature of physical reality, social reality, and the self. For example, *I believe this is a table. I believe this is an audience listening to a speech. I believe my name is Milton Rokeach.* These are all supported by one hundred percent social consensus. Type A beliefs are our taken-for-granted axioms which are not subject to controversy because we believe, and we believe everyone else believes. Such primitive beliefs are fundamental and we have evidence which shows that they are more resistant to change than any other type of belief. And we have obtained additional evidence suggesting that we become extremely upset when Type A beliefs are seriously brought into question.

8   And then there is a second kind of primitive belief—Type B—which is also extremely resistant to change. Such beliefs do not depend on social support or concensus but, instead, arise from deep personal experience. Type B beliefs are *incontrovertible* [2] and we believe them regardless of whether anyone else believes them. Many of these unshakable beliefs are about ourselves and some of these self-conceptions are positive ones—Type B+—and some are negative ones—Type B—. The positive ones represent beliefs about what we are capable of, and the negative ones represent beliefs about what we are afraid of.

9   Let me illustrate some Type B+ beliefs which most of us here probably have. Regardless of what others may think of us, we continue to believe ourselves to be intelligent and rational men, able and competent, basically kind and charitable. Type B+ beliefs represent our positive self-images which guide our aspirations and ambitions to become even better, greater, wiser, and nobler than we already are.

10   But many of us also have Type B— beliefs—negative self-conceptions

[2] Undeniable.

—which we cling to primitively, regardless of whether others may agree with us. We are often beset by phobias, compulsions, obsessions, neurotic self-doubts and anxieties about self-worth, self-identity and self-competence. These are the kinds of primitive beliefs which we only wish we were rid of, and it is these Type B— beliefs which the specialized psychotherapist is often asked to change. Other specialized persuaders are generally not trained or interested in changing Type B— beliefs, but they may be interested in exploiting them without trying to change them.

11   A third kind of belief, Type C, we call authority beliefs—beliefs we all have about which authorities to trust and which not to trust. Many facts of physical and social reality have alternative interpretations, are socially controversial, or are not capable of being personally verified or experienced. For these reasons, all men need to identify with authorities who will help them to decide what to believe and what not to believe. Is communism good or bad? Is there a God or isn't there? How do we know the French Revolution actually took place? What about evolution? No man is personally able to *ascertain* [3] the truth of all such things for himself. So, he believes in this or that authority—parents, teachers, religious leaders, scientists—and he is often willing to take some authority's word for many things. Thus, we all develop beliefs about which authorities are positive and which are negative, differing from one person to the next, and we look to such authorities for information about what is (and is not) true and beautiful, and good for us.

12   A fourth kind of belief, Type D, we call *peripheral* [4] beliefs—beliefs which are *derived* from the authorities we identify with. For example, a devout Catholic has certain beliefs about birth control and divorce because he has accepted them from the authority he believes in. I believe Jupiter has twelve moons, not because I have personally seen them, but because I trust certain kinds of authorities who have seen them. I am quite prepared to revise my belief about Jupiter's moons providing the authorities I trust revise their beliefs. Many people adhere to a particular religious or political belief system because they identify with a particular authority. Such peripheral beliefs can be changed, providing the suggestion for change *emanates* [5] from one's authority, or, providing there is a change in one's authority.

13   Finally, there is a fifth class of beliefs, Type E, which I call inconsequential beliefs. If they are changed, the total system of beliefs is not altered in any significant way. I believe, for example, that you can get a better shave from one brand of razor blade than another; I believe that a vacation at the beach is more enjoyable than one in the mountains; I believe Sophia Loren is prettier than Elizabeth Taylor. But, if you can persuade me to believe the opposite, the change is inconsequential because the rest of my belief system is not likely to be affected in any important way.

[3] To find out with certainty.

[4] Incidental, external, only slightly connected with what is central.

[5] Comes forth.

14   Let me now briefly summarize the five kinds of beliefs: every person's total system of beliefs is composed of beliefs that range in importance from the inconsequential, through the peripheral, to beliefs about authority and, finally, at the core, to primitive beliefs which are extremely resistant to change, either because they do not at all depend on social support or because they enjoy universal social support. All these five kinds of beliefs, considered together, are organized into a remarkable piece of architecture which I call the belief system. It has a definable content and a definable structure. And it has a job to do; it serves adaptive functions for the person, in order to maximize his positive self-image and to minimize his negative self-image. Every person has a need to know himself and his world insofar as possible, and a need not to know himself and his world, insofar as necessary. A person's total belief system, with all its five kinds of beliefs, is designed to serve both functions at once.

15   You might wonder what objective evidence there may be that the five kinds of beliefs I have just described really exist. There is not enough time here to tell you about all our research addressed to this question, but I would like to report that the best evidence we have comes from a study as yet unpublished in which we tried to change the five kinds of beliefs I have described through hypnotic suggestion. This work was done in collaboration with my colleagues Dr. Joseph Reyher and Dr. Richard Wiseman at Michigan State University and the results we obtained are quite clear. Our data show that all five kinds of beliefs change under hypnosis. But as we had expected, the amount of change in belief varies with the centrality of belief: the primitive beliefs, Type A and B, changed the least as a result of hypnotic suggestion. Beliefs about authority, Type C, changed more. Peripheral beliefs, Type D, changed yet more. And inconsequential beliefs, Type E, changed the most.

16   The results also show that changing one kind of belief leads to changes in the other kinds of beliefs, but changes in Type A and B beliefs exert the greatest consequences on other beliefs. Changes in Type C beliefs exert lesser consequences, changes in Type D beliefs exert yet lesser consequences and, finally, Type E beliefs—inconsequential beliefs, the ones most easy to change—exert the least effect on other beliefs.

17   Now, given these five kinds of beliefs as a frame of reference, it is possible to obtain a somewhat clearer picture of what society's specialized persuaders are trying to do, and which kinds of beliefs they wish most to act upon, to influence, and to change. As far as I can tell, there are no specialized persuaders whose main business it is to change the first kind of belief I have described—the Type A beliefs which are universally supported by social consensus. But, as already stated, it is the business of the professional psychotherapist to change the second kind of primitive belief. The psychotherapists' job is to help us get rid of our negative self-conceptions—Type B— beliefs—and to strengthen our positive self-conceptions—Type B+ beliefs.

18   Then, there are other specialized persuaders—the political and religious partisans and ideologists of various persuasions. What sorts of beliefs are they mostly concerned with? I would suggest that their main

focus is on the Type C and Type D beliefs—those I have called authority beliefs and peripheral beliefs.

19   By now, you can perhaps anticipate what I am about to say next about the kinds of beliefs which that specialized persuader—the advertising man—tries to form and to change. Without in any way wishing to deny that the results of advertising may have important economic consequences, it could be stated from a psychological standpoint that the advertising man has concentrated mainly on changing Type E beliefs—inconsequential beliefs—to the extent that his purpose is to meet the competition, and he has concentrated mainly on Type D—peripheral beliefs—to the extent that his purpose is to give information. Furthermore, the more competitive the advertising, the more it addresses itself to changing psychologically inconsequential beliefs about the relative merits of one brand over another.

20   Let me now try to explore with you some implications which seem to follow from the preceding analysis. It is tempting to suggest that at least some of the unique characteristics, problems, and embarrassments besetting the advertising industry stem directly or indirectly from its heavy specialization in changing psychologically inconsequential beliefs, and stem from the additional fact that beliefs which are psychologically inconsequential to the average consumer are highly consequential to all those who economically need to advertise.

21   I have already mentioned our finding that inconsequential beliefs are generally easier to change than other kinds of beliefs. This does not mean, however, that the consumer will passively yield to others' efforts to change such beliefs. We generally resist changing *all* our beliefs because we gain comfort in clinging to the familiar and because all our beliefs, as I have tried to suggest, serve highly important functions for us.

22   So the advertising man, while he has a psychological advantage over other persuaders specializing in changing more central beliefs, still has to find economical ways of changing the less consequential beliefs in which he specializes. This he has often tried to do by developing methods for shaking the consumer loose from his belief regarding the inconsequential virtues of a particular brand over a competitor's in order to make him believe instead that the difference does make a difference. He tries to convince the consumer that there are important benefits to be gained by changing brands, that deeper beliefs and needs will be better satisfied. The advertising industry has frequently been successful in achieving this aim and, sometimes, miraculously so.

23   How? In line with my analysis, I would suggest that the advertiser's goal is achieved by associating the fifth kind of belief, Type E—the inconsequential beliefs—with other kinds of beliefs tapping psychologically more consequential beliefs and wants.

24   But what are the other kinds of beliefs which are most frequently associated with Type E beliefs? Theoretically, it is possible to associate the inconsequential beliefs with Type D, or C, or B+, or B—, or A beliefs, but the advertising industry does not use all these combinations with equal frequency. The associations which seem to come up most often in

competitive advertising are those between Types E and C (the authority beliefs, as in testimonials) and between Types E and B— (as in the old Lifebuoy ads on B.O. or in the more sophisticated Maidenform Bra ads which exploit primitive fears or primitive self-conceptions concerning insufficient femininity).

25   Why should these two combinations come up more often than the other possible combinations? I suspect that this is due to the fact that the advertising industry has been heavily influenced by two theories in psychology—behaviorism and psychoanalysis—both having in common an image of man who is fundamentally an irrational creature, helplessly pushed around on the one hand by irrational guilt, anxiety, self-doubt, and other neurotic self-conceptions (B— beliefs) and, on the other hand, helplessly pushed around by external stimuli which, through reward and punishment, he is conditioned to form arbitrary associations. Advertising has borrowed from psychoanalysis its laws of association, and from behaviorism its principles of conditioning. Psychoanalysis tells you what to associate with what, and behaviorism tells you how to stamp it in. I would suggest that it is because the advertising profession has taken over such an irrational image of man from behaviorism and psychoanalysis that the inconsequential beliefs have been so often associated with the authority beliefs (Type C) and with the primitive beliefs (Type B—). In doing so, the advertising industry has come in for a great deal of criticism—to my mind, justified—from various sources for a style of advertising which encourages conformity, which is exploitative, debasing, lacking in taste, and insulting to the dignity of man.

26   Given the facts of our industrial society and, given what Harry C. Groome has, in a recent issue of the *Saturday Review*, called the *inevitability* of advertising, the advertising man's general strategy of associating the psychologically inconsequential with the consequential is probably the only one open to him and seems psychologically sound in principle. But in line with my presentation of the five kinds of beliefs it is now possible to at least explore systematically the other possible combinations to see where they might lead us. What would an ad look like which tries to associate an inconsequential belief (Type E) with a primitive belief which we all share (Type A)?

27   I recall having seen only one example of such an advertisement, a recent advertisement which has caught my eye as no advertisement has in many years. This ad appeared in the *New Yorker* (September 7, 1963, p. 138). It was entitled "How to keep water off a duck's back." It shows a duck wearing a raincoat. I might add that children seem to get an unusual delight in looking at this picture. Here we see an inconsequential belief about a particular brand of raincoat, associated with a primitive physical belief about the fundamental nature of a certain animal called a duck. By the process of association our primitive belief about the stark-naked duck is momentarily violated; our sanity is threatened and it is virtually impossible to turn away from the ad until our primitive belief is somehow re-established or restored to its original state. In the process the

viewer is entertained and *London Fog* gains attention. Whether *London Fog* (the brand name of the raincoat) also gains customers remains to be seen.

28   In this connection, too, let me also draw attention to the television program *Candid Camera* and to the fact that it often entertains mass audiences by having them watch what happens when there is a momentary disruption of a person's primitive belief about physical and social reality—Type A beliefs, those everyone believes. I am rather surprised that the advertising industry has not consciously applied the *Candid Camera* ideas for its own uses. The *London Fog* ad is the only one I remember seeing which seems to use a similar principle.

29   Let me next draw your attention to some psychological considerations which would favor an increasing emphasis in advertising on associations between the inconsequential beliefs (Type E) and the primitive beliefs (Type B+) which refer to the positive conceptions we strive to have of ourselves.

30   Since the end of World War II, an increasing number of distinguished psychologists have revolted against the image of Irrational Man which behaviorism and classical psychoanalysis have both helped build. Contemporary psychoanalysts talk more about the conflict-free sphere of ego functioning. The Gestalt psychologists have, for a long time, emphasized man's search for meaning, understanding, and organization. Carl Rogers has emphasized the drive for growth and maturity within all individuals. Abraham Maslow has familiarized us with man's drive for self-actualization. Gordon Allport and the existentialists talk about being and becoming. Robert White, Harry F. Harlow, D. E. Berlyne, Leon Festinger, and many others, have pointed to the fact that man has a need to know, to understand and to be competent.

31   I could say that the major way in which contemporary psychology differs from the psychology of twenty years ago is that Man is now seen to be not only a *rationalizing* [6] creature but also a *rational* creature—curious, exploratory and receptive to new ideas. This changing image of man I have represented by the B+ type of beliefs which exist side-by-side with the B— type within the belief system.

32   I can see the barest beginnings of this changing image of man on the part of the advertising industry in certain advertisements, and it may surprise you to learn which advertisement I have in mind: the Pepto-Bismol and Anacin ads. There are probably millions of Americans walking around right now with a conception of a stomach that looks like a hollow dumbbell standing on end and with a conception of a mind composed of split-level compartments. In these ads we see an image of man on the part of the advertising man which concedes that consumers—at least the ones with bellyaches and headaches—have a need to understand why they have bellyaches or headaches.

33   But at the same time the advertising man is also cynically saying that

---

[6] Making excuses.

the consumer is too stupid or irrational to understand anything well. If you or I were to learn that our children were being taught such conceptions of stomach or head by their teachers, we would demand that such teachers be immediately fired for incompetence. Why, then, should the advertising man be allowed to exploit, for money, the consumer's legitimate need to understand his bellyaches and headaches?

34   Is there not a better example of the advertising industry's changing conception of man? I think there is. David Ogilvy has expressed a more dignified and respectful view of the consumer at a conference on creativity held early in 1962. He has expressed this view in his recently published book (*Confessions of an Advertising Man*), and in his advertisements on Puerto Rico, and on travel in the United States and abroad. This dignified image of man is not true of all his famous advertisements. For example, his Schweppes ads and his Rolls Royce ads associate an inconsequential belief with unconscious primitive beliefs concerning snobbish strivings of the self—Type E with Type B—. But his travel ads try to associate psychologically inconsequential beliefs with unconscious primitive beliefs— Type B+—concerning a self which strives to become better-realized, better-rounded, and more open to experience. These ads hold out a dignified promise to let the consumer be and become.

35   But the irrational image of man still predominates in the advertising world. The more inconsequential the benefits of one brand over a competitor's the more desperately the industry has harangued and nagged and, consequently, irritated its mass audience. It's not easy work to convince others that psychologically inconsequential matters are consequential. The fact that the advertising industry attracts such highly talented people, pays them fabulous salaries, and puts them under such terrific pressure—these can all be attributed to the kinds of beliefs it specializes in changing. It is, consequently, no wonder that the advertising profession is reputed to be among the most guilt-ridden, anxiety-ridden, ulcer-ridden, and death-ridden profession in America. I think it significant that four speakers from the academic world were invited to speak to the Eastern Conference of the American Advertising Agencies about the *consumer's* interests, and I think it also significant that on no less than three separate occasions was I reminded in the process of being invited to address this group that the agency leaders who organized this meeting "are in no way seeking a whitewash of the advertising business." These facts would seem to suggest the advertising industry's alarm over its predicament, an eagerness to face up to its social responsibility, a search for conviction, and a courage somewhat in excess of conviction.

36   The advertising man's image of the consumer requires revision in order to bring it more in line not only with the broader and newer image of man, but also with the advertising man's image of himself. To the extent that the advertising man can bring himself to do so, he will gain a new respect from the consumer and in the process gain a renewed respect for himself.

Study Questions: "Images of the Consumer's Mind
On and Off Madison Avenue"

1. What key term does Rokeach define? What kind of definition
   does he give? (Explain your classification using terms you learned
   in Unit 9.)
2. Make a sketch or diagram of the conceptual structure that
   Rokeach presents—a "system of beliefs," as he calls it—and then
   summarize his thesis about advertising in terms of that diagram.
3. Not all writers are as careful as Rokeach to make their conceptual structure explicit. Why do you think Rokeach does so here?
   What advantages does he gain by doing so? Evaluate Rokeach's
   conceptual model. How has it been tested? What further information would you need to evaluate the tests? Compare your own
   experiences with his conceptual system. Cite examples from your
   own experience that tend to either support or deny Rokeach's
   classification of beliefs according to their importance or their
   resistance to change. (Recall your reading about the "stability"
   of visual and verbal concepts in Unit 9.)
4. Working within the conceptual structure he has established early
   in the essay, Rokeach implies that he has surveyed a wide range
   of examples to make an inductive conclusion. Do you think that
   he actually worked this way? or did he begin with a conclusion
   and then search for examples to support it? Explain.
5. Find ten sample ads and classify them according to Rokeach's
   system. How does your sampling confirm or deny Rokeach's conclusions about advertising?

Behavioral Study Of Obedience

1   Obedience is as basic an element in the structure of social life as one
can point to. Some system of authority is a requirement of all communal
living, and it is only the man dwelling in isolation who is not forced to
respond, through defiance or submission, to the commands of others.
Obedience, as a determinant of behavior, is of particular relevance to
our time. It has been reliably established that from 1933–45 millions of
innocent persons were systematically slaughtered on command. Gas
chambers were built, death camps were guarded, daily quotas of corpses
were produced with the same efficiency as the manufacture of appliances.
These inhumane policies may have originated in the mind of a single
person, but they could only be carried out on a massive scale if a very
large number of persons obeyed orders.

Stanley Milgram, "Behavioral Study of Obedience," Journal of Abnormal and
Social Psychology, *October 1963, 67, pp. 371–78.* © *1967 by the American
Psychological Association. Reprinted by permission.*

2   Obedience is the psychological mechanism that links individual action to political purpose. It is the *dispositional*[1] cement that binds men to systems of authority. Facts of recent history and observation in daily life suggest that for many persons obedience may be a deeply ingrained behavior tendency, indeed, a *prepotent*[2] impulse overriding training in ethics, sympathy, and moral conduct. C. P. Snow (1961) points to its importance when he writes:

> When you think of the long and gloomy history of man, you will find more hideous crimes have been committed in the name of obedience than have ever been committed in the name of rebellion. If you doubt that, read William Shirer's *Rise and Fall of the Third Reich*. The German Officer Corps were brought up in the most rigorous code of obedience ... in the name of obedience they were party to, and assisted in, the most wicked large scale actions in the history of the world [p. 24].

3   While the particular form of obedience dealt with in the present study has its antecedents in these episodes, it must not be thought all obedience entails acts of aggression against others. Obedience serves numerous productive functions. Indeed, the very life of society is *predicated*[3] on its existence. Obedience may be ennobling and educative and refer to acts of charity and kindness, as well as to destruction.

General Procedure

4   A procedure was devised which seemed useful as a tool for studying obedience (Milgram, 1961). It consists of ordering a naive subject to administer electric shock to a victim. A *simulated*[4] shock generator is used, with 30 clearly marked voltage levels that range from 15 to 450 volts. The instrument bears verbal designations that range from Slight Shock to Danger: Severe Shock. The responses of the victim, who is a trained *confederate*[5] of the experimenter, are standardized. The orders to administer shocks are given to the naive subject in the context of a "learning experiment" *ostensibly*[6] set up to study the effects of punishment on memory. As the experiment proceeds the naive subject is commanded to administer increasingly more intense shocks to the victim, even to the point of reaching the level marked Danger: Severe Shock. Internal resistances become stronger, and at a certain point the subject refuses to go on with the experiment. Behavior prior to this rupture is considered "obedience," in that the subject complies with the commands of the experimenter. The point of rupture is the act of disobedience. A quantitative value is assigned to the subject's performance based on the maximum intensity shock he is willing to administer before he refuses to

[1] Inclining (someone) to behave in a certain way.

[2] Compelling, superior in influence to anything else.

[3] Based (on), dependent.

[4] Made to look like, fake.

[5] Co-worker, co-conspirator.

[6] Seemingly, appearing to be.

participate further. Thus for any particular subject and for any particular experimental condition the degree of obedience may be specified with a numerical value. The *crux* [7] of the study is to systematically vary the factors believed to alter the degree of obedience to the experimental commands.

5   The technique allows important variables to be manipulated at several points in the experiment. One may vary aspects of the source of command, content and form of command, instrumentalities for its execution, target object, general social setting, etc. The problem, therefore, is not one of designing increasingly more numerous experimental conditions, but of selecting those that best illuminate the *process* of obedience from the sociopsychological standpoint.

Related Studies

6   The inquiry bears an important relation to philosophic analyses of obedience and authority (Arendt, 1958; Friedrich, 1958; Weber, 1947), an early experimental study of obedience by Frank (1944), studies in "authoritarianism" (Adorno, Frenkel-Brunswik, Levinson, & Sanford, 1950; Rokeach, 1961), and a recent series of analytic and empirical studies in social power (Cartwright, 1959). It owes much to the long concern with *suggestion* in social psychology, both in its normal forms (e.g., Binet, 1900) and in its clinical manifestations (Charcot, 1881). But it derives, in the first instance, from direct observation of a social fact; the individual who is commanded by a legitimate authority ordinarily obeys. Obedience comes easily and often. It is a *ubiquitous* [8] and indispensable feature of social life.

Method

Subjects

7   The subjects were 40 males between the ages of 20 and 50, drawn from New Haven and the surrounding communities. Subjects were obtained by a newspaper advertisement and direct mail solicitation. Those who responded to the appeal believed they were to participate in a study of memory and learning at Yale University. A wide range of occupations is represented in the sample. Typical subjects were postal clerks, high school teachers, salesmen, engineers, and laborers. Subjects ranged in educational level from one who had not finished elementary school, to those who had doctorate and other professional degrees. They were paid $4.50 for their participation in the experiment. However, subjects were told that payment was simply for coming to the laboratory, and that the money was theirs no matter what happened after they arrived. Table 1 shows the proportion of age and occupational types assigned to the experimental condition.

[7] The central, most difficult part.
[8] Existing everywhere.

TABLE 1
DISTRIBUTION OF AGE AND OCCUPATIONAL TYPES
IN THE EXPERIMENT

Occupations	20–29 years n	30–39 years n	40–50 years n	Percentage of total (Occupations)
Workers, skilled and unskilled	4	5	6	37.5
Sales, business, and white-collar	3	6	7	40.0
Professional	1	5	3	22.5
Percentage of Total (Age)	20	40	40	

Note.—Total $N = 40$.

Personnel and Locale

8   The experiment was conducted on the grounds of Yale University in the elegant interaction laboratory. (This detail is relevant to the perceived legitimacy of the experiment. In further variations, the experiment was dissociated from the university, with consequences for performance.) The role of experimenter was played by a 31-year-old high school teacher of biology. His manner was impassive, and his appearance somewhat stern throughout the experiment. He was dressed in a gray technician's coat. The victim was played by a 47-year-old accountant, trained for the role; he was of Irish-American stock, whom most observers found mild-mannered and likable.

Procedure

9   One naive subject and one victim (an accomplice) performed in each experiment. A *pretext* [9] had to be devised that would justify the administration of electric shock by the naive subject. This was effectively accomplished by the cover story. After a general introduction on the presumed relation between punishment and learning, subjects were told:

> But actually, we know very *little* about the effect of punishment on learning, because almost no truly scientific studies have been made of it in human beings.
>
> For instance, we don't know how *much* punishment is best for learning—and we don't know how much difference it makes as to who is giving the punishment, whether an adult learns best from a younger or an older person than himself—or many things of that sort.

[9] Cover story, front.

So in this study we are bringing together a number of adults of different occupations and ages. And we're asking some of them to be teachers and some of them to be learners.

We want to find out just what effect different people have on each other as teachers and learners, and also what effect *punishment* will have on learning in this situation.

Therefore, I'm going to ask one of you to be the teacher here tonight and the other one to be the learner.

Does either of you have a preference?

10   Subjects then drew slips of paper from a hat to determine who would be the teacher and who would be the learner in the experiment. The drawing was rigged so that the naive subject was always the teacher and the accomplice always the learner. (Both slips contained the word "Teacher.") Immediately after the drawing, the teacher and learner were taken to an adjacent room and the learner was strapped into an "electric chair" apparatus.

11   The experimenter explained that the straps were to prevent excessive movement while the learner was being shocked. The effect was to make it impossible for him to escape from the situation. An electrode was attached to the learner's wrist, and electrode paste was applied "to avoid blisters and burns." Subjects were told that the electrode was attached to the shock generator in the adjoining room.

12   In order to improve credibility the experimenter declared, in response to a question by the learner: "Although the shocks can be extremely painful, they cause no permanent tissue damage."

13   *Learning task.*   The lesson administered by the subject was a paired-associate learning task. The subject read a series of word pairs to the learner, and then read the first word of the pair along with four terms. The learner was to indicate which of the four terms had originally been paired with the first word. He communicated his answer by pressing one of four switches in front of him, which in turn lit up one of four numbered quadrants in an answer box located atop the shock generator.

14   *Shock generator.*   The instrument panel consists of 30 lever switches set in a horizontal line. Each switch is clearly labeled with a voltage designation that ranges from 15 to 450 volts. There is a 15-volt increment from one switch to the next going from left to right. In addition, the following verbal designations are clearly indicated for groups of four switches going from left to right: Slight Shock, Moderate Shock, Strong Shock, Very Strong Shock, Intense Shock, Extreme Intensity Shock, Danger: Severe Shock. (Two switches after this last designation are simply marked XXX.)

15   Upon depressing a switch: a pilot light corresponding to each switch is illuminated in bright red; an electric buzzing is heard; an electric blue light, labeled "voltage energizer," flashes; the dial on the voltage meter swings to the right; various relay clicks are sounded.

16   The upper left-hand corner of the generator is labeled Shock Generator, Type ZLB, Dyson Instrument Company, Waltham, Mass. Output 15 Volts–450 Volts.

17   Details of the instrument were carefully handled to insure an appearance of authenticity. The panel was engraved by precision industrial engravers, and all components were of high quality. No subject in the experiment suspected that the instrument was merely a simulated shock generator.**

18   *Sample shock.* Each naive subject is given a sample shock on the shock generator, prior to beginning his run as teacher. This shock is always 45 volts, and is applied by pressing the third switch of the generator. The shock is applied to the wrist of the naive subject, and has its source in a 45-volt battery wired into the generator. This further convinces the subject of the authenticity of the generator.

19   *Shock instructions.* The subject is told to administer a shock to the learner each time he gives a wrong response. Moreover—and this is the key command—the subject is instructed to "move one level higher on the shock generator each time the learner flashes a wrong answer." He is also instructed to announce the voltage level before administering a shock. This serves to continually remind subjects of the increasing intensity of shocks administered to the learner.

20   *Preliminary and regular run.* Pretests revealed that the procedure of reading words and administering shocks requires some practice before it can be handled smoothly. Therefore, immediately preceding the regular run, the teacher is given a preliminary series of 10 words to read to the learner. There are 3 neutral words in the practice series (i.e., words that the learner answers correctly), so that shocks are administered for 7 of the words, with the maximum shock at 105 volts (moderate shock). Almost all subjects master the procedure by the time the preliminary run is over.

21   Subjects are then presented with a second list, and are told that the procedure is the same as for the first list; the experimenter adds, however:

>   When you get to the bottom of the list, repeat it over again, and continue giving shocks, until the learner has learned all the pairs correctly.

The experimenter instructs the subject to

>   start from 15 volts and increase the shock level one step each time the learner gives a wrong answer.

22   *Feedback from the victim.* In all conditions the learner gives a pre-

** A related technique, making use of a shock generator, was reported by Buss (1961) for the study of aggression in the laboratory. Despite the considerable similarity of technical detail in the experimental procedures, both investigators proceeded in ignorance of the other's work. Milgram provided plans and photographs of his shock generator, experimental procedure, and first results in a report to the National Science Foundation in January 1961. This report received only limited circulation. Buss reported his procedure 6 months later, but to a wider audience. Subsequently, technical information and reports were exchanged. The present article was first received in the Editor's office on December 27, 1961; it was resubmitted with deletions on July 27, 1962.

determined set of responses to the word pair test, based on a schedule of approximately three wrong answers to one correct answer. In the present experimental condition no vocal response or other sign of protest is heard from the learner until Shock Level 300 is reached. When the 300-volt shock is administered, the learner pounds on the wall of the room in which he is bound to the electric chair. The pounding can be heard by the subject. From this point on, the learner's answers no longer appear on the four-way panel.

23   At this juncture, subjects ordinarily turn to the experimenter for guidance. The experimenter instructs the subject to treat the absence of a response as a wrong answer, and to shock the subject according to the usual schedule. He advises the subjects to allow 5–10 seconds before considering no response as a wrong answer, and to increase the shock level one step each time the learner fails to respond correctly. The learner's pounding is repeated after the 315-volt shock is administered; afterwards he is not heard from, nor do his answers reappear on the four-way signal box.

24   *Experimenter feedback.*   At various points in the experiment the subject may turn to the experimenter for advice on whether he should continue to administer shocks. Or he may indicate that he does not wish to go on. It was important to standardize the experimenter's responses to these inquiries and reactions.

25   If the subject indicated his unwillingness to go on, the experimenter responded with a sequence of "prods," using as many as necessary to bring the subject into line.

> Prod 1: Please continue, or Please go on.
> Prod 2: The experiment requires that you continue.
> Prod 3: It is absolutely essential that you continue.
> Prod 4: You have no other choice, you *must* go on.

26   The prods were always made in sequence: Only if Prod 1 had been unsuccessful, could Prod 2 be used. If the subject refused to obey the experimenter after Prod 4, the experiment was terminated. The experimenter's tone of voice was at all times firm, but not impolite. The sequence was begun anew on each occasion that the subject balked or showed reluctance to follow orders.

27   *Special prods.*   If the subject asked if the learner was liable to suffer permanent physical injury, the experimenter said:

> Although the shocks may be painful, there is no permanent tissue damage, so please go on. [Followed by Prods 2, 3, and 4 if necessary.]

28   If the subject said that the learner did not want to go on, the experimenter replied:

> Whether the learner likes it or not, you must go on until he has learned all the word pairs correctly. So please go on. [Followed by Prods 2, 3, and 4 if necessary.]

Dependent Measures

29   The primary dependent measure for any subject is the maximum shock he administers before he refuses to go any further. In principle this may vary from 0 (for a subject who refuses to administer even the first shock) to 30 (for a subject who administers the highest shock on the generator). A subject who breaks off the experiment at any point prior to administering the thirtieth shock level is termed a *defiant* subject. One who complies with experimental commands fully, and proceeds to administer all shock levels commanded, is termed an *obedient* subject.

30   *Further records.* With few exceptions, experimental sessions were recorded on magnetic tape. Occasional photographs were taken through one-way mirrors. Notes were kept on any unusual behavior occurring during the course of the experiments. On occasion, additional observers were directed to write objective descriptions of the subjects' behavior. The *latency* [10] and duration of shocks were measured by accurate timing devices.

31   *Interview and dehoax.* Following the experiment subjects were interviewed; open-ended questions, *projective* [11] measures, and attitude scales were employed. After the interview, procedures were undertaken to assure that the subject would leave the laboratory in a state of well being. A friendly reconciliation was arranged between the subject and the victim, and an effort was made to reduce any tensions that arose as a result of the experiment.

Results

Preliminary Notions

32   Before giving an account of the experimental results, it is instructive to consider how persons predict others will perform when commanded to administer powerful shocks to another person. Fourteen Yale seniors, all psychology majors, were provided with a detailed description of the experimental situation. They were asked to reflect carefully on it, and to predict the behavior of 100 *hypothetical* [12] subjects. More specifically, they were instructed to plot the distribution of obedience of "100 Americans of diverse occupations, and ranging in age from 20 to 50 years," who were placed in the experimental situation.

33   There was considerable agreement among the respondents on the expected behavior of hypothetical subjects. All respondents predicted that only an insignificant minority would go through to the end of the

10 Present but not visibly detectable.

11 Able to indicate or reveal personality traits and unconscious motivations.

12 Supposed, imagined.

shock series. (The estimates ranged from 0 to 3%; i.e., the most "pessimistic" member of the class predicted that of 100 persons, 3 would continue through to the most potent shock available on the shock generator—450 volts.) The class mean was 1.2%. The question was also posed [13] informally to colleagues of the author, and the most general feeling was that few if any subjects would go beyond the designation Very Strong Shock.

Result of Experiment I

34   *Subjects accept situation.*   With few exceptions subjects were convinced of the reality of the experimental situation, that they were administering shocks to another person, and the most potent shocks were extremely painful. In the post-experimental interview subjects were asked: "How painful to the learner were the last few shocks that you administered to him?" Subjects were instructed to indicate their answers on a printed 14-point scale ranging from "Not at all painful" to "Extremely painful." The *modal* [14] response was 14 (Extremely painful) with the mean at 13.42.

35   *Signs of extreme tension.*   Many subjects showed signs of nervousness in the experimental situation, and especially upon administering the more powerful shocks. In a large number of cases the degree of tension reached extremes that are rarely seen in sociopsychological laboratory studies. Subjects were observed to sweat, tremble, stutter, bite their lips, groan, and dig their fingernails into their flesh. These were characteristic rather than exceptional responses to the experiment.

36   One sign of tension was the regular occurrence of nervous laughing fits. Fourteen of the 40 subjects showed definite signs of nervous laughter and smiling. The laughter seemed entirely out of place, even bizarre. Full-blown, uncontrollable seizures were observed for 3 subjects. On one occasion we observed a seizure so violently convulsive that it was necessary to call a halt to the experiment. The subject, a 46-year-old encyclopedia salesman, was seriously embarrassed by his *untoward* [15] and uncontrollable behavior. In the post-experimental interviews subjects took pains to point out that they were not sadistic types, and that the laughter did not mean they enjoyed shocking the victim.

37   *Distribution of scores.*   It has been conjectured that persons would not, in general, agree to administer shocks beyond the level designated as Very Strong Shock. The distribution of maximum shocks for this experiment is shown in Table 2. The obtained distribution of scores deviates radically from the prediction.

38   Upon command of the experimenter, each of the 40 subjects went beyond the expected breakoff point. No subject stopped prior to ad-

[13] Presented.

[14] Most frequently met number in a series of numbers.

[15] Inappropriate.

TABLE 2
DISTRIBUTION OF BREAKOFF POINTS

Verbal designation and voltage indication	Number of subjects for whom this was maximum shock
Slight Shock	
15	0
30	0
45	0
60	0
Moderate Shock	
75	0
90	0
105	0
120	0
Strong Shock	
135	0
150	0
165	0
180	0
Very Strong Shock	
195	0
210	0
225	0
240	0
Intense Shock	
255	0
270	0
285	0
300	5
Extreme Intensity Shock	
315	4
330	2
345	1
360	1
Danger: Severe Shock	
375	1
390	0
405	0
420	0
XXX	
435	0
450	26

ministering Shock Level 20. (At this level—300 volts—the victim kicks on the wall and no longer provides answers to the teacher's multiple-choice questions.)

39   Of the 40 subjects, 5 refused to obey the experimental commands be-

yond the 300-volt level. Four more subjects administered one further shock, and then refused to go on. Two broke off at the 330-volt level, and 1 each at 345, 360, and 375 volts. Thus a total of 14 subjects defied the experimenter. It is instructive to reprint their remarks at the point of defiance, as transcribed from the tape recordings:

> [0124] I think he's trying to communicate, he's knocking. . . . Well it's not fair to shock the guy . . . these are terrific volts. I don't think this is very humane. . . . Oh, I can't go on with this; no, this isn't right. It's a hell of an experiment. The guy is suffering in there. No, I don't want to go on. This is crazy. [Subject refused to administer more shocks.]
>
> [0123] He's banging in there. I'm gonna chicken out. I'd like to continue, but I can't do that to a man. . . . I'm sorry I can't do that to a man. I'll hurt his heart. You take your check. . . . No really, I couldn't do it.

40   These subjects were frequently in a highly agitated and even angered state. Sometimes, verbal protest was at a minimum, and the subject simply got up from his chair in front of the shock generator, and indicated that he wished to leave the laboratory.

41   Of the 40 subjects, 26 obeyed the orders of the experimenter to the end, proceeding to punish the victim until they reached the most potent shock available on the shock generator. At that point, the experimenter called a halt to the session. (The maximum shock is labeled 450 volts, and is two steps beyond the designation: Danger: Severe Shock.) Although obedient subjects continued to administer shocks, they often did so under extreme stress. Some expressed reluctance to administer shocks beyond the 300-volt level, and displayed fears similar to those who defied the experimenter; yet they obeyed.

42   After the maximum shocks had been delivered, and the experimenter called a halt to the proceedings, many obedient subjects heaved sighs of relief, mopped their brows, rubbed their fingers over their eyes, or nervously fumbled cigarettes. Some shook their heads, apparently in regret. Some subjects had remained calm throughout the experiment, and displayed only minimal signs of tension from beginning to end.

Discussion

43   The experiment yielded two findings that were surprising. The first finding concerns the sheer strength of obedient tendencies *manifested* [16] in this situation. Subjects have learned from childhood that it is a fundamental breach of moral conduct to hurt another person against his will. Yet, 26 subjects abandon this *tenet* [17] in following the instructions of an authority who has no special powers to enforce his commands. To disobey would bring no material loss to the subject; no punishment would ensue. It is clear from the remarks and outward behavior of many participants that in punishing the victim they are often acting against their own values. Subjects often expressed deep disapproval of shocking a man in the face

---

[16] Revealed, demonstrated.

[17] Longstanding and accepted principal.

of his objections, and others denounced it as stupid and senseless. Yet the majority complied with the experimental commands. This outcome was surprising from two perspectives: first, from the standpoint of predictions made in the questionnaire described earlier. (Here, however, it is possible that the remoteness of the respondents from the actual situation, and the difficulty of conveying to them the concrete details of the experiment, could account for the serious underestimation of obedience.)

44 But the results were also unexpected to persons who observed the experiment in progress, through one-way mirrors. Observers often uttered expressions of disbelief upon seeing a subject administer more powerful shocks to the victim. These persons had a full acquaintance with the details of the situation, and yet systematically underestimated the amount of obedience that subjects would display.

45 The second unanticipated effect was the extraordinary tension generated by the procedures. One might suppose that a subject would simply break off or continue as his conscience dictated. Yet, this is very far from what happened. There were striking reactions of tension and emotional strain. One observer related:

> I observed a mature and initially poised businessman enter the laboratory smiling and confident. Within 20 minutes he was reduced to a twitching, stuttering wreck, who was rapidly approaching a point of nervous collapse. He constantly pulled on his earlobe, and twisted his hands. At one point he pushed his fist into his forehead and muttered: "Oh, God, let's stop it." And yet he continued to respond to every word of the experimenter, and obeyed to the end.

46 Any understanding of the phenomenon of obedience must rest on an analysis of the particular conditions in which it occurs. The following features of the experiment go some distance in explaining the high amount of obedience observed in the situation.

47 1. The experiment is sponsored by and takes place on the grounds of an institution of unimpeachable reputation, Yale University. It may be reasonably presumed that the personnel are competent and reputable. The importance of this background authority is now being studied by conducting a series of experiments outside of New Haven, and without any visible ties to the university.

48 2. The experiment is, on the face of it, designed to attain a worthy purpose—advancement of knowledge about learning and memory. Obedience occurs not as an end in itself, but as an instrumental element in a situation that the subject construes as significant and meaningful. He may not be able to see its full significance, but he may properly assume that the experimenter does.

49 3. The subject perceives that the victim has voluntarily submitted to the authority system of the experimenter. He is not (at first) an unwilling captive impressed for involuntary service. He has taken the trouble to come to the laboratory presumably to aid

the experimental research. That he later becomes an involuntary subject does not alter the fact that, initially, he consented to participate without qualification. Thus he has in some degree *incurred* [18] an obligation toward the experimenter.

50 4. The subject, too, has entered the experiment voluntarily, and perceives himself under obligation to aid the experimenter. He has made a commitment, and to disrupt the experiment is a repudiation of his initial promise of aid.

51 5. Certain features of the procedure strengthen the subject's sense of obligation to the experimenter. For one, he has been paid for coming to the laboratory. In part this is cancelled out by the experimenter's statement that:

> Of course, as in all experiments, the money is yours simply for coming to the laboratory. From this point on, no matter what happens, the money is yours.**

52 6. From the subject's standpoint, the fact that he is the teacher and the other man the learner is purely a chance consequence (it is determined by drawing lots) and he, the subject, ran the same risk as the other man in being assigned the role of learner. Since the assignment of positions in the experiment was achieved by fair means, the learner is deprived of any basis of complaint on this count. (A simliar situation obtains in Army units, in which—in the absence of volunteers—a particularly dangerous mission may be assigned by drawing lots, and the unlucky soldier is expected to bear his misfortune with sportsmanship.)

53 7. There is, at best, ambiguity with regard to the *prerogatives* [19] of a psychologist and the corresponding rights of his subject. There is a vagueness of expectation concerning what a psychologist may require of his subject, and when he is overstepping acceptable limits. Moreover, the experiment occurs in a closed setting, and thus provides no opportunity for the subject to remove these ambiguities by discussion with others. There are few standards that seem directly applicable to the situation, which is a novel one for most subjects.

54 8. The subjects are assured that the shocks administered to the subject are "painful but not dangerous." Thus they assume that the discomfort caused the victim is momentary, while the scientific gains resulting from the experiment are enduring.

55 9. Through Shock Level 20 the victim continues to provide answers on the signal box. The subject may construe this as a sign

** Forty-three subjects, undergraduates at Yale University, were run in the experiment without payment. The results are very similar to those obtained with paid subjects.

[18] Brought upon oneself.

[19] Rights and privileges granted to a person holding a certain position or rank.

that the victim is still willing to "play the game." It is only after Shock Level 20 that the victim repudiates the rules completely, refusing to answer further.

These features help to explain the high amount of obedience obtained in this experiment. Many of the arguments raised need not remain matters of speculation, but can be reduced to testable propositions to be confirmed or disproved by further experiments.**

The following features of the experiment concern the nature of the conflict which the subject faces.

56   10. The subject is placed in a position in which he must respond to the competing demands of two persons: the experimenter and the victim. The conflict must be resolved by meeting the demands of one or the other; satisfaction of the victim and the experimenter are mutually exclusive. Moreover, the resolution must take the form of a highly visible action, that of continuing to shock the victim or breaking off the experiment. Thus the subject is forced into a public conflict that does not permit any completely satisfactory solution.

57   11. While the demands of the experimenter carry the weight of scientific authority, the demands of the victim spring from his personal experience of pain and suffering. The two claims need not be regarded as equally pressing and legitimate. The experimenter seeks an abstract scientific datum; the victim cries out for relief from physical suffering caused by the subject's actions.

58   12. The experiment gives the subject little time for reflection. The conflict comes on rapidly. It is only minutes after the subject has been seated before the shock generator that the victim begins his protests. Moreover, the subject perceives that he has gone through but two-thirds of the shock levels at the time the subject's first protests are heard. Thus he understands that the conflict will have a persistent aspect to it, and may well become more intense as increasingly more powerful shocks are required. The rapidity with which the conflict descends on the subject, and his realization that it is predictably recurrent may well be sources of tension to him.

59   13. At a more general level, the conflict stems from the opposition of two deeply ingrained behavior dispositions: first, the disposition not to harm other people, and second, the tendency to obey those whom we perceive to be legitimate authorities.

Study Questions: "A Behavioral Study of Obedience"

Milgram experiments not only to see just how certain subjects will react in an experiment but also to learn how much we know about

---

** A series of recently completed experiments employing the obedience paradigm is reported in Milgram (1964).

ourselves and how accurately we are able to predict our own be-havior. With this general purpose in mind, answer the following questions in detail.

1. He designed this experiment to isolate an act of obedience. In that design you can find his assumptions about what obedience is. Review the description of the experiment and construct from it what seem to be the determining characteristics that make an action an example of "obedience." What kind of definition are you constructing? Why is it not sufficient, in this case, to simply construct a definition in other words?

2. Milgram spends a great deal of time discovering and discussing what a group of observers would predict the outcome of the experiment to be. What assumptions do they make about the choices the subjects will make in a crisis situation and what values will motivate their decisions? What generalizations can be made about people in general from Milgram's study? Why do you think Milgram includes this information about prior expectations?

3. What knowledge about history and what assumptions about human behavior seem to have prompted Milgram to make his experiment? What outcomes do you think *he* expected? (Give evidence from the report to support your answer.)

4. What measures does Milgram take in the report to keep the reader from making any hasty and untested conclusions? How does the organization of paragraphs 43 to 59 reflect his attempt to resist drawing final conclusions?

5. What further inferences about obedience, freedom, or human nature occurred to you as you read the report? Try to design an experiment like Milgram's for testing one of your inferences. If you can't, then explain *why* your inference cannot be tested.

6. What inductive method does Milgram use? What do you think about the validity of his method? Do you have any concern over Milgram's treatment of his subjects? If you do, what is the basis of your concern? On what assumptions is this concern built?

Eyewitness Testimony

1   The woman in the witness box stares at the defendant, points an ac-cusing finger and says, loudly and firmly, "That's the man! That's him! I could never forget his face!" It is impressive testimony. The only eye-witness to a murder has identified the murderer. Or has she?

2   Perhaps she has, but she may be wrong. Eyewitness testimony is un-reliable. Research and courtroom experience provide ample evidence that an eyewitness to a crime is being asked to be something and do some-thing that a normal human being was not created to be or do. Human

perception is sloppy and uneven, albeit remarkably effective in serving our need to create structure out of experience. In an investigation or in court, however, a witness is often asked to play the role of a kind of tape recorder on whose tape the events of the crime have left an impression. The prosecution probes for stored facts and scenes and tries to establish that the witness's recording equipment was and still is in perfect running order. The defense cross-examines the witness to show that there are defects in the recorder and gaps in the tape. Both sides, and usually the witness too, *succumb* [1] to the fallacy that everything was recorded and can be played back later through questioning.

3   Those of us who have done research in eyewitness identification reject that fallacy. It reflects a 19th-century view of man as perceiver, which asserted a parallel between the mechanisms of the physical world and those of the brain. Human perception is a more complex information-processing mechanism. So is memory. The person who sees an accident or witnesses a crime and is then asked to describe what he saw cannot call up an "instant replay." He must depend on his memory, with all its limitations. The limitations may be unimportant in ordinary daily activities. If someone is a little unreliable, if he trims the truth a bit in describing what he has seen, it ordinarily does not matter too much. When he is a witness, the inaccuracy escalates in importance.

4   Human perception and memory function effectively by being selective and constructive. As Ulric Neisser of Cornell University has pointed out, "Neither perception nor memory is a copying process." Perception and memory are decision-making processes affected by the totality of a person's abilities, background, attitudes, motives and beliefs, by the environment and by the way his recollection is eventually tested. The observer is an active rather than a passive perceiver and recorder; he reaches conclusions on what he has seen by evaluating fragments of information and reconstructing them. He is motivated by a desire to be accurate as he imposes meaning on the overabundance of information that *impinges* [2] on his senses, but also by a desire to live up to the expectations of other people and to stay in their good graces. The eye, the ear and other sense organs are therefore social organs as well as physical ones.

5   Psychologists studying the capabilities of the sense organs speak of an "ideal observer," one who would respond to lights or tones with unbiased eyes and ears, but we know that the ideal observer does not exist. We speak of an "ideal physical environment," free of distractions and distortions, but we know that such an environment can only be approached, and then only in the laboratory. My colleagues and I at the Brooklyn College of the City University of New York distinguish a number of factors that we believe inherently limit a person's ability to give a complete account of events he once saw or to identify with complete accuracy the people who were involved.

[1] Submit or yield to.
[2] Touches.

6   The first sources of unreliability are implicit in the original situation. One is the insignificance—at the time and to the witness—of the events that were observed. In placing someone at or near the scene of a crime, for example, witnesses are often being asked to recall seeing the accused at a time when they were not attaching importance to the event, which was observed in passing, as a part of the normal routine of an ordinary day. As long ago as 1895 J. McKeen Cattell wrote about an experiment in which he asked students to describe the people, places and events they had encountered walking to school over familiar paths. The reports were incomplete and unreliable; some individuals were very sure of details that had no basis in fact. Insignificant events do not motivate a person to bring fully into play the selective process of attention.

7   The length of the period of observation obviously limits the number of features a person can attend to. When the tachistoscope, a projector with a variable-speed shutter that controls the length of an image's appearance on a screen, is used in controlled research to test recall, the shorter times produce less reliable identification and recall. Yet fleeting glimpses are common in eyewitness accounts, particularly in fast-moving, threatening situations. In the Sacco-Vanzetti case in the 1920's a witness gave a detailed description of one defendant on the basis of a fraction-of-a-second glance. The description must have been a fabrication.

8   Less than ideal observation conditions usually apply; crimes seldom occur in a well-controlled laboratory. Often distance, poor lighting, fast movement or the presence of a crowd interferes with the efficient working of the attention process. Well-established *thresholds* [3] for the eye and the other senses have been established by research, and as those limits are approached eyewitness accounts become quite unreliable. In one case in my experience a police officer testified that he saw the defendant, a black man, shoot a victim as both stood in a doorway 120 feet away. Checking for the defense, we found the scene so poorly lit that we could hardly see a person's silhouette, let alone a face; instrument measurements revealed that the light falling on the eye amounted to less than a fifth of the light from a candle. The defense presented photographs and light readings to demonstrate that a positive identification was not very probable. The members of the jury went to the scene of the crime, had the one black juror stand in the doorway, found they could not identify his features and acquitted the defendant.

9   The witness himself is a major source of unreliability. To begin with, he may have been observing under stress. When a person's life or well-being is threatened, there is a response that includes an increased heart rate, breathing rate and blood pressure and a dramatic increase in the flow of adrenalin and of available energy, making the person capable of running fast, fighting, lifting enormous weight—taking the steps necessary to ensure his safety or survival. The point is, however, that a person under extreme stress is also a less than normally reliable witness. In experimental situations an observer is less capable of remembering de-

[3] Points at which a stimulus is just strong enough to be perceived.

tails, less accurate in reading dials and less accurate in detecting signals when under stress; he is quite naturally paying more attention to his own well-being and safety than to nonessential elements in the environment. Research I have done with Air Force flight-crew members confirms that even highly trained people become poorer observers under stress. The actual threat that brought on the stress response, having been highly significant at the time, can be remembered; but memory for other details such as clothing and colors is not as clear; time estimates are particularly exaggerated.

10   The observer's physical condition is often a factor. A person may be too old or too sick or too tired to perceive clearly, or he may simply lack the necessary faculty. In one case I learned that a witness who had testified about shades of red had admitted to the grand jury that he was color-blind. I testified at the trial that he was apparenly dichromatic, or red-green color-blind, and that his testimony was probably fabricated on the basis of information other than visual evidence. The prosecution brought on his opthalmologist, presumably as a rebuttal witness, but the ophthalmologist testified that the witness was actually monochromatic, which meant he could perceive no colors at all. Clearly the witness was "filling in" his testimony. That, after all, is how color-blind people function in daily life, by making inferences about colors they cannot distinguish.

11   Psychologists have done extensive research on how "set," or expectancy, is used by the observer to make judgments more efficiently. In a classic experiment done in the 1930's by Jerome S. Bruner and Leo Postman at Harvard University observers were shown a display of playing cards for a few seconds and asked to report the number of aces of spades in the display [see illustration]. After a brief glance most observers reported seeing three aces of spades. Actually there were five; two of them were colored red instead of the more familiar black. People are so familiar with black aces of spades that they do not waste time looking at the display carefully. The prior conditioning of the witness may cause him similarly to report facts or events that were not present but that he thinks should have been present.

12   Expectancy is seen in its least attractive form in the case of biases or prejudices. A victim of a mugging may initially report being attacked by "niggers" and may, because of prejudice or limited experience (or both), be unable to tell one black man from another. ("They all look alike to me.") In a classic study of this phenomenon Gordon W. Allport of Harvard had his subjects take a brief look at a drawing of several people on a subway train, including a seated black man and a white man standing with a razor in his hand. Fifty percent of the observers later reported that the razor was in the hand of the black man. Most people file away some stereotypes on the basis of which they make perceptual judgments; such stereotypes not only lead to prejudice but are also tools for making decisions more efficiently. A witness to an automobile accident may report not what he saw but his ingrained stereotype about women drivers. Such short-cuts to thinking may be erroneously reported

Who had the razor? After a brief look at a drawing such as this one, half of the observers report having seen the razor, a stereotyped symbol of violence in blacks, in the black man's hand. Gordon W. Allport of Harvard University devised this experiment.

and expanded on by an eyewitness without his being aware that he is describing his stereotype rather than actual events. If the witness's biases are shared by the investigator taking a statement, the report may reflect their mutual biases rather than what was actually seen.

13   The tendency to see what we want or need to see has been demonstrated by numerous experiments in which people report seeing things that in fact are not present. R. Levine, Isador Chein and Gardner Murphy had volunteers go without food for 24 hours and report what they "saw" in a series of blurred slides presented on a screen. The longer they were deprived of food the more frequently they reported seeing "food" in the blurred pictures. An analysis of the motives of the eyewitness at the time of a crime can be very valuable in determining whether or not the witness is reporting what he wanted to see. In one study I conducted at Washington University a student dressed in a black bag that covered him completely visited a number of classes. Later the students in those classes were asked to describe the nature of the person in the bag. Most of their reports went far beyond the meager evidence: the bag-covered figure was said to be a black man, "a nut," a symbol of alienation and so on. Further tests showed that the descriptions were related to the needs and motives of the individual witness.

14   Journalists and psychologists have noted a tendency for people to

maintain they were present when a significant historical event took place near where they live even though they were not there at all; such people want to sound interesting, to be a small part of history. A journalist once fabricated a charming human interest story about a naked woman stuck to a newly painted toilet seat in a small town and got it distributed by newspaper wire services. He visited the town and interviewed citizens who claimed to have witnessed and even to have played a part in the totally fictitious event. In criminal cases with publicity and a controversial defendant it is not uncommon for volunteer witnesses to come forward with *spurious* [4] testimony.

15 Unreliability stemming from the original situation and from the observer's fallibility is redoubled by the circumstances attending the eventual attempt at information retrieval. First of all there is the obvious fact, supported by a considerable amount of research, that people forget verbal and pictorial information with the passage of time. They are simply too busy coping with daily life to keep paying attention to what they heard or saw; perfect recall of information is basically unnecessary and is rarely if ever displayed. The testing of recognition in a police "lineup" or a set of identification photographs is consequently less reliable the longer the time from the event to the test. With time, for example, there is often a filling in of spurious details: an incomplete or fragmentary image is "cleaned up" by the observer when he is tested later. Allport used to have students draw a rough geometric shape right after such a shape was shown to them. Then they were tested on their ability to reproduce the drawing 30 days later and again three months later [see illustration]. The observers tended first to make the figure more symmetrical than it really was and later to render it as a neat equilateral triangle. This finding was repeated with many objects, the tendency being for people to "improve" their recollection by making it seem more logical.

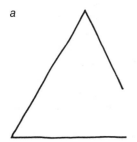 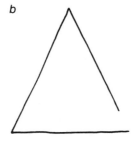 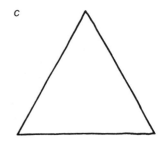

"Filling in" of details was demonstrated by a simple drawing test. Observers were shown an incomplete but roughly triangular figure and immediately afterward were asked to draw what they had seen. The typical drawing was a good reproduction of the original *(a)*. A month later observers asked to draw what they remembered produced more regular figures *(b)*. Three months after the original viewing, again asked to draw what they remembered, they drew erroneously complete, symmetrical figures *(c)*.

4 Untrue, counterfeit.

16   In analyses of eyewitness reports in criminal cases we have seen the reports get more accurate, more complete and less ambiguous as the witness moves from the initial police report through grand-jury questioning to testimony at the trial. The process of filling in is an efficient way to remember but it can lead to unreliable recognition testing: the witness may adjust his memory to fit the available suspects or pictures. The witness need not be lying; he may be unaware he is distorting or reconstructing his memory. In his very effort to be conscientious he may fabricate parts of his recall to make a chaotic memory seem more plausible to the people asking questions. The questions themselves may encourage such fabrication. Beth Loftus of the University of Washington has demonstrated how altering the semantic value of the words in questions about a filmed auto accident causes witnesses to distort their reports. When witnesses were asked a question using the word "smashed" as opposed to "bumped" they gave higher estimates of speed and were more likely to report having seen broken glass—although there was no broken glass.

17   Unfair test construction often encourages error. The lineup or the array of photographs for testing the eyewitness's ability to identify a suspect can be analyzed as fair or unfair on the basis of criteria most psychologists can agree on. A fair test is designed carefully so that all faces have an equal chance of being selected by someone who did not see the suspect; the faces are similar enough to one another and to the original description of the suspect to be confusing to a person who is merely guessing; the test is conducted without leading questions or suggestions. All too frequently lineups or photograph arrays are carelessly assembled or even rigged. If, for example, there are five pictures, the chance should be only one in five that any one picture will be chosen.

18   Research on memory has also shown that if one item in the array of photographs is uniquely different—say in dress, race, height, sex or photographic quality—it is more likely to be picked out. Such an array is simply not confusing enough for it to be called a test. A teacher who makes up a multiple-choice test includes several answers that sound or look alike to make it difficult for a person who does not know the right answer to succeed. Police lineups and picture layouts are multiple-choice tests; if the rules for designing tests are ignored, the tests are unreliable.

19   No test, with photographs or a lineup, can be completely free of suggestion. When a witness is brought in by the police to attempt an identification, he can safely assume that there is some reason: that the authorities have a suspect in mind or even in custody. He is therefore under pressure to pick someone even if the officer showing the photographs is properly careful not to force the issue. The basic books on eyewitness identification all recommend that no suggestions, hints or pressure be transmitted to the witness, but my experience with criminal investigation reveals frequent abuse by zealous police officers. Such abuses include making remarks about which pictures to skip, saying, "Are you sure?" when the witness makes an error, giving hints, showing enthusiasm when the "right" picture is picked and so on. A test that measures a need

for social approval has shown that people who are high in that need (particularly those who enthusiastically volunteer information) are particularly strongly influenced by suggestion and approval coming from the test giver.

20   Conformity is another troublesome influence. One might expect that two eyewitnesses—or 10 or 100—who agree are better than one. Similarity of judgment is a two-edged sword, however: people can agree in error as easily as in truth. A large body of research results demonstrates that an observer can be persuaded to conform to the majority opinion even when the majority is completely wrong. In one celebrated experiment, first performed in the 1950's by Solomon E. Asch at Swarthmore College, seven observers are shown two lines and asked to say which is the shorter. Six of the people are in the pay of the experimenter; they all say that the objectively longer line is the shorter one. After hearing six people say this, the naïve subject is on the spot. Astonishingly the majority of the naïve subjects say that the long line is short—in the face of reality and in spite of the fact that alone they would have no trouble giving the correct answer [see "Opinions and Social Pressure," by Solomon E. Asch; *Scientific American,* November, 1955].

21   To test the effect of conformity a group of my students at Brooklyn College, led by Andrea Alper, staged a "crime" in a classroom, asked for individual descriptions and then put the witnesses into groups so as to produce composite descriptions of the suspect. The group descriptions were more complete than the individual reports but gave rise to significantly more errors of commission: an assortment of incorrect and stereotyped details. For example, the groups (but not the individuals) reported incorrectly that the suspect was wearing the standard student attire, blue jeans.

22   The effects of suggestion increase when figures in obvious authority do the testing. In laboratory research we find more suggestibility and changing of attitudes when the tester is older or of apparently higher status, better dressed or wearing a uniform or a white coat—or is a pretty woman. In court I have noticed that witnesses who work together under a supervisor are hard put to disagree with their boss in testifying or in picking a photograph. The process of filling in details can be exaggerated when the boss and his employee compare their information and the employee feels obligated to back up his boss to remain in his good graces. Legal history is not lacking in anecdotes about convict witnesses who were rewarded by the authorities for their cooperation in making an identification.

23   In criminal investigations, as in scientific investigations, a theory can be a powerful tool for clarifying confusion, but it can also lead to distortion and unreliability if people attempt, perhaps unconsciously, to make fact fit theory and close their minds to the real meanings of facts. The eyewitness who feels pressed to say something may shape his memory to fit a theory, particularly a highly publicized and seemingly reasonable one.

24   Psychological research on human perception has advanced from the

19th-century recording-machine analogy to a more complex understanding of selective decision-making processes that are more human and hence more useful. My colleagues and I feel that psychologists can make a needed contribution to the judicial system by directing contemporary research methods to real-world problems and by speaking out in court (as George A. Miller of Rockefeller University puts it, by "giving psychology away").

25   It is discouraging to note that the essential findings on the unreliability of eyewitness testimony were made by Hugo Münsterberg nearly 80 years ago, and yet the practice of basing a case on eyewitness testimony and trying to persuade a jury that such testimony is superior to circumstantial evidence continues to this day. The fact is that both types of evidence involve areas of doubt. Circumstantial evidence is tied together with a theory, which is subject to questioning. Eyewitness testimony is also based on a theory, constructed by a human being (often with help from others), about what reality was like in the past; since that theory can be adjusted or changed in accordance with personality, with the situation or with social pressure, it is unwise to accept such testimony without question. It is up to a jury to determine if the doubts about an eyewitness's testimony are reasonable enough for the testimony to be rejected as untrue. Jurors should be reminded that there can be doubt about eyewitness testimony, just as there is about any other kind of evidence.

Study Questions: "Eyewitness Testimony"

1. In "Eyewitness Testimony" Robert Buckhout makes the assertion that eyewitnesses cannot be expected to give a completely accurate report of what they have seen. A number of other people do not share his evaluation and trust eyewitness testimony above any other kind of evidence. These two opposed views developed out of two conflicting assumptions about how we perceive the world around us. Briefly describe these two points of view and cite the paragraphs in the article where they are explained. What kind of support can be offered for each one? To what extent can each one be tested?

2. What form of argument does Buckhout use to reach his conclusion? Is the argument valid, in your opinion?

3. Beyond the problem of unreliable evidence in courts of law, what important questions about people's relationship to the world does this essay raise?

4. How closely does Buckhout's conceptual structure match your own? How did this factor affect your readiness to be persuaded by his argument? Did your conceptual structures change as you read the essay? If so, how? If not, why not?

Coming to Terms:
A Glossary
of
Important Words
and
Phrases

abstraction   the process of moving from a specific instance to a more general understanding.

active topic pattern   a sentence pattern in which the verb shows an *action;* the subject performs an action (*see* passive topic pattern).

adjective   a word that describes, or specifies, a noun.

adjective clause   an adjective word group that describes, or specifies, a noun (*see* clause, specifying pattern).

adjective phrase   an adjective word group that describes, or specifies (a noun (*see* phrase, specifying pattern).

adjective relator   a word (*who, which, that, whom, where, when*) used to signal an adjective clause (or a specifying pattern) and to connect the clause to the noun it specifies.

adverb   a word that modifies, or qualifies, a verb.

adverb relator   a word (*although, when, unless,* etc.) used to signal a qualifying pattern and to connect the pattern to the sentence.

allegorical level   that part of an allegorical writing which the reader is required to construct. It is not clearly indicated by the author (*see* literal level). In the terms of this text, it is the *second* map that the reader creates: the first one is given by the author.

allegory   a piece of narrative writing in which there appears to be more than one story. An allegory has two levels: the literal level and the allegorical level (*see* literal level, allegorical level).

alliteration   the repetition of the initial sound, usually a consonant or a consonant cluster, in two or more words.

allusion   in writing, a reference to a historical event, to another piece of writing, a famous person, etc.

antecedent noun   a noun to which a pronoun or relator refers.

associative paragraph   a paragraph in which the logic is not clearly specified, where the ideas grow through association (the associative links are not often clearly stated).

assonance   a sound similarity in which the vowel sounds of two or more words are alike.

balance   writing that is neutral (neither strongly negative nor strongly positive) is said to have balance.

balanced sentences sentences in which two similar constructions are balanced on a central point, usually a colon or a semicolon.

cause-and-effect logic a mode of inductive logic in which the thinker reasons that if Event A causes Event B in one situation, Event A will cause Event B in another, similar situation.

circular definition the practice of defining a word by words that can only be explained by the word they are attempting to define.

clause a group of words containing a subject and a verb, forming part of the sentence; in this text, meant to refer to a dependent clause that requires another clause to be meaningful.

cliché a phrase that is trite and hackneyed through overuse.

cloze testing the process of testing a reader's ability to comprehend written material by deleting some words and asking the reader to replace them.

combined sentence a sentence that is built by combining two or more very simple sentences to make a more complex one.

comparison the process of bringing two similar things together.

complex sentence in this text, meant to designate a sentence that is densely packed with clauses and phrases, with a relatively high reading difficulty.

concepts mental images or categories built out of our experiences with concrete things, events, and people.

conceptual structure the pattern of concepts that organizes our attitudes and beliefs (*see* concepts).

conclusion in argument, the logical inference that can be drawn from the facts or assumptions that have been stated.

connotation the suggestion or overtone that a word carries with it (*see also* denotation *and* public and private connotation).

context the parts of a sentence, paragraph, or discourse immediately surrounding a specified word or passage and determining its meaning.

coordinating pattern a group of words joined together by a coordinator (*see* coordinator).

coordinator a word that joins together two or more similar terms: *and, but, or, nor, for, still, yet.*

cultural myths those concepts that operate at an unconscious level that are common to all of the members of a culture. They are frequently passed along from generation to generation without close examination. (One example might be the cultural myth of heroism, or the American myth of poor-boy-makes-good.)

cumulative sentence a sentence in which clauses and phrases have been *added to* the main clause—before it, after it, in the middle of it.

deductive argument the process of arguing from *premises,* or clearly stated assumptions. In a deductive argument, the thinker begins with the general and then establishes a specific conclusion (*see* inductive argument).

definition by analysis   the process of defining a term by describing its component parts.

definition in other words   the act of defining through the use of words, rather than pointing to an object or act or showing it in operation (*see* operational definition *and* point-to definition).

denotation   the "dictionary" meaning of a word (*see* connotation).

descriptive definition   a definition built by describing the most important or characteristic features of a thing, event, or idea.

descriptive paragraph   a paragraph built by descriptive details. Descriptive paragraphs are usually organized around a spatial logic, so that the writer describes one thing, and then the thing next to it, and so on.

embedding   putting additional phrases and clauses into a simple sentence to make it convey more information.

emphasis   special stress given to a word, a phrase, or a sentence by its placement in a position where it can catch the reader's attention.

formal definition   defining a term by giving the class to which it belongs and the specific category within that class in which it is found.

frame   the graphic representation that shows the relationship of sentence components (clauses, phrases) to one another, or the relationship of sentences to one another in a paragraph, or the relationship of paragraphs to one another in a paragraph sequence.

hasty generalization   the act of drawing a conclusion too quickly from an inadequate sample of specific instances.

implicit conclusion   conclusion that is left to be drawn by the reader; a conclusion that is not stated explicitly.

implicit definition   a definition that is not clearly stated or acknowledged as a definition.

implicit topic sentence   an organizing statement that is left out so that the reader must infer it from the other sentences.

inductive argument   an argument in which the thinker proceeds from several specific instances to a general statement (*see* deductive argument).

infer   to draw a conclusion from several pieces of evidence.

interactive process   in this text, used to describe the process by which readers involve or engage themselves with the text, making meaning out of their interaction with the writer's meanings.

is of identity   the use of a form of the verb *be* to say that one thing is identical to another. Once this labeling act is complete, the important differences between the two things are often ignored.

journalistic paragraphs   paragraphs that are organized by the principle of *most important things first.* Journalistic paragraphs are usually short, and can be shortened by the deletion of sentences from the bottom up.

language code   the rules and principles that comprise the language system in a given language. The code also includes rules that govern which persons may speak to one another and what kinds of subjects they may discuss in a particular situation.

language of belief   language that is used to influence a reader to adopt a certain belief.

language of fact   language that is balanced, or neutral, and that is used to represent the objects or events it describes as accurately and factually as possible.

language of metaphor   language that describes or defines one thing by associating it with another, through *metaphor, simile, personification, allusion,* or *allegory (see each of these terms).*

literal level of allegory   the level of reading based on the actual words in their everyday meaning, disregarding any allegorical interpretation (*see* allegory, allegorical level). In the terms of this text, it is the *first* map that the author presents: the second is implicit, created by the reader.

map   in this text, used to describe a representation, usually in words, of the world (or *territory*) around us. Writers are said to build verbal *maps* which in some way describe the *territory.*

meaning   a much-debated term, used in this book to describe the process by which readers make sense out of the writer's communication.

meaning signals   marks on the page (words, punctuation marks, sentence structures, paragraph organization, and so on) by which writers attempt to confine readers to a particular meaning or set of meanings.

metaphor   a figure of speech in which a comparison is implied, rather than explicitly stated; for example, rose red (*see* simile).

modification   the process of adding specifiers or qualifiers or restatement patterns to a noun or verb in order to convey more information.

narrative paragraphs   paragraphs that tell a story, in a chronological sequence of events. Narrative paragraphs are generally organized in a *time* order.

negative slant   a technique of word choice in which the writer attempts to influence the reader's opinion by choosing and arranging words to exploit their unpleasant connotations.

neutral   neither positive nor negative, pleasant nor unpleasant; balanced.

operational definition   a definition that explains something by showing it *in action,* rather than by pointing to it or using other words (*see* point-to definition *and* definition in other words).

parallel structures   structures that are grammatically alike, joined in a series.

participating reader   a reader who is actively involved with the text and understands what kinds of devices and strategies the writer is using to affect his or her perceptions and beliefs.

passive reader   a reader who is content to let the words slip by under his or her eyes, without being actively or energetically involved with them.

passive topic pattern   a sentence pattern in which the subject is acted upon; the verb consists of a form of the verb *be* and a present or past participle of the verb.

past participle   a form of the verb ending in *-ed, -en, -t, -d,* or *-n.*

pattern of reference   in a paragraph or sequence of sentences, the connections that are made between sentences. A reference may be established by the repetition of a key word, a pronoun reference, a question-answer sequence, etc.

perceptual set   the psychological readiness to perceive an object or event in a particular way. A perceptual set is often established when a person is *told* that he or she will see something, and then sees that thing because of the expectation.

personification   a figure of speech in which a thing is given human attributes.

phrase   a word group that has neither subject nor verb (*see* clause).

point-to definition   a nonverbal definition in which the definer simply points to the object he or she wants to define.

positive slant   a technique of word choice in which the writer attempts to influence the reader's opinion by choosing and arranging words in a way that will exploit their pleasant connotations (*see* negative slant).

post hoc fallacy   a logical error in which the thinker asserts that Event A causes Event B without any other evidence than the fact that Event B occurred *after* Event A. The whole term is *post hoc ergo propter hoc* (after this, therefore because of this).

predictions   in this text, a term used to describe the guesses that readers make on the basis of their expectations about a sentence or a larger unit of discourse.

premises   the basic assumptions in an argument.

prepositional phrase   a preposition, its object, and all specifying words or phrases. A preposition is a relation or function word, such as *in, by, for, with,* etc.

present participle a form of the verb ending in -*ing*.

primer style a style that is composed almost entirely of very simple sentences, like a first-grade primer.

private connotations associations, either pleasant or unpleasant, that cluster about a word, growing out of an individual's own private experience (*see* public connotations).

public connotations associations, either pleasant or unpleasant, that cluster about a word, shared by many members of a culture.

qualifying clause clause that is used to qualify, add information to, or change a verb.

qualifying pattern a clause or phrase used to qualify a verb (*see* qualifying clause, phrase, qualifying subordinator).

qualifying phrase a phrase that is used to qualify, add information to, or change a verb.

qualifying sentence in a paragraph, a sentence that serves to change or qualify the sentence before it. Usually, a qualifying sentence contradicts, contrasts, shows cause or effect, etc.

qualifying subordinator a word that is used to signal a qualifying pattern. Qualifying subordinators include such words as *although, unless, whenever, wherever, until, if,* etc.

reading the active process of making meaning out of signs and symbols.

renaming pattern a sentence pattern in which a noun or noun word-group (even a whole clause or a sentence) is used to restate more specifically a general word or phrase.

representative sample in inductive argument, a set of instances taken from a general population and carefully selected to represent the characteristics of the larger population.

restatement paragraph a paragraph in which all the sentences refer back to the topic sentence, restating the topic sentence or a part of it in more specific form.

restating sentence in a paragraph, a sentence that restates more specifically the preceding sentence.

rhyme a similarity in end-sounds among two or more words.

samples in inductive argument, a selection taken from a larger population (*see* representative sample).

self-fulfilling prophecy a verbal prophecy, or map, that makes a prediction about a particular act or event and thereby causes that act or event to happen.

sign any thing (object, symbol, action) that can be taken to represent another thing.

simile a figure of speech in which a comparison is signaled by the words *like* or *as*.

simple sentence   a sentence that is built on a single topic pattern, without any specification or qualification or restatement patterns added.

slant   the process of influencing a reader's perception and attitudes through word choice, selection of detail, and emphasis.

specifying paragraph   in a sequence of paragraphs, a paragraph that adds examples that further specify a more general statement in the preceding paragraph.

specifying pattern   in a sentence, a clause or phrase that specifies a more general noun by adding detail to it.

specifying sentence   in a paragraph or a sequence of sentences, a sentence that adds specific details or examples to the sentence preceding it.

structural context   the structural—or organizational—pattern that surrounds a particular word, phrase or clause, or sentence.

structural signals   words or organizational patterns that the writer uses to confine the reader to a particular interpretation. Words used as structural signals may be adjective and adverb relators, coordinators, and so on.

surface structure   the surface meaning of a text, composed by the marks the reader sees on the page; the immediate meaning a reader may derive from a text.

suspended sentence   a sentence in which the topic pattern is withheld until the end (also called *periodic* sentence).

syllogism   in formal, deductive argument, the proof for the argument.

symbol   a sign, usually a verbal sign.

synonym   a word that can be substituted for another word without a great deal of change in meaning.

tachistoscope   an instrument often used in reading labs to measure the speed at which a reader can perceive words and phrases or clauses and whole sentences.

territory   in this text, a term used to refer to an area that is or can be mapped by words or other representations.

topic paragraph   in a paragraph sequence, a paragraph that serves as an "umbrella" paragraph, to organize the paragraphs that follow.

topic pattern   the subject, verb, and complement of a sentence.

topic sentence   in a paragraph, a sentence that serves as an "umbrella" sentence, to organize the sentences that follow. A topic sentence may be explicitly stated or only implied.

valid   in argument, logically sound.

verbal adjectives   verbs transformed into adjectives (past or present participles) and used to specify nouns.

visual ambiguity any visual representation or configuration that can be read in more than one way is said to be "visually ambiguous."

visual concept an "idea picture" that we hold in our heads that helps us to know what to look for. (For example, we hold an idea picture of the animal "dog" in our heads that serves as a kind of schematic model for all dogs—even though not all dogs look like our visual concept.)

wordfact a word or statement that appears to be factual and yet misrepresents the thing it seems to describe.

word order the arrangement of words in a sentence.